JUDAEO-CHRISTIAN INTELLECTUAL CULTURE
IN THE SEVENTEENTH CENTURY

ARCHIVES INTERNATIONALES D'HISTOIRE DES IDÉES

INTERNATIONAL ARCHIVES OF THE HISTORY OF IDEAS

163

JUDAEO-CHRISTIAN INTELLECTUAL CULTURE IN THE SEVENTEENTH CENTURY

A Celebration of the Library of Narcissus Marsh
(1638–1713)

edited by

ALLISON P. COUDERT
SARAH HUTTON
RICHARD H. POPKIN

and

GORDON M. WEINER

JUDAEO-CHRISTIAN INTELLECTUAL CULTURE IN THE SEVENTEENTH CENTURY

A Celebration of the Library of Narcissus Marsh (1638–1713)

edited by

ALLISON P. COUDERT

Arizona State University,
Tempe, Arizona, U.S.A.

SARAH HUTTON

University of Hertfordshire,
West Hall Campus, U.K.

RICHARD H. POPKIN

University of California,
Los Angeles, California, U.S.A.

and

GORDON M. WEINER

Arizona State University,
Tempe, Arizona, U.S.A.

KLUWER ACADEMIC PUBLISHERS

DORDRECHT / BOSTON / LONDON

A C.I.P. Catalogue record for this book is available from the Library of Congress.

ISBN 0-7923-5789-2

Published by Kluwer Academic Publishers,
P.O. Box 17, 3300 AA Dordrecht, The Netherlands.

Sold and distributed in North, Central and South America
by Kluwer Academic Publishers,
101 Philip Drive, Norwell, MA 02061, U.S.A.

In all other countries, sold and distributed
by Kluwer Academic Publishers,
P.O. Box 322, 3300 AH Dordrecht, The Netherlands.

Printed on acid-free paper

Printed in the Netherlands.

CONTENTS

INTRODUCTION

MURIEL MCCARTHY

This volume originated from a seminar organised by Richard H. Popkin in Marsh's Library on July 7–8, 1994. It was one of the most stimulating events held in the Library in recent years. Although we have hosted many special seminars on such subjects as rare books, the Huguenots, and Irish church history, this was the first time that a seminar was held which was specifically related to the books in our own collection.

It seems surprising that this type of seminar has never been held before although the reason is obvious. Since there is no printed catalogue of the Library scholars are not aware of its contents. In fact the collection of books by late seventeenth and early eighteenth century European authors on, for example, such subjects as biblical criticism, political and religious controversy, is one of the richest parts of the Library's collections. Some years ago we were informed that of the 25,000 books in Marsh's at least 5,000 English books or books printed in England were printed between 1640 and 1700.

While there is no printed catalogue of all the books in Marsh's there are some sectional catalogues which with one exception are now out of print and are only available in special libraries. The first printed catalogue was compiled by J. R. Scott and edited by N. J. D. White: *Catalogue of the Manuscripts*, published in 1913.[1] N. J. D. White also compiled *A Short Catalogue of English Books . . .Printed before MDCXLI*, 1905[2] (this contains a listing of our incunabula) and *A Catalogue of Books in the French Language* (1918).[3] *A Catalogue of the Music Books*, compiled by Richard Charteris, was published by the Boethius Press in Kilkenny in 1982.

Archbishop Marsh's Library

Marsh's Library, the first public library in Ireland, was founded by Archbishop Narcissus Marsh in 1701.[4] Marsh was born in Hannington in Wiltshire in 1638 and educated in Oxford. He was ordained a clergyman in the Church of England and became a distinguished scholar and administrator. Marsh was later appointed Principal of St. Alban Hall in Oxford and was subsequently offered the Provostship of Trinity College in

A.P. Coudert, S. Hutton, R.H. Popkin and G.M. Weiner (eds): Judaeo-Christian Intellectual Culture in the Seventeenth Century, viii–xviii.
© 1999 *Kluwer Academic Publishers. Printed in the Netherlands.*

Dublin. He accepted this position and shortly after his arrival in Trinity College in 1679 he discovered that there was nowhere to go to read or study in Dublin. The College Library was only available to the staff and students. Marsh decided to build a public library but he did not get the opportunity to do so until he became Archbishop of Dublin nearly twenty years later. The Library, which was designed by Sir William Robinson, is now one of the few eighteenth-century buildings left in Dublin which is still being used for its original purpose.

Archbishop Marsh intended that the Library should be used by 'divines and anybody who wanted to spend an hour or two upon any occasion of study'. The original rules for readers also stated that 'all graduates and gentlemen shall have free access to the said Library on the days and hours before determined provided they behave themselves . . . give place and pay due respect to their betters'.

The interior of the Library with its beautiful dark oak bookcases each with carved and lettered gables, topped by a mitre, and the three elegant wired alcoves or 'cages' where the readers were locked with rare books, remains unchanged since it was built nearly three hundred years ago. It is a magnificent example of a seventeenth century scholars' library.

There are four main collections, consisting of 25,000 books relating to the sixteenth, seventeenth and the early part of the eighteenth centuries. As one might expect, there is a large collection of liturgical works, missals, breviaries, books of hours of the Sarum use, bibles printed in almost every language, including the four great Polyglot bibles, and a great deal of theology and religious controversy. But these collectors were men of scholarly tastes, and the scope of the subjects is surprisingly wide and varied. There are books on medicine, law, science, travel, navigation, mathematics, music, surveying and classical literature in all the collections.

While most of the books in Marsh's are in the possession of other great libraries some of the editions are either unique to the Library or are held by only a few national libraries. Apart from the books there are several distinctive features which set Marsh's apart from similar institutions. One unusual feature is that the interior design of the Library has changed so little that the books remain in the same places with the same shelfmarks where Archbishop Marsh and his first librarian placed them nearly three hundred years ago. This also means that the first manuscript catalogue compiled by the first librarian can still be used.

Of the four main collections the most important is the library of Edward Stillingfleet (1635–1699) who was Bishop of Worcester.[5] In 1705

Narcissus Marsh paid £2,500 for this library of nearly 10,000 books. Bishop Edward Stillingfleet was one of the most influential divines in the Church of England in the seventeenth century. He acted as spokesman for the Anglican Church during a period of great religious conflict. It was also a period when the Bible and biblical interpretations and translations were being questioned. Stillingfleet was renowned for his controversies with atheists, Roman Catholics, Protestants, and other religious groups. He preached sermons and wrote extensively on these disputes. Stillingfleet's 'noble' library is a great tribute to his scholarship and knowledge of books and it is not surprising to find that he purchased books until a few weeks before his death.[6]

Many of the books in Stillingfleet's library bear the signatures of important previous owners. These include Archbishop William Laud, Joseph Justus Scaliger, John Dee, Nicholas Udall (who wrote the first English comedy, *Ralph Roister Doister*), Richard Bentley (Stillingfleet's chaplain), Sir Kenelm Digby and Ben Jonson.

One of the most interesting discoveries in recent years is that we have 26 books which previously belonged to one of the heroes of Renaissance classical scholarship, Isaac Casaubon.[7] Casaubon was a major theologian at the centre of the religious controversies at the courts of Henry IV of France and James I of England. It was James I who requested Isaac Casaubon to reply to Cardinal Baronius's *Annales ecclesiastici*. The copy of this work in Stillingfleet's collection contains several sheets of manuscript notes made by Casaubon. There are also 77 books which belonged to Casaubon's son, Meric.

The second collection in the Library belonged to Elias Bouhéreau, a Huguenot refugee who fled from France in 1685 and came to Ireland in 1697.[8] Archbishop Marsh appointed Bouhéreau the first librarian in 1701. His books, which he donated to the Library, relate to protestant theology and controversy and also to the protestant Académie of Saumur which he had attended. It is interesting to note that three of the most renowned scholars in the Académie of Saumur, Moise Amyraut, Louis Cappel and Taneguy Le Fèvre, were Bouhéreau's teachers. A prize book given to Bouhéreau when he was in the Académie has been signed by Amyraut and Le Fèvre.

Bouhéreau's library represents a typical scholar's library of the seventeenth century. Religious controversy, history, politics, science, medicine and many of the classical authors are well represented. There are also a considerable number of books relating to the French protestants and the Edict of Nantes. Jean-Paul Pittion, when commenting on Bouhéreau's library said that 'it constitutes a unique source of information for the study of Calvinism in seventeenth century France'.[9] In 1981 Roger Nicole from the Gordon-Conwell Theological Seminary in America informed us that 'the world's most extensive collection of Amyraut's works is to be found in Marsh's Library'.[10]

Bouhéreau's library also represents his interest in modern medicine and intellectual developments in seventeenth century France. This can be seen in his purchase of the first issue and later issues of the *Journal des Sçavans*, his medical prescriptions, and the latest publications on medicine and related subjects. Bouhéreau's only publication was a translation from Greek into French of a work by Origen, *Traité d'Origène contre Celse*, which was published in Amsterdam in 1700. It was mentioned by such notable French scholars as Bayle and Le Clerc.

The third collection consists of Marsh's own books, which he left to his Library at his death. The fourth major collection consists of the books of Bishop Stearne of Clogher (the only Irish collector). Stearne bequeathed his books to Marsh's when he died in 1745. These four great scholarly collections represent some of the finest books produced in Europe in the seventeenth and early part of the eighteenth centuries.

The Oriental Collection

Marsh's interest in languages began in Oxford where he studied oriental languages and rabbinical and medieval writers. He was part of a learned circle that specialised in oriental studies in Oxford. The members of this group exchanged gifts with each other and an example of this can be seen in a charming inscription to Marsh by a member of the Buxtorf family in a Hebrew Bible printed in Venice in 1615. The librarian of the Bodleian Library also gave handsome gifts to Marsh, including Edward Pocock's Arabic version of Hugo Grotius's *De veritate religionis christianae* (1660).

It is interesting to note the extent and provenance of Marsh's original oriental collection, which contained both printed books and manuscripts. He donated all his oriental manuscripts, consisting of over 700 items, to the Bodleian Library.[11] The choicest of these superb manuscripts were purchased for Marsh at the auction in Holland of Jacob Golius famous collection in 1696.[12] Marsh also purchased manuscripts and printed books from the widow of the Dublin orientalist, Dudley Loftus.[13] We know from his correspondence that he purchased Hebrew books from a Mr Aron Moses and that Frances Guise, the widow of the Oxford orientalist William Guise, presented him with books when he was Bishop of Ferns and Leighlin in 1690. [14]

Until recently the only information we had on the use and importance of Marsh's collection came from two sources. The first was in Professor George Stokes's *Some Worthies of the Irish Church* (London, 1900). Stokes included 'An account of Archbishop Marsh and his library', and a brief description of some of the liturgical and oriental books. The second reference was given by Louis Hyman in his book *The Jews in Ireland* (London/Jerusalem, 1972). Hyman said that 'in the presence of Rev. Dr Thomas Sheridan . . . the Rev. John Alexander and other Hebrew scholars (they) held a disputation in the public library of St. Sepulchre's in May 1733'. (Marsh's Library was originally called the Library of St. Sepulchre.) In 1994 Professor Popkin told us that when an Israeli scholar studied a microfilm of our oriental collection he said that it was the biggest list of Latin Judaica he had ever seen or heard of. Because of this new information it may be useful to give some details of the oriental books in our collections.

Biblical and Henrew Books

There are superb Bibles, Mishnas, Targums, Talmuds, oriental grammars, dictionaries, lexicons, and some poetry in the collections. Many of the Hebrew books were printed by the famous Daniel Bomberg in Venice and the well known Jewish printers in Amsterdam. The Jewish writers include Moses Kimchi, David Kimchi, Moses ben Nachman, Moses ben Jacob Kimchi, Menasseh ben Israel, Elias Levitica, Ben Naphtali Issachar, David ben Isaac de Pomis and Levi ben Gershon. Catholic writers such as Guillaume Postel, Jean Morin, Richard Simon and Gilbert Genebrard made fine contributions to Hebrew studies and they are also represented in the collections.

A copy of Edmund Castell's *Lexicon heptaglotton* (London, 1669) was given to Marsh by Frances Guise when he was Bishop of Ferns and Leighlin in 1690. This enormous work contains Persian and Arabic sections and is a great tribute to Castell's learning and knowledge of Semitic languages. The writings of the well-known professor of theology at the University of Leiden, Johannes Coccejus, are well represented, including his *Tituli duo Thalmudici Sanhedrin et Maccoth* (Amsterdam, 1629). Another professor at Leiden, Petrus Cunaeus, wrote a study of the government of ancient Israel entitled *De republica Hebraeorum* (Leiden, 1632), which was collected by Archbishop Marsh, and a later edition by

Bouhéreau. Most of the books on rabbinical and medieval Hebrew written by Johannes Buxtorf the Elder, who was professor of Hebrew in the University of Basle, are also here. Buxtorf's first description of Jewish practices and beliefs in his *Synagoga Iudaica* (Hanover, 1622) is in Bouhéreau's collection and Stillingfleet had the translation by David Le Clerc (Basle, 1641). John Pearson's editing of *Critici Sacri* was a milestone in the technical methodology in biblical interpretation and copies of his work are in Stillingfleet's and Stearne's collections.

There are three copies of one of the greatest books in Jewish philosophy, *Doctor perplexorum* (*Guide of the Perplexed*), by Moses Maimonides. The earliest is in the Stillingfleet Collection and was printed in Sabionetta in 1553. Sebastian Münster was another professor of Hebrew at the University of Basle. Münster wrote Hebrew grammars and dictionaries which were very popular with Marsh and Bouhéreau. His *Kalendari□ Hebraicum* (Basle, 1527) is in Bouhéreau's collection and Marsh had a copy of his *Praecepta Mosaica* (Basle, 1533) and *Cosmographiae universalis* (Basle, 1634).

The curator of Hebrew books in the Vatican library, Julius Bartoloccius, wrote a description of Hebrew books and their authors, which is in Stillingfleet's collection. This book, entitled *Bibliotheca magna Rabbinica de scriptoribus & scriptis Hebraicis,* was printed in Rome in three volumes between 1675 and 1683 and is still regarded as a valuable reference book. Conrad Gesner's *Bibliotheca instituta et collecta* (Zurich, 1583) was one of the first attempts to complete a bibliography of all printed books which included Jewish authors. There are two copies in Stillingfleet's collection and a copy in Bouhéreau's collection.

Since it would be impossible to mention the books in all the collections I have selected some authors who might be of special interest to scholars. They are as follows: Leon of Modena, Johannes Leusden, John Lightfoot, Philip Van Limborch, Philippe du Plessis Mornay, John Selden, John Spencer, Joseph Justus Scaliger, Brian Walton, Wilhelm Schickhard and the professor of church history at the Franeker Academy in The Netherlands, Campegius Vitringa, the Elder. The latter's *De synagoga vetere* (Franeker, 1696), which contains an account of the ancient synagogue, is in Marsh's collection, and Bishop Stillingfleet had a copy of Josephus de Voisin's *Theologia Iudaeorum* (Paris, 1647). De Voisin's book was an examination of the doctrine of God and his attributes in rabbinical thought.

Finally, a work in Hebrew by Immanuel ben Solomon of Rome, *Sepher ham-Mahbaroth*, was printed in Brescia in 1491 by Gerson ben

Moses of Soncino. It is interesting that this book, which belonged to Archbishop Marsh, was regarded by him over three hundred years ago as particularly valuable; the Archbishop inscribed the words 'Liber rarissimus' on the title-page. The printer of this book was described by S. H. Steinberg as 'the greatest Jewish printer the world has ever known'.[15]

Arabic Books and Books in Lesser Eastern Languages

Although most of the books in Arabic and in the lesser eastern languages are devoted to religious subjects, Marsh and Stillingfleet also collected books which reflect their wider interests in mathematics and astronomy. In addition to these subjects there is also a fine collection of grammars, dictionaries and lexicons.

Important religious works collected by Marsh include an edition of the Koran in Arabic, edited by A. Hinckelmannus (Hamburg, 1694), and an Arabic version of the Pentateuch (Leiden, 1622). He also collected John Selden's version of the History of the Church of Alexandria by Patriarch Eutychius (London, 1642) and a copy of Mîkhâ'il al-Fâbûrî al-Ifranjî, *Kitâb yastamil 'alá ajwibat ahl-Kanîsah al-muqaddisah al-rusûlîyah li-l'tirûdât al-muslimîn wal-yahûd wal-Harâtiqah didd al-Qâthûlîqîn*, printed in Rome in 1680.

The celebrated Dutch scholar, Thomas Erpenius, was professor of Hebrew and eastern languages in the University of Leiden. He was also a director of a printing press that published books in Hebrew, Syriac and Arabic. An edition of his *Historia Josephi patriarchae ex Alcorano, Arabice*, printed in Leiden in 1617, is in Marsh's collection. (A New Testament in Greek, Syriac and Latin printed by H. Stephanus in Paris in 1569, which originally belonged to Thomas Erpenius, also belonged to Marsh.) Apart from his religious publications Erpenius also wrote and edited Arabic and Syriac grammars, which Marsh and Stillingfleet collected.

Edward Pocock (the Elder), professor of Hebrew in Oxford, published some remarkable books which were of great interest to Marsh and Stillingfleet. Stillingfleet collected Pocock's edition of Gregory (Abu al Faraj), called Bar Hebraeus, *Specimen historiae Arabum* (Oxon, 1650) and *Historia orientalis* (Oxon, 1672), and they both had copies of Pocock's elegant version of Husain ibn 'Ali, called Al-Tughra'i *Lamiato 'l Ajam, carmen Tograi* (Oxon, 1661). They also collected the writings of Christophorus Crinesius, the German divine who taught oriental languages in Wittenberg and became professor of divinity at Altdorff. Both had copies of his *Gymnasium Syriacum* (Wittebergæ, 1611) and Stillingfleet had a copy of his *Lingua Samaritica* (Altdorphii [1628]).

While Marsh seems to have had the ability to master and to collect books in eastern languages it would be interesting to know if he was able to understand a fascinating illustrated liturgy which originally belonged to Dudley Loftus. This is part missal and is in the Ge'ez language, an old liturgical form of Amharinya used by the Ethiopian Orthodox Church. It was printed in Leiden [1660?].

Another oriental language which interested Marsh was Persian. He acquired historical works and grammars written in Latin and Persian by Ludovicus de Dieu (the Elder), a Dutch protestant minister and expert on oriental languages who was a professor in the Walloon College in Leiden. Marsh acquired many other books in Persian, including a handsome edition of *Gazophylacium linguae Persarum* by Angelus [Joseph Labrosse], published in Amsterdam in 1684 and another book in Latin and Persian which appears to be an unfinished publication. This is a copy of the Gospel of St. Matthew entitled *Quatuor evangelia*, which is dated 1652 with no place of publication.

An interesting book with a Latin annotation by Marsh stating that it is a Turkish catechism translated by William Seaman in 1666 is difficult to identify. Marsh also noted that it contained some additional religious material in Arabic. But this catechism may have been written by the English puritan divine, John Ball, and it could also be in Arabic with some Turkish words added.

A very beautiful edition of another liturgical work, *Virtute et ope trinitatis sanctissimae . . . officia sanctorum juxta ritum ecclesiæ Maronitarum,* Syriac (Rome, 1666) and two copies of what appear to be a Maronite *Horae*, printed in Rome by Dominici Basae in 1584, are in Marsh's collection. An Illyrian Breviary entitled *Breviarium Romanum Slavonico idiomate iussu S. D. N. Innocentii P.P.X. editum* [Edited by R. Levakovic and M. Terlecki, Bishop of Chelm.] (Rome, 1648) is also in his collection.

Books in the Armenian Language

There are six books in the Armenian language in Marsh's collection: four of these have only been partly identified. The first librarian, Dr Bouhéreau, entered three of them simply as 'Liber Linguâ Armenâ'. The first appears to be a poem by Nerses Claiensis[?] 'De historia creationis'. The second is possibly a missal by G. Molino [1636]. The third book has been identified as an Armenian treatise, 'Particular ceremonies which are generally practised among Mahometans, Jews etc'. by Febourean Mikhayle. It was printed in Rome in 1681. The fourth is 'A book of countries and stories' printed in Amsterdam in 1669. The fifth book is Petro Paulo's *Doctrina christiana, versa linguam armenam* (Latin & Armenian) which was printed in Paris in 1634, and the sixth is Francisco Rivola's *Dictionarium Armeno-Latinum Evangelie* (Paris, 1633).

Russian Books

One of the most exciting events in recent years was the discovery by J. S. G. Simmons of six early printed Russian books in Marsh's collection.[16] Four of these books probably exist nowhere outside Russia. Three of the books were printed by the first Russian printer, Ivan Fedorov. They consist of an Apostol (Liturgical epistles) (1564), an *Evangelie uchitel 'noe* (Liturgical gospels) (Belorussia, 1569), a Psalter and New Testament (Ostrog, 1580), a *Bukvar*, or elementary instruction book for children (Kuteino, Belorussia, 1653), and we also have a *Pouchenie o morovom yazve* written by the Patriarch Nikon and printed in Moscow in 1656. Two copies of a devotional work on the sacraments, *O sakramentakh*, printed at the Monastery of the Caves in Kiev in 1657, are also here.

Astronomy and Mathematics

In his diary and correspondence Marsh regularly mentions his interest in astronomy and mathematics. In one long and fascinating letter, dated April 1681, he gave a detailed account of a comet which he observed in Dublin, and in his diary he mentions how he often solved 'knotty problems in algebra'. A book in his collection which would have helped him to solve just such 'knotty' mathematical problems is Euclid's *Elementorum geometricorum ex traditione Nasiri Dini Tusini*, which was printed in Rome in 1594. This book was printed in the Typographia Medicea in superb Arabic letters which were probably cut by the famous French typecutter Robert Granjon.[17]

For his astronomical collection Marsh seems to have been particularly interested in the writings of Ulugh Beg, the grandson of Tamerlane and founder of the observatory at Samarkand. He acquired two important works by him, which were edited or published by John Greaves, the Savilian professor of astronomy at Oxford. They are: *Binae tabulae geographicae una Nassir Eddini Persae altera Ulug Beigi Tatari* (London,

1648) and *Epochæ celebriores astronomis* (London, 1650). Another friend of Marsh's in Oxford, whom we have already mentioned, was Thomas Hyde. Hyde was the librarian of the Bodleian Library and was, like Marsh, interested in astronomy and eastern languages. Marsh purchased a copy of Hyde's edition of Ulugh Beg's catalogue of the stars, *Sive tabulae longitudinis ac Latitudinis stellarum fixarum* (Oxford, 1665).

Although the majority of Stillingfleet's books on astronomy are in Latin, he did have a copy of Alfraganus's *Elementa astronomica*, Arab. Lat. cum notis J. Golii (Amst. 1669) and an earlier edition with a commentary by J. Christomannus (Frankfurt, 1590).

****

It has been said that Marsh's is an intellectual fossil, a collection of books frozen in time, which remain in the same place and on the same shelves where they were placed by the scholars who collected them. To study and examine the books in Marsh's is to explore a microcosm of Europe's great cultural heritage. A study of these books would make an exciting project for scholars interested in original seventeenth century collections.

We are grateful to Constance Blackwell and the Foundation for Intellectual History for generously funding the event and to Gordon M. Weiner and Allison P. Coudert for hosting the conference dinner. Thanks are also due to Gordon M. Weiner for his sterling work in typesetting the volume. We express our gratitude to Richard and Julie Popkin for all their encouragement. We are deeply grateful to the President of Ireland, Mary Robinson, for the reception given to the delegates at her residence, Áras an Uachtaráin.

Muriel McCarthy
Marsh's Library
Dublin, Ireland

1 J. R. Scott, compiler & N. J. D. White, ed., *Catalogue of the Manuscripts Remaining in Marsh's Library, Dublin* (Dublin, [1913]).

2 N. J. D. White, *A Short Catalogue of English Books in Archbishop Marsh's Library Dublin, printed before MDCXLI* (Bibliographical Society, 1905). This contains a supplement listing incunabula separately taken from T.K. Abbot's *Catalogue of Fifteenth Century Books in Trinity College, Dublin* (Dublin, 1905).

3 N. J. D. White, Compiler, *A Catalogue of Books in the French Language, Printed in or before A.D.1715* (Dublin, 1918).

4 For details on Marsh and his library see Muriel McCarthy, *All Graduates and Gentlemen: Marsh's Library* (Dublin, 1980).

5 *Dictionary of National Biography;* R. T. Carroll, *The Common-sense Philosophy of Bishop Edward Stillingfleet 1635–99* (The Hague, 1975). Cf. Sarah Hutton, 'Science, philosophy, and atheism: Edward Stillingfleet's defence of religion', In *Scepticism and Irreligion in the Seventeenth and Eighteenth Centuries*, eds. R. H. Popkin and A. Vanderjagt (Leiden: E. J. Brill, 1993).

6 See Stillingfleet, Edward, *Works; with his Life and Character* [by R. Bentley], 6 vols (London, 1709–10), vol. 1, p. 41.

7 T. A. Birrell, 'The Reconstruction of the Library of Isaac Casaubon', In *Hellinga* (Amsterdam, 1980).

8 N. J. D. White, *Four Good Men* (Dublin, 1927), 'Elias Bouhéreau of La Rochelle'.

9 See J. P. Pittion, 'Notes for a Saumur Bibliography', *Long Room* 2 (Spring 1971): 9–22.

10 Roger Nicole, *Moyse Amyraut. A Bibliography* (New York, 1981). Contains a note on upper endpapers on the Amyraut collection.

11 See Muriel McCarthy, p. 47.

12 See typewritten copy (in Marsh's Library) of the Diary of Archbishop Marsh (1690–96), p.71: 'I returned £220–00 to Dr Edward Bernard of Oxford, who takes a journey into Holland Friday the 18 on purpose therewith to purchase for my use the choicest of Jacobus Golius his oriental manuscripts. . .'.

13 See Muriel McCarthy, p. 47.

14 Marsh's correspondence in Oxford, Bodleian Library, MS Smith 52 (15,659), Extracts Letters to Dr Smith from Narcissus Marsh 1679–1709. See also Richard Mant, *History of the Church of Ireland*, 2 vols (London, 1841–40): see Marsh's letters in vol. l.

15 See S. H. Steinberg, *Five Hundred Years of Printing*, 3rd ed (Harmondsworth, 1974), p. 114.

16 J. S. G. Simmons 'Early-printed Cyrillic books in Archbishop Marsh's Library, Dublin', *The Irish Book* 11 (Spring 1963): 37–42.

17 See A. F. Johnson, *The Italian Sixteenth Century* (London, 1926), pp. 6–7.

Catalogues & Dictionaries Consulted:

British Museum: General Catalogue of Printed Books. Photolithographic edition to 1955 (London, 1965).

H. M. Adams, *Catalogue of Books Printed on the Continent of Europe 1501–1600 in Cambridge Libraries* (Cambridge, 1967).

A. W. Pollard & G. R. Redgrave, *Short-title Catalogue of Books Printed in England, Scotland and Ireland . . . 1475–1640* (New York, 1972).

D. Wing, *Short-title Catalogue of Books Printed in England, Scotland, Ireland, Wales and British America 1641–1700* (New York, 1982).

A. Chalmers, *The General Biographical Dictionary* (London, 1812–17).

Encyclopaedia Britannica (Edinburgh, 1875–89).

A. M. Hyamson, *A Dictionary of Universal Biography* (London, 1951).

D. Patrick & F. H. Groome, eds, *Chambers Biographical Dictionary* (London, 1897).

L. Stephen & L. Sidney, eds, *Dictionary of National Biography* (London, 1885–1901).

1. TWO TREASURES OF MARSH'S LIBRARY

RICHARD H. POPKIN

I should like to begin this volume about the treasures of the Marsh Library by discussing the significance of two items in the collection – the Spanish Polyglot Bible, the Complutensis, published in 1517, and the vocalized *Mishna* of 1646. These are two extraordinary publishing ventures which involved intimate cooperative effort of Jewish and Christian scholars, and which were each part of Millenarian plans and expectations of the Christian sponsors and partners. Both of these works are exceedingly rare. The Marsh copies of the *Mishna* are not presently known.[1]

To begin with the Polyglot Bible, this was probably the most intricate publishing venture undertaken since the beginning of printing with Gutenberg. The finished product, the first publication together of the Hebrew text, the Greek text, the Latin Vulgate, and the Aramaic paraphrase (the Targum Onkelos) with a Latin translation of it, all on the same page, involved enormous expense, many printers to make the fonts, and print the work, and Hebrew and Greek scholars to establish the text.[2] The project was organized, supervised and financed by Cardinal Francisco Ximines de Cisneros, 1436–1517, the Archbishop of Toledo, Primate of Spain.[3] (The cost was estimated in 1917 as 250,000 English pounds of the time, at least half of the revenues of the diocese of Toledo in the early 16th century).[4]

At first what caught my interest about this was finding out about the Hebrew scholars who were involved, since all Jews who had not converted to Christianity were expelled from Spain in 1492. So, I wanted to know who were these Hebrew scholars expert enough to prepare the Hebrew and Aramaic texts after 1492. Second, when I read a description of the contents of the six volumes of the Polyglot Bible, I saw that there was a tiny apparatus for the Greek portion (a one and half page Greek grammar) but that a large folio volume was devoted to a Hebrew dictionary, a Hebrew grammar, an Aramaic dictionary and grammar, and *a pronouncing word book* so that if one knew Latin one could find the equivalent in Hebrew or Aramaic and know how to enunciate it.[5]

I looked up who the Hebrew scholars were, and I puzzled over who in the early 16th century might need a pronouncing dictionary of Aramaic,

A.P. Coudert, S. Hutton, R.H. Popkin and G.M. Weiner (eds): Judaeo-Christian Intellectual Culture in the Seventeenth Century, 1–12.
© 1999 *Kluwer Academic Publishers. Printed in the Netherlands.*

(which I do not think ever existed before or after the Spanish Polyglot). It was claimed that Cardinal Ximines brought together the best Hebrew scholars of the time.[6] They were actually three almost unknown figures at the time; one Alfonso de Alcala, a Jewish doctor about whom nothing more is known; Pablo Nunez Coronel, who was just twelve years old in 1492, converted, and later became Professor of Sacred Scriptures at Salamanca; and the most interesting and intriguing, Alfonso de Zamora, an eighteen year old rabbinical student in 1492, who was taken in by Cardinal Ximines, became his expert on Aramaic text, and who apparently only converted in 1506 when he became professor of Hebrew at the new university at Alcala.[7] It was illegal for unconverted Jew to be in Spain after 1492, and it was a most serious crime to protect and aid an unconverted Jew at that time.[8] Nonetheless Alfonso de Zamora became chief editor of the Hebrew and Aramaic portions of the Polyglot. (A letter of his of 1544 indicates that he was not a real convert and considered himself the last of the Spanish Jewish sages).[9]

What was the point in all of the emphasis on the Aramaic text and knowledge of how to pronounce Aramaic? Cardinal Ximines when a simple priest around 1480 studied both Hebrew and Aramaic with a rabbi. His reason, he openly said was to master the languages of Jesus himself, who Ximines expected to soon return to earth. It was Ximines's original intention to devote his life to the study of Hebrew and Aramaic, to avoid any involvement in the world while awaiting the Second Coming.[10] He involuntarily became first the leader of the Reformed Franciscans, and then the Archbishop of Toledo. In his worldly capacity he then sought to construct the institutions and to find the personnel to prepare for the great events to come.[11]

The Cardinal by 1500 was the most powerful political figure in Spain, leading the country through wars, political crises, and the development of its colonial empire. At the same time he single-handedly set up the new University of Alcala in 1506 as the place where people would be trained for the world to come. Of the original forty-four chairs (including a medical school and a law school) there were four professors of Hebrew. The staff at Alcala played a central role in the Polyglot Bible project preparing the texts.[12] Ximines assembled as many of the best and most ancient manuscripts in Hebrew and Greek as he could obtain.[13] The texts were prepared with philological aids, grammars and dictionaries, but no footnotes or any critical apparatus. One of the professors at Alcala, the leading Spanish humanist of the time, Antonio de Lebrixa, wanted to amend the Greek text by showing that the passages about the Trinity are not in the earliest manuscripts or in the citations by the Church Fathers. Ximines would not let him include this in the Polyglot, which would need Vatican approval, but instead paid for a separate publication of a study on how to edit the Greek text, which is one of the first modern critical studies of Biblical scholarship.[14]

Cardinal Ximines was anxious to rediscover pure Christianity and to lead Jews and pagans to convert to this pure Christianity. He believed it was to be found first in the language which Jesus spoke,[15] then in the spirit of pure persons such as the early Spanish mystics, especially unlettered women, the original *alumbrados* of early 16th century Spain, and such as the uncontaminated Indians of Central America, preserved from the corruptions of European Christianity.[16] The Cardinal protected the early mystics. He led his order in America to the protection of the Indians. He reorganized the Inquisition so that it would not punish people just because of their Jewish or Moorish ancestry, but would recognize their equality if they had truly imbibed pure Christianity.[17] To further this he had his resident Aramaic scholar, Alfonso de Zamora editing many Aramaic biblical commentaries from ancient times, and making this fount of wisdom available to his students in Alcala and Salamanca.[18] In an unpublished work, Alfonso de Zamora brought together all of the ancient Jewish sources he had available to him, presumably for his students.[19] And this would indicate that while the Inquisition was trying to stamp out Jewish learning, Cardinal Ximines was collecting it and having it passed on to future generations.

What can be the explanation for this? As I have indicated it all seems to have been part of a Millenarian scenario which the Cardinal was living through, (in which he, himself, may have been playing a crucial role. One of his lady mystics proclaimed around 1506 that the angelic Pope who would rule just before the Second Coming was not himself a pope or a person living in Italy, but in Spain![20] The Cardinal's efforts went on globally in terms of his directions to his brethren in America to preserve the Indians and prepare them for pure Christianity, in terms of his establishment of reformed educational institutions to create a reformed educated elite (mostly sons of Jewish converts) to prepare for the Millennium, in terms of reviving what he called: 'the hitherto dormant study of the sacred Scriptures', by going back to the original sources and languages.[21]

The Polyglot Bible is thus a critical part of a great Millenarian vision. The Hebraic-Aramaic part obviously played the greatest role in terms of volumes, and effort. At a time when Greek was practically unknown in Spain except to imported Greek scholars and a couple of humanists, the aid offered for reading the Greek scripture was just a page and half grammar. And at a time when only Jews and a few odd figures like the Cardinal knew Aramaic, so much of the text in the Polyglot apparatus was devoted to making it a living language, *because* its most famous native speaker, Jesus, was soon to appear again on earth.

If this explains the Cardinal's reasons for underwriting and guiding the project, why should the Jewish scholars have cooperated? The actual putting together of the contents of the books and the printing of them took six years. We do not know how many people were involved, but the cost was immense. German printers and font makers were brought in from Lyon, Hebrew, Aramaic and Greek manuscripts were bought at very high prices, scholars were supported.[22] The Jews may have co-operated as a way of keeping alive their Jewish knowledge, and as a way of being protected while engaging in what the Inquisition would have regarded as prima facia evidence of Judaizing.[23] Another possibility which needs to be explored is that the project was used as a way of assembling a great library of ancient and medieval Jewish texts, and of training another generation to understand and utilize them. (Some of the manuscripts that Alfonso de Zamora edited in manuscript are said, on them, to be for students at Salamanca or Alcala).[24] Not only were biblical texts and ancient commentaries assembled, but also Hebrew grammars, Jewish works on Bible interpretations were also part of the collection. And, after Ximines died in 1517, this center of Jewish studies persevered another decade. Then the Inquisition managed to destroy Jewish studies at Alcala and to condemn most of its teachers as heretics and Erasmians.[25] (They included some of leaders of Spain's minuscule Protestant movement). Alfonso de Zamora stayed on at least until 1544, but his letter that I alluded to earlier reveals him as a bitter, discouraged man, who wants some outside Jewish community to know of his situation, and to carry on its Judaism.[26] At the insistence of his bosses in 1526 he wrote and published a letter to the Jews of Rome, which is so overdone as a conversion document that it is hard to believe anyone took it seriously.[27] Here one needs to examine who had copies and what they did with them. There is a copy at the University of California Berkeley which has notes in Ladino, Spanish written in Hebrew characters.[28] There may be other copies with useful information.

The Polyglot itself also needs more study. Only 600 copies were originally printed. The work seems to have been given away as presents to Church officials, scholars, political leaders, rather than sold. Only around one hundred copies survive nowadays, and quite a few are lacking the volume with the Hebrew and Aramaic apparatus. This had led some to speculate that since Jewish instruction was forbidden in Inquisition Spain, that some secret Jews used the Hebrew and Aramaic volume as a text for themselves and their students.

In recent years Prof. Michael Screech of All Soul's has been inspecting copies of the Polyglot and finding significant differences in them. I have only seen about six copies, but each has a note about Screech's observations on the copy.[29] Each set may have special features designed for its intended recipient. So it may be worth somebody's time and trouble to check whether the sets that still have the Hebrew and Aramaic apparatus have the same content, or whether there are important additions or omissions in copies of this volume. The Marsh Library copy is listed among the ninety-seven known copies of existing Polglots in Tyrell's book on Cardinal Ximines. It is number twenty-seven, and all that is said of it is that it was purchased from the collection of Edward Stillingfleet (1635–1699), Bishop of Worcester.[30] The Spanish Polyglot Bible was a joint Jewish-Christian project carried on at a time of intense hostility towards Jews in Spain. It produced a model for later polyglots and a setting for the beginning of modern Bible scholarship (if Antonio de Lebrixa's separate work on Bible interpretation is included).

The second Jewish-Christian project I want to deal with is the edition of the *Mishna* of 1646. This is the first printed copy of this ancient Jewish compilation from the second century of the common era which is vocalized, that is, has the diacritical markings that are used to indicate Hebrew vowels. It also has some commentary material from medieval Jewish writers to make the text more intelligible. I only became interested in the work because there is so much discussion of it in the writings of the Protestants Samuel Hartlib, John Dury and Adam Boreel, and there was such a vast distribution effort, sending hundreds of copies to various countries from England and France to Poland and Sweden.[31] The work, just one volume, took four years to produce, and was published in 4,000 copies by Menasseh ben Israel in Amsterdam, as the beginning of a plan to publish the text in many formats, as well as in Spanish and in Latin.[32] Work went on for about forty years on preparing the Spanish and Latin texts.[33]

When I kept running across references to the work, and the attempts to distribute it in various parts of Europe, and the failure to sell any copies, I began to start looking into what this was all about. The editorial work on the 1646 *Mishna* was done by Adam Boreel, the leader of the Dutch Collegiants, and by rabbi Judah Leon of Middleburg and later of Amsterdam. Boreel financed the project, put the rabbi and his family up in

Boreel's house, and fed them (kosher food?).[34] Boreel even went to the trouble to learn Spanish and Portuguese so that he talk more easily with the rabbi.[35] The rabbi in these four years put in the vowel markings, and Boreel chose and edited the commentaries.

Then, as I found in one of the Hartlib papers, when they were done, Boreel was told that no Jews would accept the text as genuine if the name of a Dutch Protestant was on the title page as editor, and they would only accept the text if Menasseh ben Israel, the most famous rabbi of Amsterdam was involved. So, Menasseh was enlisted to write a one page preface, and rabbi Judah Leon wrote another, and *no* mention of Boreel appeared anywhere in the volume. Some Dutch Protestants paid 2,200 guilders to Menasseh to have the 4,000 copies made.[36]

During my travels to libraries in America, Europe and Israel, I looked for a copy of this work to no avail. It did not seem to be in any collection. Had the 4,000 copies all disappeared? One day I went into the great Judaica library in Amsterdam, the Rosenthaliana, and asked my friend, Dr. Adrian Offenberg, the librarian (and expert on rabbi Judah Leon and his works) if he had ever seen a copy. He went into his rare book room and took down a copy. He told me he thought this was the only one, but he had recently learned that the late Professor Leo Fuks, a great Judaica collector in The Netherlands, also had a copy.[37] So, there were two. And here in Marsh's Library there are also two copies, one from Bishop Stillingfleet's collection and one from Bishop Marsh's, thereby doubling the number of known copies.

One can ask, what was the point in so much time and energy being expended in publishing a known Jewish text with the vowels inserted? The initiative for the project came from some English and Dutch Millenarians during the Puritan period. Dury and Hartlib wanted to establish a College of Jewish Studies in London to make Christianity less offensive to Jews and to make Jewish learning accessible to Christians, all in preparation for the conversion of the Jews to pure Christianity and for the ensuing Millennium that would start when Jesus reappeared. In the envisaged plan for the College of Jewish Studies, the staff was to consist of Adam Boreel, Menasseh ben Israel and a Christian Hebraist, J.S. Rittangel. They wanted one thousand pounds for the College. And as Dury described the unfortunate state of affairs, due to the troubles in Ireland at the time, the money was diverted to fighting there.[38] The first fruits of the plan seem to be Boreel's work with rabbi Judah Leon, both on the *Mishna* and on building an exact model of Solomon's Temple.[39] The *Mishna* contains detailed descriptions of the Temple and all of its contents. The Temple will be rebuilt, according to Christian eschatology, when Jesus reappears. Therefore the information in the book and the model is needed in order to prepare for what is to come. The information in the book is so important that it has to be made available first to those whose Hebrew is not good enough to read without the vowels, and then also for those who do not know Hebrew. The Spanish edition, which Boreel worked on with rabbi Abendana, was presumably for the Jews of Amsterdam and their friends and relatives who really did not know Hebrew. The Latin edition would be for the Christian world. Up to Boreel's death in 1661 he was having difficulties with rabbi Abendana and others in the Jewish community who were not as anxious as he to get the Spanish translation finished and published.[40] Isaac Abendana took the Latin project with him when he moved to Cambridge, England, and he was working on it there while he was Reader in Hebrew. The Regius Professor of Hebrew at Cambridge, Ralph Cudworth, supervised his work, and wrote out chits to pay Abendana as the work proceeded.[41]

From the point of view of the English and Dutch Millenarians the *Mishna* project was of great importance from 1642–1660, because of their firm belief that the Millennium would soon occur, and that its occurrence would be preceded by the conversion of the Jews. Part of the preparation for the conversion was to make the Jews more fully aware of their own religion so that they would see that Christianity was the fulfillment of it. If the Jews fully understood, through seeing the Christian relevance of texts like the *Mishna* they would gladly convert. Hartlib, Dury and Boreel, among others, worked closely with the Jews of The Netherlands, and sought the readmission of the Jews in general to England, as preparations for the conversion which they originally were convinced would occur in 1655–56. They also felt that Christians, if they genuinely knew what Judaism involved, would be anxious to assist in any way in creating conditions that would be helpful in bringing about the conversion. Presumably, making the vocalized Hebrew text of the *Mishna*, with commentary available all over Europe to Christians who knew Hebrew would assist in God's work.[42]

If that was the rationale of the Millenarian Christians who put in so much time, energy and money in their philo-semitic projects at the time, why should the Jews have joined in and assisted in these ventures? To some extent I think rabbis Judah Leon and Menasseh ben Israel, and perhaps others, shared the expectation that a Messiah was about to arrive, the long awaited Jewish Messiah, who would usher in the Messianic age. Rabbi Judah Leon's small book about his *exact* model of the ancient

Temple, published in Spanish, Portuguese, Dutch, French, English and German, shows that he sincerely believed that a most important understanding of what is going on the world can be reached through appreciating the model, and that the model can prepare everyone for the rebuilding of The Temple.[43]

Menasseh ben Israel saw his own role as significant in making Jewish and Christian readers understand the dynamics of current history, leading to the Messianic age. He tried to make Jewish learning accessible to Jews and Christians through his many publications in Spanish, Latin and Hebrew. He was the leading publisher of Hebrew texts in Amsterdam of the time. He probably saw the *Mishna* publication as related to what he himself had been doing in the 1620's, 30's and 40's. And since he was constantly in need of money, he probably was happy to get such a fat contract for printing the *Mishna*, with the prospect of many further contracts to publish larger and smaller format *Mishnas* and modern language versions.[44]

The failure of the project needs more explanation. The Jews might not have trusted the text because of rumors of Christian involvement in the edition. But why were there no Christian purchasers except for Stillingfleet and Marsh? And what finally became of the remaining 3,996 copies? All of this remains to be explored.

These two projects, the Polyglot Bible and the *Mishna* are important indications of Jewish and Christian scholarship combining at a time when there was so much mutual antagonism and distrust between Jews and Christians. We know of many cases where individual Jews worked with Christians to put out texts for Christians. We know that Jews worked with the Christian Hebrew printer, Bomberg, to put out the Hebrew Bible with three Jewish commentaries, and they worked with him to put out the Talmud, texts of importance for the practice of Judaism.[45]

However I think the two projects I have described have a special flavor because of the resonance of Millenarian expectations involved in each. And it is fortunate that such fine exemplars have survived in the Marsh Library, amongst the amazing amount of Judaica and Latin Judaica that is here.

1 The Marsh copy of the Polyglot is in the list of copies given in James P.R. Lyell, *Cardinal Ximines, Statesman, Ecclesiastic, Soldier and Man of Letters, with an Account of the Complutensian Polyglot Bible* (London, 1917). Dr. Adrian Offenberg of the great Judaica library, the Biblioteca Rosenthaliana of Amsterdam told me that the only known copies of the 1646 Mishna edition were the only in the Rosenthaliana and one in the private collection of the late Professor L. Fuks.

2 The logistics and the cost of creating the Polyglot Bible are discussed and analyzed in Lyell, Cardinal Ximenes, chap. iv, and M. Revilla Rico, *La Poliglota de Alcala* (Madrid, 1917).

3 On Ximines's life and career, see Alvor Gomez de Castro, *De la hazanas de Francisco Jiminez de Cisneros* (1569), ed. and trans. by Jose Droz Reta (Madrid: Fundacion Universitaria Espanola, 1984), Libro primero; and Carl J. von Hefele, *The Life and Times of Cardinal Ximinez* (London, 1860), chaps. 1–5.

4 This estimate is given by Lyell, p. 34, using data that appeared in 1569 by Alvor Gomez de Castro, who had conferred with people then at Alcala de Henares who either had worked on the project or knew the details of it.

5 The one and half page Greek grammar appears in the first volume. This is somewhat strange since Spain had very few Greek scholars at the time. In fact, a Greek scholar from Crete had to be brought to Spain to work on the Bible project. What is usually listed as volume 5 contains as its total contents a Hebrew grammar, a Hebrew and Aramaic lexicon, Hebrew and Aramaic dictionaries, including aids for pronunciation so that if one knew Latin one could enunciate the Hebrew and Aramiac equivalents.

6 See Jerome Friedman, *The Most Ancient Testimony. Sixteenth Century Christian Hebraica in the Age of Renaissance Nostalgia*, (Athens: Ohio University Press, 1983), p. 29.

7 For the little that is known about these Hebrew scholars, see the introduction by Federico Perez Castro to *El Manuscrito Apologetico de Alfonso de Zamora*, (Madrid: Consejo Superior de Investigaciones Cientificas Instituto Arias Montano, 1950), the articles 'Alfonso de Alcala', 'Alfonso de Zamora' and 'Pablo Coronel' in the *Enciclopedia Universel Ilustrada*, 4:612, 4:614, and 15:820; and articles 'Paul Nunez Coronel' and 'Alfonso de Zamora' in the *Jewish Encyclopedia*. The *Encyclopedia Universal Ilustrada* says that Alfonso de Alcala and Pablo Coronel were converted in 1492, and Alfonso de Zamora in 1506. The *Jewish Encyclopedia* article on Alfonso de Zamora also reports his baptism in 1506. In the Spanish article on Zamora, he is identified as a learned Spanish rabbi, *even though* he was only 18 in 1492, and Coronel as a *Docto israelita* though he was just twelve years old in 1492. The most recent review of Zamora's biography in Luis Diez Merino, *Targum de Salmos. Edicion Principe del Ms. Vila-Amil n. 5 de Alfonso de Zamora, Bibliotheca Hispana Biblica*, Vol. VIII (Madrid, 1982) pp. 5–8, states, without offering any evidence, that Alfonso de Zamora and his father, a rabbi, left Spain in 1492 and then returned later and converted in 1506.

8 According the edict expelling the Jews from Spain in 1492, anyone who harbored an unconverted Jew after August 1492 was subject to the death penalty.

9 This letter appears in Hebrew in A. Neubauer, 'Alfonso de Zamora', *Jewish Quarterly Review* 7(1895): 412–415 taken from the mansucript original in the Warner Collection, 65, in the University of Leiden Library. A Spanish translation of it is given by Frederico Perez Castro in *El manuscrito apolegetica de Alfonso de Zamora, traduccion y estudio del Sefer Hokhmat Elohim* (Madrid: Consejo superior de Investigaciones Cientificas Institute Arias Montano, 1950). I should like to thank my colleague Professor Wolf Leslau of UCLA who has carefully gone over the Hebrew and the Spanish texts and assured me that the texts are identical. I have used the Spanish translation in this study.

10 See Alvar Gomez de Castro, *De Rebus Gestis a Francisco Ximenio*, Alcala, 1569. Ximines's Millenarianism is discussed in detail in R.H. Popkin, 'Jewish Christians and Christian Jews in Spain, 1492 and After', *Judaism* 41 (1992), pp. 248–67.

11 On his career, cf. Alvor Gomes de Castro, *De Rebus Gestis a Francisco Ximenio* and Hefele, *Life of Cardinal Ximines*, chaps. 1–5.

12 Spain was ahead of other European countries in establishing chairs of Hebrew studies. France did not create a chair of Hebrew until the 1530's. Louvain was looking for a Hebrew teacher in the 1520's. England did not begin Hebrew studies until the latter part of the century. The university of Alcala had a law school and a medical school. So, the allotment of *four* chairs for Hebrew studies is even more striking. On the allotment of chairs, see Lyell, p. 25. On the founding of the university of Alcala, see A. de la Torre, *La Universidad de Alcala . . .* en *Homenaje a Menendez Pidal* (Madrid: Libraria y Casa Editorial Hernando, 1932), III, p. 377ff.

13 Alfonso de Zamora told Alvor Gomez de Castro that the Cardinal spent 4,000 gold ducats on seven Hebrew manuscripts used in the project. Gomez de Castro, pp.117–118.

14 On Antonio de Lebrixa's relations with Ximines and the Bible project, and on his *Apologie*, see Marcel Bataillon, *Erasme et l'Espagne*, nouvelle edition (Geneva: Droz, 1991), Tome I, pp. 24–47.

15 In his preface to the Polyglot Bible, Cardinal Ximines said, 'No translation can fully and exactly represent the sense of the original at least in that language in which our Saviour himself spoke . . . Every theologian should also be able to drink of that water which springeth up to eternal life, at the fountainhead itself. This is the reason, therefore, why we have ordered the Bible to be printed in the original language with different translations. . . To accomplish this task we have been obliged to have recourse to the knowledge of the most able philologists, and to make researches in every direction for the best and most ancient Hebrew and Greek Mss. Our object is to revive the hitherto dormant study of the sacred Scriptures'.

16 I have used the translation given by Lyell, *Cardinal Ximines,* pp. 26–27, which I have checked against the original Latin.

17 On all of these activities see Popkin, 'Jewish Christians', pp. 254–257.

18 Cf. Popkin, 'Jewish Christians', p. 262. From 1500 onward Alfonso de Zamora prepared various Aramaic texts for Cardinal Ximines. These texts were apparently also for the use of students at the universities of Alcala and Salamanca. A list of the known Aramaic works prepared by Alfonso de Zamora appears in Perez Castro, *El manuscrito apologetico de Alfonso de Zamora*, pp. XXXII–LX.

19 This work, *Sefer Hokmat Elohim*, was only published in 1950 by Perez Castro. The work contains a wealth of materials from the Talmud, Midrashim and medieval Jewish writers.

20 See Jodi Bilinkoff, 'A Spanish Prophetress and her Patrons: the Case of Maria de Santo Domingo', *Sixteen Century Journal*, 23 (1992): 21–34, esp. pp. 30–34. The author points out that the Cardinal may have indeed begun to view himself as that long awaited leader of Christendom, who was prophecied by Maria de Santo Domingo.

21 See Popkin, 'Jewish Christians', Hefele, *Life and Times*, and John Leddy Phelan, *The Millenial Kingdom of the Franciscans in the New World* (Berkeley and Los Angeles: University of California Press, 1956).

22 On the logistics of producing the Polyglot Bible, see Lyell, *Cardinal Ximines*, and Revilla Rico, *La Poliglota de Alcala*.

23 Possessing any Hebrew works was taken by the Inquisition as indicating that one was 'judaizing'. Explaining Jewish beliefs and practices would be seen as even more seditious at the time.

24 See Neubauer, *Alfonsa de Zamora*, and Perez Castro, *El manuuscriptoa aplogetica.*

25 Cf. Marcel Bataillon, *Erasme et l'Espagne*, Tome I. See also R.H. Popkin, 'Marannos, New Christians and the Beginnings of Modern Anti-Trinitarianism', *Proceedings of Conference, The Expulsion of the Jews, 1492 and after* (Jerusalem forthcoming).

26 The letter purports to be from a Professor Zornosa to Pope Paul III. At the end it is stated that the letter is by Alfonso de Zamora, who is 70 years of age, and who teaches Hebrew at Alcala, *and who has not yet seen happiness*. Then he said, 'I am the only Jewish wise man left in Spain since the Expulsion of the Jews from Castile, which took place in 5232 of the era of the Creation of the world as the Jews compute it'. Then the letter ends with its author praying for the Jews in the rest of the world, and signing with a symbol which will be recognized by the reader. The Hebrew text is given in Neubauer, *Alfonsa de Zamora*, pp. 412–415. The letter is in the Warner collection at the University of Leiden which was assembled in Constantinople in the middle of the 17th century. There is no evidence

of the letter in the Vatican files. This suggests that the form of the letter is a ruse in order to communicate with a Jewish community in the Ottoman Empire. It is the only document of Alfonso de Zamora that gives the date based on the Jewish calender.

27 The work is entitled *Introductionis artis grammatice hebraice nunc recenter edite* (Alcala de Henares: Academia Completensis, 1526). It makes such wild charges about Jewish beliefs, that no actual Jew would have taken it seriously as a conversion document. Compared to the major conversionist writings of Pablo de Santa Maria, Jeronimo de Santa Fe, and other New Christians, Alfonso's is not interesting.

28 This is in the Bancroft Library, call number PJ4566.A64 1526. I should like to thank Amos Funkenstein for deciphering the notes for me. Ladino was the language of Sephardic Jews in the Ottoman Empire, especially at Salonika. It is unlikely that it would have been the language of someone in Rome, the purported place where the conversionist document was directed.

29 There are interesting notes by Screech in the copy at the Detriot Public Library and in the copy at the Pitts Library at Emory University, Atlanta, Georgia.

30 Lyell, *Cardinal Ximines*, Appendix A, p.94. Lyell did not know of the copies now in the Detroit Public Library and in the Pitts Library at Emory University in Atlanta. The former belonged to the Scripps family of Detroit and the latter was formerly in the Hartford Seminary Library which has been purchased by Emory.

31 See R.H. Popkin, 'Some Aspects of Jewish-Christian Theological Interchanges in Holland and England 1640—1700', in J. van den Berg and E.G.E. van der Wall, *Jewish-Christian Relations in the Seventeenth Century. Studies and Documents* (Dordrecht: Kluwer, 1988), pp.8—11 and the references given there.

32 The contractual agreement for the various proposed editions appears in M.M. Kleerkooper, *De Boekhandel te Amsterdam voornamelijk in de 17de eeuw* (Eerste deel), ('sGravenhage 1914–16) pp. 410–412. See also L. Fuks and R.G. Fuks-Mansfeld, *Hebrew Typography in the Northern Netherlands*, 1585–1815, Part I (Leiden: E.J.Brill, 1984), p.109.

33 Cf. David S. Katz, 'The Abendana Brothers and the Christian Hebraists of Seventeenth-Century England', *Journal of Ecclesiastical History*, 40(1989):28—52. The Latin translation being made by Isaac Abendana exists in manuscript at the Cambridge University Library. Apparently some of it was used in Surhensius's Latin edition of the *Mishna*. The Spanish translation existed in manuscript in The Netherlands in the 18th century.

34 Boreel wrote Father Marin Mersenne on Sept. 3, 1646 that he had been working on the *Mishna* edition since 1639 'avec l'aide d'un Juif que j'ay eu aliment environ cinq ans pour cette affaire', *Correspondance de Mersenne*, Tome XIV (1646), p. 431.

35 See the letter of John Dury to Samuel Hartlib about Boreel, Hartlib Papers 1/6/11–13, published in Van den Berg and van der Wall, *Jewish Christians Relations*, pp. 145–149, especially p. 147.

36 ibid., loc. cit., and Popkin, 'Some Aspects of Jewish-Christian Interchanges', p. 9.

37 Prof. Fuks's great collection of Judaica was left to the city of Leeuwarden.

38 Cf. R.H. Popkin, 'The First College of Jewish Studies', *Revue des Etudes juives* 143(1984):351–64, and 'Hartlib, Dury and the Jews', in M. Greengrass, M. Leslie and T. Raylor, eds., *Samuel Hartlib and Universal Reformation. Studies in Intellectual Communication* (Cambridge: Cambridge University Press, 1994), pp. 118—136.

39 Cf. Popkin, 'Some Aspects of Jewish Christian Interchanges', p. 8; and A.K. Offenberg, 'Jacob Jehuda Leon (1602–1675) and his Model of the Temple', in Van den Berg and van der Wall, *Jewish Christian Relations*, pp. 95–115.

40 These difficulties are described in John Dury's letter to Samuel Hartlib, July 15, 1661, Hartlib Papers, Sheffield, 4/4/26, published in Van den Berg and van der Wall, *Jewish Christian Relations*, p. 158.

41 See Katz, 'Abandana Brothers'. The chits of Cudworth are in the Cambridge University Library.

---

42 Cf. Popkin, 'Hartlib, Dury and the Jews'.

43 He said, for instance, in *Portrait du Temple de Salomon*, Amsterdam, 1643, that Solomon was the architect of the Temple, but that he built it on a model and order expressly given by God himself, 'qui fut le premier ouvrier and le principal architecte de ce bastiment si merveilleux'.

44 On Menasseh and his relations with Christian Millenarians see Popkin, 'Christian Jews and Jewish Christians in the 17th Century', in R.H. Popkin and G.M. Weiner, *Jewish Christians and Christian Jews in the 17th Century from the Renaissance to the Enlightenment* (Dordrecht: Kluwer, 1994), pp. 60–64.

45 On this see J. Friedman, *The Most Ancient Testimony*.

2. QUEEN CHRISTINA'S LATIN *SEFER-HA-RAZIEL* MANUSCRIPT.

SUSANNA ÅKERMAN

Pone te in solum et scias
quod ipse ponet se totum in te

In the fall of 1650, Christina of Sweden's artistic consultant in Amsterdam, the engraver Michel le Blon (1587–1658) offered the Queen some 20 manuscripts from R. Menasseh ben Israel. One of these was entitled *Magia cabalistica*; the Rabbi spoke highly of it, Le Blon pointed out, 'duquel il fait très grand estat'.[1] Menasseh's magical manuscript has never been conclusively identified, but there is a text now preserved in Queen Christina's collection in Rome that brings us closer to evaluating Menasseh's offer. The manuscript in question is a Latin translation of the four hundred page Hebrew text on angelic invocation, *Sefer-ha-Raziel*, now MS. Reg. Lat. 1300 in the Bibliotheca Vaticana. The text is carefully copied out and the first thing that strikes the eye is that the first letter of its first line is drawn in the form of a little devil. Not without reason this text is considered one of the rarest specimens of original angelic magic and offers a Hebrew cosmology that will be seen to have had some influence during the late Renaissance. The text was known at the Imperial court of Prague and as R. J. W. Evans observes there is a Czech translation of the *Raziel* by the Rudolphine courtier Johannes Polentarius 'which is called the book of powers and mysteries, and here are seven treatises in the seven arts and the seven powers'.[2]

The sources for Renaissance Christian Kabbalism in Hebrew magical texts focus attention on the precise spread of Western translations of such documents. The Latin copies of *Sefer-ha-Raziel* in particular shows a continuation of interest in Hebrew angelology among Christian readers well after the great blooming of such concerns among Rosicrucian authors in 1614–1620. As Carlos Gilly recently has shown, several authors in the first decades of the seventeenth century suggested that the impulse for the legend of Christian Rosencreutz is to be found in a text on angelic invocation available in German transcription in 1608, the *Cabala Mystica, the Book of Sacred Magic*, attributed to Abraham ben Simon of Worms.[3] Prefaced by a memoir of his travels to kabbalists and magicians in Constantinople, Palestine, and Egypt, Abraham ben Simon offers a number

A.P. Coudert, S. Hutton, R.H. Popkin and G. M. Weiner (eds): Judaeo-Christian Intellectual Culture in the Seventeenth Century, 13-25.
© 1999 *Kluwer Academic Publishers. Printed in the Netherlands.*

of angelic spells that he learned from a profound master in 1409 near the Nile, the Aramaic speaking R. Abraham Elim. In a crucial sentence, Abraham of Worms records that before going into Egypt, he had travelled for a year in Arabia with a Christian youth that he met in Palestine, Christoph. Nothing further is said about Christoph, but literary space had been created for inventing a similar figure, as when Lutheran apocalypticists in Tübingen in about 1610 began to write the first Rosicrucian manifesto, the notorious *Fama Fraternitatis Rosaea Crucis* (Kassel, 1614).

While not identical, the angelic invocations of Abraham of Worms is parallelled by the angelic spells of the much older *Sefer-ha-Raziel,* a text that as early as in 1615 was said be foundational for the Rosicrucian Cosmology. Since the first recorded mention of the secrets of Raziel are by Eliazar of Worms in his magical text *Sode Razajja* (early thirteenth century), it is possible that there was a tradition to draw on for the magical spells attributed to Abraham of Worms.[4]

Let me begin by noting that Michel Le Blon's contact with Menasseh ben Israel fits well with the rumour that Le Blon was a Rosicrucian. Le Blon is thought to have written the *Antwort oder Sendtbrief an die Gott erleuterne Bruderschafft von Rosencreutz*, signed M. B. on 4 September 1615.[5] Through the Merian family at Frankfurt, Le Blon was related to the Rosicrucian printer Theodore De Bry at Oppenheim, and as early as in 1613, Le Blon made skillful Hermetic designs (e.g., the 'Zeus' engraving) by using the technique of parametric drawings. Such drawings are done by the sole use of the straight line and circle and were employed for seeking particular intersections of lines. Collected by members of the eighteenth century 'Cabala Club' in London, they attempt to trace the hidden designs of Hermetic engravings. Some are from specified books while others give no clues as to their origin. There are literally hundreds of such drawings now preserved in a private British collection. Le Blon's signature appears on a number of these drawings. Some of the drawings are further inscribed on the back with references to particular pages in texts written by people with high Rosicrucian profiles such as Heinrich Khunrath, Theophilus Schweighart (Daniel Mögling), and Robert Fludd. The British Library's copy of Schweighart's *Speculum Sophicum Rhodostauroticon* (1616) has identical drawings pasted at the end.[6] Note, as Frances Yates points out, that Theodore De Bry cut many engravings from scenes in Elisabethan London (including the procession of the Order of the Garter) and his son Johan Theodore printed books for the court of Heidelberg. Michel Le Blon followed De Bry in making a career in England by offering his services in the art of engraving to Charles I.[7]

While in residence in Stockholm as the Queen's artistic consultant in 1647–1649, Le Blon translated Jacob Boehme's 'little prayer book' from a manuscript he had bought in Amsterdam from the mystic Silesian exile Abraham van Franckenberg in 1642.[8] Le Blon's attempt to persuade Christina to build an Apollinic Temple of learning with antiquities designed by Artus Quillinus, and described in Reyer Anslo's poem *De Zweedse Pallas* (1647), is also rumoured to conceal a Hermetic or Rosicrucian understanding. The poem describes how the gods gather on a cloud taking them to Rostock where they hold a ceremony in honour of the Swedish Queen. In 1644, Le Blon belonged to a secret 'lodge' of some sort, along with the Flemish poets Reyer Anslo and Jost van den Vondel, who later converted to Catholicism from their respective Mennonite and Baptist origins. Le Blon is said to have recommended to the Queen a Dutch painter who was banned in the Netherlands because of his Rosicrucianism.[9] Given his contact with Franckenberg beginning in 1638, Le Blon may well have been steeped in Rosicrucian thought, while his engraving methods and Hermetic designs may show him familiar with De Bry's architectural projects in London.

Thus, I take it, the offer from Le Blon and Menasseh to the Queen in 1650 concerned a fifteenth century Latin transcript of the rare Hebrew collection of magic formulas *Sefer-ha-Razim*, sometimes described as the Book of Secrets (Raz means secret in Hebrew). Christina's copy is entitled *Liber prophetarum Evae scriptas a Raziel* and has an introduction dedicated to Alfonso the Wise of Castile (d. 1284), the great patron of magic and astronomy, who as a grandson of the Staufens sought the throne of the Holy Roman Empire. Alfonso X is known for his interest in arcana. He supported the translation of the Talmud and took an interest in the Kabbalah. One is reminded of his personal emblem: a self-wounding Pelican perched on its young, with the device 'solo pro lege et grege' — I wound myself only in defense of the law and my flock. Christina's Raziel-manuscript appears to be part of her collection of magical astronomy, she also owned a Spanish *Libro de las formas en de las ymagenes que son en los cielos* (Reg. Lat. 1283) with a similar dedication to Alfonso the Wise.[10] This text contains a passage speaking of the vicious demon Samael, with the comment 'secundo dicto Raziel'. Both manuscripts thus emanate from the same Spanish circles and deal with angelic magic and astrology.

We can thus begin to see why Queen Christina would have taken interest in these texts. *Libros de las formas e de las ymagenes* speaks of the

12 signs of the Zodiac and the 24 mansions of the moon and also develops a prophecy of a final apocalyptic struggle between the Lion and the Dragon, a clash that will destroy the Church of Anti-Christ. Ideas of a leonine cosmic war were of particular interest to Christina because the Swedes in 1631 had used the Paracelsian prophecy of 'der Löwe aus Mitternacht' (the Lion of the North), in propaganda for their intervention in the Thirty Years' War. There was even a broadsheet published in Amsterdam as late as 1644 portraying Gustav Adolf as the self-wounding Pelican, the emblem for a martyred King of Justice and of paternal love. The Raziel manuscript uses the imagery of the Lion in a handful of magical spells. These spells alone may have interested the Queen, but the text was highly esteemed also because it is foundational for a metaphysics of angelic worlds structured into degrees or levels. In a critical review of 1615, the influential alchemist Andreas Libavius suspected that the secrets of Raziel lay behind the Rosicrucian philosophy. He straightforwardly claimed that the book of *Raziel* was the founding document for a Rosicrucian cosmology of angelic spheres.[11] Libavius' observation concerning Raziel's angelic cosmology thus challenges the established eighteenth-century Masonic belief that the nine sphere angelic cosmology of Dante's *Divina Comedia*, inspired by a poem written by the Sufi philosopher Mohyiddin Ibn Arabi, is the founding document for Rosicrucian ascent to the Divine essence. For example, the colour symbolism designed in the 1730s for the Scottish Rite of the Heredom of Kilwinning draws upon Ibn Arabi. Dante's poetic world would also appear to depend on Arabic astronomical models, in particular al-Bitrujji's Ptolemaic revision introduced by Michael Scotus to the Staufen court at Sicily.[12]

The Raziel-Manuscript and the Key of Solomon

Sefer-ha-Raziel is divided in seven chapters: the book of the key; the book of wings; the book of herbal cures; the book of ages; the book of medicine and abstinence; the book of heavens; and the book of magical incantations. The third book describes 'the mother of Herbs, the (Clepid) Arthemesia', but makes it give way to Corona Regis (acylamatit), anomalously put first among herbs. The sixth book discusses the structure of the heavens and names 715 angels located throughout the cosmos, 360 of which belong to the innermost heaven. Seven superior angels (pseudo-archangels) are assigned, one to each planet and they control the planetary virtues influencing human activity. Seven celestial spheres or expansions (firmaments, *reqi`im*) are described; they are populated by angels, guardians (*soterim*), and lords of glory (*sarim*) controlling the heavens.

The angel Raziel stands on the seventh step of the second heaven. He is also called Gallizur, 'he who reveals the hidden reasons of the Rock'. Behind the Veil in the Holy of Holies, Raziel has been told everything that is going to happen in the future, and at one time he is said to have descended to tell these secrets to Elijah, the prophet enrapt into Heaven.[13] It is no coincidence that the thirteenth-century Italian Kabbalist Abraham Abulafia wrote in the name of Raziel, nor that the mid-sixteenth century orientalist Guillaume Postel claimed that he was told new ideas by an angel named Raziel.[14] The manuscript explains that Raziel wrote down his ideas on stone-slabs later hidden in a cavern by Seth; the same cavern is described by Enoch as the cavern located in the left part of Paradise. It is said that Sem showed these stones to Abraham, who showed them to Levi, who gave them to Elyseo, who then told Elyseis and thus confirmed him also in the secrets (hinting at a mutual Jewish-Greek understanding). The stone-tablets of Seth were engraved with a sacred language: a pseudo-Chaldean angelic script (simplified Hebrew letters made up of interconnected lines, curves, and hooks). The manuscript shows us these signs and spells out the forbidden name of God, the *shem hammephorash*, written in seventy-two words, each naming a particular angelic spirit; the whole unspeakable formula has been inscribed in a square by Raziel.

Another version of the same manuscript declares that the content was revealed by the Angel Raziel to Noah while he was in the Ark. Noah then wrote it on some tablets of saphire, that later were passed on to King Solomon; therefore the book is also called the Key of Solomon, the key to the mysteries of the heavens. The exact form of the Key to the Palace of the King is described in the beginning of the book. The handle of the key consists of a square for the four elements with a triangle representing man inside; the seven teeth (wardens or angels) of the key represent the seven planets. The key has some resemblance to the key illustrated in Postel's *Clavis Absconditorum* (1547) a text which discusses the restitution of the soul through the Tree of Life with the comment: 'C'est la la sentence de *Cabdiel* et *Raziel* qui nous est transmise par les monuments les plus secrets de la Theologie dans les Réponses verbales des 72 Anciens'.[15]

A second edition of Postel's *Clavis* was edited by Abraham van Franckenberg in 1646 and was published at Amsterdam by Jan Janssonius, the same printer who set up shop in Stockholm in 1649. There was an emerging market for astro-spiritual healing methods and it was known to some of these readers that *Raziel* describes the four corners of the square as containing four virtues found in 'herbs and words and grass'. Or as the text says: 'The key of this book is to write and know the place of the seven bodies about & their natures & their houses & all their vertues after that they approach the earth'.[16]

The Reception of the Raziel Manuscript

The late eighteenth-century Vatican catalogue of the Reginensis collection gives the Raziel manuscript the shelf number 1300 — which might seem to be a mere coincidence if it was not the case that the catalogue also lists Christina's copy of Jean Bodin's sevenfold dialogue on the Secrets of the Sublime, the infamous *Colloquium Heptaplomeres*, as number 1313. It appears that there has been a deliberate ordering of the catalogue, so as to make these manuscripts stand out from the rest, though not in a very benign light.[17] Number 1300, which concerns me here, is correctly catalogued as *Liber secretorum de Raziel*. Remember that the Hebrew version of the book was first printed at Amsterdam in 1701, but was then given a more accurate title: *The Book of the First Humans*, given to them by the angel Raziel (*Se sifra de Adam*, in Hebrew). Note that the Christian Hebraist Johan Christoph Wolff describes *Raziel* in his *Bibliotheca Hebraica* (Hamburg-Leipzig, 1715–1734), an important source for Swedenborg's angelic views.[18]

The angelic doctrine of the *liber Raziel* is taken up by the group of texts called *Claves Salomonis*, magical texts that in conjunction with al-Magriti's book of Arabic magic, *Picatrix*, influenced Cornelius Agrippa (Raziel is refered to in *De occulta philosophia* book II, ch. 22 and 32). Libavius published against the Kabbalah and the Rosicrucians, warning that their secret doctrine of a sevenfold succession of ages had been adapted by Johannes Trithemius and others to fit the angelic cosmology of the *Sefer-ha-Raziel*. The influence of *Raziel* and the *Libro de las formas que son en los cielos* was particularly strong during the Reformation because of allusions in them to a cosmic struggle between the Lion and the Eagle, similar to the struggle described in the apocryphal fourth book of Ezra, a text used by Protestant apocalypticists. Francois Secret shows that the *Raziel* is quoted by Thomas Aquinas, Nicolas of Cusa, Cornelius Agrippa, and the Christian Kabbalist Johannes Reuchlin. The French Paracelsian Jaques Gohory uses it in his commentaries on the magical texts of Paracelsus.[19] Secret also draws attention to the section of the *Raziel* bespeaking the Tree of Life, the tree that bears the fruits of life and the leaves of which give medicine with curative powers. The *Raziel* also has a most useful feature for the practise of angelic invocation, the names of the seven planets in seven different languages.

There appears to be no direct reference to the Hebrew magic of Raziel in Menasseh's printed texts, but he frequently employed kabbalistic spells in his hymns.[20] The offer to Christina was at the time that Isaac Vossius planned to set up an international board for studying the oriental background of the Bible, and to produce a volume on the Babylonian, Chaldean, and Egyptian background of the Testaments. James Ussher of Armagh, Henric Valesius of Paris, and Claude Saumaise of Leiden were to participate with other scholars in a vast exchange of ideas and correspondence sanctioned by the Swedish Queen. Intriguingly, even Meric Causubon, who a few years later brought out the first edition of John Dee's *Spiritual Diaries* from Prague, was called to join the Stockholm scholars, but he decided no to go.[21] The angelic invocations of the *Sefer-ha-Raziel* were hardly meant to be used in occult sessions at the Stockholm court, however. Although she was much interested in prophecy, we have no evidence that magical practises were encouraged by the Queen. Instead, the text was probably intended for study in Christina's academy as a contribution to the controversy about Hermetic origins. Menasseh thought it an opportune time to get the Swedish Queen to sponsor a series of texts, a *Bibliotheca Rabbinica*. A new Spanish edition of the Bible and of the Talmud was on his mind, perhaps as a tribute to the benevolent patronage of Alfonso X. However, money ran short and Christina began to plan her abdication.[22]

As I am in the process of showing in my study *Rose Cross Over the Baltic*, the Paracelsian Lion prophecy builds on the astrological observations on the successive conjunctions of Saturn and Jupiter in the fiery trigon, more specifically on the expected great conjunction in the zodiacial sign of Leo in 1623. For example, Cyprian Leowitz of Prague predicted a great change after the great conjunction in Cancer in 1563, and these expectations were repeated for 1623 by the Lutheran pastor Eustachius Poussel, whose calculation in turn influenced the founding document for the first Rosicrucian tracts, Simon Studion's *Naometria*. The conjunction in Leo in 1623 was then used in a Rosicrucian context by exiled Palatine supporters in The United Provinces to prepare for the election of the Danish King Christian IV as leader of the the Saxon circle. Christian IV and his allies were utterly defeated in 1626 by the Imperial army led by Count Wallenstein, but a new wave of leonine propaganda was launched in 1631–32 for the landing of the Swedes in the Thirty Years' War.

The astro-spiritual theory of the great conjunctions was first formulated by the ninth century astronomer of the eastern Khurasan, Abu Ma'shar al-Balki (d. 886), who argued that a great prophet who would supercede Mohammed would appear when these planets meet in Scorpio, as they did in 1484. His writings were held to draw upon older material from the Sabéan sect, the star-gazers at Damar in Yemen maintaining that the stars reflect the shining garment of the Deity.[23]

Abu Ma'shar's texts were translated into Latin in 1130 by John of Seville and then once more in 1150 by Herman of Carinthia, whose text was printed at Augsburg in 1489. Abu Ma'shar's works continued to be read among sixteenth-century astronomers. Copies of his manuscripts are now in Christina's Vatican collection; she also collected tracts on the great conjunctions by more contemporary astronomers such as Johannes Regiomontanus, Tomaso Campanella, and Johannes Magini (the astronomer friend of Galileo). She owned the central manuscripts by Abu Ma'shar, eg., the extract at Reg Lat. 1330, Albumasar, *De Cometis*, in a high-medieval hand. The Queen's collection testifies that the conjunctions and their periodic passage was an important element of late Renaissance esotericism.

Consider, now, in this context, an English transcription of the *Raziel*, deposited in the British Library with the listing: 'Liber Salomonis qui dicitur Cephar Raziel, containing seven treatises, said to be written by William Parry at Cliffords Inn in on 2 November 1564 at the charges of John Gwynne of Llaudloys in the county of Monmouth'. A letter written 27 July 1570 by the Welsh squire Gwynne precedes it. Here, Gwynne speaks of how inferior nature can be purged by an artificial fire that betroths it to the superior realm; this is the work of inferior astronomy, of Kabbalah, and its entire doctrine is set out in John Dee's mystical tract *Monas Hieroglyphica* (Antwerp, 1564).[24] After an angel has been invoked with the words, 'Rise, Rise, Rise and come and speak to me', one notices a Monas-sign written upside down in the margin to the Raziel manuscript (f. 137v), just where it is said, 'the figure that is Mars that he should rest & should not fight in the reign of that sign Arietis. . . Aries is a sign very hot and dry and cholerick and so is Leo and Sagittarius and they have might in the east'. Indeed, Dee's hieroglyphic monad consists of nothing else than Mercury betrothed to Aries.[25]

The Structure of Raziel's Angelic Heavens

Mordechai Margalioth argues that the central elements of *Sefer-ha Raziel* even dates from the time of the Babylonian captivity (400 B.C.E); there are also magical formulae compiled in the text from the Gaonic period (100 C.E.). He points out that the text has sections at the end called *Liber Ignis* and *Liber Semyforas*, because they describe the twenty-two Hebrew letters and the twenty-two virtues emanating from them. Also, these sections describe the seven semyphoras of Adam and Moses, by interpreting the three angles in the letter Aleph. The legend is that the text was first written by Abraham the Patriarch in Chaldean and then translated into Hebrew. In Latin the text was often entitled *Liber secretorum Dei* or as a *secreta secretorum Clavis Salomonicis*. The well known shorter magical texts that circulate as *The Key of Solomon* thus in part derive from *Raziel*, just as Libavius pointed out in 1615.

In Margalioth's reconstruction, the old core of the *Book of Secrets*, or *Sefer-ha-Razim*, has an introduction in which it is declared that the content is a revelation from the Angel Raziel to Noah while he was in the Ark. Noah then wrote it on some tablets of saphire, that later became known to King Solomon. A pledge is made that the secret magic of the book will approach the divine throne, the throne of Great Light.

Before we leave it is useful to consider the angelic content of *Sefer-ha-Raziel*. There are seven chapters each treating a celestial sphere or expansion (firmaments, *reqi'im*). They are populated by angels, guardians (*soterim*), and lords of glory (*sarim*) to control the heavens. The first heaven or firmament (*Shamaim*) contains seven levels of angels, who are served by seven guardians. These are: Orpheniel, Tiegara, Denael, Calamia, Ascimor, Peyscar, and Boel, each with a number of subservient spirits, 360 in all. The second heaven (*Raquia*) is controlled by twelve angels with corresponding guardians. In the third heaven (*Saquum*) three angels serve three guardians, in the fourth (*Mahun*) there are two groups of angels, in the fifth (*Zebul*) there are twelve angelic lords of glory. In the sixth (*Araboa*) spirits and angels are controlled by two angelic kings. In the seventh heaven there is only the Divine presence described in esoteric hymns. The first angel of the first heaven reigns over seventy-two spirits. The second heaven controls the climate by fire, rain, hail, and snow. The third contains twenty-one angels, some are bewinged horses, similar to Pegasus. The fourth heaven contains the angel of the sun, clothed by fire and surrounded by seven streams of water and seven streams of fire. The fifth heaven contains two angels of the most high controlling the twelve months, the zodiac, and the passage of seasons. The sixth heaven contains twelve lords of glory seated in thrones.

Now, this cosmological structure is coordinated with magical spells. In chapter one there are seven magical practises, in the chapter two twelve, and in chapter three, three; in the following three, on the other hand, there are more complex sets of magical practises. These practises employs the name and character of an angel, some of which are:

> The angel of fire
> the angel of flames
> the angel of silence
> the angel of knowledge and wisdom
> the angel of anger and rage
> the angel of compassion
> the angel of power and force
> the angel that runs by the stars
> the angel that stands on the third level

They can be invoked by description, for instance, on the fifth level, e.g., the first angel is invoked by saying: You who are formed by the fiery flames, your breath is fire, your habitation is in fire, you who have fire-flaming wings.

The last and seventh chapter is built up around visionary formulas of the Mercavah and Hekhalot type, datable to the first century. Thus, the *Book of Secrets* is a compilation collected by more than one writer. The text even contains two Hebrew transcriptions of Greek magical formula; one is an incantation to Helios, the sun, reproduced at the beginning of this paper. These simple formulas are found on Greek magical papyri, and Margalioth uses them to argue that the magical core of the manuscript dates from the Talmudic period. The collection as it now stands attributes the various magical ideas to a three-score source, with the alternate words dixit Hermes, dixit Salomon, dixit Raziel. A modern critical edition based on the best available manuscripts could probably enlighten us further on these intertwined traditions.

The Magical incantation: Structure and Content

According to a recent analysis by J-H Niggemeyer, the magic formula repeat a structure that can be reduced to a single pattern:

> I beseech you with the power that I set free by naming

this God or his hypostases. . . .[21]

The magic power/force (dynamis) of these words implies that the Deities have to obey, because the formula works on the principle of analogy: 'As I do this and this to this and this thing, so will it happen to this and that thing with this and that person'.

Examples:

For protection in war:

> Make a ring of iron and inscribe it with the image of a lion. Write the name of the guardian angel on a golden leaf, then take the ring in your mouth and make an invocation to the angel, then take the ring out and put it on your finger.

To put a spell on a foe:

> Save water from seven sources in seven different containers and keep it for seven days, then mix the water together in a glass. Pronounce the magic formula over the glass, and then sprinkle the water in the directions of the four corners of the earth.

Finally, Niggemeyer observes that the formula proceeds in different steps, those of:

> Pronouncing the Angel's name.
> Saying the binding formula.
> Describing the Angel with his attribute.
> Affirmation of the overall power of God.
> Resumé of the binding formula (with or without temporal clause, 'until this or that day has passed).
> Ending formula, for example: 'I have unbound you, go your way'.

1 Michel le Blon to Christina, 1651, Riksarkivet, Stockholm. Cf. Susanna Åkerman, *Queen Christina and Her Circle. The Trans-formation of a Seventeenth century Philosophical Libertine*, E. J. Brill, Leiden, 1991. p. 145ff. The text was first published as *Sefer Raziel, Liber cabalistico-magico*, Amsterdam, 1701. For a modern transcript see M. Margalioth, *Sepher-ha-Razim, a Newly Recovered Book of Magic from the Talmudic Period, Collected from Genizah fragments and Other Sources*, (Jerusalem, 1966).

2 R. J. W. Evans, *The World of Rudolph II* (Oxford: Oxford University Press, 1977), p. 238.

3 August of Anhalt-Plötzkau to Carl Wideman 29 July 1611 asking to see a copy of the *Buch der wahren Practic von der alten Magia*, see Carlos Gilly, *Adam Haselmaier. Der Erste verkünder der Manifeste der Rosencreutzer*, In *de Pelikaan* (Amsterdam, 1994), pp. 134, 146. For the question of authenticity compare the discussion of the fragmentary Hebrew copy of this text preserved at the Bodleian, Oxford MS. Opp. 594, in Raphael Patai, *The Jewish Alchemists* (Princeton: Princeton University Press, 1994), pp. 271–288.

4 See Gershom Scholem, 'Raziel' *Encyclopaedia Judaica* (Jerusalem: Macmillan, 1971). Also, his *Kabbalah Keter* (Jerusalem, 1974. New York: Dorset, 1984), p. 39. There are other Hebrew manuscripts on angelic invocation that may be indebted to the *Raziel*, for instance the *Uraltes Chymisches Wärck by Abraham Eleazer*. See Patai, *The Jewish Alchemists*, pp. 238–257.

5 For documentation of this tradition see Govaert Snoek, *De Rosenkruizers in Nederland – Voornamelijk in de eerste helft van de 17e eeuw. Een inventarisatie* (Leiden, 1991). See further n. 8 below.

6 Joy Hancox, *The Byrum Collection* (London, 1993), pp. 42, 130. The illustrations of this book are worthwhile, and the material related to Le Blon extensive, but Hancox's general interpretation (that these drawings encompass architectural designs of churches and theatres in Elizabethan London, including the Globe, the Swan, and the Rose) is not generally accepted.

7 Hancox quoting Frances Yates, *The Rosicrucian Enlightenment* (London: ARK Paperbacks, 1986), pp. 70–71. The inventor of colour engraving, Christoph Le Blon, continued the Le Blon printing shop in London.

8 Franckenberg corresponded with Menasseh ben Israel and by 1641 with the Rosicrucian authors Johannes Bureus of Stockholm and Christoph Hirsch of Eisleben. Franckenberg's text *Raphael* (in ms. by 1639) contains an engraving specified after the plate of brass in the vault of Christian Rosencreutz. See Will-Erich Peuckert, *Das Rosenkreutz* (Jena, 1924, 2nd. ed. Berlin 1973), p. 288ff.

9 Herman de la Fontaine Verway, 'Michel Le Blon, Engraver, Art Dealer, Diplomat', *Amstelodamum Jahrboek 1969*. Anslo dedicated his tragedy, *Parysche Bruiloft – Tantum Religio potuit suadere malorum* (1649), to Le Blon 'as dear to me as the light'. Anslo also praised the Latin Poet Caspar van Baerle, who corresponded with British esoterics. Cf. Jos. A. Alberdink Thijm, 'Reyer Anslo', *Dietsche Verande* 5 (1859):478–495.

10 Reg. Lat. 1283 is not, as has been argued, a fragment of the Spanish version of al-Magriti's Arabic book of magic, *Picatrix*. Cf. Carlos Gilly, 'Picatrix latinus. Conzesioni filosofico e prassi magica', *Medioevo, Rivista di storia della filosofia medievale* (Padova, 1975), pp. 237–337 esp. p. 242, n.5. On the translation of the Picatrix see Evelyn S. Procter, *Alfonso X of Castille, Patron of Literature and Learning* (Oxford, 1952).

11 Andreas Libavius, *Examen Philosophia Nova* (Leipzig, 1615), p. 25, quoted by Francois Secret, 'Sur quelques traduction du Sefer Razi'el', *Revue des études juives* 128 (1969), pp. 226–239.

12 On Dante, see the interesting work of René Guenon, *L'ésoterisme de Dante* (Paris: Gallimard, 1957), based on the views of Paul Sédir. On Al-Bitrujji see *Dictionary of Scientific Biography* (New York: Scribners), 1970.

13 *Encyclopaedia Judaica* (1971). Note that the gematria of Raziel is 248 which is equal to the gematria of Abraham and of the number of commandments in the Torah. The angel Raziel is mentioned in the Slavonich version of the second book of Henoch and in the Apocalypse of Baruch. In this context Francois Secret recommends J. A. Pentheus, *Voarchydymia–Henoch descriptus* (Wittenberg, 1670), on the use of amulets.

14 Cf. R. J. W. Evans, (1977) p. 238. For some further observations on Raziel, see Marion Leathers Kuntz, *Guillaume Postel. Prophet of the Restitution of all Things. His Life and Thought* (The Hague: Martinus Nijhoff, 1981). Queen Christina owned Postel's MS. *Thrésor des Profeties de L'Univers* (1547), see Åkerman p. 173 cited in Vossius' Antwerp catalogue, now MS Vat. Lat 8171. Note that Postel's manuscript at Basel, *Chavae sive Evae omnium viventium*, adds prophecies from the Bahir and from the Raziel.

15 Guillaume Postel, *Clef des Choses Cachées (Absconditorum Clavis)*. This is a reprint of the first French translation (Paris, 1899; Milan: Sebastiani-Arché, 1977), p. 77.

16 Cf. note 24 below.

17 Christina's 2100 manuscripts were catalogued before her death by the Order of St. Maur, but new listings were made later. The collection contains many rare items, for example the *Veritas Hermetica*, Ms. Reg. Lat. 1218. Bibliotheca Vaticana. In this text, on f. 37, Father Binet, S. J., discusses the distillation of dew by the Fratres Rores Cocti and refers to Michael Maier, perhaps to the 11th section of his *Themis Aurea* (1618).

18 Raziel is described by Wolff in vol. II, p. iii and IV, p. 771, 1033, See Francois Secret (1969) p. 235. Several Latin manuscript versions of the *Sefer-ha-Raziel* are extant, Secret mentions one at the Bibliothèque National, Fonds Latin 3666.

19 Jacques Gohory, *Paracelsi philosophiae et medicinae utriusque universae compendium* (Paris, 1568). See Secret 'Sur quelques traduction du Sefer Razi'el', p. 225.

20 In Menasseh ben Israel's *The Hope of Israel* (Amsterdam, 1650) there is mention of Claude Duret's *Thrésor des Langues de L'Univers* (1613), a text on the origin of languages that reports of the book of Raziel in some detail, see Secret, 'Sur quelques traduction du Sefer Razi'el', pp. 242, 244.

21 Åkerman, *Queen Christina and Her Circle*, p. 104.

22 ibid. p. 135. Christina took these manuscripts with her to Rome, which perhaps indicates that she was fully aware of their value. In 1657, she gave most of the Hermetic books from Prague to her former aid Isaac Vossius, later librarian at Windsor. See P. C. van Boeren, *Codices Vossii Chymici, Codices Manuscripti no. 17* (Leiden, 1975).

23 See 'Abu Ma'shar' *Encyclopaedia of Islam* (Leiden: E. J. Brill, 1960), I:139. On the reception of these ideas by Pierre D'Ailly and Roger Bacon, see Eugenio Garin, *Le Zodiaque de la Vie* (Rome-Bari: Laterza, 1976; Paris: Les Belles Lettres, 1991), pp. 37–39, 141–143. The classic work is Daniel Chwolson, *Die Ssabier und der Ssabismus* (St. Petersburg, 1856).

24 As Ron Heisler has been kind to inform me there is a sixteenth-century collection of alchemical manuscripts belonging to John Gwynne in the Bodleian Library at Oxford. Gwynne is however difficult to identify since it is a very common Welsh name.

25 English transcript, MS Sloane 3846, British Library ff. 129–157ff. Letter at ff. 127–128. Latin Versions entitled *Clavis Salomonis sive Sepher Raziel* are also at the Sloane, MS. 3826, 3847, 3853/2 and 3848/17 (a treatise on the seven planets by Paracelsus).

26 J.H. Niggemeyer, *Beshwörungsformeln aus dem 'Buch der Geheimnisse - Sefär ha-razim' - Zur Topologie der magischen Rede* (Hildesheim: Olms, 1975).

3. HENRY MORE, ANNE CONWAY AND THE KABBALAH: A CURE FOR THE KABBALIST NIGHTMARE?[1]

SARAH HUTTON

In this paper I argue that Anne Conway's *Principia philosophiae* meets the objections that Henry More levelled against the kabbalah which he set out in his *Fundamenta philosophiae* printed in the second part of the first volume of the *Kabbala denudata*. Her treatise may therefore be read as an answer to More's objections, or at least as a demonstration that kabbalist-inspired metaphysics need not be incompatible with Christian philosophy. But in so doing, I want to emphasise that Anne Conway's kabbalism does not in itself constitute a break with Henry More. Although her position is vey different from his, they were both working within the same Christian-Platonist interpretation of kabbalah.

Henry More's Nightmare

The last piece by More to be included in the *Kabbala denudata* is entitled *Fundamenta physica, sive cabbala aeto-paedo-melissae*.[2] This consists of a set of objections to positions extracted by More from the Lurianic kabbalah, followed by *scholia* in which he recounts a vivid dream he had featuring the 'eagle-boy-bee' of the title.[3] This work could be described as the nadir of More's interpretation of kabbalah. More was particularly critical of the Lurianic account of creation: the *Fundamenta philosophiae*, amounts to a *summa* of his objections to the Lurianic kabbalah, deriving from denial of *creatio ex nihilo*. According to his account of it, there is no matter in nature, but all things consist of uncreated spirit, separated from the the divine essence and contracted into particles or monads. Contrary to the explicit statement that all things are made of spirit More interprets this account as materialistic: in his view, the account itself contradicts that claim. He concludes that because the deity and created beings are of the same substance, the deity itself is material. Luria is therefore guilty of the combined errors of Hobbes and Spinoza. More attributes his errors to a dangerous cocktail of reason and imagination. The *Fundamenta* could be described as the culmination of More's comments and criticisms on kabbalistic wisdom, in particular his criticisms of the kabalist account of

A.P. Coudert, S. Hutton, R.H. Popkin and G. M. Weiner (eds): Judaeo-Christian Intellectual Culture in the Seventeenth Century, 27-42.

the relationship of God to the world. But the dream bears out More's view that the kabbalah nonetheless contained at its core important elements of true wisdom (the bones beneath the scrawny exterior of the eagle in the dream). At best, therefore, the kabbalah gives insight into only part of the truth. The value of this was made questionable by the fact that these nuggets of truth were dispersed among corrupt wisdom and corrupting untruths (i.e. the 'pretious gold in this Cabbalisticall rubbish').[4]

The *Fundamenta* is followed in the *Kabbala denudata* by nearest thing we have to More's kabbalistic conversations with Van Helmont: *Ad fundamenta cabbalae aeto-paedo-melissaeae dialogus.*[5] This was subsequently printed in English as a slim book entitled *A Cabbalistical Dialogue in Answer to the Opinion of a Learned Doctor* (1682). In this a thinly disguised Van Helmont (called the 'Compiler') answers questions put by an equally thinly disguised Henry More (called 'Cabbalista Catechumenus'), in the course of which Van Helmont expounds his belief in such heterodox doctrines as the transmigration of souls and denial of *creatio ex nihilo*. He insists that creation is a process of forming beings out of pre-existing spiritual substance. There is no attempt to meet More's objections that the monads formed in this way are, on the one hand, not distinguished from the deity and on the other confused with matter. There is, in other words, no attempt to address the charges of pantheistic and polytheistic materialism which More makes in the *Fundamenta*. Thus Van Helmont's heterodox opinions can only have corroborated More's reading of the Lurianic kabbalah as fundamentally dangerous to the Christian religion. But, as I shall show, this negative view is not representative of More's assessment of kabbalah in general, and it does not amount to a complete revision of More's interpretation of kabbalah.

More and the Kabbalah

Francis Mercurius van Helmont first met Henry More in 1670. This was an encounter enormous consequence both for the two of them and for their associates, More's friend and pupil, Anne Conway, and Van Helmont's friend and collaborator, the Christian kabbalist, Christian Knorr von Rosenroth.[6] At this meeting More was directly exposed to genuine (Jewish) kabbalism apparently for the first time. It seems certainly to have been his first introduction to the kabbalist writings of of Isaac Luria. And he was put into contact with Knorr von Rosenroth who was then engaged in making the Latin translation of Jewish kabbalistic writings which appeared in three volumes as the *Kabbala denudata* (1677 & 1684).[7] His ensuing correspondence with Knorr resulted in More being represented (disproportionately to his expertise) in the critical apparatus of the *Kabbala denudata*. The meeting with Van Helmont also led directly to Van Helmont making the acquaintance of More's pupil Anne Conway, with the result that her mature philosophy departs radically from that of her teacher Henry More.[8] In consequence of his encounter with Van Helmont, More revised his view of the kabbalah, or at least of part of it — More's kabbalistic discussions with Van Helmont resulted in his explicit denunciation of the philosophical implications of kabbalah, described above.

Henry More's interest in kabbalism was both complex and long-standing.[9] Long before he ever read the Zohar, he had written a kabbalah of his own invention, his *Conjectura cabbalistica* (1653). His acquaintance with kabbalism at this stage of his life was through Reuchlin, Agrippa and Meursius, from whom he took the idea that Pythagoreanism incorporated the secrets of the philosophy of Moses and was therefore a version of kabbalism.[10] Fundamental to More's philosophical reading of Genesis, 1, is the equation of the Pythagorian 'denarium', the symbolic numbers 1–10, with the ten *sepiroth*. In *Conjectura cabbalistica* he talks of 'Pythagoras, speaking the mystical language of the Jewish Philosophy', and twenty-five years later he still insisted that the 'Pythagorean system was indeed the same as that of the ancient Jews'.[11] According to More, it was through Pythagoras, that this ancient Jewish wisdom, both philosophical and scientific was passed to the ancient Greeks among whom it came to be the foundation stone of Greek philosophy. He calls the Pythagoreans *kabbalisti graeci*. In More's view the history of philosophy comprised this heritage handed down piecemeal, often diluted and corrupted by later accretions. All Western European philosophy could be seen as either a version of part of this tradition or a corruption of it. More undertook a detailed reconstruction of this Pythagorean kabbalah in his *Defence of the Threefold Cabbala* (1653) and his *Appendix to the Defence of the Philosophick Cabbala*, included in the reprint of *Conjectura cabbalistica* in his *A Collection of Several Philosophical Writings* (1662). More was particularly excited at being able to identify his favourite modern philosophy, that is to say Cartesianism, as heir to this tradition. In his discussions of what he calls the philosophical kabbalah, he presents Descartes as the reviver of ancient atomism, that is of the natural philosophy of Democritus deriving from Pythagoras himself.

More's continuing interest in kabbalah surfaces again in his *Divine Dialogues* (1668) where he offers an interpretation of the *mercava*,

Ezechiel's vision of the chariot. His comments in this account suggest that he had been reading Jewish sources. But it was not, apparently, until after 1670 that More had any extensive first-hand experience of kabbalist writings. More's response to reading the genuine Jewish kabbalah (or, rather, as much of it as he could understand for he freely admitted his ignorance of Hebrew) was, as I have said, complex. His early reaction is recorded in a letter to Lady Conway of 1672. It bespeaks both disappointment and curiosity, excitement and caution. He described to her his reaction when he first attempted to read the 'Cabbalisticall papyrs' sent him by Knorr:

> At my first reading them over wch was the same evening they came, it was if I had lickt a peece of rough iron with my tongue, so little pleasure or savour I found in them, understanding the reason of nothing there, nor what they contributed to the Christian life, in so much that they left me with sadnesse.[12]

In the same letter he explains the difficulty of reading these texts as in part due to the corruption of the Hebrew tradition: 'there are severall names that signify nothing but the ignorance of the later Pythagoreans, and . . . the later Jewes may have cast much trash in nothing to the purpose'.[13] On balance, he concludes: 'there is pretious gold in this Cabbalisticall rubbish, which the discerning eye will easily discover'. The discerning eye he has in mind is, of course, his own: he goes on, 'I met with may things that did very much please men, and such as are likely highly to gratify posterity'.[14] And he lost no time in trying to make sense of the 'Cabbalisticall Papyrs' which Van Helmont brought him. He shared his enthusiasm with Lady Conway, supplying her with copies of the texts he received, and communicating his reactions to Knorr.

It is notable that in almost all his readings of the genuine kabbalah More's general view of the kabbalah accords with the interpretation set out in *Conjectura cabbalistica*: in 1679 he is still trying to find support for his original pre-conceptions about the kabbalah, interpreting the genuine kabbalah to fit his own Reuchlinian/Neoplatonic model, notably the Pythagorean thesis. More's first response on receiving the 'cabbalistical papyrs' from Knorr in 1672 was to produce an explanatory diagram as an alternative to the 'tables' supplied by Knorr.[15]   Entitled *Tabula sephirotharum Graeciana sive Pythagorica*, this was designed to show up the Pythagorianism underlying the sepiroth. Furthermore, he offered a Neoplatonized reading of the *ma'seh merkavah* which was printed in *Kabbala denudata*. In this he insisted that, 'The cabbala of Mercava contains the highest and deepest conceivable mysteries, which are scarcely

credible to the vulgar philosopher'.[16]   His exposition of it adduces
Pythagorean principles, as the sub-title makes clear: *Visionis Ezechieliticae
sive Mercaveae expositio, ex principiis philosophiae pythagoricae
praecipuisque theosphiae judaicae reliquiis concinnata.* Besides, More
clearly looked for and found confirmation of his own kabbalistical
conjectures, not to mention his own philosophy. Just as, in *Conjectura
cabbalistica*, he had found an uncanny agreement between Cartesianism
and the book of Genesis when he subjected the latter to a philosophical
reading, so also, in the 'Cabbalistical papyrs' supplied to him by Knorr, he
found traces of Cartesianism *avant la lettre* — for example in 'Postulatum
III' he asserts, with reference to his own interpretation in *Conjectura
cabbalistica*,

> The whole world in its primeval state was either diaphanous or illumined, that is the
> ethers or vortices were were distributed in transparent suns and heavens.
>   This may be established with certainty from the interpretation of the fourth day's
> work in our *Philosophical Kabbala*, which, for brevity's sake, I won't repeat here. The
> matter may be easily understood out of Cartesian philosophy.[17]

Again, he interprets the whirlwind of Ezechiel's vision as a vortex of ether,
'non absimilem eis a *Cartesio* descriptis'.[18]

More's detection of glimmerings of Cartesianism was facilitated
by the fact that he considered Cartesianism to be a version of ancient
Pythagoreanism, exactly as he had done in the *Appendix to the
Philosophick Cabbala* published in his *Collection of Several Philosophical
Writings* in 1662. These Pythagorean principles are, he claims in the
opening paragraph of *Visionis Ezechieliticae sive Mercaveae expositio*,
akin to the postulates of Cartesianism.[19] Furthermore, he interpreted
Ezechiel's vision as containing an enigmatic statement of some of his own
most cherished theories, *Postulatum* II proposes the pre-existence of souls.
In *Postulatum* III he calls the spirit driving whirlwind the spirit of nature.[20]
In his fourth postulate, More cites the authority of Knorr for bringing the
spirit of nature into the interpretation of the two elements of the world,
natural and divine:

> There are two chief elements of the material world, one natural, the other divine. The
> first is subject of the operations of the spirit of nature which the cabbalists call
> Sandalphonis, the latter the vehicle of the holy spirit, and truly that heavenly manna,
> which is the food and bread of holy souls and angels. I call the Spirit of Nature here
> Sandalphonis on your authority.[21]

More's *Enchiridion metaphysicum* adduces kabbalistic learning in support
of his own metaphysical theories. This is especially true of the *scholiae*

added when it was printed in More's *Opera omnia* in 1679, at around the same time as the *Kabbala denudata* appeared.[22]

Although More invokes Knorr's authority for this particular interpretation, his overall view of the kabbalah and the approach to be taken to it differed fundamentally from Knorr's. The letters printed in More's *Opera omnia* and the *Kabbala denudata* show that for all the mutual respect between them, neither could persuade the other to accept his overall view. More thought that the kabbalah should be interpreted in a Christian manner. Indeed he insisted that its true meaning of Jewish wisdom could only be understood by persons with suitably enlightened minds, that is Christians. This explains why, for instance, the Jews failed to see that Ezekiel's vision of the chariot was a prophecy about Christ and the church. Not only that, but the kabbalah contained other revelations enigmatically concealed in a shroud of symbolism. Perhaps the most important of these, for More, was confirmation of the Trinity, which was, naturally, not accessible to non-Christians. Knorr was particularly cautious about reading the kabbalah through Christian spectacles. But for More, such an approach was consistent with his view that kabbalah was a version of the same body of ancient wisdom preserved in the *philosophia perennis* fostered by Pythagoras, who was, after all, indebted to the ancient Hebrews for his learning. Furthermore, the fact that Jews were unable to fathom the deepest mysteries of kabbalah was confirmation of the fact that, although ancient in its origins, kabbalah was a corruption of the original wisdom revealed by God. Thus kabbalah both preserves in hidden form elements of ancient truth and garbles aspects of that wisdom. More's addition to Knorr's kabbalistical tables show just how much kabbalah matches and mismatches the original framework of ancient wisdom.[23] And More's readings of the texts are largely concerned with identifying what the Jewish interpreters got right and what they got wrong — separating out the 'gold' from the 'Cabbalisticall rubbish'.

A central concern of More's assessment of kabbalah could be described as Trinitarian, but this has important metaphysical dimensions. More insists on separating off the first three sepiroth from the other seven, interpreting them as the persons of the Trinity. In his letter *Ad clarrisimum et eruditissimum virum Christianum Knorrium de usu decemsphirotharum* (a reply to Knorr's comments on his cabalistical tables), More makes a distinction between the first three sepiroth and the remaining seven, explaining these last as spiritual emanations from God ('omnem omnino spiritualitatem quae a Deo in creaturam emanat').[24] A similar interpretation obtains in *Quaestiones ac considerationes in libri Druschim*, where the first three are interpreted as a trinity distinguished from the other seven, which are metaphysical virtues emanating from God at creation ('classes metaphysices divinarum virtutum, quas Deus in Creationem emittit').[25] The separation of the two groups of sepiroth is important not simply as a means of eliciting a Trinitarian reading, but also for distinguishing God from creation. More commends Knorr's second table because 'the distinction between eternal divinity and the divine emanations which flow out in creation is very clear' ('distinctio inter aeternam deitatem et divinas emantiones in creationem profluentes, magis est manifesta').[26] More identifies problems in the hierarchical scheme which make it difficult to accommodate it to a Trinitarian one, confident that the problems are not that Trinitarianism was never there, but that recent interpreters of the kabbalah ignorantly explain things in such a way as to fail to distinguish God from His creation. This tendency to pantheism introduces basic materialist errors. In his discussion of 'uxor Dseir Anpin' of the second 'table' he says that the Jews fail to distinguish the soul of the messiah from the eternal logos. They mistakenly describe the logos as the soul of the messiah extended throughout the world, because they did not understand hypostatic union clearly.[27]

These strands of criticism culminate in *Fundamenta*. But it must be recognised that even though More is directly critical of the emanationist doctrines of the Lurianic kabbalah, he himself employed such ideas. In *Conjectura cabbalistica* he puts forward a concept of prime matter, which he calls 'metaphysical hyle'. Citing Aquinas as his authority, he describes creation as an emanation from God. It is not a physical but a metaphysical emanation, emanation of potential being, the 'mere possibility of being' — *ens in potentia* which he insists is 'as truly *ens* as *ens actu*'.[28] More also employs the term 'monad' in his conception of basic physical substance as corpuscular, 'consisting of actual perfect Parvitudes and of nothing else which are so many Physical Monads and utterly indivisible in themselves as the incorporeal Beings created the first day are'.[29]

Anne Conway and the Kabbalah

It is clear from *The Conway Letters* that Anne Conway launched herself into the study of the genuine kabbalah with as much alacrity as Henry More. Copies of Knorr's papers were supplied to her from 1671 onwards. Furthermore, she had the advantage of the presence of Van Helmont in her household to assist her in her studies. There are no documents recording her immediate reactions to the kabbalah, but her one philosophical treatise, her *Principles of the Most Ancient and Modern Philosophy* shows unmistakably, the impact of kabbalism on her thought. Anne Conway's *Principia philosophiae* is radically different from Henry More, in so far as she proposes a monistic ontology instead of his dualistic account of the relationship between soul and body. (In fact it contains a point-by-point critique of Henry More's philosophical dualism without actually naming him as the target of her anti-dualist arguments.)[30] Nonetheless, it is a work which is shaped by the presence of Henry More. Thus it is that, in so far as Conway propounds a system consistent with the Lurianic account of the nature of God and created substances, and of the relation of God to His creation, and in so far as it is immune from the kind of criticism which More makes in the *Fundamenta*, it can be said to be an answer to More. What I want now to argue is that Van Helmont's *Cabbalistical Dialogue* was not the only response to More's objections to the kabbalah: that Anne Conway's *Principia philosophiae* should be read in relation not simply to her reading of the kabbalah, but to Henry More's reading of it. Anne Conway's system is one which can be said to meet the Henry More's objections to the kabbalist account of creation, without abandoning basic elements derived from kabbalistic thought. Furthermore, there are aspects of her application of kabbalist thinking which correspond closely to his.

Lady Conway proposes a philosophical system based on monistic vitalism, in which all created things are, like the deity, composed of spirit, not matter. But she is at pains to avoid the imputations of materialism, pantheism and atheism. This is evident from her specific repudiation of the arch-materialist Hobbes and and the materialist-pantheist, Spinoza. It is also implicit in the metaphysical hierarchy of being which she proposes.

Conway's philosophical system is deduced, *a priori* from her idea of God, whom she conceives of as "Spirit, Light, and Life, infinitely Wise, Good, Just, Mighty, Omniscient, Omnipresent, Omnipotent, Creator and Maker of all things visible and invisible'.[31] Created things must be like their creator, but they must be differentiated from the creator, or else they would be God. As in the Lurianic kabbalah, for Conway all things consist of spirit. To this extent created things are composed of the same substance as the God. There is no matter in nature, matter being by definition the contrary of God:

> And seeing the Goodness of God is a living Goodness, which hath Life, Power, Love
> and Knowledge in it, which He communicates to his Creatures, How can it be, that any

dead Thing should proceed from him, or be created by Him, such as is mere Body or Matter . . .?[32]

As in the Lurianic account of creation, Conway's 'creatures' are composed of spirit contracted into particles or monads. Where More interprets the Lurianic version of this assertion as materialistic, Anne Conway was sensitive to the charge that her system might be interpreted as a variant of Hobbism or Spinozism. She identifies the root of the materialism and pantheism which she attributes to them as their making the deity of one substance with created things:

> *Hobbs* himself affirms God himself to be Material and Corporeal; yea nothing else but Matter and Body, and so confounds God and the Creatures in their essences, and denies that there is any Essential Distinction between them . . . *Spinosa* also confounds God and Creatures together, and makes but one Being of both; all which are diametrically opposite to the Philosophy here delivered by us.[33]

Conway categorically denies that in her philosophy, 'God and Creatures are one Substance':

> For in all Transmutations of Creatures from one *Species* into another . . . there can never be a Progression or Ascension made unto God, who is the chiefest of all Beings, and whose Nature still infinitely excels a Creature placed in his highest Perfection; for the Nature of God is every way unchangeable, so that it doth not admit of the least Shadow of a Change: But the Nature of a Creature is to be changeable.[34]

The very principle by which she differentiates her system from Hobbist or Spinozistic monism, are also the criteria which meet the kind of objections More had itemised in his *Fundamenta philosophiae*. I shall discuss three: her hierarchy of being and with it the role of Christ; her perfectionism and, in so far as it is possible to reconstruct it, her account of the formation of the monads. Paradoxically perhaps, it is the underlying (though modified) Neoplatonism of Anne Conway's system, its tripartite descending heirarchy, that rescues it from charges of pantheism or of monistic materialism. But, let us recall, Henry More too tried to reduce kabbalah to a Neoplatonic hierarchy of being as part of his attempt at an orthodox reading of it.

As I have already stated, Anne Conway's vitalistic and monistic concept of substance satisfies her Platonic view that there must be an affinity between the creator and that which is created. Through her concept of substance, she underlines the *likeness* of God to His creatures. At the same time, however, her division of being into three orders, *differentiates* God from His creation. The decisive distinction between divine and created substance is that God is immutable, and created things subject to change. God is eternal, creatures subject to time:

That all Creatures in their own Nature are changeable, the distinction between God and Creatures, duly considered, evidently evinces and the same is by daily experience confirmed. Now if any Creature be in its own Nature changeable, it hath this Mutability, as it is a Creature, and consequently, all Creatures will have the same according to that Rule: Whatsoever agrees to anything as placed under this or that *Species* agrees to all comprehended under the same *Species*; but Mutability agrees to a Creature (which is the most general name of that *Species*, under which all Creatures are comprehended), and from thence it is manifest, for there would no distinction between God and the Creatures. For if any Creature were of it self and its own Nature unchangeable, that Creature would be God, because Immutability is one of his incommunicable Attributes.[35]

Anne Conway's insistence on a clear distinction between the communicable and incommunicable attributes of God underlines the ontological separation of created things from God, without sacrificing the analogy between God and created things.[36]

The differentiation between God and His creation is re-inforced by the role of Christ, the middle nature, in her system. Christ, the *logos* or Adam Kadmon, is an indespensible part of her hierarchy of being — his function understood here primarily in a metaphysical rather than a religious or salvific sense, though the invocation of kabbalah is obvious from the terminology. God does not have contact with created things except through Christ, conceived as a mediator between being and becoming, between the eternal and immutable deity and the temporal and changeable world.[37] Anne Conway is at pains to stress that this mediation should not be understood simply physically or spatially, like 'the Trunk of the Body is between the Head and Feet', but rather ontologically 'as Silver is between Tinn and Gold or Water between Air and Earth' — though she dissociates herself from the materialistic implications of these analogies ('which are but gross comparisons in regard of the thing it self').[38] Christ, as middle nature invested with the communicable attributes of God, which He communicates to created things. In nature, Christ also admits of change, but only in the sense of a tendency towards the good, a capacity for increasing goodness. Thus he participates in both divine being and created being. Christ bridges the gap between God and creation, but Christ also separates creation from God. Although Christ as middle nature participates third order, that of created things, there is no question of the this being construed as the soul of the messiah extended throughout the world, as More had objected to the kabbalist account of the logos.

Conway's optimistic conception of change, allows that all created things may increase in perfection, a Body may always be more and more spiritual *ad infinitum*; because God, who is the First and Supreme Spirit, is Infinite and doth not nor cannot partake of the least Corporeality.; whence such is the Nature of a Creature . . . that it always draws nearer and nearer to God in likeness.[39]

Nonetheless, Conway's concept of perfectionism ensures that while created things may increase in perfection, *ad infinitum*, they cannot become fully perfect. For to do so would be to transcend the limits of their nature, to transgress the ontological boundary separating the God—

. . . God, or the Chiefest Being is altogether unchangeable. Now seeing the, the Nature of Creatures is really distinct from the Nature of God, so that there are some Attributes of God, are incommunicable to Creatures, among which is reckoned Immutability: Hence it necessarily follows that Creatures are changeable, or else they would be God himself.[40]

To express the perfectibility of created things which at the same time does not result in their becoming God, Conway uses a geometric analogy, arguing that just as no polyhedron can become a circle, so no creature can become God:

We have an Example of Figure in a Triangular Prisme, which is the first Figure of all right lined solid Bodies, whereinto a Body is convertible; and from this into a Cube, which is a perfecter Figure, and comprehends in it a Prisme; from a Cube it may be turned into a more perfect figure . . . and so it ascends from one Figure, more imperfect, to another more perfect, *ad infinitum* . . . and yet can never reach to the Perfection of a Globe, although it always approaches nearer unto it; the case is the same in divers degrees of Life, which have indeed a beginning, but no end; so that a Creature is always capable of a farther and perfecter degree of Life, *ad infinitum*, and yet can never attain to be equal with God.[41]

Anne Conway's *Principia* does not, it is true, include an account of creation. But in what she does say about the relationship of God to created nature, I think we can say she is more careful and precise than Van Helmont when he writes on the same subject. She does actually not express an opinion on the issue which so troubled More: *creatio ex nihilo*. Nor does she give an account of the formation or production of her monads.[42] She does, however, concur with Van Helmont in maintaining that creation is a continuous process, though she does argue that it has a beginning in time, and she conceives of creation taking place through Christ. She also insists that God creates freely, and not out of the necessity of His nature.[43] It is not clear whether she conceives of creation as a process of emanation from the Godhead. But she does write of the coming into being of Christ as an emanation:

> And his Production is rather a Generation or Emanation from God rather than a
> Creation, if the word be taken in a strict sence; although, according to the larger sense
> and use of this Word he may be said to be created or formed.[44]

This statement suggests that she distinguishes between *emanation* and *creation* and that therefore created spirit is not to be understood as something extruded from God. Elsewhere, she does talk in emanationist terms with regard to creation:

> . . . if the Word Create respects the Universal Seeds, and Principles of all Things which
> (in subordination to God, who is the Principal Beginning of all Things) are as it were
> Springs and Fountains from whence Creatures flow forth in the order of their
> succession; so it may be said that all Creatures were Created together.[45]

But even here where she seems to endorse emanationism, her terminology is carefully non-literalist. Created things do not bud off from or ooze out of divine substance, but it is the principles of their creation which emanate from God. Moreover, it is only through Christ that such principles or seeds can be said to become created things — 'Christ, who is the First Begotten of all Creatures, by whom all Things are said to be made; as *John* declared it, and *Paul* expressly affirms, that by Christ all Things were made both visible and invisible'.[46]

There are many features of Conway's philosophical system which must give pause to orthodox Christians. But by making careful metaphysical distinctions, Conway preserves her monadic vitalism from the possible imputation that she confuses God with His creation, makes the world the body of God, or derives her monads from the Divine essence. Conway's *Principia* is notably free from allegorical interpretations of kabbalistic images. It is also highly selective in what it incorporates. In these respects it is a model of the kind of philosophical enterprise in which the Cambridge Platonists, and above all, Henry More engaged. Indeed, her choice of a tri-partite system concurs with Henry More's Pythaogrean interpretation of the sepiroth and his stress on the first three in a bid to preserve a vesitige of Trinitarianism. Anne Conway's tri-partite order of being is certainly not Trinitarian, though it accords great significance to the concept of a divine triad underlying all being. She also Christianises her reading of kabbalah to the extent that she elides Christ with Adam Kadmon and adduces New Testament support for some of her positions.[47] Her *Principia* shows that by careful philosophical analysis, kabbalistic doctrines can be considered as compatible with a Christian outlook (though not perhaps with orthodox Christian theology). I do not mean that Anne Conway made adjustments to her interpretation of the kabbalah in order to satisfy Henry More. On the contrary, hers was a monistic philosophy which departed radically from the modified mechanistic dualism espoused by Henry More. No doubt he would have regarded some of her positions as prime examples of how too much kabbalism can turn ones head. But if we read *Principia philosophia* with More's reactions to the kabbalah in mind, I think it is possible to see the work not simply as *influenced by* kabbalism, but, as a philosophical interpretation, if not defence, of kabbalah. And in this in turn helps us to see the differences between Anne Conway and Van Helmont, for all their agreement in points of doctrine. Anne Conway's *Principia* therefore stands in closer relation to the Christian Platonist reading of kabbalah than the negative assessments in his *Fundamenta philosophiae* might lead us to assume.

1 My title alludes to Allison Coudert's classic article, 'A Cambridge Platonist's Kabbalist Nightmare', *Journal of the History of Ideas*, 35 (1975), pp. 633–652.

2 *Kabbala denudata seu doctrina hebraeorum transcendentalis et metaphysica atque theologica opus antiquissimae philosophiae barbaricae variis speciminibus resertissimum.* vols. 1–2 (part 1)(Sulzbach, 1677), vol. 3 (part 2) (Sulzbach 1684), (hereafter cited as *KD*), part 1, vol. 2, pp. 293–307. (Modern reprint , Hildesheim and New York: Olms, 1974).

3 See Coudert, art. cit. for a vivacious account of this vivid dream. On the kabbalah of Isaac Luria, see G. Scholem, *Major Trends in Jewish Mysticism* (New York: Schocken Books, 1954. First published 1941).

4 *Conway Letters the Correspondence of Anne, Viscountess Conway, Henry More and their Friends, 1643–1684*, ed. M.H. Nicolson, revised ed. Sarah Hutton (Oxford: Clarendon Press, 1992), p. 529.

5 *KD*, pp. 308–310.

6 More's contributions to the apparatus of the *Kabbala denudata* are to be found in the second volume. They are as follows: *Tentatus rationem reddendi nominum & ordinis decem sephirotharum in duabus tabulis cabbalisticis ex scriptura, Platonismo, rationeque libera D. Henrici Mori Cantabrigensis* ; *Quaestiones ac considerationes in libri* Druschim *D. Henrici Mori Cantabrigiensis.*; *Ad Clarissimum ac eruditissimum virum N.N. [i.e. Henry More] De rebus in Amica sua Responsione contentis Ulterior Disquisitio*; *Visionis Ezechielis seu Mercavae expositio; Fundamenta philosophiae seu cabbalae aeto-paedo-melisseae.*

7 On Knorr see, K. Salecker, *Christian Knorr von Rosenroth* (Leipzig, 1931). *Christian Knorr von Rosenroth Dichter und Gelehrter am Sulzbacher Musenhof. Festschrift zur 300 Wiederkehr des Todestages* (Sulzbach-Rosenburg 1989, Literaturarchiv und Stadt Sulzbach-Rosenburg); Allison Coudert, *Leibniz and the Kabbalah* (Dordrecht: Kluwer, 1995).

8 On Van Helmont's impact of Lady Conway's mature philosophy, see S.Hutton, 'Ancient Wisdom and Modern Philosophy. Anne Conway, F.M. van Helmont and the seventeenth-century Dutch Interchange of Ideas', *Questiones infinitae*, 9 (1994); eadem, 'Of Physic and Philosophy: Anne Conway, Francis Mercury van Helmont and Seventeenth-century Medicine', in A. Cunningham and O.P.Grell (eds), *Religio medici* (London: Scolar Press, 1997).

9 There is no comprehensive study of More's interest in the kabbalah, but see Stuart Brown, 'Leibniz and Henry More's Cabbalistic Circle' and David Katz, 'Henry More and the Jews', both in S. Hutton (ed.) *Henry More, 1617–1687. Tercentenary Studies* (Dordrecht,Kluwer, 1992); and Allison Coudert, 'Henry More, the Kabbalah and the Quakers', in R. Kroll et al. (eds), *Philosophy, Science, and Religion in England (1640–1700)* (Cambridge: Cambridge University Press, 1992), pp. 31–67.

10 See J.J. Blau, *The Christian Interpretation of the Cabala in the Renaissance* (New York: Columbia University Press, 1944), chapter 4.

11 Henry More, *Opera omnia, tum latine, tum quae anglice scripta sunt* , 3 vols. (London, 1675–9), vol. 2, *Opera philosophica*, p. 449, 'Pythagoricum vero Systema idem fuisse quod antiquorum judeaorum'. More applied the same method of reading kabbalah as *prisca sapientia* or ancient wisdom, as he did with the writings of Jacob Boehme. See S. Hutton, 'Henry More and Jacob Boehme', in Hutton, *Henry More.*

12 *Conway Letters*, ed. cit., p. 529.

13 ibid., pp. 529–30.

14 ibid., p. 530.

15 More supplemented Knorr's *Tabula sephirotharum cabbalistica ac Judaica vulgaris,* with *Tabula sephirotharum Knorriana, in sublimionis cabbalae clavem Zoaristicam destinata* and *Tabula sephirotharum Graeciana sive Pythagorica ab H.M. restituta.* Only the first of these is printed in *KD.* All three are printed together with More's explanatory notes in his *Opera philosophica.*

16 'In Cabbala *Mercavae* summa contineri, quae concipi possunt, & profundissima Mysteria, vulgarique Philosopho vix credibilia', *KD*, vol. 2, p. 225.

17 'Totum Mundum Materialem in primaevo suo statu aut diphanum fuisse aut lucidum, hoc est, in Soles, transparenteque Coelos, aethereosve Vortices fuisse distributum.

'Hoc certe constare potest ex *Cabbala* nostra *Philosophica* in Interpretatione Operis quarate Diei. Nec permittit brevitas ut eadem hic repetamus. Res facile intelligitur e Philosophia *Cartesiana*.' *KD*, vol. 2, p. 226.

18 ibid., 241.

19 'Postulata quaedam, aut antiquae Pythagoreorum Philosophiae (a quo non multum abludit, quantum ad eas res, ad quas nos respicimus, Cartesiana)', *Mercavae expositio*, *KD* 2, p. 224.

20 'Spiritus movens Turbinem est Principium *Hylarchicum* (de quo in *Enchiridio* meo *Metaphysico*) sive *Spiritus Naturae, aeterni Spritus* Instrumentum'. ibid. p.242.

21 'Duo quasi esse praecipua Mundi Materialis Elementa, *Naturale* alterum, alterum *Divinum. Prius autem esse subjectum Operationum* Spiritus Naturae *quem* Cabbalistae Sandalphonem *appellant,* Posterius *Spiritus S.* vehiculum, verumque illud Manna coeleste, quod Cibus Panisve sit Sanctarum Animarum ac Angelorum. *Spiritum Naturae* hic *Sandalphonem* appello tua Autoritate adductus'. ibid. p. 226.

22 Henry More, *Opera philosophica,* vol.1, i.e. vol. 2 of his *Opera omnia,* On More's use of kabalistic doctrines in support of his arguments for the infinity of space in his *Enchiridion metaphysicum,* see Brian Copenhaver, 'Jewish Theologies of Space in the Scientific Rvolution: Henry More, Joseph Raphson, Isaac Newton', *Annals of Science,* 37 (1980), pp. 489–548.

23 See note 15 above.

24 *Opera Omnia,* vol. 2, p. 424.

25 ibid., p.449.

26 ibid., p. 433.

27 '. . . humanam creatamque naturam Christi sive Messiae, hoc est, Animam ejus, quam & *Logon* esse, qui incarnatus est, esse volunt, per totum Mundum extendunt, id profecto nullo modo admittendum est . . . quod Animae Messieae cum Aeterno Logo, unionem quam vocant Hypostaticam non satis distincte intelligerent . . .Logon autem incarnatum non esse Animam Messiae per totum Mundi extensam' *Opera omnia,* 2:437. Later More makes clear that this error in interpretation is the direct result of the Jews not recognising͵Christ as the Messiah. This failure lead them into all sorts of distorted interpretations ('in varios labyrinthos eos aduxisse'). But knowledge that Christ is the Messiah is the true golden key which Christians have for unlocking the secrets of the kabbala and restoring it to it pristine purity, 'ad referenda pretiossisima Mysteria Cabbalae Theosophicae... & antiqua Cabala pure ac sincere restituatur'. ibid., p. 456.

28 op. cit., p. 138, in *A Collection of Several Philosophical Writings* (London, 1662).

29 ibid., p. 142.

30 See my 'Anne Conway, critique de Henry More: l'esprit et la matière', *Archives de Philosophie* 58 (1995), pp. 371–84.

31 Anne Conway, *The Principles of the Most Ancient and Modern Philosophy,* ed. P. Loptson (Dordrecht: Kluwer, 1982), ch.1.1, p. 149. This is a reprint of the 1692 translation of the Latin first printing of Conway's philosophy, *Principia Philosophiae antiquissimae et recentissimae* (Amsterdam, 1690).

32 Conway, *Principles,* Ch. 2.2, p. 196.

33 ibid., Ch.9.4, p. 222.

34 ibid., Ch. 9.5, p. 224.

35 ibid., Ch. 6.1, pp. 175–6.

36 In Anne Conway's account, God's communicable attributes include goodness and justice, and his being life and spirit. The incommunicable attributes include besides immutability, omnipotence, omnipresence, eternity, omniscience.

37 ibid., 168ff. Compare Plotinus' second hypostasis relationship to the first and third hypostases in *Enneads,* 5.1.

38 ibid.,169. The analogy with metals is alchemical.

39 Conway, *Principles,* Ch.7, p. 192.

40 ibid., Ch. 5.3, p. 168.

41 ibid., Ch. 9.7, p. 226.

42 This does not mean that she did not have an opinion on the subject, but the absence may be accounted for by the possibility that these parts of her treatise were illegible —according to the preface to her treatise, much of the manuscript was illegible.

43 ibid., chapter 2.

44 'eisuque productio est generatio vel emanatio a Deo, quam Creatio, si vox haec stricto accipiatur sensu: quamvis secundum latiorem sensum usumque hujus vocis ipse etiam dici queat creatus esse vel formatus'. ibid., 5.4, p. 170.

45 ibid., ch. 4.1, p. 165.

46 ibid.

47 See chapter 5.

4. SEVENTEENTH-CENTURY CHRISTIAN HEBRAISTS: PHILOSEMITES OR ANTISEMITES?

ALLISON P. COUDERT

Several years ago my husband, Gordon Weiner, and I both gave papers at a conference of historians. My husband's paper was on Jewish attitudes towards Christians in the early modern period, while mine was on Christian attitudes towards Jews. In my paper, I argued that it was entirely appropriate to label Christian attitudes towards the Jews before the nineteenth century as antisemitic rather than anti-Judaic. To my mind, this was a rather innocent and uncontroversial suggestion because it was so easy to document that hostility towards the Jews involved much more than their religion. So, imagine my surprise when, after we had presented our papers, a man got up and said that he was very confused by the panel. One participant — he pointed to my husband — had given a very scholarly presentation, while the other, and that of course could only be me, was a 'mere popularizer'. I later learned that the man who had so strenuously objected to my paper was a Lutheran theologian and that I had deeply offended him.

The response of this theologian set me thinking more deeply about the appropriateness of using either the term antisemitism or philosemitism to describe Christian attitudes toward Jews before the nineteenth century. For the purposes of this paper, I am particularly interested in the use of these terms in regard to the attitudes of seventeenth-century Protestant — primarily Lutheran — Hebraists, for while the term philosemitic has been used to describe at least one of these Hebraists, namely Johann Christoph Wagenseil, the worst most historians have said about the others is that they are anti-Judaic.

I chose to investigate the work of seventeenth-century Protestant Hebraists for several reasons. First, Protestants were generally more interested in Jews, Judaism, and Hebraica than Catholics, especially after the Council of Trent reaffirmed the Vulgate as divinely inspired.[1] Second, by looking specifically at seventeenth-century Protestant Hebraists, I hoped to place the work of the two Christian Hebraists I know best, Christian Knorr von Rosenroth (1636–1689) and Francis Mercury van

A.P. Coudert, S. Hutton, R.H. Popkin and G. M. Weiner (eds): Judaeo-Christian Intellectual Culture in the Seventeenth Century, 43–69.
© 1999 *Kluwer Academic Publishers. Printed in the Netherlands.*

Helmont (1614–1698), in a broader context to see how representative their views were. Von Rosenroth was a devoted Lutheran and an accomplished Hebraist, who has won the praise of no less an authority than Gershom Scholem.[2] The religious views of van Helmont are far harder to categorize, as we shall see, for although he was born a Catholic, he became a Quaker for a short period, and died, according to Leibniz, a 'Seeker' without any specific religious affiliation.[3]

The distinction between religiously motivated anti-Judaism and racially motivated antisemitism was first made in the late nineteenth century and picked up again after World War II by Christians wishing to exonerate Christianity from the charge of contributing to the racist policies of the Third Reich. The distinction between anti-Judaism and antisemitism had and still has obvious appeal for many Christians because it allows them to describe the manifest intolerance towards Jews as impersonal and theologically valid, or at least understandable. But the line between impersonal, rational, and religiously motivated anti-Judaism and irrational, racially motivated antisemitism is virtually impossible to maintain in the medieval and early modern periods. I would go further and argue that antisemitism is and always has been a potential aspect of Christianity from its inception.

Thus the conclusion I have reached and which I will try to substantiate in this paper is that while the term antisemitism may be anachronistic if applied before the nineteenth century, its use is nevertheless entirely appropriate when characterizing the views of the majority of Christians, including those of seventeenth-century Christian Hebraists. We do, after all, speak of 'proto-capitalism', 'the rate of productive investment', and 'the gross national product' in connection with earlier epochs that had no such concepts, and we apply modern sociological and psychological theories to periods that knew no such disciplines. Had religion been the only issue involved in Christian attitudes towards Jews, anti-Judaism would indeed be the correct term. But Christian criticism of Jews involved more than religion, and this extra, basically ethnic, or what in the seventeenth century was often called 'national', dimension explains why many Jews who converted to Christianity were never fully accepted, as theoretically they should have been. But while I will argue that the term antisemitism is entirely appropriate, I have come to the opposite conclusion about the term philosemitism. As far as I can judge, it is not appropriate or even applicable, for what has been described as Christian philosemitism really has little to do with actual Jews or Christians for that matter.[4] As a number of scholars have pointed out, the vast majority of those Christians who have been described as philosemitic did not like Jews as Jews but only as potential converts to Christianity.[5] And for that tiny fraction of Christians who actually liked Jews enough to emulate their rituals and practices — the kind of Christians described by David Katz, for example[6] — the only good Jew was a dead Jew, an ideal Mosaic type, not actual Jews living at the time. In fact, as both Katz and Po-chia Hsia point out, many Protestants simply appropriated the idea of a 'New Israel', designating themselves as the true 'Chosen People'. Thus reverance for Judaism and the Old Testament could coexist nicely with antisemitism because Jews had been effectively removed from their own history.[7] Given this state of affairs, I would argue that true philosemitism was really only possible for two kinds of Christians: heretics and converts to Judaism — in other words for non-Christians. As the work of the Lutheran Hebraists I discuss below reveals, there were inerradicable aspects of orthodox Christian and Lutheran beliefs that made philosemitism impossible and antisemitism inevitable.

I am, of course, not the only scholar to use the term antisemitism to characterized pre-nineteenth-century Christian attitudes. In recent years a number of historians have applied the term.[8] While earlier centuries may not have had a clear idea about race, can one really argue that nineteenth and twentieth-century antisemites had or have a valid understanding of precisely what race is? For that matter, does anyone to this day? But more importantly, what makes anti-Judaism and antisemitism indistinguishable is that both were based on a demonic view of Jews as a sub-human or, more accurately, non-human group united in a conspiracy to destroy the human race. Norman Cohn made this point years ago in *Warrant for Genocide*:

> As I see it the deadliest kind of antisemitism, the kind that results in massacre and attempted genocide, has little to do with real conflicts of interest between living people or even with racial prejudice as such. At its heart lies the belief that Jews — all Jews everywhere form a conspiratorial body set on ruining and then dominating the rest of mankind. And this belief is simply a modernized, secularized version of the popular medieval view of the Jews as a league of sorcerers employed by Satan for the spiritual and physical ruination of Christendom.[9]

Thus the racial element is not really the issue. The issue is the consistent way in which Jews over many centuries and largely as a result of Christian doctrine and dogma were demonized and dehumanized to the point that were as easy to kill as the dogs, swine, lice, and inhuman monsters with whom they were constantly identified. The idea that Jews routinely killed little Christian children because they needed their blood for food and medicine may no longer be a common aspect of antisemitic beliefs, but the notion that Jews are murderous parasites on the body politic who suck non-Jews dry still is. The old charge of ritual murder, or 'Blood Libel', thus lived on in a new guise, transformed in the early-modern period — not the nineteenth century — from a suppposedly physical to an economic reality. As James Harrington said in the mid seventeenth century, '[Jews]. . . of all Nations never incorporate, but taking up the room of a Limb, are of no use or office unto the body, while they suck the nourishment which would sustain a natural, and useful member'.[10] The City Council and Guilds of Regensburg had lodged the same complaint against the Jews a century earlier. In a petition to Emperor Maximilliam they complained that Christians had been 'sucked dry, injured in their body and goods, and without doubt, also blemished in their soul's salvation and all felicitous estate'.[11] Johann Jacob Schudt, whose work is discussed below, availed himself of the same vampire image when he describes the Jews as 'bleed[ing] so many poor Christians dry'.[12] There is a similar continuity with the other charges against the Jews. For example the Shylock stereotype of the Jew as a grasping materialist was a reworking of the much more ancient idea that Judaism was a materialistic religion, based on tangible rewards in the physical world.[13] However much accusations against the Jews seem to have changed over the centuries there is an underlying core uniting them all: Jews are the quintessential 'Other', and this 'Otherness' flows in their blood from generation to generation regardless of their religion. If they are traditional Jews, they are Jews. If they are Spinozists, they are Jews. Even if they convert to Christianity, they are still Jews. There is therefore no radical break between the supposedly 'religious' Jew-hating of the medieval period and the 'racial' or 'scientific' anti-Semitism of modern times. As Sander Gilman has argued in *The Jew's Body,* the medieval stereotype of the Jew as the destroyer of Christian culture through the shedding of Christian blood or the mass poisoning of wells continued on into the nineteenth and twentieth centuries with the development of pseudo-scientific theories about the Jews as diseased parasites destroying society from within. It is the Jew's body, not his beliefs, that is the locus of danger. In Gilman's view there is therefore no distinction between religious and racial hatred of the Jews; Christianity provided the rational for both:

> The rhetoric of European anti-Semitism can be found within the continuity of Christianity's image of the Jew. It is Christianity which provides all of the

vocabularies of difference in Western Europe and North America, whether it is the most overt 'religious' language or in the secularized language of modern science. For it is not merely that the Jew is the obvious Other for the European, whether the citizen of the Roman Empire or of the Federal Republic of Germany. Anti-Semitism is central to Western culture because the rhetoric of European culture is Christianized, even in its most secular form. This made the negative image of difference of the Jew found in the Gospel into the central referent for all definitions of difference in the West.[14]

Gilman is unequivocal in laying the blame for Western antisemitism on Christianity. To my mind he is entirely right. As I said at the beginning of this paper, in the early-modern period only heretics and converts to Judaism could truly be philosemitic. Even the most supposedly philosemitic of the Lutheran Hebraists, Johann Christoph Wagenseil, could not escape from the inherent antisemitism of his Lutheranism.

But before we get to Wagenseil, a word should be said about Lutheran attitudes towards the Jews in general. Everyone is aware of Luther's vicious attack on the Jews in his treatise *On the Jews and their Lies*, which appears to mark a radical change from his earlier *Jesus Christ was born a Jew*. Historians by in large attribute Luther's change of attitude to his disappointment at the failure of the Jews to convert en masse to Lutheranism.[15] But as Wilhelm Maurer has shown, Luther was never as sympathetic to the Jews as this early tract might suggest if read in isolation. His Lectures on Psalms, delivered between 1513 and 1515, and his Lectures on Romans (1515–16) contain all the charges he would level at the Jews towards the end of his life.[16]

Little work has been done on Lutheran attitudes towards Jews in the seventeenth century. Martin Friedrich is one of the few to have devoted a book to this subject in recent years. He criticizes the prevailing view that the birth of the Pietist movement within Lutheranism heralded a new and more positive attitude towards the Jews.[17] He argues instead that when it came to Jews, the opinions of orthodox and pietist Lutherans were not very different. While both groups gave lip service to the notion that the conversion of the Jews was an ideal to be actively encouraged, in actual fact they both saw conversion as less and less possible or even probable. The degree to which Lutherans believed in the possibility of the conversion of the Jews readily correlates with their view of Jews as a whole. Those who thought conversion unlikely, if not out of the question — and these were the majority — were overtly hostile to Jews and describe them in ways that can only be described as antisemitic. Zedler's article 'Juden' is a case in point. Zedler's *Lexikon* was *the* Lutheran lexicon. It represented Lutheran opinion in general, and when this opinion concerned Jews there is

very little to distinguish Zedler's antisemitism from the virulent
antisemitism of Luther's later life. Zedler repeats many of the calumnies
leveled against Jews. They are the 'sworn enemy' of Christians. Having
killed the son of God, they have no compunction about killing other
innocents and routinely murder Christian children, crucifying or
pulverizing them with a mortar and pestle. They are 'thieves' and liars and
have committed infinitely greater sins than their father, the devil. They are
all these things not because of their religion but because of their 'nature'.
As Zedler says 'God has marked them in their nature. Indeed, a Jew has
something about him that one soon recognizes and which separates him
from other men'. They are 'loathsome' and 'horrible' and have a 'repulsive
smell'. The so-called 'foetor Judaicus', or Jewish stench, had a long
history before and after Zedler wrote — in fact, the Nazis claimed to have
'scientifically' verified the 'faint-sweet' racial odor of Jews.[18] As the
following long passage from Zedler's article on the Jews shows, his
polemic has very little to do with the beliefs of the Jews and everything to
do with their 'character' or 'nature'. Hence anti-Judaism is not a fitting
description of his views:

> They elevate their Talmud so far over the Bible and regard it as the source of such
> wisdom that even God himself must study it. . . . They are our sworn enemy. And
> how often have they not killed Christian children, crucified them and crushed
> them with a mortar and pestle? They are the worst thieves, and fraud marks their
> true character. Every time they must take a serious oath, they swear falsely, since
> they can soon be absolved by a Rabbi or three Jews. . . . God has marked them in
> their nature. Indeed, a Jew has something about him that one soon recognizes and
> which separates him from other men. The are loathsome and horrible, and they
> have the repulsive smell and feculence which they were threatened with in Deut.
> 28: 37, 46. The worst thing about the Jews is that their rejection is eternal. They
> are not absolutely rejected by God to the point that he will not offer mercy to any
> (Rom. 11, 12). God has a few among them who will convert, since for all those
> who believe in the Gospel, the door of mercy and entrance to the Kingdom of
> Christ is open. But they are rejected and disowned so that they will never again be
> the God's people or achieve the state of grace and holiness they had in the Old
> Testament. They made themselves very mighty with their golden ass and sought
> great consolation in it (Lev. 26, 44). However, they do not deserve consolation,
> unless they convert. In the meantime, is there any wonder that they lie under a
> perpetual curse? God punished them with only 70 years imprisonment. But now
> that they have been repudiated for almost 1700 years, they must have committed
> infinitely greater sins than their father [i.e. Satan]. Admittedly, they killed the son
> of God and crucified the Lord of Lords. This blood still oppresses them and
> fulfills the judgment, as they themselves say. They rage to this day against the
> Gospels. Must they not therefore bring upon themselves the judgment of God for
> such persistent and deep-rooted lack of faith? . . . For the most part they are
> money-changers, usurers, tax collectors, middlemen, apothecaries, doctors, and

interpreters. They can give information to anyone about all the merchandise to be found in a city and tell its actual worth and price. . . . Other Western people, like the Greeks and Armenians, Turkish and Eastern Christians report that every Good-Friday, in order to allow their hatred of the Christian religion to see the light of day, they murder a Christian slave. However, after they have had many different meals in order to keep this a secret, they are severely punished because of this abominable deed. In the West they have also often killed children as well as other older people, especially those in their midst who reveal a love for Christianity.[19]

Admittedly Zedler was not a Hebraist. His antisemitism might therefore simply be attributable to his lack of exposure to Jewish thought and Jewish people. But did the superior knowledge and broader experience of seventeenth-century Lutheran Hebraists make them more tolerant of the Jews? Unfortunately not in the case of the Lutheran Hebraists I have studied. In varying degrees, and largely as a function of how much or how little they believed in the possibility of converting the Jews, their works can and must be described as antisemitic. To start with Johann Jacob Schudt (1664–1722).

Zedler gives a glowing account of Schudt as a man of great learning with a prodigious skill in languages.[20] Schudt's imposing four volume work entitled *Jüdische Merkwürdigkeiten*, or *Jewish Peculiarities*, was published in Frankfurt and Leipzig in 1714. Frank Manual has described Leipzig as a 'center for Judeophobic publications well into the eighteenth century'.[21] It is therefore not surprising that Schudt's book should have been at least partially published there, for Schudt's 'Judeophobia', or what I would call more accurately antisemitism, is readily apparent. This is perhaps strange in a man who takes great pains in the preface to establish his impartiality and objectivity. He insists he knows Jews well and that most of his information comes from what he has seen with his own eyes. When he includes second hand information, he promises the reader that he has been careful to verify it from other sources. He insists that his work is not intended to be polemical, that unlike all too many other Christians, his purpose is not to attack or insult Jews with harsh words or scolding harangues but simply to describe their customs and beliefs with the hope of encouraging their conversion to Christianity. He assures the reader that his approach is even-handed. Where there are good things, he will be sure to point them out; but he will be equally sure to point out bad things, and in this case sharp words will be appropriate. He also insists that he has no wish to attack the 'whole Nation' of Jews or to stir up Christian hatred. But in essence his voluminous work does precisely that. The overall impression one is left with after reading it is that regardless of his obvious interest in the Jews and regardless of the many personal contacts he had with Jews, Schudt simply cannot transcend stereotypes; and this means that he could not conceive of Jews as fully human, fellow beings.

Schudt is a good example of a Christian Hebraist whose very knowledge of Jews and Judaism set up a conflict in his thinking. While he is aware, as ordinary, uneducated Christians were not, of precisely the kind of historical discrimination practiced against the Jews and the way this forced them into trade and money-lending, he still has to look for deeper motives to explain why Jews engage in the business practices they do. As one might expect, he discovers these reasons, not so much in their circumstances as in their character. I quote the following section entitled 'On Jewish Usury and Haggling' because it so clearly shows the ambivalence in his thinking, an ambivalence between what his intellect knows and what his gut feelings about Jews tells him:

> If there is anything in the world that makes the Jews so hated, it is without doubt that damnable and traditional practice of usury with which they bleed so many poor Christians dry with the result that they were expelled from Spain, England, France, Nuremberg, Worms and again from France in 1614. Our forefathers complained about this practice very much in 1612. [For which reason] we would like to insert something here about their usury.
>
> The reason the Jews practice usury so readily is partly due to Christians and partly to Jews. Christians are responsible because they do not allow them to practice any trades and because they do not allow them to possess any real estate or till the land or raise livestock. So, all that remains is trading, haggling, and usury. One of the greatest obstacles to their conversion is probably that they generally grow up and spend most of their lives in idleness and commonly earn their living through trading and haggling and yet really do not work. This is not altogether their fault since they do not have land to farm and in most places they are not allowed to learn or practice trades. Yet they can be faulted because even if they were allowed to work, they would not know how to go about it because of their laziness. Regarding those who are poor among them, whose number, as among Christians, is always the greater part, it is a sheer impossibility that anyone who has very little money can through trading turn this into enough to make ends meet and support a family without shady practices and fraud. As a consequence, these miserable people can ponder and think of nothing but how to maintain their poor lives through cunning, intrigue, fraud, and theft. . . .
>
> It is on this account that the famous jurist from Halle D. Böhmer . . . and some others are of the opinion that one should, on the contrary, encourage the Jews to learn trades so that they will have to earn their bread by the sweat of their brow. But since Christian craftsmen would hardly allow them to enter the guilds and to work with them, one should let them [the Jews] practice trades on their own. But, according to my humble opinion, this would cause many problems since the Jews would ruin the trades with their bungling as much as they have bungled trading.

He goes on to give an example of Jewish' bungling' worthy of Monty Python were it not so deadly serious:

> For example, some Jews practice trades in Holland and it happened that a certain Jewish carpenter circumcised the apostate Speeth, but rather unfortunately, as both Herr Diefenbach . . . and I were told by a learned and noble friend, who heard from Speeth's own mouth what great pain he had to suffer for a long time on account of such a botched circumcision. It serves the apostate right![22]

One would have thought that at least the profession of Jewish carpentry would be immune from attacks! Schudt further blames the Jews' own laziness for their predicament, and, in doing so, equates them with flees and lice (another version of the vampire stereotype), an analogy that had a long history and would enjoy a long future, culminating in *Mein Kampf*:

> From the point of view of the Jews, their poverty comes from the fact that they are prohibited from practicing handicrafts, trades, or farming, and yet they wish to live and feed themselves. In addition to this is the fact that for over three hundred years their young people were not used to working. Add to that the pleasure of idleness and laziness compels them to practice usury, and like lice and fleas they have the bread from the sweat and blood of others. Add to that their misconception that it is a sign of God's care, love, and grace that other people work hard and toil, while they can live in idleness and peace and have enough to eat. As it says in the Talmud *(Tract. Jebamot,* page 63): 'With 100 florins made through trade, one can enjoy meat and wine daily; but 100 florins made from farming hardly buys salt and cabbage.[23]

Schudt's claim to even-handness becomes even more suspect when one realizes that he had read Johann Andreas Eisenmenger, the 'arch Jew-hater', as Ettinger has called him,[24] whose work was used by nineteenth-century antisemites and republished during the Nazi era, another bit of evidence indicating that the distinction between anti-Judaism and antisemitism is specious. Schudt takes over and adds to Eisenmenger's examples showing the dreadful consequences of allowing the Jews 'too great freedom'. Holland, of course, provides the worst example of such freedom. The fact that Jews are allowed to practice their religion openly there is something Schudt is totally against because he is convinced this openness encourages Christians to convert to Judaism:

> A second example of the too great freedom of Jews in Holland and especially in Amsterdam is the fact that Christians openly and without hesitation accept Jewish beliefs and allow themselves to be circumcised, which is not permitted in the Holy Roman Empire but is punished by death. Although Herr Wülfer. . . deems such a forcing of one's conscience too severe, it is, however, proper and just because the apostasy from Christianity to Judaism cannot happen without blaspheming the holy Trinity and without scandalous scorning of our blessed savior Jesus Christ

(even and especially among Christians this behavior merits death). For this reason, the law demands death for those Jews who seduce a Christian to Judaism, as Herr Diefenbach shows in *Jud. Convers.*, para 14, p. 128. For this reason Nicol Antonius, a reformed minister, was hanged in Geneva in 1632 for converting to Judaism.[25]

Schudt's palpable worry about conversion is something of a leitmc̆f throughout his enormous work. For example, he refers to Eisenmenger's description of the conversion of three Chistians and immediately after to a legal case in Frankfurt against one Abraham zum Drachen, who was responsible for converting — through bribery, of course — a Christian tailor from Bergen, by the name of Philipp Heyland, and his wife.[26] The fear that Christians will convert to Judaism if the Jews are not prohibited from proselytizing is a constant theme in the work of many other Christians and Christian Hebraists as well. Why this fear should have been so pronounced is difficult to comprehend in real terms since the number of such conversions was minuscule. Such fear is perhaps only understandable as a sign of the anxieties and doubts Christians had about a religion that had become so fragmented and divisive.

Speeth's conversion to Judaism is an example Schudt comes back to several times in his work. The way the story escalates as he retells it is especially interesting in psychological terms. The first time he mentions Speeth, Schudt suggests that the Jews may actually have poisoned him because he had doubts about Judaism:

> We have a completely new example in our own time of the wretched Johann Peter Speeth, who was born in Augsburg and raised in the Catholic religion, later converted to Lutheranism, then back to the Papists, and after that to the *novatoribus*, the newest and most eccentric sects of our time, and finally adhered to the Quakers and Socinians. (In book 6, chapter 29, paragraph 7 we will have more to say about this wavering spirit which led him to Judaism when he had himself circumcised and took the name of Moses Germanus in Amsterdam in 1697.) The letter which he wrote to Herr Dr. Petersen's wife, describing his apostasy, was published by Herr Bucher in quarto in Danzig in 1699. I initially intended to insert it here, but with good reason I omitted it on account of the infuriating statements about Christ spewed out by this villain for fear that they might give the wrong idea to those with weak faith. . . . Herr Bücher was greatly suspected for printing this godless letter in Danzig and for allowing it to circulate in Saxony, since it happened both in Danzig and in other places that not only were various people led astray from Christianity by it but also had it in mind to deny the Christian religion. But those people were rightfully helped again by other pious Christians and given a stronger foundation [for their beliefs].
>
> Speeth married an honest German Jewess and had children by her (since a noble friend saw a little son at his home). He led a miserably poor life because the Portuguese and other Jews cared little about him. Not only did he make very

little money teaching Jewish children but he also begged in writing for a single gulden from a good Christian friend, who had visited him previously in Amsterdam to alleviate his extreme poverty, which he received. This friend assured me that, as one could clearly see from his conversion, the new Moses Germanus suffered from uncertainty, doubt, and anxiety, which caused the Jews, having certainly observed this, to worry about his return to Christianity. And because it happened that he was so opportunely plucked from the earth, having taken to his bed on April 26, 1701, dying on the 27th and having been buried by the Jews on the 28th, it is understandable that doubt arose as to whether he died so quickly naturally, or took his own life, or whether his life was made shorter by the Jews.[27]

When Schudt returns to this point later, Speeth's murder has become a reality, which proves, of course, that even such a reprobate as Speeth finally recognized the truth of Christianity. In Schudt's mind Speeth is a good example of what can happen if one becomes too immersed in Jewish literature. Speeth had, after all, assisted Knorr von Rosenroth in editing the *Kabbala denudata* (1677, 1684), the largest collection of Hebrew Kabbalistic texts published in Latin up to that time:

> We have already said quite a bit about this rare bird and apostate Speeth. . . but we can now offer the gracious reader a further and even more curious report about him. Our highly esteemed patron Herr Professor Joh. Christoph. Wolffius has given a full report, especially of his published writings in his Bibliotheca Hebraea, p. 811. . . and Herr de la Croze reports that Herr Knorr von Rosenroth employed Speeth in the publication of his *Cabbala denudata*. Some years after his apostasy the Jews got him out of the way with poison because he would not condone all their Talmudic fabels. And one can read in Herr D. Spener . . . how hard he tried to get him away from the papists and later from the Jews.[28]

Schudt presents further descriptions of the terrible consequences of Jewish freedom in Holland. For example, Jewish houses are much too splendid. But, he adds that however beautiful they may be on the outside, on the inside there are only Jews stinking of garlic! Schudt's disparagement of Jews has nothing to do with theology and everything to do with their physicality. As he says:

> However well-built, expensively furnished, and gorgeously embellished the Jewish 'palaces' may be, when one enters them one only finds within Jews reeking of garlic, as one can see in the engraving of an old Jewess in a magnificent garden reading a book with glasses resting on her great Jewish nose.[29]

Schudt was not by any means the worst of the seventeenth-century Christian Hebraists in terms of antisemitism. I have already mentioned Eisenmenger, whose work laid the foundation for what Manual has called 'scientific Judeophobia'.[30] Eisenmenger made it a practice to interpret every negative Rabbinical statement about Christians as literally as possible, even and especially when they were meant metaphorically or represented a minority or discredited opinion. He then methodically organized all these statements by topic. The unwary reader comes away with a truly frightful impression of the Jews. But it is not with such an obvious antisemite that I would like to end my paper. Instead I would like to concentrate on the work of Johann Christoph Wagenseil because later writers have so radically differed in their assessments of the man. For some Wagenseil represents the great Jewish 'defender', the 'Jews' friend', and a prime example of Lutheran philosemitism,[31] while for others, including myself, his views are basically antisemitic. Although his antisemitism is far less vicious and blatant than that of Eisenmenger, it is antisemitism none the less.

What has primarily given Wagenseil the reputation as a philosemite and defender of the Jews is his categorical rejection of the charge of 'Blood Libel'. Wagenseil is fully aware of the effect the charge has on the Jews, making them detest Christians and the religion that would countenance such absurd stories. And he is fully aware of how contradictory and nonsensical the charges essentially are. As he says:

> It is certain that these lies and the untruths accompanying them arouses in them [the Jews] nothing but a hate against Christians and makes them at the same time have a horror of their religion. Common sense convinces a person naturally that God loves truth and hates lies more than anything. Therefore, one can conclude that must be the true religion which serves God and is free of lies and cannot be joined with lies. The conclusion is also valid that when a religion is afflicted with falsehood, provided that these shameful vices are only afflicting those who confess the religion, this is a blemish on the people and not on the confession. Therefore, if one wishes to deal with this in a constructive manner, one must show the Jews that these untruths, with which they have been attacked, only come from unthinking men with whom pious, reasonable men and especially Christian doctrine itself has no part. Among those lies (as Luther calls them) the biggest and bitterest which Jews are forced to suffer at the hands of Christians is that they are publicly accused of needing Christian blood, although, indeed, no one agrees what such a need consists of. At one time this and at one time that explanation will be offered to pull the wool over people's eyes and to mislead them. For example, some say, as Luther pointed out, that the Jews must have Christian blood so that they will not stink; others say that they need it for Easter to prepare sweet bread and Easter cake and also to put in the wine of Easter Sunday itself. Others say that they stop the bleeding of their children with it during circumcision; others that they secretly cure illness with it; still others that it is needed when the bride and groom are being blessed under the canopy; still others that the priests must have their hands smeared with it when they bless the people; others that they use it to ease the pain and help the convalescence of their women experiencing difficult child birth; others that by means of it one makes sacrifices pleasing to God. Most

say that when a Jew wants to die, one smears him with Christian blood and whispers secretly in his ear, 'the Messiah in whom Christians believe and trust is the promised and true Messiah. Therefore this blood of an innocent Christian who was also killed will bring you eternal life'.

Help, dear God! How can the truth be found in such contradictory accusations, which always cancel each other out? Who does not immediately see that all these dealings in which Jews are supposed to use Christian blood are worthless gossip that should not come out of a Christian's mouth? And if all that happened was idle gossip! But because of those damned lies the Jews have been plagued, tormented, and many thousands of them cruelly executed. Such things should have moved the stones to pity and made them cry![32]

Not only does Wagenseil reject the accusation that Jews murdered Christian children, but he went to look at the body of Simon of Trent to prove his point. He gives an eye-witness account refuting descriptions of Simon's body as scarred with an 'orderly rows of holes made by large awls', through which his blood was supposedly drained:

The dead body of Simon lies for all to see completely naked and rather black in the middle of the altar in St. Peter's Church in Trent surrounded by bright glass. And no stranger will come to Trent who will not ask to see this hall-mark of the city. I myself did this with a friend when I traveled to Italy. We were allowed — which does not happen often — to walk onto the highest step of the High Altar and a priest pointed out several marks, like wounds made with a knife. But certainly orderly rows of holes made by large awls on either side of the body of the child were not to be seen. So too must the painting on the bridge tower at Frankfurt be false.[33]

Wagenseil is not only completely aware of how terribly Christians have treated and still treat Jews, but this awareness has provoked his sympathy for such a persecuted people:

The Jews cannot travel safely in our country, nor walk on the street, or remain in their houses. There is no end to the repeated grumbling, defaming, cursing and totally horrible, lying charges that they need Christian blood. A Jew is considered by some much less than a dog. People push and beat them, pelt them with stones and filth in summer and with snow balls in winter. People slap them in the mouth with a piece of pork before they know what's happening, tear their clothes, cheat them when they can and want, rob them of their possessions with force as often as possible, and force them to give up their dice and to say that Christ is risen. Young children pull them by their coats and grown men by their beards. If people enter their schools, they mock them and do not let them attend to their business nor say their prayers. Who could say enough about all the insults, mockery, and grief which the Jews are forced to suffer daily? Indeed, although honorable and sensible people abstain from the nonsense described above, the Jews in Germany, with the knowledge and sanction of the authorities, have a very hard life, and Episcopius. . . charges us not without cause, [saying], 'that it is permitted that they be beaten if they do not keep to themselves their gambling dice or if a public official is not present to oversee them; that they are ordered to live like lepers apart from other men; that they are compelled to wear yellow badges on their clothing so that others will flee from them as if they are abominable; and especially that if they have committed some crime they are afflicted with horrible and unusual punishments and are hanged above by the feet between two dogs, who tear them apart'.[34]

One might think that the picture Wagenseil gives of the ways Jews were treated was sufficiently horrific to appall most Christians, but of course that was not the case. If anything, most Christians believed Jews were treated all too well. Why then was Wagenseil so unusually sympathetic? The answer is that his sympathy was a conditional one. The reason he describes the indignities and torments the Jews suffer with so much passion and detail is because he is convinced that such treatment stands in the way of their conversion. Wagenseil is sympathetic to Jews as long, and only as long, as there is the potential for their conversion. When there is no such potential, he his not sympathetic; he is antisemitic. This accounts for the clear change in tone from treatise to treatise. In his book significantly titled *The Hope of the Salvation of Israel* his care and concern for Jews is readily apparent. But his Janus-faced attitude towards Jews comes out in his *Tela Ignea Satanae,*[35] a work in which he studiously collected, translated, and rebutted texts written by Jews defaming Christ and Christianity. Consequently, although Wagenseil defended the Jews against the charge of 'Blood Libel', he perpetuated the charge of deicide, and by translating and making the relatively few works written by Jews defaming Christianity available to Christians at large, he provided additional evidence of the Jews' perfidy, hardness of heart, and basic criminality.

The notion that Jews were 'Christ-killers' had, I would argue, racial implications, for the charge did not only apply to those Jews who were alive at the time of Jesus' crucifixion, but to all Jews forever after. Their responsibility was, so to speak, in their blood. While it was theoretically possible for Jews to cease being Jews by converting to Christianity, there is too much evidence to show that the possibility of such conversions was considered less and less likely, especially among Lutherans. Oberman's attempt to exonerate Luther from the charge of antisemitism on the grounds that for him 'Jew' did not stand for a racially or ethnically distinct individual but for any enemy of the true Gospel, is impossible for me to accept. When attacking those he viewed as enemies, Luther did distinguish between Christians and Jews. Only Jews have ineradicable physical characteristics that distinguish them from other men. And these characteristics stem directly from the fact that Jews killed Christ and keep on killing Christians. Their criminality has literally become embodied. As Luther says:

> . . . we are . . . at fault in not avenging all this innocent blood of our Lord and of all the Christians which they shed for three hundred years after the destruction of Jerusalem and the blood of the children they have shed (*which shines forth from their eyes and their skin*). We are at fault in not slaying them [italics added].[36]

While certain theologians, including Luther, may at times have used the term 'Jew' to characterize reprobate Christians, the metaphor was generally lost, and the Jew became the archetype of the reprobate.[37] Even the Quaker William Penn, a great advocate of toleration, repeatedly used Jews as negative examples, as the title of one of his pamphlets makes abundantly clear, *Judas and the Jews Combined Against Christ and His Followers* (1673).[38]

By the end of his life Luther shared the Iberian view that baptism was not effective, that conversion in any meaningful sense was impossible for Jews. In a sermon preached on 25 September 1539 he tells several anecdotes to drive this point home. One concerned a baptized Jew from Cologne, who eventually became dean of the cathedral. But this supposed model of Christian piety and devotion was revealed to be a fraud after his death, however, for in his will he ordered the figure of a cat and mouse to be erected on his grave. As Luther explained, this indicated that a Jew can as little become a Christian as a mouse a cat, with the added implication that like cats and mice, Jews and Christians cannot live together amicably. The same reference to a cat and mouse appeared in the cathedral in Freising in an inscription under the picture of a *Judensau*: 'As surely as the mouse never eats the cat, so surely can the Jew never a true Christian become'.[39] This became the prevailing view among later Lutherans, and indeed, among the majority of Christians.[40] To give just one of many possible examples, the converted Jew Victor von Carben (ca. 1430–1515),[41] who was Luther's contemporary, makes it perfectly clear that conversion did not remove the stigma of Jewishness. In his autobiographical account of his conversion, he refers to the same image of the cat and mouse:

> O, God, I well know how often many come to me and cunningly ask whether I had been a Jew. When I answer, yes, they reject me with mocking words, 'go to Cologne to St. Andrew's church to see a cat and a mouse, and a dog and a cat. Their meaning was, as little as true friendship is possible between a cat and a mouse, or a dog and a cat, so little might I be a good Christian. They expressed such things with words that were easily understood and said, 'you may well show yourself as a Christian with your demeanor. It is to be feared, however, that you still have Jewish malice in your heart. The *agleister* never loses its hop'.[42]

Von Carben was a Catholic, but he was also a German.[43] During the seventeenth century Germany was recognized as being the worst place Jews could live, that is apart from Spain and Portugal. Obviously, any blanket statement such as this one needs to be refined, but there does seem to have been a tendency for German Christians, especially Lutherans, to envision Jews as wholly different and wholly threatening and to react accordingly. The medieval stereotype of all Jews as essentially Judases with red hair, hook noses, thick lips, and strange clothing — hideous creatures who are greedy, treacherous, and bent on the destruction of all Christians — had become too ingrained. The very ugliness of the Jewish stereotype had potent implications, for from Plato onwards beauty has been associated with truth and virtue. The sinister appearance of the Jews consequently excluded them from all three. In Germany, and apparently exclusively in Germany, another element was added to this horrific picture of the Jew, the so-called *Judensau*. As I mentioned earlier, Jews were frequently compared to animals, an effective way to dehumanize them. One has only to remember Shakespeare's reference to Shylock as the 'Jew dog'. The canine analogy was so fixed in Christian minds that Jews convicted of crimes were sometimes hanged between two dogs, as Wagenseil pointed out. Evans describes two cases in which Christians who married or cohabited with Jews were charged with the crime of bestiality and executed.[44] But only in Germany were Jews also depicted together with swine.[45] The motif of the *Judensau* has been painstakingly (and painfully) documented by Isaiah Shachar. Shachar describes the truly disgusting carvings on churches and cathedrals as well as the many illustrations in which Jews are shown being suckled by pigs and eating their excrement. He argues that this stereotyping of Jews was an important factor in making it all but impossible for men of the Enlightenment and later ages to extend their sympathy to Jews as fellow human beings.[46]

A number of historians have argued that the seventeenth century marked the beginning of the change in the attitude of European society towards the Jews[47] on the grounds that mercantilism and the new political philosophy emphasizing the practical interests of the state encouraged rulers to see the financial advantages that Jews could provide. Puritanism and millenarianism have been suggested as additional reasons for the more tolerant attitude towards Jews.[48] But as I mentioned at the beginning of this paper, Puritans really only liked Jews who were long dead, and millenarians only like Jews as potential converts. The burst of enthusiasm for the Jews in mid-century England was really just a blip. As Healey has pointed out, 'The readmission movement failed because not enough

English believed that the Jews were future Christians and harbingers of the millennium'.[49] Speaking of millenarians, Ettinger has made the rather sobering comment that 'those who spoke in favor of the Jews did not actually believe in the permanence and future of human political society'.[50] Their endorsement of the Jews was therefore not only conditional on their conversion but totally unrelated to actual political or social life. Thus, while some or all of these factors may have contributed to the growing atmosphere of tolerance, to my mind one is forced to conclude that whatever change in attitude there was towards the Jews in the seventeenth century was the result of practical considerations and the fragmentization and consequent weakening of Christianity, but that neither of these had any real effect in dispelling the negative stereotype of the Jew.

I end where I began with the premise that during the seventeenth century only two kinds of Christians could actually be philosemitic: heretics[51] and converts to Judaism. Orthodox trinitarian Christianity was inseparable from the notion that Jews had killed God, and implicit in the charge of deicide are all the elements that coalesced in the stereotype of the demonic Jew. For any human being who would willfully kill God could only be of the devil's party. The description of the Jews as the children of the devil, which appears in the Gospels, thus provided a firm foundation for the kind of dehumanization and demonization at the heart of Christian antisemitism. For someone like Francis Mercury van Helmont (1614–1698), however, who did not believe in Christ's unique and essential role in salvation, there was a genuine possibility of philosemitism. Two of the charges brought by the Inquisition against van Helmont were 1) that he did not believe in the historical existence and divinity of Christ but accepted the mystical and Quaker teaching of 'Christ within', and 2) that anyone could be saved whatever his religion.[52] Thus because van Helmont was a heretic, he could be a genuine philosemite and accept Jews as Jews and not simply as potential converts. But from the point of view of the Catholic Inquisition van Helmont's philosemitism made him a 'judaizer', for which he was duly arrested and imprisoned. From the records dealing with van Helmont's case, one can see the way philosemitism was construed as tantamount to conversion to Judaism. One of the witnesses who testified against van Helmont described him as 'soaked with Judaism'.[53] In another passage van Helmont is likened to a 'filthy money-lender'. It may be stretching things too far, but the immediate association of this epithet with 'filthy pig pens' raises at least in my mind the specter of the *Judensau* with all the negative associations that image carried. The Inquisition effectively stereotypes van Helmont as a Jew:

> Whatever things are revealed to Helmont by the inner light are nothing but trifling, laughable matters of a very dark mind — for example, the filthy pig pens, which, like a murderous money-lender [sicarius negotiator], Helmont tried to persuade the prince to build in abundance (within the palace grounds), where the flock of pigs might feed. Thus, the courtyard of the prince would look like a farm or rustic dwelling.[54]

To make this charge against van Helmont comprehensible, it should be pointed out that the Prince in question was Christian August of Sulzbach, who had asked van Helmont to help restore the economy of the Sulzbach territories, which had been ravaged by the Thirty Years' War. Van Helmont suggested various farming and manufacturing activities, among which was the raising of pigs.[55]

John Toland is another example of someone whose unorthodoxy allowed him to accept Jews as ordinary human beings without any of the diabolical traits Christians routinely associated with them. Toland utterly denied that the Jews had any national characteristics whatsoever:

> . . . since their dispersion, they have no common or peculiar inclination distinguishing them from others; but visibly partake of the Nature of those nations among which they live and where they were bred. The ordinary sentiments and manner of the Portuguese or Italian Jews, differ not from those of the other Portuguese or Italians; the Germans differ from the Polish Jews, as much as Poles do from Germans.[56]

Toland's rejection of the idea that Jews as a group represented the quintessential 'Other' was unfortunately impossible for the vast majority of Christians. It was impossible because this negative stereotype of the Jews was a vital element in the affirmation of Christianity as the true religion. From its inception Christianity had to explain why Jews as a group did not follow the Jew, Jesus. To simply admit that Jews did not accept the evidence adduced by Christians to prove that Jesus was the Messiah and the son of God, who had died and been resurrected, only reinforced doubts. But to argue, as the Gospel of Matthew so clearly does, that only the blind or the malicious (or both) could fail to accept these truths could be persuasive. It was not a big step to go from this argument to the next, namely that the Jews really did believe Jesus was the Messiah but because such an admission would destroy their identity as a group, they determined to destroy the evidence and kill Jesus. As I said earlier, implicit in the charge of deicide are all the elements that eventually contributed to the stereotype of the demonic Jew. One might think that the growth of secularism and atheism would have improved the image of the Jew. But, unfortunately, just because one ceases to be a Christian did not mean that one ceases to be an antisemite. The Christian past was too deeply rooted in the European conscience for the stereotype of the demonic Jew to be eradicated. It lived on, simply in a more secular form.

Many years ago Gordon Allport argued that religion is never merely religion. As he says:

> The chief reason why religion becomes the focus of prejudice is that it usually stands for more than faith — it is the pivot of the cultural tradition of a group. However sublime the origins of a religion may be, it rapidly becomes secularized by taking over cultural functions.[57]

Gavin Languir devotes the greater part of his book *Towards a Definition of Anti-Semitism* to arguing the same point. Religious conflicts have historically played themselves out in racial terms, and even if earlier centuries did not have our clear sense of what a race is, they nevertheless had a clear sense of the physical and cultural differences separating different ethnic groups. As Alan Davies persuasively shows in his book *Infected Christianity*, the idea expressed by Paul in Galatians 3:28 that conversion to Christianity obliterates distinctions of race, caste, class, or gender has failed to take root to this day. How then can we expect it to have been accepted in earlier centuries when religion was inextricably tied up with an individual's personal, social, and political identity?

1 For an insightful discussion (and comparison) of Catholic and Protestant Hebraists see Jerome Friedman, *The Most Ancient Testimony: Sixteenth-Century Christian-Hebraica in the Age of Renaissance Nostalgia* (Athens, OH: Ohio University Press,1983) and Frank E. Manual, *The Broken Staff: Judaism through Christian Eyes* (Cambridge, MA: Harvard University Press, 1992). See also David Katz, *Philo-Semitism and the Readmission of the Jews to England, 1603–1655* (Oxford: Oxford University Press, 1982).

2 'Knorr von Rosenroth, Christian', *Encyclopedia Judaica* (Jerusalem: Keter Publishing House), v. 10, p. 1117.

3 Klopp, O. ed., *Correspondenz von Leibniz mit der Prinzessin Sophie* (Hanover, 1873), 2 vols, repr. (Hildesheim: Olms, 1973), v. 2, p. 8.

4 H. J. Schoeps has argued for the existence of philosemitism, but I as I argue in this paper the philosemites he describes are only philosemites because they are Christian heretics. See *Philosemitismus in Barock* (Tübingen: J. C. B. Mohr, 1952).

5 David Katz, 'The Abendana Brothers and the Christian Hebraists of Seventeenth-Century England', *Journal of Ecclesiastical History* 40 (1989): 32: 'As was almost always the case when Christians took an interest in the spiritual welfare of Jews, the ultimate aim was their conversion'. Ernestine van der Wall, 'The Amsterdam Millenarian Petrus Serrarius (1600–1669) and the Anglo-Dutch Circle of Philo-Judaists', *Jewish-Christian Relations in the Seventeenth Century. Studies and Documents*, eds. J. van den Berg and E. van der Wall (Dordrecht: Kluwer Academic Publishers, 1988), p. 73: '. . . philo-Judaism has to be seen in a conversionist light, which at once indicates the limits of their pro-Jewishness: their philo-Judaism was a conditional sympathy'. Jacob Katz refers to 'these so-called philo-Semites' and says they 'retained the Christian vision of the absorption of the Jews after their conversion'. See his article, 'Reflecting on German-Jewish History', *In and Out of the Ghetto: Jewish-Gentile relations in late medieval and early modern Germany*, eds. R. Po-chia Hsia and Hartmut Lehmann (New York: Cambridge University Press, 1995), p. 3.

6 *Sabbath and Sectarianism in Seventeenth-Century England* (note 1).

7 R. Po-chia Hsia, 'The Usurious Jew', *In and Out of the Ghetto* (note 5), pp. 173–4. This idea goes back to St. Paul, who distinguished between children of the 'spirit' (Christians) and children of the 'flesh' (Jews). See Galatians, ch. 5 (especially 5:16–21, where the children of the 'flesh' are effectively demonized).

8 For example, Joshua Trachtenberg, *The Devil and the Jews: The Medieval Conception of the Jew and its Relation to Modern Anti-Semitism* (Philadelphia: The Jewish Publication Society, 1993; first published 1943); Leon Poliakov, *The History of Anti-Semitism* (London: Routledge & Kegan Paul, 1965; first published in French, 1955); James Park, *The Conflict of the Church and the Synagogue: A Study in the Origins of Antisemitism* (New York: Atheneum, 1969); Yosef H. Yerulshamlmi, 'Assimilation and Racial Anti-Semitism: The Iberian and the German Models', Leo Baeck Memorial Lecture 26 (1982); Jerome Friedman, 'Jewish Conversion, the Spanish Pure Blood Laws and Reformation: A Revisionist View of Racial and Religious Anti-Semitism', *Sixteenth Century Journal* 18 (1987): 4–29; *idem*, 'Sebastian Munster, the Jewish Mission, and Protestant Anti-Semitism', *Archiv für Reformations-Geschichte* 70 (1979): 238–59; William Nicholls, *Christian Antisemitism: A History of Hate* (Northvale, NJ: Jason Aronson Inc, 1993).

9 Norman Cohn, *Warrant for Genocide* (New York: Harper & Row, 1966), p. 16.

10 James Harrington, *Oceana*, ed. S. B. Liljegren (Heidelberg: C. Winter, 1924), p. 11.

11 June 28, 1518. Quoted in R. Po-chia Hsia, 'The Usurious Jew' (note 5).

12 J. J. Schudt, *Jüdische Merkwürdigkeiten. . . sammt einer vollständiger Frankfurter Juden-Chronik. . .* (Frankfurt and Leipzig, 1714), pt. 2, bk. 6, ch. 12, par. 1: '. . . sie so viel arme Christen biß auffs Blut aussaugen. . . '.

13 F. E. Manual, *The Broken Staff* (note 1), p. 186: 'That the ancient Jews did not believe in the soul's immortality became a deist historical-religious dogma and fed the time-worn Christian notion that Judaism in its origins was carnal, dependent on rewards in this world that were concrete,

objective, and visible. The Jewish conception of God was material, fleshy and anthropomorphic. The temple was like a bourse: the Jews offered sacrifices to God and received equivalents in wordly goods. It was but a step from there to the accusation that the Jews' absorption with accumulating money was an offshot of their religion and inextricably bound up with the worship of mammon'.

14 ibid., pp. 18−19.

15 Except for Friedman, who takes the opposite position, arguing that the attitude towards Jews in sixteenth-century Germany was similar to that described by Yerulshalmi in fifteenth-century Spain (note 1). Luther's anti-Semitism was therefore the defensive reaction of a Christian afraid that the assimilation of Jews and Judaism had gone too far (See Friedman's article, 'Jewish Conversion, the Spanish Pure Blood Laws and Reformation', note 8).

16 W. Maurer, 'Die Zeit der Reformation', *Kirche und Synagoge: Handbuch zur Geschichte von Christen und Juden: Darstellung mit Quellen*, eds. K. H. Rengstorf and S. von Kortzbleish (Stuttgart, 1968), v. 1, pp. 363−75.

17 Martin Friedrich, *Zwischen Abwehr und Bekehrung: Die Stellung der deutschen evangelischen Theologie zum Judenthum in 17. Jahrhundert* (Tübingen: J. C. B. Mohr, 1988), p. 6: '. . . die These eines absoluten Gegensatzes zwischen pietistischer und vorpietistischer Judenmission kann auf Anhieb kaum überzeugen'.

18 Trachtenberg, *The Devil and the Jews* (note 8), p. 49.

19 Zedler, Johan Heinrich, *Grosses vollständiges universal Lexikon aller Wissenschafften und Künste*. . . (Leipzig u. Halle, 1743), p. 1499: 'Juden'. . . Ihren Talmud erheben sie weit über die Bible und achten ihn von solcher Weisheit, daß auch GOTT selbst noch darinnen studieren muße (p. 1499). . . . Sie sind unsere geschworne Feinde. Und wie offt haben sie nicht Christen-Kinder geschlachtet, gecreutziget, im Mörser zerstossen. Sie sind die ärgsten Diebe, und Betrug ist ihr eigentliches Wahrzeichen. Alle Mahl schwören sie falsch, wenn sie gleich die entsetzlichsten Eide ablegen müssen. Denn sie können (p. 1500) bald von einem Rabbi, oder drey Juden davon absolutiret werden. . . . GOTT hat sie auch in der Natur gezeichnet: Gewiss, ein Juda hat etwas an sich, daran man ihn bald erkennen, und von andern Menschen unterscheiden kann. Sie sind einem ein Eckel-und-Grauen, und Stanck und Unflat machet sie abscheulich, wie ihnen gedrohet worden. Deut. 28, 37, 46. Das härrteste aber über die Juden ist dieses, daß ihre Verwerffung ewiglich währet. Nicht sind sie absolut von GOTT verstossen, daß er gar keinen zu Gnaden annehmen wolle; Rom., 11, 12. GOTT hat noch welche darunter, die sich bekehren. Denn allen, die an das Evangelium glauben wollen, stehet die Gnaden-Thür und der Eingang in das Reich Christi offen. So aber sind sie verworffen und verstossen, daß sie immermehr wieder GOTTES Volck werden, noch in den Stand der Gnaden und Seligkeit glangen, wie sie in A. Testament gewesen sind. Sie machen sich zwar mächtig breit mit ihrem goldenen Assen, und suchen einen gewaltigen Trost darinnen, Lev. 26, 44. allein der Trost gehöret weiter nicht vor sie, als in so ferne sie sich bekehren. Inzwischen ists kein Wunder, daß sie unter dem immerwährenden Fluche liegen. Ihre greulich Sünden der Abgötterey straffete GOTT nur mit 70jährigem Gefängniss. Da sie aber nun bey nahe 1700 Jahr verstossen sind, müssen sie unendlich grössere Sünden, als ihre Vater, gegangen haben. Freylich, denn sie haben denn Sohn GOTTES getödet, und den HERRN der Herrlichkeit gecreutziget. Dessen Blut drücket sie noch, und erfüllet das Urtheil, welches sie sich selbst sprachen. Sie rasen noch auf heutigen Tag wieder das Evangelium. Muss denn nun nicht solcher beharrlicher und eingewurtzeller Unglaube die Gerichte GOTTES täglich über sie führen? . . . (p. 1501) Sie sind mehren theils Wechsler, Wucherer, Zöllner oder Gleits-Leute, Mäckler, Apothecer, Aertzte und Dollmetscher. Sie können einem von allen Waaren, so in einer Stadt anzutreffen, Nachricht geben, und dessen Güte und Preis gantz eigentlich benennen. . . . Die Türcken und Morgenländischen Christen erzählen insgemein von ihnen, dass sie aller Char-Freytage, um ihren Abscheu vor den christlichen Religion an den Tage zu legen, einen christlichen Sclaven ermorden, jedoch so, dass sie dieses sehr geheim hielten, nachdem sie unterschiedliche Mahl wegen dergleichen abscheulicher That nachdrücklich gestraffet worden. Im Occident haben sie öffters so wohl junge Kinder, als alte Leute ermordet, absonderlich aber die jenigen so aus ihrem Mittle einige Liebe zum Christenthum von sich blicken lassen'.

20 ibid., pp. 1328–29: . . So bald er zu denjenigen Jahren, darinnen man der Unterweisung fähig ist, gekommen war, so wurde alsbald ein sehr munterer und aufgeweckter Geist an ihm wahrgenommen. Wie er denn, nachem er im Jahr 1671 in das berühmte Gymnasium daselbst geschicket worden, einen gantz unermüdeten Fleiß gewiesen, so, daß er 1680 den Cursum Classicum rühmlich zu Ende brachte, und zu denen öffentlichen Lectionen gelassen wurde. Weil es aber mit diesen Lectionem wegen des hohen Alters derer damahls Lehrenden, etwas langsam vorgieng, so begab er sich auf Einrathen des damahligen Seniors D. Speners, noch in eben diesem Jahr nach Wittenberg. Hier ließ er sogleich seinem rühmlichen Fleiß sehen, indem er noch im schon gedachten Jahre unter dem Vorsig Johann Helvie Willemers, damahligen Adjunctens der Philosophischen Facultät, de Essaeis, Secta Judaeorum, öffentlich disputierte. ... Er besaß eine grosse Gelehrsamkeit, sonderlich aber eine vortreffliche Wissenschafft in Sprachen, unterhielt einen starcken Brief-Wechsel, und war gantz unermüdet.

21 Manual, *The Broken Staff* (note 1), p. 249.

22 Schudt, *Jüdische Merkwürdigkeiten.*, pt. 2, bk. vi, ch. 12, 169–170: 'Ist etwas in der Welt/ so die Juden verhaßt macht/ so ist es gewisslich der verdammliche übermachte Wucher/ so sie treiben/ damit sie so viel arme Christen biß auffs Blut aussaugen/ darüber sie aus Spanien/ England/ Frankreich/ Nürnberg/ Wormbs und auch an 1614 aus Franckreich gejagt worden/ worüber auch unsere Vorfahren an 1612 sehr geklaget haben: Wir wollen von solch ihrem Wucher auch hier etwas mit einrücken.

2. Die Veranlassung/ daß die Juden so gern wuchern/ ist enstanden theils von denen Christen/ theils von denen Juden; Von denen Christen kommt die Veranlassung her/ weil man ihnen keine Handwercke zu treiben erlaubet/ und weil sie keine eigenthümliche unbewegliche Güther besitzen dürffen/ können sie keinen Ackerbau noch Viehzucht treiben/ bleibet also nichts als die Handlung/ Schacherei und Wucher übrig; Eines der grössen Hindernüssen (ihrer Bekehrung) ist wol/ daß sie insgemein alle von Jugend auf in Müßiggang aufwachsen/ das Leben meistens in solchem zubringen/ und sich insgemein alle von handeln und schachern nähren/ hingegen zu keiner Arbeit kommen. Das theils ohne ihre Schuld geschiehet/ indem sie eignes Land zu bauen nicht haben/ auch an meisten Orten zu Handwercken/ sie zu lernen/ oder zu treiben/ nicht gelassen werden/ theils aber ists nicht ohne eigene Schuld/da ob sie zu arbeiten gelassen/ aus Faulheit sich nicht darzu verstehen würden. Was nun arme unter ihnen sind/ dero Anzahl so wol als bey den Christen allezeit den grössensten Theil machet/ ists eine pure Unmöglichkeit/ daß einer ohne Practiquen und Betrug/ da er kaum wenige Thaler zum Capital hat/ dieses durch Handlung also umsetzen könnte/ dass er davon/ wie genau er sich behilfft/ mit einer Famille solte leben können; Daher die elende Leute Tag und Nacht auf nichts anders sinnen und dencken können/ als wie sie mit List/ Räncken/ Betrug und also Diebstahl ihr armes Leben hinbringen. . . .

3. Dahero der berühmte Hallische Jurist Herr D. Böhmer. . . und andere mehr/ der Meynung sind/ man solle die Juden allerdings anhalten/ daß sie Handwercker erlernen/und im Schweiß der Angesichts ihr Brod verdienen müssen/ und da die Christl. Handwercker dieselbige wohl schwerlich für zünfftig passiren und als Mitmeister unter sich leyden würden/ so solte man sie die Handwercker für sich treiben lassen; welches aber/ meines wenigen Erachtens/ eben so wol viele Beschwehrden würde nach sich ziehen/ und durfften die Juden mit ihre Stümperey die Handwercker eben so sehr verderben/ wie sie die Handlung verstümpeln; Gleichwol treiben einige Juden in Holland Handwercker/ wie dann ein jüdischer Schreiner es gewesen/ der den abgefallenen Speeth beschnitten/ aber ziemlich unglücklich/ davon Herr Diefenbach Jud. Convers. 15. p. 154 und mir aus den Speeth Mund ein gelährter vornehmer Freund hier erzehlet/ was große Schmertzen er lange Zeit von solcher übel verrichteten Beschneidung ausgestanden; ist dem abtrünnigen Vogel recht geschehen. . . .'.

23 ibid., pp. 173–4: '5. Von Seiten der Juden kommt die Noth/ weil sie keine andere Handthierung haben/ Handwercker und Ackerbau ist ihnen versagt/ und wollen doch leben und ihre Nahrung haben; es kommt darzu die lange Gewohnheit von so vielen 300 Jahren und daß sie von Jugend an zu keiner Arbeit gewöhnet; es kommt darzu die Annehmlichkeit dess Müßiggangs und Faulheit/ daß sie bey dem Wucher müßig gehen/ und wie Läuss und Flöh/ von anderer Schweiß und

Blut ihre Nahrung haben; es kommt darzu die falsche Einbildung/ daß solches ein Zeichen Göttl. Vorsorge/ Liebe und Huld gegen sie seye/ daß ander Völcker hart und sauer arbeiten/ sie aber in Müßiggang und Ruhe leben könten/ und doch gleichwol vergnüglich ernehret würden/ wie dann im Talmud Tract. *Jebamot* p. 63 stehet: . . .100 fl. in Handlung machen/ daß man täglich Fleisch und Wein genießen kan aber 100 fl. auf Ackerbau/ verschaffen kaum Saltz und Kraut'.

24 S. Ettinger, 'The Beginning of the Change in the Attitude of European Society Towards the Jews', *Scripta Hierosolymitana* 7 (1961): 208.

25 Schudt, *Jüdische Merkwürdigkeiten*, pt. 1, bk. 4, p. 270ff., par. 4: 'Von den Juden in Holland und Friesland: Eine allzu grosse Juden-Freiheit in Holland ist es/ II. daß in Holland/ sonderlich zu Amsterdam/ die Christen öffenlich und ohne Scheu den Jüdischen Glauben annehmen und sich beschneiden lassen/ welches im Römischen Reich nicht gelidten/ sondern am Leben gestrafft wird; Ob wohl solches Herr Wülffer *Animadvers. ad Theo. Jud.* C. 3. para 16. p. 21*1* seq. für zu hart und einen Gewissens-Zwang hält/ ist es doch allerdings billig und recht/ weil der Abfall vom Christlichen Glauben zu dem Judenthum nicht ohne Gotteslästerung der Hochheiligen Dreyeinigkeit/ und schandliche Schmähung des gebennedeyten-Heylandes JESU CHRIST (so ja allerdings/ sonderlich bey einem Christen/ den Todt verdienet) geschehen kan/ dahero auch so gar die Rechte denen Juden/ die einen Christen zum Judenthum verführen/ die Todtes-Straffe setzen davon unterschiedlicher Juristen Zeugnüss anführen/ Herr Diefenbach im *Jud. Convers.* para 14. p. 128. So ist Nicol Antonius, ein Reformirter Prediger in Genffer-Gebieth/ als er ein Jud worden/ anno 1632 erstlich gehenckt und hernach verbrandt worden'.

26 ibid., pt. 2, bk. 18, p. 997.

27 ibid., bk, iv, p. 273, par. 5: '. . . Wir haben zu unsern Zeiten daß gantze neue Exempel des unseeligen Joh. Peter Speeth, welcher von Augspurg bürtig/ in Catholischer Religion gebohren und erzogen/ herrnachmahls Lutherisch worden/ dann wieder zu den Papisten hernach zu denen *Novatoribus* und Sonderlingen unserer Zeit/ ferner zu den Quäckern und Socinianern sich sehr gehalten/ (wie wir von seinem Schwindel Geist unten Libr. VI cap. 29, para 7 ein mehres reden werden) die ihm den Weg zum Judenthum gebahnet/ da er sich zu Amsterdam anno 1697 beschneiden und Moses Germanus nennen lassen; Ein Brief/ den er an Herrn D. Peterssens Ehliebste/ seines Abfalls wegen geschrieben/ ist von Herrn Bücher aus Dantzig anno 1699 in 4 heraus gegeben worden/ welchen ich anfänglich hier mit einzurucken vorhabens war/ allein wegen der ärgerlichen Reden von Christo/ so der Böswicht ausgegossen/aus Furcht eines Anstosses bey Schwachgläubigen/ billig habe unterlassen. . . . Herrn M. Bücher sehr verdacht worden/ daß er den gottlosen Brief in Dantzig drucken und in Sachsen divulgiren lassen/ alldieweil sowohl an andern Ortert/ als vornehmlich in Danzig/ wahrhafftig geschehen seye/ dass unterschiedliche Menschen dadurch nicht nur an ihrem Christenthum irre gemacht worden/ sondern auch die Christlicher Religion zu verläugnen im Sinne gehabt hätten/ denen aber durch andere fromme Christen wieder seye zurecht geholffen/ und ein besserer Grund angewiesen worden. Diefenbach *Jud. Convers.* para 15, p. 139. Es hat der Speth auch eine saubere Teutsche Jüdin geheirathet/ und mit ihr Kinder gezeuget/ wie dann ein Christlicher vornehmer Freund bey ihm ein Söhngen gesehen; Er hat aber sein Leben/ weil die Portugiesische und andere Juden sich seiner wenig angenommen/ in socher kümmerlichen Dürfftigkeit zubringenmüssen/ daß er nicht nur um ein gar geringes der Juden Kinder informiret/ sodern auch von einem Christlichen guten Freund allhier/ der ihn vormahls in Amsterdam besucht gehabt/ durch Schreiben um einen eintzigen Gulden/ zu Sublevirung seiner außersten Armuth gebetten/ und auch erhalten/ welcher Freund dann mich versicherte/ daß der neue Moses Germanus, wie man aus seinen Reden deutlich abnehmen können/ in lauter Ungewißheit/ Zweiffel und Gewissens-Angst gewesen/ welches dann die Juden wohl an ihm gemerckt/ und seinen Rücktritt zu der Christlichen Religion werden besorgen haben; und weil er. . . so gelingen von der Erden weggerafft/ indem er den 26. April 1701 sich zu Bette gelegt/ den 27 gestorben/ und den 28. von den Juden begraben worden/ so ist billig ein Zweifel entstanden/ ob er natürlich/ oder durch seine/ oder der Juden Verkürtzung/ so geschwind davon gefahren. . . '.

28 ibid., bk. 4, ch. 18, p. 192, par. 2: 'Wir haben von diesem abtrünnigen Vogel dem Speeth schon in denen *Jüdischen Merkwürdigkeiten* Lib. 4. Cap. 18. par. 5. p. 273 ff. ein ziemliches angeführet/ doch können wir jetzo dem geneigten Leser mit mehrer und curieuserer Nachricht von ihm an Händen gehen; Es hat unser hoch-geschätzter Gönner Herr Professor Joh. Christoph. Wolffius in seiner *Bibliotheca Hebraea* p. 811. sonderlich von seinen heraußgegebenen Schrifften gute Nachricht gegeben/ auch aus des Berlinischen Bibliothecatii Herr de la Croze *Vindiciis Veterum Scriptorum* p. 61 seq. angeführet/ daß Herr Knorr von Rosenroth den Speeth/ bey Heraußgebung seiner *Cabbala denudata/* gebraucht/ es hätten ihn auch die Juden/ einige Jahr nach seinem Abfall/ mit Gifft aus dem Weeg [sic] geräumet/ weil er alle ihre Talmudische-Fabeln nicht billigen wollen/ wie sich Heer [sic] D. Spener bemühet/ den Menschen von denen Papisten/ und nachmahls von denen Juden wieder abzuziehen/ ist in seinen Teutschen *Consiliis Theolog.* P. III. p. 534. f. 961. f. P. IV. p. 623. und in *Consiliis Latinis Theol.* P. III. p. 430 zu lesen'.

29 ibid., p. 278: 'Der Juden Palläst mögen noch so fürtrefflich gebauet und mit Haußrath kostbahr meubliret und aufs herrlichste gezieret seyn/ wo man hinein kommt/ so findet man nach Knoblauch stinckende Juden drinnen/ wie dann in solchen Kupfferstichen in einem vortrefflichen Garten ein alt Juden-Weib/ mit einer grossen Juden-Nase und einem Brill darauf/ in einem Buch lesende/ vorgestellet wird...'.

30 Manual, *The Broken Staff* (note 1), p. 153.

31 Friedrich, *Zwischen Abwehr und Bekehrung* (note 17), p. 143.

32 Johann Christoph Wagenseil, *Benachrichtigungen wegen einiger die Judenschafft angehende wichtigen Sachen. Erste Theil worinnen 1. Die Hoffnung der Erlosung Israelis oder klarer Beweiss der annoch bevorstehenden und wie es scheinet/ allgemach herannahenden grossen Juden-Bekehrung/ samt unvorgreifflichen Gedencken/ wie solche nechst Verleihung Göttlicher Hülffe/ zu befordern. 2. Wiederlegung der Unwarheit dess die Juden zu ihrer Bedürffniss Christen-Blut haben mussen. 3. Anzeigung/ wie leicht es dahin zu bringen/ daß die Juden forthin abstehen mussen/ die Christen mit Wuchern und Schinden zu plagen.* Leipzig: bei Johann Heinichens Wittwe, 1705, Pt. 1, ch. vii, pp. 129-31: 'Gewiss ist es/ die Lügen und Unwarheiten/ mit denen man sie beleget/ können nicht anderst als einen Haß gegen die Christen bey ihnen erwecken/ und zu gleich machen daß sie für ihrer Religion einen Abscheu haben. Die gesunde Vernunfft überzeuget einen Menschen aus natürlichen Trieb daß Gott die Warheit liebe/ und die Lügen auffs ärgste hasset/ schliesset man demnach/ es müsse die wahre Religion/ als welche in dem Dienst Gottes bestehet/ der Lügen befreyet seyn/ und könne mit derselben sich nicht vereinigen. Diese Folge ist auch richtig/ wann die Religion selbst mit Falschheit behafftet; Sofern aber dieses schändliche Läster nur denen anhängig ist/ die zu einer Religion sich bekennen/ gereichet solches diesen/ nicht der Glaubens-Bekänntnüss zum Schandfleck. Demnach will man erbaulich verfahren/ muß man denen Juden zeigen/ daß die Unwarheiten/ mit welchen sie von denen Christen angegriffen werden/ nur von unbedachtsamen Menschen herkommen/ als an welchen fromme verständige Leute/ bevorab die Christliche Lehr selbsten keinen Theil haben. Unter denen (wie sie Lutherus nennet) Lügenvertheidungen aber/ welche die Juden von denen Christen erleiden müssen/ ist sonder Zweiffel diese die größte und bitterste/ dass man sie öffentlich beschuldiget/ wie sie Christen-Blut zu ihrer Bedürffnüss haben müssen/ ob zwar/ in dem/ einer mit dem andern nicht leicht überein kommet/ in was solche Bedürffnüss haben müssen bestehe/ und bald dieses/ bald jenes auff die Bahn gebracht wird/ den Leuten einen blauen Dunst für die Augen zu machen/ und sie zu bethören. Es sagen nemlich/ wie auch Lutherus anzeigt/ einige/ es müssen die Juden Christen-Blut haben/ damit sie nicht stincken; andere geben für/ dass sie solches gegen das Oster-Fest/ zu Bereitung der süßen Brodt oder Oster-Kuchen/ wie auch am Ostertag selbsten in Wein gebrauchen. Andere sagen daß sie davon zur Liebe zwingende Artzneyen bereiten; Andere/ daß die damit den Kindern in der Beschneidung das Blut stillen; Andere/ daß sie durch dessen Hülff heimlich Kranckheiten curiren; wieder andere/ dass man dessen benöthigt/ wann Bräutigam und Braut unter den über ihnen gehaltenen Himmel ein gesegnet werden; noch andere/ daß die Priester/ wann sie dem Volck den Seegen ertheilen/ die Hände damit bestrichen haben müssen; Andere/ dass man dadurch denen Weibern/ so schwerlich zur Geburt arbeiten/ eine Linderung schaffe und ihre Genesung befordere; Andere/ dass man die Opffer Gott

dadurch angenehm mache; Die meisten geben für/ dass wann ein Jud sterben will/ man selbigen mit Christen-Blut bestreiche/ und ihm heimlich in das Ohr sage: Wann der Messias/ an welchen die Christen glauben/ und in ihn ihre Zuversicht setzen/ der versprochene wahre Messias ist/ so heißt dir dieses unschuldig ertödteten Christen-Blut zu dem ewigen Leben.

Hilff lieber Gott! Wie kan die Warheit bey so widrigen Beschuldigungen/ deren immer eine die ander aufhebt/ statt finden? Wer siehet nicht alsobalden/ dass alle diese Händel/ wozu die Juden das Christen-Blut gebrauchen sollen/ ein faules Geschwätz seyn/ so aus keines Christen Mund gehen solte? Und möchte es endlich hingehen/ wann es bey den blossen Geschwätz bliebe/ daß aber wegen dieser vermaledeyten Unwarheit die Juden sind geplagt/ gepeinigt und deren viel tausend auf grausame Weise hingerichtet worden/ hätte auch die Steine zum Mitleiden bewegen/ und schreyen machen sollen'.

33 ibid., p. 181: '. . .Es liegt des todten Knaben Simeonis Leib zu Trident in der Peters-Kirchen zu aller Menschen Beschauung gantz nackend und ziemlich schwartz mitten auf dem hohen Altar/ mit hellen Crystall umgeben/ und wird mir kein Frembder nach Trident kommen/ der nach demselben als dem Wahrzeichen der Stadt nicht fragen solte. Ein solches hab auch ich/ wie ich nach Italien reisete/ mit meinem Gefehrten. . . . Es ward uns/ welches nicht leicht geschiehet/ vergönnet/ ganz hinzu/ auff die oberste Stuffe des sehr erhabenen Altars zu tretten/ und zeigte uns ein Priester mit dem Finger/ einige Merckmalen/ gleichsam als mit einem Messer eingeschnittener Wunden. Gewiss aber is dass keine ordentlich Reye zu beyden Seiten/ als mit großen Pfriemen eingestochener Löcher an dem Leibe des Kindes wahr zu nehmen/ wird auch keine gewiesen. Und also muß das Gemähl an dem Bruck-Thurn zu Frankfurth falsche seyn'.

34 ibid., pp. 98ff: '. . . die Juden können bey uns nicht sicher über Land reisen/ auf der Straße gehen/ noch gar in ihren Häusern bleiben. Des Nach-Gruntzens/ Lästerns/ Scheltens/ und gantz entsezzlichen lügenhafften Fürwerfens/ daß sie Christen-Blut zu ihrer Bedürffniß haben müssen/ ist kein Ende. Ein Jud wird von manchen viel weniger geachtet als ein Hund. Man stößet und schlägt sie/ man wirfft sie des Sommers mit Steinen und Unsauberkeit/ des Winters mit Schneeballen; Man fähret ihnen/ ehe sie sich es versehen/ mit einem Stück Schweinen-Fleisch um den Mund; man zerschneidet ihnen die Kleider/ betruget sie wo man kan und mag/ beraubet sie/ so offt nur Gelegenheit sich hierzu ereignet/ des ihrigen mit Gewalt/ nöthiget sie Würffel herzugeben; zu sagen Christus ist erstanden; die jungen Kinder zupffen sie bey den Mänteln/ und die Erwachsenen bey den Bärten/ kommt man in ihre Schulen/ da verspottet man sie/ und läßet sie daselbst ihres Thuns nicht warten/ noch ihr Gebet verrichten/ und wer wolte allen Schimpff/ Spott und Verdruß/ so die Juden täglich erleiden müssen/ mit Worten gnugsam ausprechen? Zwar enthalten sich dergleichen Unfugs/ wie auch oben angezeigt worden/ erbare und verständige Leute/ allein wie dem allen/ so haben doch die Juden in Teutschland/ mit Vorwissen und Einwilligung der Obrigkeiten/ ein sehr hartes Leben auszustehen/ und wirfft uns der Episcopius Tom I. Oper. p. 438 nicht ohne Ursach für: Quod permittitur ut vapulent, si penes se non habeant talos lusorios, aut minister publicus non adsit, qui eos ducat: quod separatim ab aliis hominibus leprosorum instar habitare jubentur, quod in vestibus notas flavi coloris gestare coguntur, ut caeteri eos tanquam abominabiles fugiant: & speciatim quod, si scelus aliquod perpetraverint, inusitatis & horrendis suppliciis afficiuntur, vivi pedibus suspenduntur inter duos canes, a quibus lacerantur'. On the hanging of Jews by their feet between live dogs, see Guido Kisch, 'The 'Jewish Execution' in Medieval Germany and the Reception of Roman Law', *L'Europa e il diritto romano. Studi in memoria Paul Koschaker*, vol. 2 (Milan, 1954), pp. 63–93; Otto Ulbricht, 'Criminality and Punishment of the Jews in the Early Modern Period', *In and out of the Ghetto* (note 5), pp. 66–7.

35 *Tela Ignea Satanae. Hoc est Arcani, & horribiles Judaeorum adversus Christum Deum, & Christianam Religionem Libri. . .* Altdorf, 1681 (repr. Gregg International Publishers Ltd, 1970).

36 *On the Jews and Their Lies, Luther's Works*, ed. Franklin Sherman (Philadelphia: Fortress Press, 1971), pp. 47, 267.

37 Robert Healey makes this point in his article, 'The Jew in Seventeenth-Century Protestant Thought', *Church History* 46 (1977): 74: 'Preachers and writers constantly used the example of the Jews or of 'Judas and the Jews' to illustrate the meaning of apostasy. Much as their concern may have

been to stimulate Christian self-examination in their hearers and readers, the result was exactly what Lichtenburg has called 'harsh and contemptuous preaching'. Here 'doctrinal anti-judaism. . . filtered down to the masses', relentlessly hammering home the lesson that the Jew was the archetype of the reprobate'. The work Healey quotes from is Jean Paul Lichtenberg's *From the First to the Last of the Just* (Jerusalem: Ecumenical Theological Resarch Fraternity in Israel, 1972).

38 See also his *Advice to his Children* (1726).

39 Joshua Trachtenberg, *The Devil and the Jews* (note 8), p. 218. Ulrich Zasius also argued that baptism did not turn a Jew into a Christian: 'the acceptance of faith does not destroy the native element' (*Quaestiones de parvulis Judaeorum baptisandis*, 1508, 29b).

40 For further examples of the irradicable 'Otherness' of Jews, see R. Po-chia Hsia, 'The Usurious Jew' (note 5), pp. 169, 173.

41 Interestingly enough, Victor von Carben was involved in the Pfefferkorn controversy. He was one of the four imperial commissioners appointed to examine Jewish books for blasphemy against Christianity. Reuchlin, Pfefferkorn, and Hochstraten were the others on the committee. See James H. Overfield, *Humanism and Scholasticism in Late Medieval Germany* (Princeton: Princeton University Press, 1984).

42 Victor von Carben, *Jude Büchlein. Hyerinne würt gelesen/ wie Herr Victor von Carben/ welcher ein Rabi der Juden gewesst ist/ zu Christlichem glaubem kommen. Weiter findet man darinnen ein köstliche disputatz eines gelerten Christen/ und eins gelerten Juden/ darinne alle irrthumb der Juden durch ir eygen schrifft auffgelösst werden. Eyn Underredung vom Glauben/ durch Herr Micheln Kromer/ Pfarherr zu Cunitz/ und einem Judische Rabien/ mit namen Jacob von Brucks/ geschehen zu Cunitz. Auffs new corrigiert und gebessert,* 1550 (first published 1508), ch. 3, A5v–A6v: 'O Gott ich weyß wol wie dick und manig mal etlich zu mir kommen/ und arglistiglich fragen/ ob ich ein Jude geseßt were/ und so ich inen dann ja antwortet/ so wysen sye mich dann mit spotworten vorgeben Coln für Sact Andres Kirchen zu besehen/ ein Katz und ein Mauß/ ein Hundt und ein Katz/ der meynung was/ so wenig die Katz mit der Mauß/ und der Hundt mit dem Katzen/ ware freundschafften haben müchten/ also wenig wer ich gut Christ/ truckten solichs auch mit worten gnugsamlich auß und sprachen/ du magst dich wol Christlich mit deiner geberde erzeygen. Es ist aber zu besorgen du habst noch die Judischen duck in herzen/ die Agleister last irs huppens nit. . . '.

43 I am aware of the problem of using the terms 'German' or 'Germany' in relation to the early-modern period. But I follow the precedent of other historians for the sake of convenience and to refer broadly to the territories in the Holy Roman Empire.

44 E. P. Evans, *The Criminal Prosecution and Capital Punishment of Animals* (1906).

45 The association of Jews with swine also occurred in Spain, where the term Marrano was applied to New Christians. Farinelli argues that this word was derived from the Spanish word for swine (A. Farinelli, *Marrano: Storia de un Vituperio,* 1925).

46 Isaiah Shachar, *The Judensau: A Medieval Anti-Jewish Motif and its History* (London: Warburg Institute, 1974), p. 3: '. . .the attitude expressed in the *Judensau* towards the Jews is not just scurrilous. There was a further element or sub-motif present in all its representations: the Jews belong to the sow, the sow to the Jews. These people, in other words, belong to another and abominable category of beings; they are the sow's offspring and turn to their mother for their proper nourishment. . . . The Jews are by this association with the animal, implicitly but clearly labelled as not being human 'like Us': not, as the German would put it, *unsereiner*. . . . It would not be necessary to mention this partly concealed meaning if the question of the common humanity of the Jews had not become so important in Germany since the eighteenth century. In that connection the long association of Jew and sow assumes historical significance, for it was then that its latent psychological impact became clear. If it was so impossible for men in the age of enlightenment, and later, to conceive of the Jews as their fellow humans, it was not just because of religious differences but also because of less conscious factors'.

47 This is actually the title of an article written by S. Ettinger (note 24).

48 For example, Trevor-Roper argues that 'Protestant philo-Semitism was a product of Protestant millenarianism' ('Europe's Brief Flood Tide of Philo-Semitism', *Horizon* 3, 1960). David Katz, *Philo-Semitism and the Readmission of the Jews to England 1603–1655* (note 1).

49 Healey, 'The Jew in Seventeenth-Century Protestant Thought' (note 37), p. 77.

50 Ettinger, 'The Beginnings of the Change in the Attitude of European Society Towards the Jews' (note 24), p. 202.

51 Of course, there were plenty of these. As Gottfried Arnold argued in his *Unparteiische Kirchen und Ketzerhistorie* (1699–1700), the true history of Christianity is the history of its heretics.

52 The inquisitorial records of van Helmont's case can be found in the 'Archivio Segreto Vaticano, Archivio della Nunziatura di Colonia 81'. They have been printed as an appendix to Klaus Jaitner's article, 'Der Pfalz-Sulzbacher Hof in der europäischen Ideengeschichte des 17. Jahrhunderts', *Wolfenbüttler Beiträge*, hrsg. Paul Raabe, 1988, pp. 395–404. The fourth document sets forth the charges against van Helmont, among which appears his unorthodox view of Christ: ' . . . 14. Loqueretur, si viveret, Eminentissimi Domini Electoris Maguntini quondam consiliarius et ablegatus in conventu Francofurtensi, Nobilis Dominus Philippus Otto ab Herzelles, nuper defunctus, de pluribus nefariis Hemontii dogmatibus, quae ipse eidem instilare plus semel conatus est, scilicet nihilominus esse credendum de iis, quae Sancta Catholica Ecclesia docet de conceptione, nativitate, passione, resurrectione Christi Servatoris Nostri. Allegorice haec omnia intelligenda, non secundum litteram, Christum in veris Christianis, id est Helmontianis, quotidie concipi, nasci, pati, mori, resurgere; nec aliter haec intelligi debere de virgine sacratissima, quae ab Helmontio plus semel constanter audivisse variis narravit antedictus Herzelles, ita ut ipse Elector Maguntinus et Dominus Breuing, Sanctissimae Theologiae Doctor et parochus ac scholasticus ecclesiae Francofurtensis, qui dicto Herzelles in extremis adfuit, cognitionem habeant sufficientem, cuius etiam probatio in facili est, modo ab eisdem rite petatur'. In the second document van Helmont is accused of believing in universal salvation: 'Informatio de Helmontio (Mai/Juni 1662): . . . Errores et doctrina Helmontii. . . . 4. Interdum auditus est dicere, quemlibet in sua fide salvari posse secundum singulare ipsius lumen et lumen conscientiae'.

53 ibid., Document 5 (Examination of the Witness, Chancellor Franz Gise): 'Judaismo tinctus sit'.

54 ibid., Document 2: 'Information de Helmontio. . . . Summa. Quidquid Helmontio ex lumine interiore manifestatur, mera tenebrossissimae mentis ludibria sunt usque ad impura suilia, quae Helmontius quasi sicarius negotiator persuadere conatus est principi, ut in arce plurima aedificare mandaret, ubi greges porcoum alerentur, ut vel sic principis aula esset similis villae vel domui rusticanae'.

55 See van Helmont's *Memoirs*, London, British Library, Sloane MS 530.

56 Ettinger (note 24), p. 217.

57 Gordon W. Allport, *The Nature of Prejudice* (Reading, MA: Addison-Wesley Publishing Co, Inc.,1979; first published 1954).

5. THE PREHISTORIC ENGLISH BIBLE

DAVID S. KATZ

The Bible tells us that history has a beginning and an end, so it is only natural that the history of the Bible should be structured upon the same model. Every (English) school-boy knows that the Creation of the English Bible occurred in 1525 A.D., when William Tyndale (1494?–1536) printed his translation of the New Testament. William Tyndale, the Creator of the English Bible, and much more: M.M. Knappen, in his influential history of Tudor Puritanism, made him the Creator of that too.[1] Historians shy away from admitting that they write according to models: indeed, the very word 'model' makes us cringe with loathing. Yet it is undeniable that for many centuries, the history of the world, of Parliament, of religion, was written on the biblical model. It was a search for King Edward I, the Creator of the Model Parliament; Martin Luther, the first Protestant; or the anonymous First Jew in Hampstead. Even after Butterfield warned us against ends-oriented Whig History, the biblical model remained most satisfying, especially by the generation which saw during the Second World War what one man could do to change the course of history.

During the past fifteen years, historians have revised their views on how to understand history in general, and the history of the English Reformation in particular. We now see how little most people really wanted change, and were not very satisfied with the changes once they came. The biblical model has given way to a more evolutionary one. Luther becomes much more understandable as a passenger on a history train with express stops at Wyclif and Hus, on a line beginning with Augustine. The so-called 'precursors' of the biblical model – those lucky fellows who had the wit to proclaim the 'correct' concepts of the future, like religious toleration or heliocentrism – can now be seen in some cases to be genuine contributors to a view that becomes more developed down the evolutionary path. If we are interested in finding the actual *sources* of the English Bible, as opposed to its *precursors*, in looking behind Tyndale for the prehistoric English Bible, then we need to begin with the humanists who made his achievement posssible.

Burckhardt writes not only about the rise of humanism, but also about its decline, and the fall of the humanists themselves: 'Though they

A.P. Coudert, S. Hutton, R.H. Popkin and G.M. Weiner (eds): Judaeo-Christian Intellectual Culture in the Seventeenth Century, 71–89.
© 1999 *Kluwer Academic Publishers. Printed in the Netherlands.*

still served as models to the poets, historians and orators, personally no one would consent to be reckoned of their number'. The chief charges against them were self-conceit, profligacy, and irreligion:

> Why, it may be asked, were not these reproaches, whether true or false, heard sooner? As a matter of fact, they were heard at a very early period, but the effect they produced was insignificant, for the plain reason that men were far too dependent on the scholars for their knowledge of antiquity — that the scholars were personally the possessors and diffusers of ancient culture. But the spread of printed editions of the classics, and of large and well-arranged handbooks and dictionaries, went far to free the people from the necessity of personal intercourse with the humanists, and, as soon as they could be but partly dispensed with, the change in popular feeling became manifest. It was a change under which the good and bad suffered indiscriminately.[2]

Compare Burckhardt's description of the position of the Italian Greek and Latin humanists, with that of their contemporary Jewish counterparts. Rabbi Elijah Menahem Halfan described the newfound popularity of Jewish scholars as somewhat exasperating. 'In the last twenty years', he wrote:

> knowledge has increased, and people have been seeking everywhere for instruction in Hebrew. Especially after the rise of the sect of Luther, many of the nobles and scholars of the land sought to have thorough knowledge of this glorious science (Kabbalah). They have exhausted themselves in this search, because among our people there are but a small number of men learned in this wisdom, for after the great number of troubles and expulsions, but a few remain. So seven learned men grasp a Jewish man by the hem of his garment and say: 'Be our master in this science!'[3]

In both cases, the scholar was tolerated only as long as he was necessary. 'About the middle of the sixteenth century', Burckhardt ex-lains, 'these associations seem to have undergone a complete change. The humanists, driven in other spheres from their commanding position, and viewed askance by the men of the Counter-reformation, lost the control of the academies'.[4] History is written in the academies, the universities, and the story that is told does not always given credit to the Hebraic humanists who made the English Bible possible.[5] This is a shame, because Tyndale's Old Testament has an especially rich pre-history, in the Hebrew grammars and lexicons which have some claim to be seen as comprising the prehistoric English Bible.

William Tyndale was born in the Welsh border country and entered Magdalen Hall, Oxford in 1510, when he was probably about sixteen years old. He took his MA in 1515, and left shortly thereafter for Cambridge, where he stayed until the end of 1521. Tyndale thus managed to just miss both John Colet at Oxford and Erasmus at Cambridge, but something of their spirit must have remained at both institutions. He spent some time as a tutor at Gloucestershire, and at some point resolved to translate the New Testament into English.[6] 'And so I gat me to London', Tyndale recalled, and presented a Greek translation to Sir Henry Guildford the master of the horse, 'the king's grace controller'. This gift opened the door to the famously taciturn Cuthbert Tunstall, who recently had been created bishop of London. Although in some ways the model of a Renaissance prelate, Tunstall was in no mood to make any changes that smacked of Protestantism. Tyndale presented his plan for an English Bible, 'Whereupon my lord answered me, his house was full, he had more than he could well find, and advised me to seek in London, where he said I could not lack a service'.[7]

Tyndale was forced to delay his project, and became preacher at St Dunstan's-in-the-West: 'And so in London I abode almost a year', he recounted, 'and marked the course of the world'.[8] Among those who were impressed with Tyndale's vision was Humphrey Monmouth (d.1537), a cloth merchant with Lollard connections. Monmouth took Tyndale into his own house under the guise of a chaplain. Tyndale was able to remain there for nearly half a year, where, according to Monmouth, 'he lived like a good priest', that is, 'He studied most of the day and night, ate only sodden meat, drank small single beer, and never wore linen'.[9] Despite these advantages, insufficient progress was being made on his translation, and he 'understood at the last not only that there was no room in my lord of London's palace to translate the new testament, but also that there was no place to do it in all England, as experience doth now openly declare'.[10]

Tyndale removed to the Continent in May 1524, first to Hamburg and then to Wittenberg, to consult with Luther in the place where the Protestant Revolution began. Monmouth continued to support Tyndale, sending him £10 to pray for his parents' souls, and then a year later, £10 more.[11] Tyndale returned to Hamburg the following April, working all the while on his English New Testament, assisted by William Roy (fl. 1527).[12] They soon moved on to Cologne, where they contracted with Peter Quentell to print the work. The printers got as far as the signature K (ten sheets) when another patron of the same publishing house got wind of what was coming off the presses, and denounced Tyndale to the town senate, which issued an injunction stopping all further printing.[13]

Tyndale and Roy took the printed pages and fled to Worms, arriving in October 1525. There, in more sympathetic surroundings, they agreed with a printing house, probably that of Peter Schoeffer, to produce the entire work again. Unauthorized versions of Scripture had been banned in England in 1410 at the beginning of the Lollard movement, so sufficient legal menace existed to render Tyndale's project precarious. Bishop Tunstall of London no doubt had cause to remember the man who had asked for a humanist's help a few years back, but now was determined to crush the work that he might equally have approved. In October 1526, he denounced it from St Paul's Cross, and gave orders to his archdeacons to pass on the word that all copies of Tyndale's translation which had been spirited into England were to be turned in within thirty days on pain of excommunication. Tunstall then summoned the booksellers of London and ordered them not to sell Tyndale's New Testament.[14] Tyndale in turn revised the manuscript himself once again, and published his definitive translation in octavo at Antwerp in 1535.[15]

From our point of view, and certainly in terms of humanistic achievement, however, it was Tyndale's translation of parts of the Old Testament which attracts our attention.[16] Tyndale's Pentateuch, the first edition in English, was printed at Antwerp, although the title page claims that it came from the press of Hans Luft at Marburg.[17] This information comes from the colophon at the end of Genesis, which also supplies the date: 17 January 1530. It is a handy book, an octavo in 378 leaves, and not entirely in black letter, unlike the previous English Bibles. The book includes a certain number of woodcuts, and in addition to the prologues, many marginal notes for which Tyndale would become notorious.[18] Tyndale followed the Pentateuch with the book of Jonah, apparently printed by Martin de Keyser of Antwerp in 1531.[19] In addition, Tyndale left in manuscript the entire Old Testament from Joshua to Chronicles, which was printed in the 'Matthew' Bible of 1537.

Greek and Latin were part of the intellectual baggage of any Renaissance intellectual, and it is no surprise that Tyndale should have been able to utilize existing linguistic tools in the service of biblical scholarship. Hebrew was another matter entirely. The English Bible was born, if not quite created. Most general histories of the English Bible note laconically that unlike a good many of his fellow translators, William Tyndale actually could read Hebrew. Sometimes a bare list of Bibles, grammars, and dictionaries is appended, which gives no indication of the richness of this literature and the lives of the men who wrote and published it. These sources are the set texts of the prehistoric English Old Testament, and provide testimony to that unique period in the eighty or so years before the Counter-Reformation when Jewish and Christian scholars might work together to elucidate the common elements of the Judaeo-Christian tradition. Without their efforts, Tyndale might well have stayed in London.

The Renaissance emphasis on textual analysis, on reintegrating the classical text with the original classical meaning, was bound to have consequent religious implications. No longer was Greek and Roman literature to be used as a vehicle for demonstrating Christian values and ethics; now it came to be seen again as texts written within a specific temporal and cultural context. Beginning with Erasmus, if not before, these methods were applied to Holy Scripture, although at first with the New Testament alone, which was always seen to be more the work of man than of God, and therefore a legitimate proving ground for philological tinkering.[20] Every jot and tittle of the Old Testament might still be seen as divinely inspired, written with the finger of God on Mount Sinai, but it was inevitable that one day the Renaissance would come to the Pentateuch as well.

That revolution in biblical studies was long delayed, for not until the seventeenth century, even in Roman Catholic circles, was the Old Testament considered to be fair game. Nevertheless, the initial interest of Renaissance scholars in the Old Testament was not narrowly textual, but included many occult applications of the biblical message. It was Pico della Mirandola (1463–1494) who was the first to introduce the Jewish mystical tradition, the Kabbalah, as a Christian tool for biblical analysis. Through Pico's influence, Johannes Reuchlin (1455–1522) was led to kabbalistic and hebraic wisdom, which he studied in Italy under Jacob ben Jehiel Loans, the Jewish court physician of Frederick III. Reuchlin produced in 1506 the first Hebrew grammar in Latin, and published the first full treatises on Kabbalah written by a gentile.[21]

Certainly, to some extent, the fascination which Pico and Reuchlin had for Hebrew and Kabbalah was part of Renaissance eclecticism, the notion that the truth could be found scattered in a wide variety of sources. Yet, more importantly, there was also the belief that the Kabbalah was part of the original divine message given by God on Mount Sinai, and that it had remained pure, untainted by the intervention of the rabbis and their obfuscating Talmud. Those drawn to Jewish sources soon found themselves in dire need of guidance, such as could only be had from living Jews. Many Jewish rabbis and even medical doctors found themselves in demand by their intellectual Christian neighbours as purveyors of whatever Hebrew knowledge they might have had, no matter how haphazardly it had been acquired. Eventually, their monopoly would be weakened both by the printing of kabbalistical works, and the rise of Lurianic Kabbalah, the new variety of the mystical tradition which was being developed at Safed in Palestine, but for nearly a century, the market for Jewish teachers was very active.

Pico had his Rabbi Yohanan Isaac Allemanno, whom he met in Florence in 1488 and engaged as his teacher. We know little about Allemanno, but it appears that he was acquainted with Lorenzo de Medici as well.[22] Flavius Mithradates (c.1450, fl.1489), that mysterious Sicilian Jew who converted to Christianity, translated kabbalistic texts for Pico, and taught Hebrew, Aramaic, and Arabic not only in Italy, but in France and Germany as well. He also translated the Koran into Latin for the duke of Urbino, and preached a sermon before the pope on the suffering of Jesus.[23]

Indeed, the point has been made that the entire direction of translation was altered. Before the Renaissance, many philosophical treatises were translated into Hebrew by Jews for the use of other Jews. From the beginning of the fifteenth century, on the other hand, Jews and converts from Judaism were translating Hebrew works into Latin or Italian and writing themselves in these languages.[24] The Reformation strengthened this interest and respect for Jewish learning, not so much in the kabbalistic vein, but more directly for the Jews as the guardians of the Old Testament, which came to be seen as their most important historical function.[25] The Word of God was His legacy to mankind, and His word was in Hebrew. The principle of *sola scriptura* demanded a mastery of the Hebrew language. Yet even in rationalistic Protestantism, Hebrew soon acquired mystical signification and kabbalistic intonations. Hebrew was the vernacular of Adam and Eve in the Garden of Eden, when Adam gave names to the animals and there was no poetic ambiguity between words and the things to which they referred. The Bible tells us that God created the universe by speaking, and the language He spoke was almost certainly Hebrew. There was always the hope that one day mankind might recreate this entire technology by a study of the intricacies of the Hebrew language, and thereby take part in the divine process.[26]

During the first half of the sixteenth century, then, both Protestants and Roman Catholics alike were united in the belief that in order to reach full Christian understanding it was necessary to study the Old Testament, the Hebrew language, and even the Jewish mystical tradition, the Kabbalah. The Jews of Europe, and especially in Italy, were therefore given positive associations, and a number of Jewish intellectuals found themselves popular and in demand as representatives of an entire people.

That, at least, was the theory, but even Erasmus was defeated by the prospect of learning Hebrew 'by the strangeness of the language, and at the same time the shortness of life'.[27] A difficult language at the best of times, one can only gnash one's teeth at the challenge which faced the Christian humanists and the Renaissance Hebraists at the end of the fifteenth century. The very first Hebrew grammar written by a Christian was the work of Conrad Pellican (1478–1556), twenty quarto leaves, printed from woodcut blocks at Strasburg. It was an extract from a larger work, and was more an account of how Pellican divined the rules of Hebrew grammar on his own. The little grammar itself is a mere nineteen pages, followed by a sampler of texts from Isaiah and Psalms (five pages), and a short list of Hebrew words, with their Latin and Greek equivalents.[28]

Johannes Reuchlin, the German humanist politician, produced his more substantial *De Rudimentis Linguae Hebraicae*, published in 1506 and printed back-to-front like a Hebrew book. Reuchlin had to pay Jews to teach him the language, and this first proper grammar in Latin of the Old Testament language was pathbreaking, not the least because, as Reuchlin lamented, 'before me among the Latins no one appears to have done this'. Reuchlin's book was part grammar (very briefly done), part dictionary, and part primer: mere description of the Hebrew alphabet for absolute beginners.[29]

Other such works would follow throughout the sixteenth century,[30] but Hebrew studies after Reuchlin's death would not receive its next boost until the appearance of Sebastian Münster at Basle. Sebastian Münster (1489–1552) was a second-generation Christian Hebraist, a pupil of Pellican, and by 1524 (like him) a Protestant, having abandoned the Franciscans who had accepted him while still a very young man. Münster taught Hebrew at Heidelberg, and in 1528 was appointed professor of Hebrew at Basle, where he remained until his death. Münster was not only a Hebraist, of course, but also mathematician, cosmographer, and cartographer. But his Hebraic studies alone were prodigious and pioneering. His first Hebrew grammars were unexceptional, published in 1520 and 1524.[31] At about this time he discovered the work of Elijah Levita, the great Jewish grammitician, who had already published both a Hebrew grammar at Rome and an Aramaic dictionary at Isny. Münster immediately recognized the futility of trying to hack a pathway through the Hebrew woods on his own: 'In all the grammatical works written by Christians before Elias began his work', he confessed, 'the true

fundamental [grounding] was missing'. Indeed, he lamented, 'We have
become teachers before being students'.[32]

Elijah Levita (1468?–1549), also known as Eliyahu Bachur, was
not only a leading Hebrew philologist and lexicographer, but one of those
Jews during the period of the Renaissance who actively promoted Christian
Hebraism, as a point of principle. Although born near Nuremburg, Levita
lived most of his life in Italy, and was in contact with most of the leading
Christian Hebraists of his day.[33] Guillaume Postel (1510–81) claimed
Levita among his closest friends in Venice.[34] At Rome, Levita lived for
thirteen years (1514–27) in the home of Cardinal Egidius da Viterbo, the
General of the Augustinian Order, and taught him Kabbalah while
translating manuscripts for him. Acting on the recommendation of one of
his pupils, King Francis I invited Levita to lecture at the Collège Royal in
Paris. Levita refused, explaining that being the only Jew allowed to live in
France would be detrimental to his religious observances.[35]

Levita's life changed in the sack of Rome (1527), which ruined
him. He returned to Venice and from about 1529 for ten years worked as a
proofreader for Daniel Bomberg's press, which was a Christian business
publishing Hebrew books. Levita remained in Venice, except for the period
1539–44 when he took a job with Paul Fagius's press at Isny and printed
there some of his most important works.[36] Levita's Hebrew grammars and
dictionaries, and his Aramaic dictionary and biblical concordance, brought
him to the attention of the Christian scholarly world. His *Bove-Bukh*, a sort
of Jewish *Decameron* written in Yiddish, brought him fame among Jews
everywhere, and gave him a lasting place in the history of Yiddish
literature. But for Sebastian Münster, what was important were the books
that Levita wrote and published at Rome in 1518 and 1519, and which
seemed even to gentile scholars to put the field on an entirely new
footing.[37]

To his credit, Münster immediately gave up significant creative
work and dedicated himself to bringing Levita before the gentile Latin-
reading public. These ponderous products were inherently unobjectionable.
So too was his translation of the Old Testament into Latin, the first such
achievement by a Protestant, printed in parallel columns to the Hebrew.[38]
Even Münster's Aramaic grammar of 1527, the first written by a Christian,
was very nearly beyond reproach.[39] What annoyed his fellow humanists
was Münster's attraction to aspects of the Jewish tradition which did not
seem to have much bearing on biblical scholarship. How could one explain
his work on the Jewish calendar,[40] or his editions of the books of Joel,

Malachi and Isaiah with the commentary of David Kimchi?[41] Münster also published a translation of a medieval Jewish catalogue of the 613 commandments,[42] and Maimonides's Thirteen Articles of Faith.[43] Worst of all, however, was his translation of the Gospel of Matthew into Hebrew, the first Hebrew translation of any portion of the New Testament, and dedicated to King Henry VIII of England, no less.[44] Even Postel, who was no saint, was outraged, and attacked Münster in print.[45]

Apart from the not inconsiderable difficulty of actually learning the language, there was the slow development of Hebrew printing. Despite the fact that the technology of printing was most advanced in Germany, it was in northern Italy that the Hebrew language was first set in moveable type. The first surviving example of Hebrew printing is a Psalter which appeared in Bologna in 1477, and is therefore the first part of the Hebrew Bible to be printed.[46] This was followed in 1482 at Bologna by a Pentateuch with vowels, cantillation marks, the Aramaic paraphrase of Onkelos, and Rashi's standard commentary.

But Hebrew printing really came of age near Mantua in the town of Soncino when a family of South German Jews inaugurated their press in 1484 by printing the Talmudic tractate *Berachot*. The way in which they arranged the commentaries around the Aramaic text would become standard practice. The following year they published a Hebrew edition of the Prophets, and in 1488 made history by printing the first edition of the complete Hebrew Bible. A second edition followed in 1491–3, printed without date or place of publication, but thought by scholars to be the work of the Soncino press transmigrated to Naples. Except for a brief three-year hiatus bewteen 1494 and 1504 the Soncino press was the only Hebrew publishing house in the world. Their work was not only of intrinsically high quality, but like Erasmus' Greek New Testament had a great effect on subsequent scholarship since there was no effective competition. Luther used the Soncino third edition printed at Brescia in 1494 as the basis of his translation of the Old Testament. This indeed was the last production of the Hebrew Bible or parts thereof until 1510–11, when Gershom ben Moses Soncino (d.1533 or 1534) published a beautiful edition of the former Prophets with the commentary of Isaac Abrabanel (1437–1508). This gap in Hebrew publishing may have some historical significance or it may reflect the vicissitudes of the Soncino family. Abrabanel was himself a Spanish refugee who fled to Italy and there lived out the remainder of his life in contemplation of the disaster that had befallen the Jewish people in 1492. Jewish life was turned upside down in the *fin-de-siècle*

Mediterranean world, and it may be that Hebrew publishing by Jews was one of the victims.[47]

By the time the Soncino family left Italy in the 1520s, Hebrew printing was no longer a Jewish monopoly. Daniel Bomberg (d.1549?1553?) of Antwerp settled in Venice as a young man and with a good deal of Jewish help published during his lifetime about two hundred Hebrew books. The most famous was his first rabbinic Bible, the Hebrew text with standard commentaries, which appeared at Venice in 1516–17.[48] Bomberg's Bible was meant primarily for a Jewish readership, it would appear, although he went to the trouble of turning to the Medici pope Leo X for a licence forbidding any other printer from producing a rabbinical Bible until 1525.[49]

Bomberg's chief Hebrew adviser was the apostate known as Felix Pratensis (d.1539), and after his death, Bomberg would return to Antwerp.[50] Bomberg followed up the success of the rabbinical Bible with the first complete edition of both the Babylonian and Jerusalem Talmuds (1520–3), and his pagination in this work has remained standard among Jews until today. So too was Bomberg's second rabbinical Bible, published at Venice, 1524–5, an important model for all later editions. His Jewish assistant, later baptized, was Jacob ben Hayim, a refugee from Tunisia who set the text which is still used by most Jews today. This edition utilized full massoretic equipment and was based on fourteenth-century manuscripts.[51] Although somewhat of a calm followed Bomberg's storm, a number of other Hebrew Bibles did appear before the next great edition, the Royal Polyglot of Antwerp (1569–72). Nevertheless, Sebastian Münster's Hebrew Bible in two volumes at Basle (1534–5) used the Hebrew text of Bomberg's first edition as the basis for his own Latin translation.[52] William Tyndale was the heir to all of this Hebraic activity, and had access to these printed sources, and especially in Germany, to living Jews who most likely were consulted in their utilization. His tragedy was that his political sense was far inferiour to his scholarship.

One of the most interesting shifts of policy during the Tudor period was the government's 'to-ing and fro-ing' over the question of the vernacular Bible. In May 1530, Tyndale was denounced as a heretic and a perverter of God's word. Within less than a year, however, King Henry VIII was ordering Thomas Cromwell, his henchman and architect of Tudor authority, to scour the European countryside for Tyndale and to offer him the job of producing an authorized version of the English Bible. Cromwell in turn wrote to Stephen Vaughan (d.1549), an English merchant at

Antwerp, giving him the job of convincing Tyndale to come home at once and set to work.

What had happened to cause such a dramatic turn-about in English religious policy? Thomas Cromwell has been left with the image of a cruel and devious politician, but he was also an intellectual, almost a humanist. Foxe claimed he had memorized Erasmus's New Testament during a journey to and from Rome.[53] Anne Boleyn may have had some influence: the British Library has her copy, printed on vellum, of Tyndale's New Testament of 1534.[54] She made Henry read Tyndale's polemical work on *The Obedience of a Christian Man* (1528), a very erastian document which promoted the notion of the king who would arise to deliver the people from the powerful and corrupt Catholic Church.[55] It may simply be that Henry was warming to the idea of being Supreme Head of the Church, and conceived of this as an active job involving policy-making.

In any case, the romance between Tyndale and King Henry VIII was short-lived. In April 1531, Vaughan reported to Henry that he had had a meeting with Tyndale in a field outside Antwerp, and enclosed with his letter a manuscript copy of Tyndale's reply to the attacks of Thomas More.[56] This latest document disabused Henry of any hope of cooperating with the cantankerous cleric, made manifest in Tyndale's book about the *Practice of Prelates* (1530) in which he positively denounced Henry's divorce.

In 1534, Convocation under Cranmer wrote formally to Henry asking for an English translation of Scripture, and a new project was underway. The English Bible carried on even without Tyndale, or so it would seem. In 1535, an English Catholic tricked Tyndale into leaving the safety of the English House in Antwerp, whereupon he was arrested. Despite appearances, this was apparently done without English collusion. Stephen Vaughan, who had worked so hard to bring Tyndale home, wrote to Cromwell on 13 April 1536, pleading that 'If now you sende but your lettre to the Pryvey Counsail, I could delyver Tyndall from the fyre, so it came by tyme, for elles it wilbe to late'.[57] But this was too much to ask: Tyndale was condemned as a heretic, and given the mercy of being strangled before his body was burnt by the Imperial authorities. His last words at his martyrdom at Antwerp in October 1536, according to Foxe, were 'Lord, open the King of England's eyes!'[58]

The work of producing the first full edition of the Bible in England was given to Miles Coverdale (1488–1568), a Yorkshireman educated at Cambridge, a former Augustinian friar who had worked with Tyndale at Hamburg on the first Pentateuch. He would become bishop of Exeter in

1551 under Edward VI, and after return from his Marian exile, would be given a quiet rectory in London under Elizabeth.[59] Why a man with a biography so similar to that of the rejected Tyndale was chosen for this work is not clear, but it may be a combination of a more pliant nature and the promise of a groveling dedication to the king which made him more attractive. Coverdale's Bible, published at either Cologne or Marburg in 1535, made no pretense of being an original work, but was rather 'faithfully and truly translated out of Douche [German] and Latin'.[60]

Coverdale's Bible was just a stop-gap, however, made more unsatisfactory in August 1536 when Cromwell, as deputy to the Supreme Head of the English Church, issued injunctions to the clergy to provide both Latin and English Bibles for parishioners to read in church.[61] Cromwell was enough of a humanist to realize that the martyred Tyndale's translation was too good to lose. In August 1537 he licensed a folio edition of the Old and New Testaments which was said on the title page to have been 'truly and purely translated into Englysh by Thomas Matthew'. Cromwell knew that 'Thomas Matthew' did not exist, and that the man behind the edition was John Rogers (c.1500–55), later to be the first martyr in Mary's persecutions, but meanwhile chiefly known as the late William Tyndale's close associate. Essentially, this version of the Bible is a melding of the best of Coverdale and Tyndale. From Ezra to the end of the Apocrypha, including Jonah, is Coverdale's version, but the entire stretch from Joshua to Chronicles is almost certainly Tyndale's, drawn from a manuscript given to Rogers for safe keeping. The Pentateuch and the New Testament are basically Tyndale's as well. Even the place of publication and the name of the printer are mysterious, although the work was probably done in Antwerp. It is more than likely that not even King Henry VIII knew that he was endorsing the work of the awful William Tyndale when he allowed the book to appear 'with the Kinges most gracyous lyèce'.[62]

Thomas Cromwell was therefore able to issue a second set of royal injunctions in September 1538, ordering each parish to obtain 'one book of the whole Bible of the largest volume in English' by the following Easter, set up in church for people to read. At the same time, he commissioned a revision by Coverdale of Matthew's Bible, corrected with further application to Sebastian Münster's Latin translation of the Hebrew Old Testament (1534–5), with due attention to Erasmus's Latin New Testament and the Complutensian Polyglot. The work was begun in Paris, but when many of the finished sheets were confiscated at the end of 1538, they shifted the entire lot — presses, type and printers — to London, where the so-called 'Great Bible' was finished in folio by April 1539.[63] Cromwell spent a good deal of his own money in this project, but by the time of his execution the following year, had managed to get printed enough copies for all of the eight and one-half thousand English parishes, although few of those outside London were willing to lay out the subsidized cost of purchase. 'Cromwell's Bible' almost fell with him, but assiduous work by Cranmer out-maneuvered the opposition. In the end, a royal proclamation of 1541 ruled that parishes had six months to purchase a Bible or to pay a £2 fine. It was finally cheaper just to buy the holy book. By the end of 1545, most churches had them, and the royal commissioners two years later made sure that the last recalcitrant parishes obeyed. Tyndale, in one form or another, was finally set up throughout England.[64]

William Tyndale was a great man, and not merely because he was the first to translate and publish (most of) the English Bible. Tyndale was the beneficiary of a good deal of pioneering scholarship in the Greek and Hebrew text, right in the middle of the period when there was still a modicum of cooperation between Jewish and gentile scholars, before the Counter-Reformation put an end to all that. In his appreciation and utilization of these advances, Tyndale put himself squarely in the Renaissance tradition. But he was also a champion and publicist for the Protestant Reformation, as his 'pestilent glosses' and various polemical writings abundantly show. We have become accustomed to thinking of the Renaissance and the Reformation as two separate historical tunnels, especially after Luther made it quite clear to Erasmus and the humanist world in 1525 that he would have nothing to do with newly developed notions of human free will.

Tyndale the Protestant, however, demonstrates a good deal of Renaissance spirit, especially if we take note of P.O. Kristeller's controversial claim that the humanists were more interested in how ideas were obtained and expressed than in the content of those ideas themselves. Rhetoric, eloquence, and style were their primary concerns. As long as the views expressed were derived from antiquity and presented in an elegant and learned format, then it really did not matter if you were Platonist or Aristotelian. The cover was almost as important as the book.[65]

A good deal of printers' ink has been spilled over such questions as 'Did Tyndale really know Hebrew?', or 'How much did he rely on previous translations', and the killer question, 'How accurate a translation from the Hebrew is Tyndale's Old Testament?'[66] We could do worse than to listen to Tyndale himself, keeping Kristeller in mind. Concluding the preface to his Pentateuch, Tyndale asked his readers to remember that:

> Notwithstanding yet I submit this book and all other that I have either made or translated, or shall in time to come, (if it be God's will that I shall further labour in his harvest) unto all of them that submit themselves unto the word of God, to be corrected of them, yea and moreover to be disallowed and also burnt, if it seem worthy when they have examined it with the Hebrew, so that they first put forth of their own translating another that is more correct.[67]

Tyndale was far less concerned than his modern critics with providing the ultimate translation into English of the Old Testament. The important thing was to publish a basic text of Holy Writ over which scholars could argue, a standard basis for discussion, a *printed* English translation which came to the scholar's library, instead of him having to seek it out under the beds and behind the cupboards of Lollards up and down the country. In this, Tyndale was just like his hero Erasmus, who was quite happy to publish the Greek text of the New Testament out of defective late medieval manuscripts. When he found the last folio of the Book of Revelation lacking, he just made it up for himself, translating the Vulgate back into Greek. This was not forgery; he made no attempt to hide this literary slight-of-hand, for it was perfectly in keeping with the main purpose behind the entire enterprise — to provide a basic text over which all further discussion could centre.[68]

Tyndale thus combines both Renaissance and Reformation trends, and stands at the beginning of a new enterprise – the printed English Bible. But he also marks the end of another line of medieval biblical scholarship represented by the Lollard followers of Wyclif. The Lollards thought it enough to produce a vernacular text, any English Bible, even if it was merely a translation of the increasingly inaccurate Vulgate. They would no more have thought of turning to the Hebrew and the Greek, searching out and collating early biblical manuscripts, than an Italian humanist would think of praising Scholasticism. Like in everything else, the Lollard underground had to give way to the heavy artillery of the Reformation.[69]

We all know that there is nothing so permanent as temporary, and Tyndale's achievement turned out to be well-nigh eternal. About 90-per cent of the King James Authorized Version (1611) is verbatim Tyndale, and even the Revised Version of 1881 retains Tyndale to the degree of 80-per cent.[70] Not only did Tyndale introduce the word 'Jehovah' into English,[71] but numerous phrases such as 'powers that be', 'die the death', 'eat drink and be merry' and many others as well. Tyndale proclaimed that 'the properties of the Hebrew tongue agreeth a thousand times more with the English than with the Latin'.[72] That this could be made a permanent part of the English legacy was due to the Hebraic pioneers, both Jew and Gentile, of the prehistoric English Bible.

1 M.M. Knappen, *Tudor Puritanism: A Chapter in the History of Idealism* (Chicago, 1939), ch. 1.

2 Jacob Burckhardt, *The Civilization of the Renaissance in Italy: An Essay* (Phaidon edn, London, 1960), pp. 162–3, from 2nd German edition (1868), trans. S.G.C. Middlemore.

3 Quoted from a manuscript source in Moshe Idel, 'The Magical and Neoplatonic Interpretations of the Kabbalah in the Renaissance', in B. Cooperman, ed., *Jewish Thought in the Sixteenth Century* (Cambridge, 1987), pp. 186–242, esp. pp. 186–7. See also idem, 'Hermeticism and Judaism', in I. Merkel and A. Debus, (eds), *Hermeticism and the Renaissance* (Washington, 1988), 59–76.

4 Burckhardt, *Renaissance*, p. 170.

5 See generally, A.W. Pollard, *Records of the English Bible* (London, 1911); C. Anderson, *Annals of the English Bible* (London, 1845–55); D. Wilson, *The People and the Book: The Revolutionary Impact of the English Bible, 1380–1611* (London, 1976).

6 On Tyndale generally, see J.F. Mozley, *William Tyndale* (London, 1937); R. Demaus, *William Tyndale* (London, 1871).

7 *Tyndale's Old Testament*, ed. D. Daniell (New Haven & London, 1992), 'W.T. To the Reader', p. 5. Cf. John Strype, *Ecclesiastical Memorials* (Oxford, 1822), i/2, pp. 364, 367; Mozley, *Tyndale*, pp. 44–50.

8 C. Haigh, *English Reformations: Religion, Politics and Society under the Tudors* (Oxford, 1993), p. 59.

9 Petition of Humphrey Monmouth, draper, of London, to Wolsey and the Council, 19 May 1528: *Letters & Papers of Henry VIII*, iv (2), #4282. Cf. John Foxe, *Acts and Monuments*, ed. S.R. Cattley & G. Townshend (London, 1837–41), vol. IV, p. 618.

10 *Tyndale's Old Testament*, ed. Daniell, p. 5.

11 Petition of Humphrey Monmouth, draper, of London, to Wolsey and the Council, 19 May 1528: *Letters & Papers of Henry VIII*, iv (2), #4282.

12 According to A.G. Dickens, *The English Reformation* (London, 1964), p. 74, Roy was 'born of Jewish stock in Calais'.

13 The unhappy customer was Johann Dobneck (Cochlaeus), dean of the church of the Blessed Virgin at Frankfurt, who was having printed an edition of the works of Rupert, a former abbot of Deutz [DNB]. The only surviving copy is the fragment in the Grenville Collection of the British Library, which is missing the title page: 31 ff. in all, ending suddenly in the middle of Matthew xxii. Quentell's name does not appear in the text that we have, but he was almost certainly the printer: *Historical Catalogue of Printed Editions of the English Bible 1525–1961*, ed. A.S. Herbert, *et al.* (London & N.Y., 1968), p. 1.

14 S. Brigden, *London and the Reformation* (Oxford, 1989), p. 159, with MS. citations; W.A. Clebsch, *England's Earliest Protestants* (New Haven, 1964), pp. 139–42; *Original Letters*, ed. Ellis (3rd ser.), ii. 86 [DNB]; Haigh, *Reformations*, p. 60. Cf. *Letters & Papers of Henry VIII*, iv (2), p. 1158n., referring to Tunstall's order, printed in Foxe, and cited by Strype, *Memorials*, i. 165.

15 It seems to have been printed by Martin de Keyser for Govaert van der Haghen: *Historical Catalogue*, ed. Herbert, pp. 7–8 [#15]. This is therefore often called the 'G.H.' edition.

16 As was usually the case, the first portion of the Old Testament to be translated into the vernacular was the Book of Psalms, which according to the title page appeared on 16 January 1530. The publisher was given as 'Francis foxe'; the place of publication as 'Argentine', that is, Strasburg. In fact, as everyone knew, the book of 240 leaves was printed by Martinus de Keyser at Antwerp: *Historical Catalogue*, ed. Herbert, p. 3; *The Library*, Sept. 1947/8, p. 85. There are copies in both the British Library and the Bodleian. The translator, however, was not Tyndale, but almost certainly his associate George Joye. Like Tyndale, Joye used many aliases, including Clarke, Geach, Gee and Jaye, but he was the Bedfordshire fellow of Peterhouse, Cambridge who became a well-known Protestant controversialist and Bible translator. Thomas More at least thought that Joye was the one who had translated the Psalms, and Stokesley, the bishop of London, included 'the psalter in English by Joye'

as one of the forbidden books in his list of Advent Sunday, 1531: *DNB., s.v.* 'Joye, George (d.1553)'. The author of the entry, however, doubts that Joye was the translator, noting that 'the verbal differences are too thorough to render this theory probable'. A.S. Herbert, in his *Historical Catalogue*, p. 3, catagorically lists the book [#3] as Joye's. Joye also produced eight preliminary leaves of a translation of Isaiah [#5] (1531: Martin de Keyser at Antwerp) [Bodleian]; another Psalter [#9] (1534: Martin Emperour [de Keyser]); Proverbs [#10] (1534?: Thomas Godfray, London); Jeremiah [#11] (1534: widow of Christopher of Endhoven alias C. Van Ruremund, Antwerp) [Brit.Lib., C.25.d.7.(2)]; a version of Tyndales NT 'diligently ouersene and corrected', [#12] (1534, same printer, Antwerp) [Brit. Lib., only copy, G.12180]; a carefully revised edition of Tyndale's 1525 NT and including a second preface in which Tyndale defends his own translation against Joye's corrections, [#13] (1534, Martin Emperour [de Keyser], Antwerp) [Brit.Lib. C.23.a.5]; a further reprint of his 1534 modification of Tyndale's NT, now also in [#17] (1535: Catharyn Widowe [of. . .]) [Brit.Lib., only copy, C.36.bb.3].

17 *Historical Catalogue*, ed. Herbert, p. 3; *The Library*, Sept. 1947/8, pp. 85 ff. There are copies in both the British Library and the Bodleian.

18 See the edition edited by David Daniell.

19 Only one copy exists, in the British Library, discovered in 1861 by Lord Arthur Hervey, later bishop of Bath and Wells.

20 See generally, J.H. Bentley, *Humanists and Holy Writ: New Testament Scholarship in the Renaissance* (Princeton, 1983).

21 Johannes Reuchlin, *De rudimentis Hebraicis* (Pforzheim, 1506); idem, *De verbo mirifico* (Basle, 1494); idem, *De arte Cabalistica* (Haguenau, 1517). For an interesting discussion of the Egyptian tradition, see Martin Bernal, *Black Athena* (London, 1987).

22 Allemanno's son Isaac taught Pico's nephew Giovanni Francesco: Idel, 'Magical', p. 212.

23 C. Wirszubski, *A Christian Kabbalist Reads the Law* [Hebrew] (Jerusalem, 1977); Flavius Mithridates, *Sermo de Passione Domini*, ed. idem (Jerusalem, 1963); S. Simonsohn, 'Some Well-Known Jewish Converts During the Renaissance', *Revue des études juives*, 148 (1989), pp. 17–52.

24 Idel, 'Magical', p. 187.

25 See also H.H. Ben-Sasson, 'The Reformation in Contemporary Jewish Opinion', *Proc. Israel Academy of Sciences and Humanities*, 4 (1970), pp. 239–326.

26 D.S. Katz, 'The Language of Adam in Seventeenth-Century England', in Hugh Lloyd-Jones, Valerie Pearl, and Blair Worden, eds, *History and Imagination: Essays in Honour of H.R. Trevor-Roper* (London, 1981), pp. 132–45.

27 *The Collected Works of Erasmus* (Toronto, 1974): *Correspondence.*, vol. 2, p. 87.

28 [Conrad Pellicanus], *De modo legendi et intelligendi hebraevm* (Strassburg, 1504), printed by J. Grÿuuninger. The work was originally leaves F ix–xxviii of Gregorius Reisch, *Margarita philoophica* (Basle, 1535: earliest edn in Bodleian), a famous compendium of useful knowledge: cf. facimile printed in pamphlet form by E. Nestle (Tÿuubingen, 1877). Pellican was Swiss, originally a Franciscan monk, who became a Protestant about 1526 and professor of theology and librarian at Zurich.

29 Johannes Reuchlin, *De Rudimentis Hebraicis* (Pforzheim, 1506).

30 Reuchlin's lead was followed by Wolfgang Fabricus Capito, who published a small Hebrew grammar at Basle in 1518. See esp. the Hebrew grammars by the Roman Catholic scholars Nicolaus Clenardus of Louvain (Paris, 1540) and Sanctes Pagninus of Lucca (Lyons, 1529). The latter's Hebrew grammar of 1546 was printed by Robert Estienne and thereby became the best presented Hebrew grammar of its time.

31 Sebastian Münster, *Epitome Hebraicae grammaticae* (Basle, 1520), printed back to front; idem, *Institutiones Grammmaticae in Hebraeam Linguam* ([Basle], 1524), including a polyglot text of the Book of Jonah.

32 From the prefaces, respectively, of Münster's *Opus grammaticum consummatum* (Basle, 1542) and his *Absolutissima* (1525) [see below], as quoted in J. Friedman, *The Most Ancient*

Testimony: Sixteenth-Century Christian-Hebraica in the Age of Renaissance Nostalgia (Athens, Ohio, 1983), pp. 44–8.

33 Generally, see G.E. Weil, *Elie Levita humaniste et massoréte 1469–1549* (Paris, 1963).

34 In his *Linguarum duodecim characteribus differentium alphabetum* (Paris, [1538]), fol. 3: 'Elias Germanus, quo usus sum Venetiis'. Postel's pupil Guy Le Fèvre de la Boderie praises Levita in the preface to his *Dictionarium Syro-Chaldaicum* (Antwerp, 1573), originally part of the Antwerp Polyglot Bible (1572).

35 The pupil was Georges de Selve, who later became the French ambassador to Venice.

36 Paul Fagius also supplied a Latin forward to Levita's Aramaic dictionary, *Lexicon Chaldaicvm* (Isny, 1541).

37 These books were: 1) *Sefer ha-Harkavah* (Rome, 1518), 2) *Sefer Ha-Bachur* (Rome, 1518), later called *Dikduk Eliyyah ha-Levi* (Isny, 1542), and further editions.

38 Sebastian Münster, *Hebraica Biblia* (Basle, 1534), with annotations and commentary.

39 Sebastian Münster, *Chaldaica Grammatica* (Basle, 1527). Levita had published an Aramaic dictionary at Isny in 1514.

40 Sebastian Münster, *Kalendarum Hebraicum* (Basle, 1527).

41 Sebastian Münster, *Ioel et Malachias* (n.p., 1530). David Kimchi (1160–1235), also known as 'Radak' from the initials of his name, was one of the members of the medieval Jewish family of grammarians and biblical scholars in Narbonne, Provence.

42 Sebastian Münster, *Praecepta Mosaica* (Basle, 1533).

43 Sebastian Münster, *Tredecim articuli fidei Iudaeorum* (n.p., 1529).

44 Sebastian Münster, *Evangelium secundum Matthaeum in lingua Hebraica cum versione Latina* (Basle, 1537), dedicated to Henry VIII on sigs. a2r–a4r. The Bodleian's copy of the Basle, 1557 edition [8o Z 202 Th] has the signature on the title page of 'Joannes Dee 1562' and a few underlinings and notes. The dedication to Henry VIII is sigs. aa2r–8r in the 1557 edn. Münster's translation derived from an imperfect MS copy of Matthew's gospel in Hebrew made in 1385 for polemical purposes by Shem Tob b. Shaprut, a Jew of Tudela in Castile. The book is 154 pp. Actually, it is not quite true that Münster was the first to translate Matthew: Jacob ben Reuben's *Milkhamot ha-Shem* (c.1170) has some of Matthew in Hebrew, and Raymond Martini has some quotations in Hebrew from the New Testament.

45 In the concluding section of his *De orbis terrae concordia* ([Basle, 1544]).

46 It was printed without vowels with David Kimchi's commentary.

47 The Soncinos for their part removed to the Ottoman Empire, printing their works in Salonica (1527) and from 1530 in Constantinople. By mid-century they were in Cairo, printing until 1557. The Soncinos published altogether about one hundred Hebrew and an equal number of Latin works.

48 Bomberg's first Hebrew work was a Pentateuch (Venice, Dec. 1516).

49 Bomberg obtained a privilege to print Hebrew books for Jews in 1516.

50 Other Jews who worked for Bomberg included Elijah Levita, David Pizzighettone, Kalonymus ben David, and Abraham de Balmes. Bomberg had Felix Pratensis' Latin translation of Psalms (Venice, 1515) printed at his own expense at another publishing house.

51 The next edition of a rabbinical Bible was that published by the Adelkind brothers at Venice in 1548.

52 Robert Estienne (1503–59), the great Protestant printer of Geneva, preferred to use the more accurate Jacob ben Hayim text as the basis for his quarto Old Testament published between 1539 and 1544: generally, see E. Armstrong, *Robert Estienne: Royal Printer* (rev. edn, Sutton Courtenay, 1986): 1st edn (Cambridge, 1954). Bomberg's son worked for Christopher Plantin (c.1520–89), the leading crypto-Protestant printer who fled France for the Low Countries and began publishing books at Antwerp from 1555. By the mid-1570s he had more than twenty-two presses, an empire which in one form or another survived until the mid-nineteenth century. Plantin's copy of Bomberg's rabbinical Bible in its second edition was very successful, not the least among North African Jews.

53 Foxe, *Acts and Monuments*, vol. 5, pp. 363–5 (cf. vol. 4, p. 635).

54 *Historical Catalogue*, ed. Herbert, p. 7 [#13].

55 See M. Dowling, 'Anne Boleyn and Reform', *Journal of Ecclesiastical History*, 35 (1984), pp. 30–46; E.W. Ives, *Anne Boleyn* (London, 1986), chapters 13–14.

56 [Vaughan to Henry VIII], [18 Apr.] 1531: *Letters & Papers of Henry VIII*, v, #201. The book in question was *An Answere unto Sir Thomas Mores Dialogue Made by Willyam Tindale* ([London, 1530]): also ed. H. Walter (Parker Soc., Cambridge, 1850). See also *The Confutation of Tyndale's Answer* in Thomas More, *Complete Works* (New Haven & London, 1963–), viii. See generally, J.A. Guy, *The Public Career of Sir Thomas More* (Brighton, 1980).

57 Vaughan to Cromwell, 13 Apr. 1536: *Letters & Papers of Henry VIII*, x, #663.

58 Mozley, *Tyndale*, chap. 13.

59 See generally, J.F. Mozley, *Coverdale and his Bibles* (London, 1953).

60 *Historical Catalogue*, ed. Herbert, pp. 9–11 [#18]: copies in both the British Library and the Bodleian. Coverdale's sources were the Vulgate, Tyndale's translations, the German version of Zwingli and Leo Juda (Zurich, 1524–9), Pagnini's Latin (1528) and Luther's German version (finished 1532). Coverdale's version of 1537 [#32] was the first folio Bible printed in England, produced by James Nycolson at Southwark. The same year also saw the production of a quarto version of the same [#33], the first Bible of that size printed in England as well.

61 *Documents Illustrative of English Church History*, ed. H. Gee & W.J. Hardy (London, 1896), pp. 269–74.

62 *Historical Catalogue*, ed. Herbert, pp. 18–19 [#34]: a copy is in the British Library. Cf. Haigh, *Reformations*, p. 135.

63 *Documents*, ed. Gee & Hardy, pp. 275–81; Haigh, *Reformations*, p. 135. The second edition of April 1540, a folio with Cranmer's prologue, became the standard text, 'Cranmer's Bible': *Historical Catalogue*, ed. Herbert, pp. 29–30 [#53].

64 Haigh, *Reformations*, pp. 156–9. For Gardiner's opposition to Cranmer on this issue, see G. Redworth, *In Defence of the Church Catholic* (Oxford, 1990), pp. 160–4. For some examples of local leaders (the mayor of Sandwich and the vicar of Faversham) trying to outlaw Bible reading, see L. & P., Henry VIII, xviii (2), 546, pp. 299, 308, 358.

65 P.O. Kristeller, *Renaissance Thought: The Classic, Scholastic, and Humanist Strains* (New York, 1961), chap. 5: first pub. 1955.

66 See, e.g., G.L. Jones, *The Discovery of Hebrew in Tudor England: A Third Language* (Manchester, 1983), pp. 115–22; D.M. Karpman, 'William Tyndale's Response to the Hebraic Tradition', *Studies in the Renaissance*, xiv (1967), pp. 110–30; G. Hammond, 'William Tyndale's Pentateuch: Its Relation to Luther's German Bible and the Hebrew Original', *Renaissance Quarterly*, 33 (1980), pp. 351–85; idem, *The Making of the English Bible* (London, 1982); *William Tyndale's Five Books of Moses Called the Pentateuch*, ed. J.I. Mombert (London, 1884) [new edn ed. F.E. Bruce (Arundel, 1971)]; Clebsch, *Protestants*, p. 138.

67 *Tyndale's Old Testament*, ed. Daniell, pp. 5–6.

68 Note that Erasmus and Tyndale died at almost the same time, Erasmus in July 1536 and Tyndale in October of the same year.

69 The metaphor is A.G. Dickens's: *English Reformation*, p. 37.

70 N.b. that there were 14 edns of the English Bible produced in the 1560s; 25 in the 1570s; 26 in the 1580s; and 31 in the 1590s, mostly drawing on Tyndale: Haigh, *Reformations*, p. 276, from the *Short-Title Catalogue*.

71 Although the word 'Jehovah' first appears in the thirteenth century.

72 Tyndale, *Obedience*, preface: quoted in *Tyndale's Old Testament*, ed. Daniell, p. xv.

6. APOCRYPHA CANON AND CRITICISM FROM SAMUEL FISHER TO JOHN TOLAND, 1650-1718

JUSTIN A.I. CHAMPION

Perusing the manuscript catalogue of Stillingfleet's library held in Marsh's library one thing becomes immediately apparent: that is the proliferation of Biblical material of all varieties. Whether in folio, octavo or otherwise Stillingfleet owned at least seventy-two variant editions of Scriptural texts. Among this collection he owned texts as varied in time and place of publication as the famous Complutensian edition, Brian Walton's polyglot and more obscure versions such as the Anglo-Saxon translation published at Dordrecht in 1665 or the Bible in Irish (1690). As well as owning translations of the Bible in Hebrew, Chaldaic, Greek, French, Latin and many others, Stillingfleet also possessed a full compliment of commentaries and criticism from the early Church fathers to modern critics such as Father Simon, Jean LeClerc and John Locke. To say that Scripture and biblical studies formed the basis of Stillingfleet's collection might not be an overstatement.[1]

Indeed the authority of Scripture was at the heart of Stillingfleet's intellectual world: defending its authenticity as the true word of God, whether against papists or socinians, or against atheists or heathens was a backbone of his theological strategy.[2] In *Origines Sacrae* (first published in 1662 but reprinted many times into the eighteenth century) Stillingfleet took his stand against 'the affronts and indignities which have been cast on Religion; by such, who account it a matter of judgement to disbelieve the Scriptures'. Focusing on the 'most popular pretences of the Atheists of our Age', especially their suggestions regarding 'the irreconcileableness of the account of times in Scripture, with that of the learned and ancient Heathen nations', Stillingfleet inverted the blasphemies of such proposals and instead upheld the 'excellency of the Scriptures' against the failings of non-divine texts.[3] Indeed throughout the *Origines Sacrae* Stillingfleet took the text of received Scripture as a canon and standard against which Heathen sources could be compared and disabled. Deviation from the historical certainties found in Scriptural accounts was a means of illustrating and exposing the forgeries, inaccuracies, and mistakes of non-biblical material. Throughout *Origines Sacrae* however the tools of

A.P. Coudert, S. Hutton, R.H. Popkin and G.M. Weiner (eds): *Judaeo-Christian Intellectual Culture in the Seventeenth Century*, 91-117.

philological criticism turned so effectively against pagan sources remained undirected at Scripture itself. In a similar manner Stillingfleet's polemic against the Catholic Sergeant, *A Rational Account of the Grounds of Protestant Religion* was premised upon defending the 'Protestant way of Resolving faith': the 'certain grounds which we build our Faith upon' were achieved by applying 'reason' to 'testimony' to create a reasonable belief. The determining testimony was not patristic, conciliar or papal but scriptural. For Stillingfleet, Scripture was 'God's infallible testimony' and as such was superior to all forms of human tradition.[4] Again throughout Stillingfleet's argument 'Scripture' was assumed to be a given and identifiable quantity, something real and concrete which had to be defended against the doubts of atheists, the ignorance of papists, and the manipulations of socinians.[5]

Stillingfleet's powerful attempt to defend scripture as 'God's infallible testimony' engaged with what we might call a meta-scriptural problem. He was concerned to defend the place of 'scripture' within the wider context of belief and doctrine: part of this strategy was deliberately contrived to sidestep discussions of the authenticity of Scripture itself. Between the 1650s and the 1700s however there were attacks not just upon the role scripture played in the texture of intellectual conviction but more fundamentally upon the text and accuracy of Biblical material itself.[6] In this paper an attempted outline of some of the central components of this attack on the Bible and its significance in the intellectual ferment of the mid to late seventeenth century will be proposed. One of the main purposes of this sketch will be to re-inscribe the continuity of public strategies of assault upon religious orthodoxy between the days of the English Revolution and the early eighteenth century. The second proposition will focus upon the connection between what might be called the technical history of Biblical 'scholarship' and practical purpose of radical criticism in the period. In this discussion there is neither the physical nor intellectual space to pay any more attention than a mere gesture towards the profundity, complexity, and sheer amount of scholarly industry devoted to what could be termed orthodox biblical scholarship in England from the 1630s through to the 1720s. It is perhaps enough to say that there was a continuity of technical hermeneutical investigation, both in terms of intellectual agendas and scholarly and political relations, from the days of Archbishop Laud to those of Richard Bentley. The starting points for disinterring this continuum of theologically orthodox criticism should focus upon the circles surrounding key figures such as Archbishop James Usher and later in the century the Oxford critic John Mill.[7] Although this paper will not explore the nature of this orthodox scholarly enterprise it should be thought of as the backcloth to the examination of what non-orthodox critics attempted to achieve. Indeed, one of the suggestions made here will be that the vast quantity of philological, hermeneutic and textual scholarship undertaken by orthodox Anglican theologians became a resource that was vunerable to being plundered and publicised by critics of the established Church.[8]

Revising Protestant Certainties

Some of the first public moves against Protestant certainties and the authenticity of Scripture were made at two levels during the 1640s and 1650s. At a practical and popular level mechanic preachers, prophets and millenarians burnt, defaced and re-wrote the text of received Scripture.[9] Such was the orthodox fear of popular anti-scripturalism that the Blasphemy Acts of 1648 and 1650 placed at the centre of concern a defence of Holy Scripture: those who challenged the canon of the Bible would be subject to imprisonment and ultimately much more severe punishment.[10] Importantly this concern with defending the sanctity of Scripture was reiterated in stentorian terms in the rubric of the 1698 Blasphemy Act. Although the legal proscriptions against tampering with the text of Scripture were severe this did not restrain many inspired men and women throughout the period. An officer in the early 1650s was dismissed from his commision for insisting 'that the Scripture is no more to be beleeved but as the Turks Alchoron, or other books of men's writings, so far as it is truth, and that there are many things in it contradictory one place to another'.[11] A more interesting case can be found described in the autobiographical narrative of the Quaker Mary Penington whose transition from the Church of England to Quakerism was accompanied by an abandonment of faith in the Bible. As she became more disenchanted with the rituals and rubrics of the Laudian Church she literally deconstructed the sacred text by first tearing out of the bound volume 'the common prayer, the form of prayer, and also the singing psalms, as being the inventions of vain poets'. Ultimately she abandoned reading Scripture at all.[12] A more public and violent example of hostility towards the Bible can be found in the case of John Pennyman, merchant draper of the City of London who in the early 1670s repeatedly stated that it was his intention to burn the holy text in public at the Exchange as he had done to his collection of Quaker pamphlets. As Henry More commented in September 1670, 'Neither do I think that it is so far from the spiritt of a reall Quaker to burn the bible, when as the letter is so little believed by them. For that unbelief takes away the very sense of the bible, the fire consumes only the paper'.[13] At a more cerebral level Thomas Hobbes was responsible for launching a much more profound deconstruction of scriptural certainties in his *Leviathan* (1651).[14] Importantly in Chapter Thirty-two 'of the number, antiquity, scope, authority, and interpreters of the books of Holy Scripture' Hobbes made his point with almost uncharacteristic succinctness: 'who were the originall writers of the severall Books of Holy Scripture, has not been made evident by any sufficient testimony of other History, (which is the only proof of matter of fact); nor can be by any arguments of naturall reason'.[15] Hobbes continued to insist that the only real method for addressing issues of authors and composition was to examine the matter contained in the 'bookes themselves'. Famously he went on to suggest that the Pentateuch, the Books of Joshua, Samuel, Kings and Chronicles (among others) were probably written by others than those traditionally assumed to have composed them. As an important component of Hobbes' critique of protestant certainties not only did he raise questions about authorship but also about the 'authority' of received texts: as he put it 'It is a question much disputed between the divers sects of Christian Religion, *from whence the Scriptures derive their Authority*; which question is also propounded sometimes in other terms, as, *How wee know them to be the word of God*, or *Why we beleeve them to be so*'. Hobbes' repy to these typically blunt questions was simply: men could have no knowledge 'that they are God's word' but only 'beleefe' so the real question 'truly stated is, *by what authority they are made law*'. Scripture only became canonical or law by the authority of the sovereign within the Commonwealth.[16] Although the first canon had been drawn up in AD 364 by the Council of Laodicea, the implication for Hobbes was clear: there was an historicity to Scripture.

Hobbes' doubts about authorship and canonicity were not isolated in the 1650s. It is clear from the fragmentary surviving sources that between 1652 and 1657 many theologians and politicians in the Republic and the Protectorate were concerned about the authenticity of the public Bible. The Grand Committee for Religion summonsed printers who had issued defective editions 'grossely misprinted' and confiscated the faulty copies.[17] Later between 1656 and 1657 a subcommittee was convened, that included Brian Walton and Ralph Cudworth under the care of the Lord Commissioner Bustrode Whitelocke, to look into the possibilities of a new and more accurate translation of the Scriptures: it was only the dissolution of the Protectorate Parliament that rendered the business fruitless.[18] Calls for a reaffirmation of the text of Scripture can be found in the writings of more orthodox Anglican Churchmen like Robert Gell, sometime Chaplain to Archbishop Laud and vicar at St Mary Aldermanbury in the City of London, who in his 1659 essay argued that the King James version 'may be improved . . . by many instances'. Gell, in collaboration with Dr Thomas Drayton, William Parker and Richard Hunt, spent two sharp winters work researching the defects of the authorised version consulting variant editions (amongst many others) in Greek, French, Spanish, Italian, and High and Low Dutch. Mistranslations, misinterpretations and human deceit conspired to make the 'necessity of an exact and perfect translation of the Holy Bible' urgent. The wrested and partial translation of 1611 'speaks the language, and gives authority to one sect or another'. Gell's aspirations in cleansing Scripture were clear: to preserve a true text was essential to upholding the authority of the priesthood. Citing Malachi 2.7, 'They shall seek the law at the mouth of the Priest', Gell insisted that an accurate and authentic translation of Scripture was essential to reinforcing the authority of the Christian priesthood.[19] For Gell, only learned priests could give the true sense of the Bible.

Concern with the authenticity of received scripture, exemplified in Walton's polyglot edition published in six volumes between 1654 and 1657, was in one sense a result of the coincidence of the need for the Church to reinforce its social authority and the growth of scholarly interest in ancient scriptural manuscripts.[20] As Hobbes had already made clear there was a history to both the composition and reception of the Old and New Testaments. Walton's polyglot had used manuscripts in nine different languages: the New Testament appeared in Greek, Latin, Syriac, Arabic, Ethiopic and Persian. The libraries of Oxford and Cambridge, repositories of important manuscripts such as the Codices Beza and Alexandrinus, provided series of variant readings of a supposedly fixed Biblical text. Indeed Walton had included many of these variations in the Greek New Testament (borrowed from Usher) in volume six of his work. Here is clearly not the place to attempt any more than a superficial discussion of the impact of manuscripts on the Biblical culture of the period but clearly the availability of non-standard material, combined with the destabilisation of religious authority (at both the level of the printed word and as a social and political institution) provided in tandem a resource that the orthodox needed to integrate with established versions but also a potential source of hostile criticism.[21] In other words the mere existence of variant manuscripts combined with an increasingly sophisticated scholarly discourse meant that

ancient manuscripts and their interpretation became a cultural resource that
needed careful definition.

From Apocrypha to Apocryphal

One of the most powerful strategies adopted by non-orthodox writers was
to disinter scriptural material from the university libraries and private
archives that challenged the established canons. Debates about the
distinction between canonical and non-canonical scripture had persisted
from the early days of Christianity: doubts about the authority of the
Apocypha became more pronounced from the fourth century. As early as
AD 156 Montanus had attempted to redraft the number and scope of
authoritative scriptural texts.[22] The substitution of apocryphal for canonical
texts was one of the means that radical critics employed from the 1650s to
the 1700s to undermine the cultural power of the established Church.
Indeed the question of the sacredness of apocryphal literature had
bedevilled the established Church from the reformation period in England.
Throughout the later part of the sixteenth century precise Protestants had
objected against the inclusion of the Apocrypha in printed editions of the
Bible although the 39 Articles of the Church of England (Canon 6)
recognised that they were useful texts for the examples of life. Indeed the
Kalenders of readings from Scripture established by the Book of Common
Prayer (between 1561 and 1661) suggested that on at least fifty days of the
year lessons would be taken from the Apocryphal books. Archbishop
Abbott had forbidden the sale of Bibles without the Apocrypha as early as
1615, but from at least 1599 they were omitted from English editions of
the Geneva Bible, and from the 1620s were also being left out of some
printings of the Authorised Version. Biblical scholars such as Hugh
Broughton (1549–1612) had indicted the inclusion of Apocrypha with
canonical texts: as he commented 'all who hold the Apocrypha part of the
Holy Bible make God the author of lying fables and vain speech, whereby
wisdom would they should not come side by side with the Holy Books, nor
under the same roof'.[23] The Hebrew scholar John Lightfoot in a sermon to
the House of Commons in 1643 demanded the Apocrypha be left out of
printed editions and indeed the Long Parliament banned their use in
Church services after 1644: as the Westminster Confession insisted the
Apocrypha had no authority in the Church of God. John Vicars in his
Unwholesome henbane between two fragrant roses (1645) made the case
against the Apocrypha in no uncertain terms when addressing the
Westminster Assemby and Parliament: 'it is not only thus indecent and

uncomely, but indeed, most impious, and unlawful to misplace them in the midst of God's Book, or, indeed, in any part thereof'. The Apocrypha was 'meer humane stinking breath, between the two sweet and most sacred lips'. They were erroneous and deviant: contrived only to encourage popish superstition and formalism. Carrying on the work of the Reformation the apocryphal books had to be 'utterly expunged and expelled out of all Bibles'.[24] Even after the Restoration much controversy between Dissenter and Anglican was focused upon the re-establishment of the Apocrypha to the Church service.[25]

The simple point to be made here was that there was even in terms of the accepted biblical material disputes amongst the Godly about what might be counted as the word of God: defining the legitimate circumferance between scriptural and non-canonical texts was a profoundly problematic debate.[26] Defining the limits or inclusiveness of the canon was a critical enterprise. It was into this context that Samuel Fisher (1605–1665) projected his scholarship and criticism. Fisher's intellectual oddessy and ecclesiastical career is a valuable casestudy for the examination of transformations of radical protestants into radical critics in the crucible of the English Revolution. The son of a Northampton haberdasher Fisher was educated at Trinity College from 1623 but being puritanically inclined transfered to New Inn. By 1632 he had been made vicar at Lydd in Kent. From the early 1640s he became increasingly unorthodox: in 1643 much to the devout horror of the Churchwardens he allowed two Anabaptists messangers of God to use his pulpit at Lydd. By 1649 he had renounced his cure and was debating the merits of infant baptism with other ministers before huge crowds in Lydd market place.[27] In the 1650s he continued his polemics against the orthodox Church and travelled throughout northern and southern Europe. At the Restoration he again engaged in public disputes at Sandwich in Kent, eventually moving to London where he kept conventicles, and thereupon was imprisoned in Newgate. He died in a Southwark prison in the Great Plague of 1665.

Fisher has been subject to important examination by Christopher Hill and Richard Popkin who have both insisted upon the radical innovation of his critique of the Bible and his proximity and indeed intimacy with Spinozist arguments, especially in his massive *Rusticos ad Academicos* (1660). Fisher, opposing the collective arguments of four of the 'Clergy's Chieftains' John Owen, Thomas Danson, John Tombs and Richard Baxter, had in the latter work thrown doubt upon the accuracy of the received text because of textual variations and mistranslations. Indeed by comparing Fisher's criticism of the texts of the Bible with that of

Robert Gell's proposals for reforming the authorised translation it is possible to high light in the most defined chariascuro how theories of translation and Biblical scholarship were enmeshed with the politics of social authority and religion. For Gell the purpose of restoring the scriptural text was to disable the prerogatives of private opinion in interpretation. The fact that the spirit of opinion rather than the spirit of God guided the understandings of those who interpreteted the Bible meant that 'Africa semper aliquid apportat novi, some hideous shape or other daily is brought forth; and every one fathered on the Scripture'. Translation should avoid all rhetorical '*colours* in favour of *perspicacity*, as the best elegancy'. Plain work rather than fashionable embroidery was the divine method. For Gell the imperative of translation was to follow the 'clue of the original tongues': thus Hebrew texts should be rendered exactly into English without imposing our own sense upon it. As Gell acknowledged a literal translation rather than a stylish one would make the text uncouth and strange to the unlearned reader. This, for Gell, however was the central point. The unlearned private man did not have the authority to understand: that was the business of the priesthood. As he insisted, 'it will be the Preachers *duty*, *business*, and *comfort*, to explain it unto the people, together with the *Spiritual meaning of it*'. Gell reviled those who at least in their own opinion claimed to be so skillfull in the *Letter* of the Scripture. Without divine ordination these people perverted Scripture to their own by-ends and purposes, 'they make them speak everyone their *own sense* and *private interpretations*'. As he reiterated, 'Jesus maketh the Ministers of the New Testament able ministers, not of the Letter, but of the Spirit': understanding the Bible was not then a process of grammatical explication but a gift implicit in the *ordo* of priesthood.[28]

It is at this point that the difference between Gell and Fisher can be seen at its clearest. Fisher in the *Rusticus Ad Academicos* (1660) took as his starting point that the orthodox clergy claimed to be the 'misty ministers of the meer letter' while the Apostles had been ministers of the mystery of the New Testament or the Spirit.[29] It was Fisher's point (following Spinoza) that since the text or letter was corrupt the spirit of Scripture must exist outside of the pen and ink of manuscripts and bound volumes: thus the indeterminacy of the received text enfranchised the private spirit of each man. For Fisher, on the one hand, then the textual indeterminacy established by sacred scholarship and philological criticism was an argument for reforming the 'poor Priest-ridden British Nation'; for Gell, on the other hand, using much of the same technical scholarship, textual obscurity and imprecision reinforced the claims of the priesthood.

Central to part of Fisher's argument was a discussion of the concept of canonicity which he undermined by including extended discussion relating to the existence of other valuable scriptural texts regarded as non-canonical by orthodoxy.[30] Fisher considered 'some of thy Cloudy Conjectures & Conceits concerning the bounds of the Canon'. His main point was that the notion of canonicity was human — or more precisely priestly: as he explained, 'where learnest thou all these lessons, but from the Lectures and Lying Legends, and voluminious lexicons of the illiterate Literatists of the World, that are always laying on, and loading one another with their endless, boundless, and bottomless Scribles about the outward Original Text, and Transcriptions of the Scripture in their tedious Tomes, Talmuds, and Talmudical Traditions till they are lost from the very letter'.[31] The congregationally constituted, synodically composed, ecclesiastically authorised, clerically conceived canon was an obscure and partial thing. Who was it? Was it God, or was it man that set such distinct bounds to the Scripture, Is all Extant? All Remaining? were questions that exploded from Fisher's text.[32] His reply was devastatingly simple: 'There's not all in your Bible by much, and by how much who knows?'[33] To compound these points Fisher included lists of apocryphal works. So for example he lauded the 'Testament of the Twelve Patriarchs' which was 'now extant' and the Book of Enoch.[34] Importantly Fisher also commented upon New Testament apocrypha describing a list of material that included Paul's letters to the Laodiceans and to Seneca and the correspondence between King Agbar of Edessa and Christ.[35] An illustration of the attitude Fisher contrived towards orthodox understandings of the canon can be seen in his account of public debate with Thomas Danson at Sandwich about the authenticity of Paul's letters to the Laodiceans. Danson refused to acknowledge even the existence of such a text until one of the audience stood up, and said he had the book: it was Fisher's point not to probe too carefully the authenticity of the letters but merely to establish that there was at least a script to work with.[36] Generally it was Fisher's case to contrive enough doubt about the accuracy and comprehensivity of canonical scripture: he lambasted orthodox scholars who insisted they could establish a text with 'Sacred Truth and Certainty'. Theologians wandering from library to library collating and comparing might produce 'to a tittle entirely true and exactly corrected copies' but this was but the 'Dead Corps of Scripture'.[37]

Importantly Fisher probably popularised this attack upon the canon by publishing a much shorter and more accessible pamphlet that reiterated his point more concisely: the work is titled *Something Concerning*

Agbarus, Prince of the Edesseans and can probably be dated to 1660, although importantly there were reprints of it in 1680 and 1697 and there is some evidence that manuscript variants were in circulation both in England and the American colonies.[38] The text which also has material in common with works published by George Fox in 1659–1660 is intriguing.[39] Not only does it include transcriptions of the letters exchanged between Agbar and Christ, and Paul and the Laodiceans, but also a list of those scriptures which are mentioned, but not inserted in the Bible and several scriptures 'Corrupted by the Translators'.

That Fisher almost certainly took the Agbar material from Eusebius' *History of the Church* which included a transcription of the exchange between King Agbar the Black and Jesus is evidenced by the inclusion of Eusebius' commentary in the introduction to *Something Concerning Agbarus*.[40] Indeed although Fisher acknowledged both Jerome and Eusebius 'whose credit herein is not small' as ancient sources for the tradition the way in which he presented his copy emphasised the historical ambiguity of the republication. Fisher was concerned to stress the historical authenticity of his text: 'the Reader hath an approved Testimony of these things in writing, taken out of the recorded Monuments of the Princely City Edessa, for there are found inrowled in their publique Registry things of Antiquity, and which were done about Agbarus' time, yea and preserved unto this day'.[41] 'Yea and preserved unto this day' reinforced Fisher's intention of presenting the documents as historically accurate and authentic: as he continued 'there is no reason to the contrary but that we may have the epistles themselves, copyed out of their Registry, and translated by us out of the Syrian Tongue in this manner'. *The Letters of Agbarus* were translated word for word out of their original script. Fisher projected his work as accurate historical scholarship: the irony of this literary use of a language of scholarly authenticity is to be found in the fact that it was lifted from Eusebius' original history: without acknowledgement Fisher transformed Eusebius' words into his own voice. Fisher's pamphlet continued in the same vein of scholarly imposture with the transcription of Paul's epistle to the Laodiceans. As he noted, the epistle was found in the oldest Bible that was printed at Worms and in the Jerome Vulgate translated by John Hollybushe and printed in Southwark by James Nicholson in 1538, but more importantly 'in a certain Ancient Manuscript of the New Testament Text, which I have seen and can produce written in Old English 340 years since'. Cadbury suggests that the latter manuscript was probably a Wycliffite version that Fisher had access to.[42] The point again was that Fisher was popularising quite profound and academic knowledge: the thrust of his presentation of these partial and obscure texts was to emphasise their antiquity and genuineness. Having published such genuine transcripts of lost texts Fisher supplemented his case with a Catalogue of still more examples: the implication being that these scriptural materials could too be republished if they could only be found.[43] The intention of the work in destabilising the authenticity of the established Bible was further highlighted in the last section where Fisher included a short list of places in the authorised version where mistranslation had corrupted the original meaning.

Clearly Fisher's text could be read in a number of ways. At one level *Something Concerning Agbarus* was simply making the intensely intricate and learned polemic of *Rusticos ad Academicos* available to a non-learned audience. In the latter Fisher had simply stated that the *Letters of Agbarus* were as 'worthy (as particular as it is) to stand in your standard, and claim a room in your Canon, as that particular letter of Paul to Philemon'.[44] Crucially, in the shorter work, Fisher did not interlard his transcriptions, lists and catalogues with any pronounced authorial instruction: that is he did not point explicitly to the subversive implications of the work but simply presented the material for private understanding. This undirected interpretation could have read the meaning of the text in a number of ways. Fisher himself did point rather quietly to one possible implication in citing 2 Timothy 3.16 'All Scripture given by inspiration of God, is profitable to teach, to improve' perhaps suggesting that he was merely reclaiming scriptural material for Godly purposes.[45] Clearly, as Cadbury acutely proposed,[46] the publication of the *Letters of Agbarus*, Christ and Paul in a double-columned format which could have easily been inserted into the the canonical editions was not only an intellectual threat to Scripture but also a practical assault on the canon of the orthodox Bible. Fisher was not only propagating new *sacred* material for edification, but at the same time he was also suggesting that the received canon was defective and/or corrupted by proposing a list of other texts that either existed or had been lost. Fisher's pamphlet not only gave the unsuspecting and unlearned reader something new (but authentic) to examine, but also subtly insinuated a doubt about the comprehensiveness of the received text.

Fisher's *Something Concerning Agbarus* is an intriguing text. It shows that he had access to a series of manuscript and printed sources: for example he cites from the Codex Beza and Syriac and Wycliffite editions as well as early printings by Tyndale and Coverdale. In the case of the Letters to and from Agbar Fisher uses Eusebius as his source complemented by 'Jerome and other grave writers'. Contemporary scholarship suggests that the Agbar text originated in second century Eddessean desires to establish lineage with the primitive church. Although the text survives in Syriac, Greek, Latin, Armenian, Arabic, Coptic, Slavonic and Irish it was rejected by the Gelasian decree as apocryphal.[47] Orthodox scholarly opinion following the humanist scholarship of Lorenzo Valla (via Erasmus' annotations) also exposed it as forgery. It is unclear whether Fisher believed in the text or not: what is clear however is that the form in which he presented it to a non-learned public meant that it looked authentic on the printed page.

Cataloguing the Apocrypha

Trying to assess the impact of Fisher's assault upon the Bible within the limited confines of this piece is difficult. Fisher's works were republished in 1680 and 1697. It is clear that other Quakers published apocryphal texts in the 1650s and after the Restoration, as well as making the more general arguments against the comprehensivity and accurancy of the Authorised Version.[48] The Quaker assault upon the Bible has not been treated as anything other than a marginal aspect of their confessional history. However if the writings of Fisher are considered in a wider cultural context than simply that of Quakerism it is possible to suggest that the particular assault upon orthodox scripture was the product of a much more profound and persistent radical tradition. Too commonly historians have adopted an interpretative myopia when examining the religious radicalism of the 1650s. The world may have been temporarily inverted in the interregnum but was firmly placed upon its feet in 1660. Although Ranters, Quakers and Fifth Monarchists may have terrorised the souls of orthodox Christians these were projected rather than real anxieties. The history of the Restoration has thus become testimony to the muscularity of the Church of England and the defeat of both speculative and practical radicalism. The radicalism that survived 1660 was resolutely secular in political idiom.[49] Part of the suggestion in this piece will be that try as they might historians of the seventeenth century should not (just like the Church men of the period could not) underestimate the impact and cultural consequences of the 1650s in determining many of the intellectual and literary problems that confronted the pillars of political orthodoxy. The polemics of men like Fisher against the Bible provided both a literary resource and cultural example for later generations of radical critics. This is not to suggest some form of teleological narrative where radical religion of the 1650s mutated into the critical freethought of the 1700s but simply to point to continuities of discourse in the period. Again to reiterate the point I do not intend to imply that there was (somehow) a causal relationship between the intentions of authors in the 1650s and those in the 1700s, but that the cultural crisis of the 1650s did in some sense redefine the mental and cultural landscape which enabled later writers to think and argue in new ways.

As a case study the reputation and criticism of the letters exchanged between King Agbar and Christ also form a convenient literary bridge between the days of Samuel Fisher and the times of John Toland.[50] Indeed there does seem to be an important and unacknowledged intellectual affinity between Fisher the collaborator with Spinoza and Toland whose nick-name was 'Tractatus-Theologicus-Politicus'.[51] The specific congruence between the intentions and polemics of the two men can be proposed by a consideration of the relationship between Fisher's *Something Concerning Agbarus* (1660) and Toland's *A Catalogue of Books . . . as Truly or Falsely ascrib'd to Jesus Christ, his Apostles, and other eminent persons* (1726)[52] and *Nazarenus* (1718). Toland the scholar and freethinker needs little introduction but his *Catalogue* probably does. The full length work was published in the posthumous collection of works in 1726 but had its origins in works written defending John Milton's life and works in the late 1690s. Toland had in passing reflected upon the supposititious Royal authorship of *Eikon Basilike* (1649) and drawn a parallel between such secular forgeries and the foisting of illegitimate works upon Christ and the Apostles. His original comments both on Charles I's penning of the *Eikon* and apocryphal scriptural works fomented much orthodox complaint that Toland was challenging the received canon of sacred literature.[53] Reluctant to withdraw from a contentious debate Toland girded his pen with scholarship (both patristic and modern criticism) and redrafted and much expanded his orginal *Catalogue*. Citing a full range of antique sources as well as cutting edge modern criticism such as Simon, Grabe, Sykes, Fabricius and Pfassius, Toland simply compiled a list of potentially sacred material, that drew very little distinction between items that were clearly spurious, non-existent or downright fictitious. Indeed the very literary form of Toland's catalogue was provocative: as David McKitterick has pointed out, the 1690s heralded an expansion of scholarly cataloguing as a means of organising knowledge. Edward Bernard's attempt at a national union catalogue of manuscripts in Britain was intended to facilitate orthodox, pious, respectable scholarship. Although Toland's literary form adopted the orthodox style of a catalogue its intentions were anything but pious.[54]

The fifty-page work catalogued Toland's reading of a variety of Biblical criticism and historical commentary. It was projected as a work of scholarship. Toland proudly acknowledged the reception his researches had received upon the continent: Professor Fabricius of Hamburg had treated it with particular favour while Christopher Pfaffius, Professor at Turinge, called it a 'remarkable Catalogue' in his own critical dissertations upon the New Testament.[55] The structure of the catalogue from Chapter I to XV ran through the list of spiritual authors starting of with Christ and Mary, and working through the apostles from Peter to Barnabas. Chapter XVI dealt rather contentiously with various Jewish texts (some of which his dismissed as pious Christian frauds) before Toland jogged his own elbow with the reminder, 'But I forget that I am in this CATALOGUE reciting the spurious books of the Christians, and not of the Jews, who were very near as fertil and expert in forgeries'.[56] Chapters XVII to XX dealt with 'General Pieces' a bland title that allowed Toland to discuss works such as the Gospel of the Hebrews, the Apostolic Constitutions, the Gospel of Nicodemus and the Epistle of Lentulus. The final analysis leapt 'over the monstrous and infinite impostures down from the fourth century to this day' to expose the gospel 'of his own framing' that the Jesuit Xavier imposed upon Persian converts to Catholicism. Altogether Toland provided critical discussions of nearly 150 distinct apocryphal texts. Peter had fourteen texts fathered upon him, while Paul was the supposed author of at least nineteen works.

Toland's catalogue 'to modern readers' might seem a rather dull work: but every entry and the very structure of the list would have needled orthodox scholars and theologians. The simplicity of the organisation of the text, title of apocrypha, sources and references for the literary tradition, and occasionally direction to modern editions or extant manuscripts, conspired to leave the unlearned reader with the impression that there existed, or had existed, a plethora of spurious and fictional holy material. With each entry the principle of an authorised canonical scripture was rendered more fragile. Part of the literary power of the catalogue was its simplicity. Toland baldly listed the title and its bibliographic sources invariably without passing scholarly comment. The example of the entries for Paul provide an apt illustration of Toland's deliberate technique of scholarly austerity. Take entry 3 'THE *Epistle of* PAUL *to the Laodiceans*. Coloss. 4. 12. Tertul. adversus Macion. l. 5. c. 11,17. Hieronym. in Catal. c. 5. Epiphan. Haeres. 42. n. 9:& alibi. 'Philastr. Haeres. 88. Theodret. Commentar. ad Coloss. 4. 12. tom. 3 Legantur etiam Theophylactus, Gregorius Magnus, & Council. Nicen. II. act. 6. part. 5'. Here the title of the text is followed by a dense thicket of references. The learned reader might examine the supporting evidence and assess their value. The unlearned reader might simply deduce that the scholarly references (especially the scriptural reference to Coloss. 4.12 which does not obviously support the existence of an Epistle to the Laodiceans) uphold the genuiness of the assertion. The next entry suggests the existence of a third epistle to the Thessalonians and then continues that this was 'forg'd in his own life time, as some deduce from Thes. 2.2'. Again Toland accrued credit to his scholarship by using authentic scriptural texts to establish the authority (or not) of suppositious works. Two last examples will illustrate the literary trickery of the work:

> 8. ARCHBISHOP USHER, and Dr. JOHN GREGORY, have seen an Armenian Manuscript of Sir GILBERT NORTH'S, where there was an *Epistle of the Corinthians* to PAUL, with PAUL'S *answer* to the same: and both these *Epistles* are lately publish'd at Amsterdam, in the Armenian and Latin tongues, by Mr. DAVID WILKINS, now Doctor of Divinity, and Library Keeper at Lambeth.

> 10. THE *Epistles of* PAUL *to* SENECA, with those *of* SENECA *to* PAUL. These have been so far approv'd, that JEROME, on this account, places SENECA among the Christian writers, if not Saints: and they are defended as genuine by FABER *d'Estaples*, SIXTUS SENESIS, ALPHONSIUS SALMERON, and others. The ancient authorities for them are, *Hieronym. in Catal.* c.12. *Augustin. de Civit. Deo* L 6. c.10. *Idem in Epist.* 15. *Edit Benedictin. scilicet ad Macedonium. Joan Sarisberiens. in Polycrat.* l. 8. c.13. If I may reckon this last among the ancients? The *Epistles* however are still extant.[57]

In entry 8, Toland implicates scholars of high reputation into his scheme: Archbishop Usher and John Gregory have seen the manuscript in question. The authenticity and reality of the document is further established by the fact that a critical edition has been published by the librarian of Lambeth Palace. Again there is no assessment of the value of these remarks, just simple statement: the mere mention of Usher, might to the unlearned, vouchsafe the authenticity of the ancient manuscript, Wilkins publication made it potentially available to everyone. In entry 10 Toland's straightfaced lack of embellishment reached a high point. The texts under dicussion, the exchange of letters between Paul and Seneca, had been subjected to profound scholarly criticism, and although there was an humanist tradition that had insisted upon Christianising Seneca, by the 1700s the commonplace view would have denied their authenticity.[58] Again Toland plainly rehearsed the modern and ancient sources and concluded the entry with 'The *Epistles* however are still extant'. No discussion, just assertion masked by a veneer of scholarly reference.

The point to be emphasised here is that although the catalogue may strike the modern reader as a profoundly dull piece of work it was in fact, given the scholarly conventions of contemporary Augustan literary discourse, an intensely sophisticated irritant for orthodox readers. The catalogues of theologian critics like Grabe and Dodwell were discursive and analytical: they presented collations of ancient manuscripts with judicious and careful assessments of their historicity and authorship.[59] A Grabe or even a Whiston might write many hundreds of pages reviewing the evidences for the authenticity of just one text. Toland pillaged these researches and abstracted them into short digests that evaded the scholarly delicacy of the originals.

Important for establishing a link with the sort of cultural criticism that Fisher engaged in the first item on Toland's list was 'The Letter of Jesus in answer to that of Abgarus King of Edessa', supported by citations from Eusebius, Nicephorus, Procopius, Cedrenus and Constantinus Porphyrogennetus and finished with the simple word 'extant'. Indeed a rough comparison between the catalogue of books not inserted in the Bible listed in Fisher's work and that of Toland shows an intriguing coincidence. Four of the missing texts, the Revelation of St Peter, the Epistle of Barnabas, the Prophecy of Enoch and the Epistle to the Corinthians, occur on both lists. Toland also gives full coverage to works mentioned elsewhere in Fisher's work — Paul's letters to the Laodiceans and to Seneca, the Letter of Lentulus and the Testament of the Twelve Patriarchs. Indeed, as already discussed above, one of the intriguing aspects of Toland's catalogue is the problem of trying to distinguish his research from the publications of clearly orthodox Biblical critics. A case in point to illustrate this ambiguity concerns commentary upon the *Letters of Agbarus* undertaken by orthodox divines: John Ernest Grabe, closely associated with the Oxford circle surrounding John Mill, published the text in his *Spicilegium* (1698) as did Fabricius in his *Codex Apochryphus Novi Testamenti* (1719). Both these scholars were devout Christians and accomplished Biblical critics. As Grabe's work transcribing the Septuaguint from the *Codex Alexandrinus* suggests (1707–1709), the intellectual and theological concerns of this group of scholar theologians were to preserve the word of God in its most authentic form. To this end they produced comprehensive and learned, but importantly Latin, discussions of the textual evidences and testimonies concerning particular documents. Toland on the other hand, clearly competant in his own right in the fields of linguistics and criticism, not only plundered the orthodox volumes of scholarship for textual variations and potentially controversial documents, but then published such commentatries and discussions in plain and lucid English, rendering the scholarship transparent to non-expert comprehension. Although much more comprehensive than Fisher's project Toland's intentions seem to have had a similar purpose and one correctly identified by clerical contemporaries of undermining the established canon with the tools of biblical scholarship.

Assessing the relationship between Fisher's and Toland's intentions can only be speculative. There is little direct evidence that Toland knew Fisher's work although it was available in recently published collections. Certainly Fisher and Toland shared a common intellectual interest and perhaps personal connection with Spinoza and his circle. Fisher collaborated with Spinoza in the publication of a Hebrew edition of Margaret Fell's *A Loving Saluatation*.[60] Although Toland never had direct contact with Spinoza he certainly did know the philosopher's physician Dr Henri Morelli who was involved in the clandestine circulation of irreligious ideas.[61] That Toland was familiar with Quaker writings and attitudes towards apocryphal texts is also hinted at in the *Catalogue* where the *Epistle of Lentulus* was acknowledged as text that 'was formerly in high credit with the Quakers'.[62] In some sense, given the Spinozist connection, it might be possible to see some sort of lineage between Fisher and Toland. This is not however to suggest that Toland simply acted as a legatee of the Quaker. Although both writers were engaged in a similar polemic against the literary foundations of the authority of the established Church the audience for the different authors was distinct. Fisher's work was contrived as part of a confessional polemic against the corruption of the Presbyterians and Anglicans. The tone of *Rusticos ad Academicos* was sharp and brontolare: the text is one that confronted and ridiculed orthodox beliefs. It would be difficult to imagine an unsuspecting reader picking up Fisher's writings and mistaking them for a calm detached review of the problems of canonicity and Biblical criticism. Toland's work, on the other hand, was exactly calculated for such a reception. By assuming the literary style of detached unembellished criticism it seems likely that Toland hoped to insinuate doubts about the established canon. Far from representing himself as defending any particular confessional interest Toland constructed the *Catalogue* as a work of objective discussion: he deliberately set out to engage with scholarly discourse. When reading Fisher's writings it is difficult not perceive his point; with Toland's *Catalogue* the simple listing of titles, references and classmarks devolved the meaning of the text away from the author to the reader. This was precisely to Toland's wider polemical purpose: that every individual might create their own sense of religious conviction rather than being led by a *ecclesia docens*.

Practical Criticism

In conclusion it is important to consider the relationship between orthodox biblical scholarship and religious dissidence in this period. The affinities between Fisher's and Toland's strategies of publicising and disseminating non-canonical material are ample testimony to the continuities of the radical attack upon clerical orthodoxy between the 1650s and the 1700s. The one question that remains concerns the irreligious intentions and motivations of these writers: how sincere was Fisher when he republished the *Letters of Agbarus*? The case of Toland is even more ambiguous. His reputation as a scholar was widely acknowledged although (almost) always invariably with a rider that doubted his committment to established Christianity. This strategy of popularisation worked upon two levels: the intellectual and the practical. Opening the question of the authenticity of established Scripture posed a theoretical doubt, but publishing vernacular extracts of non-canonical texts gave literate but non-scholarly readers real material to consider. Fisher achieved this on a small scale with his publications of the *Letters of Agbarus,* Toland was to go one step further in his publication of *Nazarenus* (1718). Directly related to the project of the *Catalogue* in *Nazarenus* Toland took the opportunity to give an extended account of two early (apocryphal) Christian texts, the Gospel of Barnabas and 'an Irish manuscript of the 4 Gospels' described by Toland as the 'Codex Armachanus'.[63] Here is not the place to give a detailed analysis of Toland's reading of these two apocryphal manuscripts. It is enough to say that in *Nazarenus* Toland brought to practical fruition some of the suggestions he made in the *Catalogue* by disinterring two manuscripts which he had located in continental archives and publishing them in the literary style of orthodox biblical criticism. However, much to the devout disgust of many churchmen, Toland's expert hermeneutics were refined to produce an argument that overturned many of the shibboleths of orthodox Christian doctrine and ecclesiology. Priestcraft and clericalism were refuted: the Church was not originally 'a political empire, or an organis'd society with a proper subordination of officers and subjects; but the congregation of the faithful thro-out the world'.[64] Original Christianity had none of the liturgies or rituals of either contemporary Catholicism or Protestantism: 'faith consisted in a right notion of God, and the constant practice of Virtue'.[65] Once again a series of political and theological arguments had been built on the foundations of biblical criticism.

The question remains about the priority of scholarship and dissidence in the thought of people like Fisher and Toland. Did their readings of ancient manuscripts and learned commentaries lead them to radical criticisms, or was the rhetoric of Biblical criticism a convenient and effective instrument to project their non-orthodox opinions? One answer to such an inquiry might point to the changing cultural context of Biblical scholarship in the period. The long legacy of humanist interest in the manuscript remnants of antiquity, combined with the pious injunctions of a Church that needed a primitive heritage produced a literary culture encumbered with the dusty odour of codex and documents. The spirit of the antiquarian collector melded with the Protestant historical ideology of *renovatio* produced a cultural infrastructure of historical artefacts that became the subject of intense scholarly scrutiny and polemical struggle.[66] Put simply, because of the endeavours of men like William Laud and James Usher, by the mid-seventeenth century, there were many collections of sacred and holy manuscripts deposited in private, college and national archives that became the focus of earnest scholarly and theological interest.[67] A brief illustration of these cultural practices can be seen in the account of Zacharius Conrad Von Uffenbach's travels around the libraries and museums of England in the summer of 1710. Visiting various Oxford and Cambridge college collections Von Uffenbach made it his business to search out the oldest or most eminent manuscripts: a Wycliffite Bible at Emmanuel, the Baroccian Mss at the Bodeliean, Saxon Gospels in London, and the high point of his visit a meeting with Dr John Grabe in October 'where we at last saw the Codex Alexandrinus'.[68] Von Uffenbach, a reknowned collector of manuscripts and books himself, clearly had a scholarly map of important texts to examine while in England. In examining the holdings of the Oxbridge colleges Von Uffenbach was concerned to explore and assess the authenticity of the texts themselves and scholarly opinion about them. He was keen to examine the Codex Alexandrinus and also to meet and discuss the Biblical researches of John Mill. From the times of Walton's polyglot there seems to have been an almost collective enterprise of collecting and collating sacred materials into what Fisher vilified as an 'exact copy'. The business of discovery, criticism and assimilation of ancient sacred texts was considered part of the intellectual economy of religious life. Reinforcing and establishing an authentic and accurate text was essential to refurbishing and maintaining the social and political authority of the established Church and priesthood.[69]

Scholars, theologians and critics who engaged in analysis and commentary on ancient texts were not simply undertaking literary studies, but given the bibliocratic nature of the Church, were actually employed in activities that fashioned the cultural dimensions of social power.[70] Biblical scholarship and criticism, then, ought not to be thought of as a pure discipline independent of politics or theology but as a literary technology for establishing where the authoritative power of Scriptural interpretation resided.[71]

Thinking about Biblical criticism and scholarship not just in terms of literary encounters but as part of a debate about the location and distribution of cultural power must cause some revision of the nature of the radical attack on organised religion (for convenience sake it can be labelled deism). It is perhaps an historical commonplace that a central plank of the deist attack on organised religion was a rejection of revelation. As one commentator has recently put it, 'the characteristic current of mainstream deism [was] a negative rejection of revealed truth'. This rejection was contrived in terms of a rational challange to the veracity of the mysteries of revealed doctrines: reason was above religion.[72] Although there is clearly much sense in this analysis, to insist that the deist assault upon scripture was simply the product of rational discourse would be an overstatement. Central to the tradition of the 1650s (Hobbes, Spinoza and Fisher) was an historical, rather than a purely rational, critique of Scripture. Similarly with the writings and criticism of John Toland (carrying on the Hobbist and Spinozist traditions): the critique of orthodoxy was borne not from reason alone, but from the results of textual exegesis. Toland employed the very same tools that orthodox Biblical critics used for very different purposes: he, and others, were not stepping outside the cultural parameters of orthodox discipline but bending them to new purposes. What Fisher and Toland undertook was to challenge the fundamentalism of Anglican Biblical criticism not by rejecting revelation but by extending the textual basis for what revelation was on to uncertain grounds. That this sort of enterprise might be designed for devout purposes is clear from the examples of men like William Whiston, who, appealing to the testimony of 'original' documents like the *Apostolic Constitutions*, attempted to reform the doctrines and institutions of the Church of England.[73] Although it is not possible to ascribe the same level of piety to either Fisher's or Toland's ambitions and intentions, it is important to acknowledge the methods they adopted in their attempted revisions of established religion. It is possible, at least in the case of John Toland, to write with a little more confidence about the irreligious intentions of his public biblical criticism. In October

1701, while on a diplomatic mission relating to the Hanoverian Succession, Toland engaged in private discussion with Isaac Beausobre, an Huguenot cleric at the court of Sophia, electress of Hanover, about the authenticity of Scripture. Although Toland initially acknowledged that he was a Christian he expressed that 'il avoit de grande scruples sur l'authorité des livres du N. Testament'. While he commenced his discussion by casting doubts upon specific texts (2 Peter and parts of the Gospel of Matthew) the results of his arguments suggested that much of Scripture was little more than fable and popular superstitition. It was Beausobre's opinion that after two hours intense discussion that Toland was a man of little or no religion who had 'rendre L'Ecriture douteuse'.[74] Further evidence of the gap between Toland's published attitude towards Scripture and the true extent of his private opinions can be explored in two other manuscript pieces. One of Toland's favourite past-times was composing rough plans for new works usually in the form of a draft title page and list of chapter headings: 'Christopaedia: or an account of the puerile studies of JESUS CHRIST' is one of the most contentious of his proposals. Given the proposed content it is hardly surprising that he never dared to publish such a work.[75] Pretending to translate the work from a German text Toland intended to discuss a non-scriptural history of Christ drawing in particular on the messiah's books, tomes and manuscripts (27 volumes in all!). The publication of such a work could have been no other than an attempt to parody the life of Christ by employing deeply suspect, if not downright forged, historical materials. Importantly the one piece of apocryphal material Toland named was 'an Epistle to Abgarus King of Edessa'. In another unnoticed manuscript Toland adopted a less ridiculous tone towards the issue of canonicity as a direct response to criticism of his *Amyntor*: the privacy of his own notes however allowed him far more license than he had employed in his published texts. In an extended commentary upon the orthodox theologian Henry Dodwell's views on the canon employing the full rigour of a Spiniozist and Simonian vocabulary, Toland not only exposed the historical uncertainty of the formation of the Protestant canon, but also suggested that the very notion of a universal revelation in the form of scripture was deeply problematic if not actively unlikely.[76] There can be small doubt then that Toland's private convictions led him to articulate profound scepticism about the divinity of the text of revelation. There is similarly little doubt that Toland adopted an explicitly Spinozist attitude towards the heuristical function of Scripture.[77] Knowing Toland's private opinions about the authenticity of Scripture thus allows a greater insight into the exoteric purpose of his publication of *Nazarenus*. On one level

Toland was engaging in deliberate literary forgery but as Grafton has discussed in other contexts this 'forgery' had explicitly pragmatic purposes in undermining popular perceptions of canonicity and the authenticity of scripture.[78]

1 See *Catalogue of Marsh's Library*. Much work needs to be undertaken analysing the nature of the collection. It is clear the library held not only orthodox but also many volumes of heterodox material. Much of the latter may have come from the library of Richard Smith: see E.G. Duff, 'The Library of Richard Smith', *The Library* 8 (1907), pp. 113–133, and J.A.I. Champion and R.H. Popkin, 'Bibliography and Irreligion: Richard Smith's 'Observations on the Report of a Blasphemous Treatise by some affirmed to have been of late years published in print of three grand impostors' c1671', *The Seventeenth Century* 10 (1995), pp. 77–99.

2 See S.Hutton, 'Science, Philosophy, and Atheism: Edward Stillingfleet's defence of religion', in R.H. Popkin (ed.), *Scepticism and Irreligion in the Late Seventeenth Century* (Leiden, 1993), pp. 102-120; 'Edward Stillingfleet, Henry More, and the decline of *Moses Atticus*: a Note on Seventeenth Century Anglican Apologetics' in R. Kroll, R. Ashcraft, P. Zagorin (eds.), *Philosophy, Science and Religion in England 1640–1700* (Cambridge, 1992), pp. 68–84. See also R.T. Carroll, *The Commonsense Philosophy of Religion of Bishop Edward Stillingfleet* (The Hague, 1975); R.H. Popkin, 'The Philosophy of Bishop Stillingfleet' *Journal of the History of Philosophy*, 9 (1971), pp. 303–319.

3 E. Stillingfleet, *Origines Sacrae* (1680 edition) Preface 1, main text 2.

4 E. Stillingfleet, *A Rational Account of the Grounds of Protestant Religion* (1710 edition) pp.195–196.

5 For Stillingfleet's polemic against the Socianianism of men like Johan Crell and other radical biblical critics see G. Reedy, *The Bible and Reason. Anglicans and Scripture in Late Seventeenth Century England* (Philadelphia, 1985) *passim* but also pp. 145–156.

6 For two important contributions see D. Katz, 'Isaac Vossius and the English Biblical Critics 1670–1689' and J. Force, 'Biblical Interpretation, Newton and English Deism' in R.H. Popkin (ed.), *Scepticism and Irreligion*. See also C. Hill, *The English Bible and the Seventeenth Century Revolution* (1993).

7 A brief sense of the community of scholars focused upon the person of James Usher can been achieved by examining his correspondence: see *The Life of James Usher* (1686). Many thanks to Michael Hunter for drawing my attention to these materials. For the later period the context of orthodox scholarship in the 1690s and 1700s can be reconstructed from (amongst others) the letters of John Locke and Isaac Newton as well as the diaries and remarks of Thomas Hearne. I am currently engaged in exploring these connections.

8 For the context to this attack upon the Church of England, see J.A.I. Champion, *The Pillars of Priestcraft Shaken. The Church of England and its Enemies 1660–1730* (Cambridge, 1992).

9 See C. Hill, *The World Turned Upside Down* (1972); idem, *The English Bible*; N. Smith, *Perfection Proclaimed* (Oxford, 1989); idem *Literature and Revolution* (Yale, 1994).

10 For the text of the law see C.H. Firth and R.S. Rait, *Acts and Ordinances of the Interregnum 1642–1660* (1911) 3 volumes.

11 See *A List of some of the Grand Blasphemers and Blasphemies, which was given to the Committee for Religion* (1654).

12 *Experiences in the life of Mary Penington Written by herself* (London, 1911) p. 26.

13 S. Hutton (ed.), *The Conway Letters* (Oxford, 1992) pp. 306 and 512.

14 For Hobbes' attitudes towards Biblical Criticism see Champion, *Pillars of Priestcraft*; A.P. Martinich, *The Two Gods of Leviathan. Thomas Hobbes on Religion and Politics* (Cambridge, 1992) Chapter 11; D. Johnson, *The Rhetoric of Leviathan* (Princeton, 1986); L. Strauss, *Spinoza's Critique of Religion* (New York, 1965) has some useful passages comparing Hobbes and Spinoza on scripture.

15 T. Hobbes, *Leviathan*, ed. R. Tuck (Cambridge, 1991) p. 261.

16 Hobbes, *Leviathan*, pp. 266–267 and 356.

17 See J. Stoughton *Religion in England, from the opening of the Long Parliament to the end of the Eighteenth Century* (1881) II 142–143, see also 96. See *Commons Journals*, 20th November 1656 (at 456) and 11th June 1657 (at 554) for concerns about misprinted Bibles. For earlier Parliamentary debates about translation see *Commons Journals* 11 Jan 1653 and 4 March 1653. For further details

see Thomas Burton's account in *The Diary of Thomas Burton*, ed. J.T. Rutt, 4 volumes (1828) I, pp. 348, 351n, and 352. See also *CSPD* 21 October 1656 for the composition of the committee on religion.

18 *Commons Journals*, p. 351.

19 See R. Gell, *An Essay toward the Amendment of the last English Translation of the Bible, or a Proof, by many instances, that the last Translation of the Bible into English may be improved* (London, 1659) xxv, xxvi, xxxvi.

20 For a general discussion of Walton see A. Fox, *John Mill and Richard Bentley* (Oxford, 1954) pp. 47–49.

21 Identifying where the different codices were would be an important project towards establishing who had access to the material. A start can be made for the later seventeenth century by consulting the Unitarian Joseph Hallet's (1691–1744) *Index to Mill* (1728) which includes an appendix with lists of mss and library locations.

22 See J.N.D. Kelley, *Early Christian Doctrines* (London, 1980) Chapter 3.

23 D. Norton, *A History of the Bible as Literature. From Antiquity to 1700* (Cambridge, 1993) p. 139.

24 J. Vicars, *Unwholesome henbane between two fragrant roses. or reasons and grounds proving the unlawful and corrupt and most erroneous Apocrypha between the two most pure and sacred Testaments* (London, 1645) pp. 2, 3, and 7–8.

25 See B. Metzger, *An Introduction to the Apocrypha* (OUP, 1957) pp.190–198; F.F. Bruce, *The Canon of Scripture* (1988) pp. 105–109; F. Procter and W.H. Frere, *A New History of the Book of Common Prayer* (1961) pp. 172–173 and 378. See also W. H. Daubney, *The Use of the Apocrypha in the Christian Church* (Cambridge, 1900).

26 See B.F. Westcott, *A General Survey of the History of the Canon of the New Testament* (7th edition, Cambridge, 1896).

27 See for a context to Fisher's confrontations A. Hughes, 'The Pulpit Guarded: confrontations between Orthodox and Radicals in Revolutionary England' in A. Laurence, W.R. Owens, and S. Sim (eds) *John Bunyan and his England 1628–88* (London, 1990), pp. 31–50.

28 R. Gell, *An Essay toward the Amendment of the last English Translation of the Bible, or a Proof, by many instances, that the last Translation of the Bible into English may be improved* (1659) Preface ii–iii, xxvi, xxix, xxxv.

29 S. Fisher, *Rusticos ad Academicos* (1660) To the Reader pp. 31–32. For a fuller discussion of Fisher see R.H. Popkin, 'Spinoza and Samuel Fisher', *Philosophia*, 15 (1985), pp. 219-234, and C. Hill, *The World Turned Upside Down* (London, 1972) Chapter 11.

30 For more detail on Fisher see W.C. Braithwaite, *The Beginnings of Quakerism* (2nd Edition, London, 1979) pp. 288–294; A. Wood, *Athenae* III col 700–703; N. Penney (ed.) *The Journal of George Fox* (Cambridge, 1911), I p. 429; of particular importance for the question of Fisher and apocrypha is H.J. Cadbury, 'Early Quakerism and Uncanonical Lore', *Harvard Theological Review* XL (1947), pp. 177–205.

31 S. Fisher, *The Testimony of Truth Exalted* (London, 1679) *Ad Academicos*, pp. 264 and 268.

32 ibid., pp. 269 and 274–275.

33 ibid., pp. 274–275.

34 ibid., pp. 274–275.

35 ibid., pp. 277 and 281–289. On the Epistle from Laodicea see J.B. Lightfoot, *St Paul's Epistles to the Colossians and to Philemon* (London, 1875) pp. 340–366.

36 Fisher, *Ad Academicos*, p. 282.

37 ibid., pp. 299–300.

38 See Cadbury, 'Early Quakerism'.

39 See G. Fox, *The Great Mystery of the Great Whore Unfolded and Antichrist's Kingdom revealled unto destruction* (1659) in G. Fox, *Works*, volume III (Philadelphia, 1831: new edition 1990) at pp. 581–583.

40 See Eusebius, *The History of the Church*, G.A. Williamson (ed.) (1981) pp. 65–70. Translations of Eusebius were widely available in the mid 1650s.

41 *Something Concerning Agbarus* p. 2; compare with Eusebius *History*, p. 66.

42 For details see Cadbury, 'Early Quakerism', pp. 186–187 esp. footnotes pp. 26–28.

43 It is perhaps worth giving the full list of Biblical references included in Fisher (p. 8): Jude 14 – The Prophecy of Enoch; 2 Chron. 20.34 – The Book of Jehu; Num. 21.14 –The Book of the Battles of the Lord; 2 Chron. 9.29 Nathan the Prophet, the Book of Iddo, the Prophesie of Abijab; 2 Chron. 12.15 Shemaiah the Prophet; 2 Sam. 1.18 – Book of Jashar; 1 Chron. 29.29 – Book of Gad; 1 Cor 5.9 – Epistle to the Corinthian, the Books of Henoch; 1 Kings 4.32–33 – the Books of Solomon, the Epistle of Barnabas.

44 Fisher, *ad Academicos*, p. 277.

45 The *AV* reads 'All Scripture is given by inspiration of God, and is profitable for doctrine . . .'

46 Cadbury, 'Early Quakerism', p. 187.

47 See *Dictionary of Christian Biography*; M.R. James, *The Apocryphal New Testament* (Oxford, 1924) pp. 476–77; J.K. Elliott, *The Apocryphal New Testament* (Oxford, 1993) p. 538; E. Henneck et al, *New Testament Apocrypha* (1963) pp. 438–39. For background on the Agbar legend see J.B. Segal, *Edessa. 'The Blessed City'* (Oxford, 1970). May thanks to J. Phillips for this reference.

48 For example as well as owning, publishing and circulating in manuscript editions of the Testament of the Twelve Patriarchs and the Book of Enoch, works such as the Letters between Paul and Seneca, and the Gospel of Nicodemus were disseminated: see Cadbury, 'Early Quakerism', pp. 186–191.

49 For a revision this view see T. Harris, P. Seaward, and M.A. Goldie (eds), *The Politics of Religion in Restoration England* (Oxford, 1990) and T. Harris, *Politics under the Later Stuarts* (1993).

50 For Toland, see J.A.I Champion, *The Pillars of Priestcraft Shaken*; idem 'John Toland: the Politics of Pantheism' in *Revue de Synthèse* 116 (1995) pp. 259–280; idem (ed.) *John Toland Nazarenus* (Voltaire Foundation, 1998). The best intellectual biography of Toland remains R. Sullivan, *John Toland and the Deist Controversy* (Harvard, 1982).

51 J. Toland, *A Collection of Several Pieces* (1726) 2 volumes, I. liv.

52 Toland, *Collection*, II 350–403.

53 Toland made the first assertion in his edition of Milton's works, *A Complete Collection of the Historical Political and Miscellaneous Works of John Milton* (Amsterdam, 1698), pp. 26–30. The first version of the catalogue can be found in *Amyntor* (1699) at pp. 20–41. For an important unnoticed manuscript response by Toland to the latter see British Library Birch 4372 (pp. 37–43) 'Dodwell Mss' and below. For a full account of the bibliographical exchanges see F.F. Madan *A New Bibliography of the Eikon Basilike of King Charles I* (Oxford, Oxford Bibliographical Society Publications, 1949), pp. 139–146. I will be pursuing this debate in more detail my 'Introduction' to a critical edition of *Nazarenus*.

54 See D. McKitterick, 'Bibliography, Bibliophiliy and the organisation of knowledge' in D. Vaisey and D. McKitterick (eds.), *The Foundations of Scholarship: Librarians and Collecting 1650–1750* (William Andrews Clark, University of California, 1992), esp. pp. 31–33.

55 Toland, *Collections* II, p. 356. Ironically, Pfaffius' work was designed to rebut the deistical criticism of men like Toland: for a typically ascerbic commentary see T. Hearne, *Remarks and Collections* (1709), pp. 274–276.

56 Toland, *Collections* II, p. 383.

57 ibid., pp. 379–380.

58 For the history of Renaissance criticism see L. Panizza, 'Gasparino Barzizza's commentaries on Seneca's Letters' *Traditio* 33 (1977), pp. 297–358, and idem 'Biography in Italy from the Middle Ages to the Renaissance: Seneca, Pagan or Christian?' *Nouvelles de la Republique des Lettres* 2 (1984), pp. 47–98. For a modern discussion of the correspondence see J.K. Elliott, *The Apocryphal New Testament* (Oxford, 1993), p. 547. The Correspondence is available in C.W. Barlow, *Epistolae Senecae ad Paulum: Papers and Monographs of the American Academy in Rome* 10 (1938).

59 For John Ernest Grabe see G. Thomann, 'John Ernest Grabe (1666–1711): Lutheran Syncretist and Anglican Patristic Scholar', *Journal of Ecclesiastical History* 43 (1992), pp. 414–427.

60 See R.H. Popkin, 'Spinoza's relations with the Quakers' *Quaker History* 73 (1984), pp. 14-28; idem 'The Hebrew translation of Margaret Fell's 'Loving Salutation'. The first publication of Spinoza?' 21 *Studia Rosenthalia* (1987).

61 On Morelli see R.H. Popkin, 'Serendipity at the Clark: Spinoza and the Prince of Condé' *The Clark Newsletter*, 10 (1986), pp. 4–7. For the connection with Toland see Champion, *The Pillars of Priestcraft Shaken*.

62 See Toland, *Collections* II, p. 396. The description of Christ in the letter was meant to bear a striking resemblance to the leading Quaker figure James Naylor. See also Cadbury, pp. 189–190.

63 There is an important account to be written of the Codex Armachanus: the manuscript which Toland examined had been in the possession of Archbishop Ussher. The codex complete with marginal annotations by Ussher is now in Marshes Library, Dublin. For a brief account see A. Harrison, 'John Toland and the discovery of an Irish Manuscript in Holland', *Irish University Review* 22 (1985), pp.33–39. See also C. Graves, 'On the date of the manuscript commonly called the Book of Armagh' *Proceedings of the Royal Irish Academy* III (1847).

64 Toland, *Nazarenus* (1718) Part II, pp. 34–35.

65 ibid., pp. 16–17 and 19ff.

66 These statements, of course, compress many cultural and religious transformations of the early modern period: for a brief outline of some of the themes see D.R. Kelley, *Foundations of Modern Historical Scholarship* (New York, 1970); J. Levine, *The Battle of the Books. History and Literature in the Augustan Age* (Cornell, 1991). I intend to pursue the question at greater length elsewhere.

67 On Laud's interests in the collection of Oriental Biblical material see H.R Trevor-Roper, *Archbishop Laud 1573–1645* (London, 1940); on Usher idem *Catholics, Anglicans and Puritans* (Chicago, 1988), pp. 120–166.

68 See J.E.B. Mayer (ed.), *Cambridge Under Queen Anne* (Cambridge, 1911), pp. 142, 167, 390, 391, and 400.

69 See R.W.F. Kroll, *The Material Word. Literate Culture in the Restoration and Early Eighteenth Century* (Baltimore, 1991).

70 For some preliminary discussions along these lines see J.O. Newman, 'The Word made Print: Luther's 1522 New Testament in an age of mechanical reproduction', *Representations* 11 (1985); G. Brennan, 'Patriotism, Language and Power: English Translations of the Bible, 1520–1580', *History Workshop Journal*, 27 (1989), pp. 18–37.

71 See D. Lawton, *Faith, Text and History. The Bible in English* (Brighton, 1990).

72 See J. Force, 'Biblical interpretation, Newton and English Deism', p. 282.

73 See W. Whiston, *Primitive Christianity Reviv'd* (London, 1711).

74 See J.P. Erman, *Memoires pour servir à l'histoire de Sophie Charlotte reine de Prusse* (Berlin, 1801), pp. 200–208.

75 BL Add Mss 4295 folio 69. 'Christopaedia:/or/An acount of the *pueril studies*/of/JESUS CHRIST,/What languages he learnt, what callings he followed, &/What books he wrote, with several other remarkable/things concerning his Education, not contain'd in ye/Scriptures of the New Testament./By/The Reverend and very worthy divine,/Mr Christian Hilscher,/Minister/of Old Dresden in Saxony/After three days they found him in the Temple, sitting in the/midst of the Doctors, both hearing them and asking them questions./ – and Jesus encreased in wisdom and stature, and in fa/vor with God & man. Luc.2.44,52/London printed&/The Contents/Christ for a time laid aside the exercise of his divine nature. Sect 1/He did in the same manner with other men, increas'd in wisdom –11/He becam a school boy, and had for masters Lachus, ano/ther nameless one much given to whipping, also Josua the/son of parachia, & Elkanan — III/Of his dispute with the Doctors iin the Tmple, & what it concern'd IV/Whether he learnt to write or no, & probably yt he did not V/Whether, besides his mother tongue & Hebrew, he understood/Greec and Latin VI/That he was conversant in the books of

the Jews, and as Rabbi, Doctor and Priest VII/His learning vindicated against his townsmen of Nazareth VIII/That he was not a Conjurer IX/That he was not an Apparitor, Dyer, or [insert in pencil 'the maker of false images'] a Painter X/That he as a Messianic; but controverted whether a mason, carpenter, blacksmith, or Goldsmith; or whether a Cartwright, shipwright [insert in pencil illegible] joiner, or Architect; and the dispute reconciled, by his having a smater of all XI/The books said to be written by him, as XXVII tomes wch he left at his ascension into heaven, a treatise of magic address'd to Peter and Paul, an Epistle to Abgarus King of Edessa, a hymn wch he secretly taught his disciples, his parables and sermons,his subscription, seal, and manuscripts XII/An advertisement concerning the whole, or the conclusion address'd to all sober Christians XIII/'.

76 See BL Add. Mss 4373 'Dodwell Mss' I intend to publish the manuscript with commentary in the near future.

77 See Champion, *The Pillars of Priestcraft Shaken*; idem 'The Politics of Pantheism'.

78 See A. Grafton, *Forgers and Critics. Creativity and Duplicity in Western Scholarship* (London, 1990); see also idem 'Higher Criticism Ancient and Modern: the lamentable deaths of Hermes and the Sybils', in A.C. Dionisotti, A. Grafton and J. Kraye (eds.), *The Uses of Greek and Latin. Historical Essays* (Warburg Institute Surveys and Texts, XVI, 1988); see also on Scriptural forgeries B.M. Metzger, 'Literary forgeries and canonical pseudepigrapha', in *New Testament Studies. Philological, Versional, Patristic* (Leiden, 1980).

7. 'LIBERATING THE BIBLE FROM PATRIARCHY:'[1] POULLAIN DE LA BARRE'S FEMINIST HERMENEUTICS

RUTH WHELAN

That, indeed, is the chief source of patriarchal power:
that it is embodied in unquestioned narratives.
C. G. Heilbrun[2]

To find glimmers of this truth in submerged and alternative traditions
through history is to assure oneself that one is not mad or duped. Only by
finding an alternative historical community and tradition more deeply
rooted than those that have become corrupted can one feel sure that in
criticizing the dominant tradition one is not just subjectively criticizing the
dominant tradition but is, rather, touching a deeper bedrock of authentic
Being upon which to ground the self.
R. R. Ruether[3]

It seems anachronistic, even bizarre, to present François Poullain de la Barre — a Cartesian, sometime Roman Catholic priest, and later Protestant convert[4] — as an early modern feminist theologian. Contemporary critics, whatever their discipline, commonly define feminism not only as a critique of the gender bias in culture and society and its relationship to power, but also as a commitment to correcting that bias in favour of women. In other words, feminism, as we understand it, is not simply a critical stance, it is also a political movement.[5] While this definition is appropriate in our own time, it cannot be generalized to the early modern period. In societies where women and men were disenfranchised, thinkers might denounce the injustice of the position of women, might even imagine a society in which women took an active and equal part in public life, but they were understandably unable to envisage a programme for social change.[6] Nonetheless, their failure to articulate pragmatic political goals is not a sufficient basis, in my view, for denying them a place in the intellectual and social history of feminism.[7] As contemporary feminists have shown,

A.P. Coudert, S. Hutton, R.H. Popkin and G.M. Weiner (eds): Judaeo-Christian Intellectual Culture in the Seventeenth Century, 119–143.
© 1999 *Kluwer Academic Publishers. Printed in the Netherlands.*

criticism of the androcentric bias of culture and society is a political act in as much as it seeks to change the consciousness of readers and, thereby, necessarily, their relationship to their culture and society.[8] That is to say, although early modern feminists were not political activists, they were active critics — and Poullain is no exception — of the gender bias in the politics of knowledge.

In fact, Poullain's radical critique of androcentric power structures, his onslaught on essentialist notions of gender and his contention that women 'are also [fit] to govern others and to share in the professions and in the offices of civil society'[9] have guaranteed him a place in the history of feminism, particularly in France.[10] His importance for the history of philosophy has also been recognized. Poullain is, to quote a recent study, 'a brilliant example' of the application of Cartesian philosophy to the socio-political question of the status of women.[11] However, while Poullain's own contemporaries noted the connection between his feminism and his exegesis,[12] his place in the history of feminist theology has not yet been established.[13] There are a number of reasons for this neglect.

On the one hand, seventeenth-century specialists have concentrated almost exclusively to date on Poullain's first feminist treatise, *De l'égalité des deux sexes* (1673).[14] Although this treatise lays the foundation for his feminist theology and hermeneutics, it is only in the *De l'éducation des dames* (1674) and the *De l'excellence des hommes* (1675) that he engages explicitly with theology and the Bible. On the other, theologians seeking a historical tradition for feminist theology find it chiefly in alternative countercultural movements in early christianity and church history,[15] but they have not yet turned their attention to the exegesis of the dominant tradition. Some feminist theologians also conflate feminism with political activism, situating the inception of feminist hermeneutics in the nineteenth century.[16] Finally, if they do look beyond the nineteenth century, feminist theologians tend to privilege the writings of women, forgetting, as the case of Poullain suggests, that even in the early modern period masculinity does not *necessarily* preclude a writer from being a feminist.[17] To neglect voices like Poullain's, as I hope this essay will demonstrate, is to impoverish the intellectual history of feminist theology. This early modern 'man in feminism' reveals that the alternative historical community sought by contemporary theologians may also lie *within* the dominant tradition, a tradition which finds in Poullain a neglected but no less articulate voice of self-criticism.

The central insight informing Poullain's feminism is inspired by Cartesian dualism, that is the radical distinction of mind and matter. If our bodies (or material substances) cannot be identified with our minds (or spiritual substances), it follows that 'it [= the mind] is sexless [. . .] it is equal and of the same nature in all people — and capable of all kinds of thoughts'.[18] Cartesian dualism enables Poullain to limit sexual difference to biological function and to conclude that there is no *natural* reason why women, intellectually equal to men, should not also be their social equals. That they are not is obvious, and Poullain offers a socio-political explanation of the inferior status of women. The following themes — drawn from his, at times, rambling arguments — are relevant, I believe, to the development of his feminist hermeneutics. Although his terminology is different from twentieth-century analyses, Poullain offers a 'speculative anthropology,'[19] as it has been called, or a theoretical reconstruction of the origin of patriarchy. He reflects on the politics of knowledge, revealing an awareness of both the close association between patriarchy and the church, and also the social construction of gender as a means of legitimizing the patriarchy.

Not surprisingly, then, we find him recommending a hermeneutics of suspicion,[20] since the androcentric bias of knowledge turns culture into so many forms of patriarchal narrative. The Bible progressively becomes the focus of this critical feminist hermeneutics and we shall see Poullain struggle to retain it as an authority, while dissociating it not simply from androcentric interpretations but also from the patriarchal bias *within* the biblical texts. Finally, we shall appreciate that Poullain's critique of the Bible is inspired by an alternative, although barely articulated, vision of God and society, which denounces patriarchy and its God as a form of alienation from true humanity and true divinity. Startling as this feminist theology may be, we should not, however, expect Poullain to be absolutely coherent. As we shall see, his feminist vision is often trammelled by the masculinist assumptions more typical of his time.

Inspired, no doubt, by natural law philosophers, Poullain grounds his feminist social theory on a hypothetical reconstruction of the natural state,[21] that is before 'government, education, [the] profession[s], or religion' were established. While he sees the nuclear family as the basis of sociality in the state of nature, Poullain argues that relationships were based on principles of equality and mutuality: 'Men and women, who were at that time simple and innocent, labored equally at cultivating the earth or hunting — as savages still do. Man went his way, and woman went hers. The one who produced most was also most honoured'.[22] Childbirth and care, according to Poullain, did place women at a disadvantage because pregnancy prevented them from working, making them more dependent on their husbands, but this dependence did not cause any radical alteration in women's natural liberty.[23] In Poullain's view, the shift from a relationship of equality between men and women to one of domination and subjugation was caused by the evolution of the nuclear into the patriarchal family.

The expansion of the family unit to include other families, related by kinship, resulted in a hierarchical relationship based on physical force. Naturally, women, children and younger males were compelled to yield to the stronger and, therefore, more dominant male: 'We [. . .] see the mistress submitting to her husband, sons honoring their father, he ruling his children'.[24] With the patriarchal family also came a division of labour based on difference of gender: 'women, forced to remain at home to raise their children, took care of the indoors; [. . .] men, being freer and more vigorous, assumed responsibility for the out-of-doors'.[25] In short, Poullain's outline of evolution within the state of nature is an implicit rejection of the findings of natural law theorists, like Pufendorf, who present the patriarchal family as both natural and normative. In Poullain's theory, patriarchal domination goes against nature, it upsets the natural order founded on freedom, equality and mutuality.[26]

The hierarchical relationships typical of the patriarchal family, as Poullain describes it, precipitated the creation of primitive associations organised on a similar principle of domination and subjugation. According to Poullain, the death of a patriarch was followed by a power struggle between dominant males within the same family; those who refused to submit to the victor banded together and, having no independent resources, preyed on the existing kinship groups. The warring factions seized the goods of the wealthiest patriarchal families, re-enacting the pattern of domination, but this time both the conquered males and their families were subjugated.[27] Although Poullain does not use the term, he is in fact sketching the emergence of the patriarchy from the primal family. That is to say, in his view, primitive society is a graded pyramid of male power based on the subjugation and exploitation of the weak.[28] Women occupy the lowliest position in this pyramid of power: regarded as a spoil of war by the marauding males, they became an item of exchange and were appropriated with the other chattels. As Poullain sees it, exogamy only served to reinforce their subjugation because, in the eyes of the conqueror, the vanquished are always inferior.[29]

Inferiority was transformed into utter powerlessness in the period of political expansion which, Poullain says, followed the creation of these primitive associations. Hegemony, the will to power, or — as Poullain puts it — 'the lust for dominion'[30] was their political goal, and was achieved by militarisation. Lacking in brute force and, Poullain maintains, 'being too humane' to participate in the 'violence and injustice' necessary to dominion, women were left at home and, consequently, marginalised, because, in the aftermath of war, the conquerer appointed his comrades in arms to positions of power.[31] Consequently, to quote a recent study, in primitive societies, authority quickly became 'a male prerogative'.[32] In other words, Poullain is pointing up a radical discontinuity between the state of nature and the political organisation of primitive societies. In as much as patriarchy, in his understanding, is based not on consensus but on usurpation, and is enforced by militarism, it is a perversion of justice and natural rights, which illegitimately enslaves women while protecting the male pyramid of power.

In Poullain's schematic account, the constitution of civil society, which followed the creation of patriarchy, only served to institutionalise the alienation of power into male hands. The shift from patriarchy to monarchy — his model of social organisation — was a simple one.

> When a lord saw himself master of a people and a considerable country, he formed a kingdom. He made laws to govern it, chose officers from among his men, and elevated to positions of authority those who had best served him in his projects. So notable a preference for one sex over the other caused women to be even less appreciated.[33]

Simplistic as this account may be, it nonetheless serves to highlight a crucial point in Poullain's understanding, namely, that *civil* society is no more than *male* sociality. That is, a society organized by and for men which makes women objects rather than co-agents of the social process.

Inevitably, the civil institutions created in this context reflect and, indeed, legitimize male domination. Civil law, according to Poullain, was defined not to reflect the *public* interest, but rather 'all laws seem to have been made just to maintain men in possession of what they already have'.[34] As for religion, given that it was institutionalized 'only after formal societies were set up [. . .] men, who already controlled the government, did not fail to take over the management of religious affairs'.[35] The androcentric pattern is repeated, as Poullain sees it, in institutions of learning: men 'congregated in various places where they could talk at their ease. Academies were founded to which women were not admitted; and, in this way, women were excluded from learning as they were from everything else'.[36] The hidden patriarchal interests which Poullain sees at work in the constitution of society ensured, then, that men became the sole lawmakers, ritualists and definers of culture. This male monopoly of civic and intellectual life means that, relegated to the domestic sphere, women

were also reduced to silence.[37] In fact, the survival of civil society as male
sociality actually depends, as Poullain is aware, on the silence and
exclusion of women, or on what is now referred to as the politics of
knowledge.[38]

Poullain's analysis, as a contemporary feminist expresses it, of 'the
power base and power relations which are inherent in the codification of
knowledge,'[39] helps to explain why women, who do not lack 'natural
capacity or merit', nevertheless 'endure their condition' and 'regard it as
their natural state'.[40] Taking the example of God, whom women know
'only from men's report,'[41] Poullain suggests that men are the unchallenged
mediators between women, the world and God. The misogyny Poullain
sees in philosophy, literature, history and painting reveals that the resulting
culture is neither neutral nor objective but, in fact, gender-encoded.[42]
Furthermore, the culture arising out of male sociality — whether it be
Aristotle's view of woman as monster, or the poet Sarasin's image of her
as temptress — is, according to Poullain, the history of male constructions
of women which relegate women to a position of inferiority and deviance
from an unspoken male norm.[43]

Since men control the institutions of both power and learning,
Poullain argues that the educational curriculum, devised by men for the
women of his time, is an instrument of socialisation, ensuring that women
conform to male constructions of their gender, thereby fixing them in
patterns of behaviour designed to facilitate the continuance of the
patriarchal social order.[44] As consumers rather than producers of
knowledge, women have neither the power, nor the critical vantage point
from which to question the self-perpetuating androcentric cultural
tradition.[45] This is clearly why education occupies such a central position in
Poullain's feminism, and why he urges women to adopt the Cartesian
method, with its rational critique of authority and tradition, as an
instrument of emancipation.[46] In the meantime, however, Poullain attempts
to defuse the power of androcentric knowledge by adopting a stance of
radical doubt: 'everything that men have said about women must be
suspect, for men are both judges and defendants in this case'.[47] This
lapidary statement, picked up by Simone de Beauvoir,[48] encapsulates
Poullain's hermeneutics of suspicion and paves the way for his feminist
critique of the Bible.

It is only toward the end of his life that Poullain articulates at
length the principles implicitly at work in the critical feminist
hermeneutics he practices in the seventies while still a Roman Catholic. In
La Doctrine des protestans sur la liberté de lire l'Ecriture sainte (1720),

the interplay between Cartesianism and what Poullain defines as a Protestant hermeneutics is such as to suggest that Descartes' philosophy is the key not only to Poullain's feminism but also to his later conversion to the reformed tradition. The Bible, for Poullain, is the sole rule of faith and behaviour: 'the Scriptures are [. . .] authentic [. . .] they contain the true religion and all the principles on which it is based'.[49] While he recognises that tradition and custom are useful indicators of what people believe, he explicitly rejects the Roman Catholic understanding of them as normative, insisting instead on the right of individual examination of the Scriptures without the mediation of ecclesiastical authority or tradition.[50] In fact, according to Poullain, the Bible must be read 'in the same spirit, in the same frame of mind, and according to the same rules with which we read and should read all good books'.[51] This spirit is rationalistic.[52]

In a manner reminiscent of Pierre Bayle's *Commentaire philosophique* (1686), Poullain insists on the primacy of reason in all the intellectual disciplines, including theology, and makes reason the rule of truth in biblical criticism: 'when reading the sacred Scripture, it is [. . .] lawful to reject as false any meaning which seems contrary to the rules of sound reason, and to accept what is found to agree [with reason]'.[53] This hermeneutical principle places a significant limitation on the authority of the Bible, since it allows the exegete to set aside as no longer normative those parts of the Scriptures seen to conflict with reason. The implications for feminist exegesis are obvious but Poullain does not dwell on them in the *Egalité*. If equality between the sexes is in accordance with reason, as Poullain argues, then the biblical injunctions against women are only of antiquarian interest. They tell us 'what the sacred authors said with regard to the customs of their time,'[54] but they cannot be accepted as a norm for all times. By 1675, however, it is clear that Poullain realises that the patriarchal tone of the Bible cannot be so conveniently dismissed.

The form of Poullain's treatise *De l'excellence des hommes contre l'égalité des sexes* (1675) alerts us to his heightened awareness of the complex relationship between the Bible, patriarchy and the politics of knowledge. The feminist hermeneutical arguments, which open and close the book, are answered in the central section by a male voice seeking to establish the inferiority of women and legitimize their subjugation by reference to the Scriptures. In other words, Poullain uses the form of a debate to dramatise the way the Bible is made to function as a religious justification of patriarchy.[55] In his view, this oppressive use of the Bible occurs because theologians fail to implement the 'philosophical rule': they allow prejudice ('prévention'), instead of reason, to guide their interpretation. That is to say, they impose meanings on the text which they think are true but which in fact are the result of intellectual habits usually acquired in childhood.[56] Hence the importance of Poullain's rejection of tradition as a criterion of religious truth, since tradition enshrines the androcentric prejudices of a male magisterium.

However, in 1675, it is impossible for Poullain simply to turn instead to the Bible as his rule of faith, even a Bible tested against the rules of 'sound reason'. Poullain now appreciates that the patriarchal tone of the Scriptures cannot be limited to its injunctions against women. The misogyny he sees expressed throughout its pages implies that the whole social context and redactional bias of the Bible is patriarchal.[57] In a passage worthy of the best burlesque writing of the period, he uses the patriarchal interlocutor to express the view that the Bible is a male text.

> [My opponent] might say that this history [that is, the Scripture] — which is the story of all humankind — is, on the contrary, just an account of our own sex. Scripture speaks for the most part only of men, it reckons the generations, families and empires only by reference to them, and it hardly mentions women in the lists of genealogies. Scripture teaches us that men invented the arts and sciences, founded cities, created civil society, founded kingdoms, governed states, in a word, that men alone had the superintendence of everything to do with peace, war and religion.[58]

The Bible's patriarchal prejudice makes it inevitably one more narrative of male sociality and, as such — if it is to be read like all other 'good books' — it too must be subject to the hermeneutics of suspicion.[59] Nonetheless, once the androcentric bias throughout the text is acknowledged, Poullain's rationalistic hermeneutics becomes too blunt an instrument: it would lead him to reject the Bible in its entirety as irretrievable for feminism.[60] Given that Poullain clearly wishes to retain the Bible as sacred Scripture, he must therefore find a way of liberating it from patriarchy.[61]

There is a second hermeneutical principle, mentioned by Poullain in 1673, which inspires his attempt to separate the biblical writings from patriarchy. In the preface to the *Egalité* he observes that 'the Scripture serves simply as a rule of human conduct according to the ideas of justice it [= Scripture] provides'.[62] In other words, Poullain discerns an ethical norm in the Bible by which the biblical texts themselves can be criticized. This second principle refines his rationalistic hermeneutics, making it more pointed in its discernment: those biblical passages which legitimize or even command injustice may be either set aside as not normative, or interpreted differently in accordance with the normative ethical principle of justice as defined by both reason and the Scriptures. Not surprisingly, given his reconstruction of the state of nature, Poullain's exegesis is driven by an understanding of justice as human equality and mutuality.[63]

Throughout the treatise *De l'excellence des hommes contre l'égalité des sexes*, Poullain returns obsessionally to the biblical texts which seem to lend divine authority to the subordination of women. He is determined to divest these scriptural passages of their oppressive power. His treatment of Genesis 3.16 is a case in point, revealing both the thrust and the limitations of his feminist criticism. Instead of reading the story traditionally as an indictment of women which legitimizes their subjection to men, Poullain reads the statement — '[your husband] shall rule over you' — as descriptive rather than prescriptive.[64] As he expresses it, '[God] was warning [Eve] that the sin in which she had shared would so derange [Adam] that, unconcerned for their mutual equality, he would take the opportunity to dominate her'.[65] In this way, Adam became the first of the patriarchs.[66] This, as so many of Poullain's other remarks, is hardly an example of critical biblical scholarship even — if we remember Spinoza or Richard Simon — by the standards of his own time. Nonetheless, over two centuries before the publication of *The Woman's Bible* (1895),[67] Poullain succeeds in appropriating biblical authority as part of a critique of patriarchy. In his reading of this verse, the subordination of women is neither normative nor ethical but rather sinful, a derogation of the state of nature which, in Poullain's interpretation, is implicitly conflated with the biblical state of innocence. It is this moral feminist exegesis, primitive as it may be, which enables Poullain to detect in the Bible a tradition capable of empowering women.

Although the Bible, as patriarchal narrative, shows little concern for the spiritual journeys of women, Poullain refuses to endorse it as an instrument of oppression. Instead, with characteristic sensitivity, he has a woman, Eulalie — one of the female interlocutors in the dialogues on the education of women — express her own experience of the Scriptures as a liberating force.[68] Timandre, one of the male voices in *De l'éducation des dames* (1674), asks her to explain how she escaped from the subjugation common to the women of her time. Eulalie replies that, having borrowed a New Testament from a friend, she was empowered as a woman by its teachings on the moral life. Far from relegating women to a subordinate role, the New Testament teaches, in her view, both the moral and intellectual equality of men and women: since 'both [sexes] will be punished and rewarded in the same way for the same behaviour', they must have equal access to knowledge.[69]

Furthermore, even in the misogynist writings of the apostle Paul, Sophie — the second female voice in the treatise — detects women in positions of power in the early church. She points to Phoebe, deacon of the church at Cenchreae, and to Paul's advice on the selection of widows, as examples of women in early Christian ministry, arguing that 'the diaconesses were ordained with almost the same ceremonial as the deacons'.[70] Stasimaque — the male interlocutor who seems to speak for Poullain — suggests that this was a ministry by women for women, 'to gain access for the teaching of the Lord to places where men could not go,'[71] but he also discerns more general leadership roles for women recorded in the New Testament. He singles out Priscilla, wife of Aquila, noting that her grasp of theology must have been superior to that of the women of his own time, because it was she and her husband who led Apollos to a deeper understanding of his faith.[72] Although sketchy, Poullain's hermeneutical procedure here signifies an attempt to restore biblical history to women, and women to biblical history.[73]

Poullain's concentration on the female characters in Scripture is matched by the way he attempts to make the Bible allow women to speak for themselves. That is to say, he provides a startling revision, from the woman's point of view, of the patriarchal adages typical of the wisdom literature. This early example of what might be called 'the woman's Bible' — quoted in full as an appendix to this essay — reverses the sexism of the Scriptures against men, by the simple procedure of substituting the word 'man' where the biblical authors use the word 'woman'. In this way, Poullain creates, as he himself suggests, a matriarchal text which expresses the advice a female biblical author might have given to her daughter. In short, his hermeneutical practice reveals a commitment to distinguish the Word of God from the patriarchy of the biblical writings, thereby opening up the text for women. By recovering or creating the neglected or lost female voice, Poullain makes sacred Scripture a force for the liberation of women.[74]

It would be a mistake, however, to reduce Poullain's feminist hermeneutics simply to antipatriarchalism because, in fact, his deconstruction is inspired by a more positive, constructive theology.[75] God, as we might expect, is defined by Poullain as spirit, truth and love.[76] The corollary of this is that biblical anthropomorphisms are merely imaginative representations of the divine, permitted by God in recognition of human weakness, since 'human beings have difficulty thinking about anything in other than gross sensuous terms'.[77] Thus, anthropomorphisms do image forth God, but they are not to be conflated with the divine nature which is immaterial. This commonplace theological insight is the basis for Poullain's more unusual critique of the sexism of the received symbols of God. As far as he is concerned, men have appropriated revelation to their own ends: 'men believe that they are more like God and are more valued [by God] because they make him speak like them, saying that he is a king, a lord, a father etc., and not a queen, a lady, a mother etc.'.[78] Consequently, although male images of God persist in Poullain's writings, he also deliberately privileges female representations of the divine.

For example, he repeatedly refers to truth, and by implication to God, as 'an accomplished lady who is worthy of everyone's services and attention'.[79] This image, as the context reveals, is drawn from the courtly love tradition and, as such, might be read as leaving the hierarchy of male to female in place. A second metaphor — of woman-truth as sun — suggests a more active female image of the divine: '[truth] is bright and shining [as the sun]. She enlightens our souls, strengthens and delights them'.[80] The metaphor is female, then, but not passive, God as woman-sun empowers and supports all human (including male) life. A third metaphor, the divine mother, clinches Poullain's association of transcendence (normally thought of as male) and the feminine. While, on the one hand, he defines God as 'the Being who has produced and begotten the world', he qualifies this androcentric image with the feminocentric representation of 'divine omnipotence which produces [the world] in her immensity, as in a vast womb'.[81] Femaleness in this image is neither subordinate nor devalued, God as matrix is both the original source and sustainer of the world. That is to say, Poullain's metaphorical theology points up the androgynous imagery of God which he discovers and mediates through the experience of women. Androgyny, of course, is also only another metaphor of the divine, an analogical language pointing to the otherness of God.[82] As Poullain expresses it — albeit in clumsy essentialist terms — 'truth is male for women and female for men'.[83] In a word, the use of metaphors for God, based on the experience of both genders, enables women and men to transcend the limitations of their own experience and embrace the strangeness of the divine Other.

It follows from Poullain's androgynous imagery of the divine that both genders are living metaphors of God, expressing divinity analogically: 'the divine characteristics are present in women as they are in men'.[84] In fact, as his mixed metaphor of God as procreator *and* matrix of the world implies, divine revelation is mediated through love and mutuality, whether between women and men, or between God, human beings and the world.[85] However, as Poullain's speculative anthropology indicates, mutuality and equality in love are features of pre-patriarchal times, that is of the state of nature. Not surprisingly, then, in the closing pages of *De l'excellence des hommes*, Poullain introduces a female voice — whom it is tempting to see as a seventeenth-century personification of woman-wisdom[86] — denouncing patriarchy, and placing women at the centre of the revelatory, even redemptive experience. In her view, the desire for glory, or as we might say, the will to power is 'the most empty of all the spectres forged by men', since it leads them to make enemies of their fellow human beings and to put their own and other lives in danger. Given that such behaviour paradoxically sees often violent death as the pathway to immortality, it is, she affirms, contrary to the natural and divine law which uges us to preserve life.[87]

From this point of view, the militarism of patriarchy appears as a form of alienation from true humanity, while the marginalisation of women ironically ensures that they are in harmony with the natural state: 'in accordance with the dictates of religion and reason, we like to live apart from strife and armed conflict'.[88] Indeed, women's stance against the patriarchal value system, their pacifism, compassion and sensitivity grant them a privileged relation to the Mother-Father-God.[89] Women's motherhood and superior grasp of 'the art of loving' ensures that they are more authentic images of divine love, 'imitating [God's] goodness, wisdom, mercy and providence quite differently from men'.[90] By privileging the female, Poullain's woman-wisdom simultaneously highlights the distorted, oppressive social relations of patriarchy and points to possible alternatives for a redeemed humanity, regrounding itself in the original harmony of the primordial procreator-matrix.

Over two hundred years before the appearance of *The Woman's Bible*, Poullain clearly appreciated that to establish the equality of women on a doctrine of God, imagined as both male and female, consecrated their dignity as the divinely ordained equal of men.[91] He also understood that the Bible as patriarchal narrative was in need of revision, in order to reclaim it as an authority for the women who had been largely excluded from its pages.[92] Furthermore, by grounding women's equality on Cartesian dualism, he was able to break the essentialist connection between women and matter, and forge a philosophically convincing connection — for its time[93] — between women and mind, thereby subverting the confinement of women to the domestic sphere of child-rearing and nurturing. Finally, his sense of the injustice of patriarchal subjugation of women, and, conversely, the justice of women's right to be equal and free makes him one of the most indisputably feminist voices of early modern France. While he does not call for social or political revolution,[94] his theological, hermeneutical and philosophical arguments undoubtedly alter his readers' perception of the traditional status of women.[95] Nonetheless, it is legitimate, by way of conclusion, to ask if Poullain's theology is ultimately liberating for women.

As we have seen, the alternative metaphor of God as procreator-matrix, which Poullain proposes, reveals his concern to subvert the traditional hierarchy of active male to passive female by making the male and female images of the divine co-equal and co-active. However, as his privileging of the feminine as a revelation of God indicates, he is still operating within the essentialist notions of gender which have functioned historically in favour of the subjugation of women. That is to say, by arguing that the providence of God is most clearly seen in the sensitivity, compassion and care of women, and more particularly of women as mothers, he leaves in place the connection between female biological identity and the capacity to be intuitive or caring.[96] That such a perpetuation of traditional gender stereotypes ultimately works against the liberation of women is obvious from Poullain's insistence on the complementarity of the sexes, equal in dignity but separate in function. Sexual equality does not mean, in his understanding, that women should abandon the domestic for the public economy: 'the bearing and education of children, which is women's function, is at least as important and noble as everything men do'.[97] In a word, the feminist thrust of his arguments is blunted by masculinist assumptions of which he seems unaware.

Poullain's privileging of the feminine has a second consequence. It follows from his conflation of the states of nature and innocence that patriarchy is a social sin from which women were spared by virtue of their marginalisation. In fact, Poullain idealizes woman as a representation of 'unspoiled nature' and as an example of more integrated humanity.[98] Of course, his argument for the superiority of women is an attempt to counteract not only the rampant misogyny of his time, but also the traditional interpretation of the myth of human origins which makes woman the source of all evil and woes. However, if women are more representative of the lost state of nature or innocence, then the restoration of the equality and mutuality between the sexes which characterized the natural state will only occur — within the terms of this paradigm — at the end of historical time, when all humanity is redeemed. To put it another way, Poullain's feminism is utopian, and is consequently deprived of pragmatic significance. As a result, although his criticism of the dominant tradition anticipates the theological and hermeneutical positions of nineteenth-century feminism, women would wait for centuries to be liberated from patriarchy.[99]

Appendix: *De l'excellence des hommes contre l'égalité des sexes* (1675), pp. 94-96.

Et ce qu'elle [= l'Ecriture] dit contre les femmes se peut aussi justement appliquer aux hommes en substituant le mot d'*homme* à celuy de *femme*. En effet une mere qui voudroit instruire sa fille, ne pourroit-elle pas luy parler de cette sorte?

    Ma fille, ne vous trouvez point parmy les hommes; ne vous laissez point surprendre à leurs artifices, à leurs promesses & à leurs cajolleries.[100] Souvenez-vous que le peché a commencé par eux & qu'ils sont cause du malheur de toutes les femmes;[101] que l'iniquité de la femme vient de l'homme; & que le mal que fait une femme est preferable au bien que veut faire un homme.[102] Ne vous arrétez point trop à considerer la beauté, la bonne mine, ny tout ce qui donne de la grace aux hommes, de peur que cela n'allume en vous le feu de la concupiscence,[103] & ne vous soit un sujet de chute & de scandale, comme à tant d'autres de vôtre sexe que je pourrois vous nommer, & qui estoient auparavant extrémement sages & vertueuses. Eloignez vous donc de leur compagnie autant qu'il vous sera possible. Il vous sera toûjours plus avantageux de n'avoir nul commerce avec eux, non pas mesme par le mariage,[104] & sçachez que celles qui suivent l'Agneau par tout où il va, ce sont celles qui sont vierges[105] & ne sont point soüillées par les hommes.

    Neanmoins comme je ne pretens pas forcer vostre inclination,[106] si elle vous porte à vouloir un mary, songez à le bien choisir. Car il est entierement rare d'en trouver un bon. C'est un present que vous ne devez attendre que du ciel.[107] Un homme de vertu & de bon sens, & qui aime sa femme, est un sujet continuel de joye & de consolation, & est plus à estimer qu'une couronne & que tous les thresors du monde.[108]

    Mais au contraire, c'est le dernier malheur pour une femme, d'avoir un mary sujet aux disputes, à la colere, à la jalousie. Il vaudroit mieux demeurer dans les deserts avec les tigres, les dragons & les bestes les plus farouches.[109] C'est comme un toît qui degoute continuellement au milieu de l'hyver,[110] & un vent rude & fâcheux qui gronde sans cesse. C'est pourquoy pensez y bien.

    S'il vous arrive d'avoir des enfans, prenez un soin particulier de les garantir du vice. Les garçons demandent une garde & une exactitude tres-grande, de peur qu'ils n'échappent & ne se perdent.[111] Et pour peu que vous y voyïez d'ouverture, redoublez vostre vigilance & vos soins, de crainte qu'ils ne se laissent aller à la premiere occasion. Et vous ne pourrez rien faire de mieux pour vostre repos, & pour leur avantage, que de leur

donner une femme qui ait de l'esprit & de la vertu; pour les retenir par sa
modestie & par sa douceur dans de justes bornes où ils ont bien de la peine
à demeurer.

And what it [= Scripture] says against women can also justifiably be
applied to men by substituting the word *man* for that of *woman*. Indeed,
could a mother who wanted to advise her daughter not speak to her as
follows?

     My daughter do not go with men; do not allow yourself to be
caught unawares by their devices, promises and flattery. Remember that
sin began with them and that they are the cause of the downfall of all
women; that the iniquity of the woman comes from the man; and that the
evil which a woman does is preferable to the good a man wants to do. Do
not stop too much to consider the beauty, good looks or anything which
makes men attractive, for fear that it may arouse the fires of concupiscence
in you, and be a cause of downfall and scandal for you, as [it has been] for
so many others of your sex whom I could name, and who used to be
extremely well-behaved and virtuous. Keep your distance from them as
much as possible. It will always be more to you advantage to have no
dealings with them, not even in marriage; and you should know that those
who follow the Lamb wherever he goes, are virgins and are not sullied by
men.

     Nonetheless, as I do not mean to override your natural inclinations,
if they drive you to desire a husband, think carefully about choosing one.
Because it is extremely rare to find a good one. It is a gift which you may
expect only from heaven. A virtuous and sensible man, and who loves his
wife, is a constant source of joy and solace, and he is more valuable than a
crown and all the riches in the world.

     But on the contrary, it is an utter calamity for a woman to have a
husband subject to quarrelling, anger and jealousy. It would be better to
live in the desert with tigers, dragons and the wildest animals. He is like a
roof which leaks continually in the middle of winter, and a harsh, tiresome
wind which growls without ceasing. So think it over carefully.

     If you happen to have children, take particular care to
protect them from wickedness. Boys require watching and a great deal of
firmness lest they get out of control and lose their way. And if you should
see any relaxation [of discipline], increase your vigilance and attention, for
fear that they let themselves go at the earliest opportunity. And you could
do nothing better for your peace of mind and their advantage than to give
them an intelligent and virtuous wife whose modesty and gentlessness will

restrain them within the bounds of righteousness where they have great difficulty remaining.

1 I have borrowed this phrase from P. Trible, 'Jottings on the journey', in L. M. Russell (ed.), *Feminist Interpretation of the Bible* (Philadelphia: The Westminster Press, 1985), p. 147.

2 C. G. Heilbrun, 'What was Penelope unweaving?', *Hamlet's mother and Other Feminist Essays on Literature* (London: The Women's Press, 1991), p. 109.

3 R. R. Ruether, *Sexism and God-talk: Toward a Feminist Theology* (Boston: Beacon Press, 1983), p. 18.

4 Very little is known about the life François Poullain (1647–1723), who added de la Barre to his name when he left France in 1688. He was awarded his Master of Arts in 1663; at about age twenty (1667), he became disillusioned with the scholastic philosophy prevailing in higher education at the time. His disillusionment was probably precipitated by his discovery of Cartesianism. He spent the next ten years tutoring in Paris, also publishing his three major works: *De l'égalité des deux sexes* (Paris: Jean du Puis, 1673); *De l'éducation des dames pour la conduite de l'esprit dans les sciences et dans les moeurs. Entretiens* (Paris: Jean du Puis, 1674), and *De l'excellence des hommes contre l'égalité des sexes* (Paris: Jean du Puis, 1675). In 1680 he was ordained priest and was appointed to a parish in Flamangrie in Picardie, and later (1685) to the parish of Saint-Jean Baptiste de Versigny. In 1688 he left for Paris, already a convert — it seems — to the the Reformed faith; by December 1689 he had sought refuge in Geneva. He married a Genevan magistrate's daughter in 1690 and they had two children, a daughter later in 1690, and a son in 1696. In 1720 Poullain published *La Doctrine des Protestants sur la liberté de lire l'Ecriture sainte, le service divin en langue entenduë, l'invocation des saints, le sacrement de l'Eucharistie; justifiée par le missel romain & par des réflexions sur chaque point; avec un commentaire philosophique sur ces paroles de Jesus-Christ, ceci est mon corps; ceci est mon sang* (Geneve: Fabri & Barrillot, 1720). Poullain also published two works on the French language which I shall not refer to in this essay. These biographical details are taken from M. Alcover, *Poullain de la Barre: une aventure philosophique, Papers on French Seventeenth-Century Literature, Biblio 17* (Paris, Seattle, Tübingen 1981), pp. 9–20.

5 See J. A. Sabrosky, *From Rationality to Liberation: the Evolution of Feminist Ideology* (Westport and London: Greenwood Press, 1979), pp. 13–14. Sabrosky's definition of feminist ideology includes the 'delineation of both short- and long-term programs and strategies to implement feminist prescriptions and long-range goals'. See also, C. Venesoen, *Études sur la littérature féminine au XVIIᵉ siècle* (Alabama: Summa Publications, 1990), p. 9: 'Depuis que le concept [du féminisme] a été forgé en France, la doctrine s'est accompagnée d'actions multiples pour élargir les droits et le rôle des femmes dans la société. C'est pourquoi la définition du féminisme devrait aussi inclure les pratiques et non seulement la doctrine'. Venesoen uses this definition of feminism to question not only the validity of feminist analyses of seventeenth-century French literature but also to question the legitimacy of identifying certain seventeenth-century French authors as feminists. However, if this definition were accepted, Poullain, whom Venesoen considers a feminist (see p. 10), would automatically be eliminated from the intellectual tradition of feminism, since, as we shall see below, Poullain cannot be said to be committed to a programme for social change.

6 This point is made by L. Abensour, *La Femme et le féminisme avant la Révolution* (Genève: Slatkine-Megariotis Reprints, 1977 [1923]), pp. 421, 424.

7 The majority of writers on historical feminism make this distinction, some even argue that it is anachronistic to associate the feminist ideology of the past with the argument for equal rights. Many critics suggest that, given the socio-economic position of women, any argument in their favour (even those which suggest women are superior to men) and any identification of gender imbalance in society and culture are historical manifestations — appropriate to their time and place — of what we now call feminism. See M. Albistur and D. Armogathe, *Histoire du féminisme français du moyen âge à nos jours* (Paris: Editions des femmes, 1977. 2 vols), I, pp. 9–10; P. Hoffmann, *La Femme dans la pensée des Lumières* (Paris: Ophrys, 1977), p. 19; I. Maclean, *Woman Triumphant: Feminism in French Literature 1610–1652* (Oxford: Clarendon Press, 1977), pp. vii–viii.

8 See J. Fetterly, *The Resisting Reader: a Feminist Approach to American Fiction* (Bloomington: Indiana University Press, 1978), p. vii: 'Feminist criticism is a political act whose aim is not simply to interpret the world but to change it by changing the consciousness of those who read and their relation to what they read'; quoted by J. Culler, *On Deconstruction: Theory and Criticism after Structuralism* (London: Routledge & Kegan Paul, 1983), p. 52.

9 F. Poullain de La Barre, *The Equality of the Two Sexes*, tr. A. D. Frankforter and P. J. Morman (Lewiston, Lampeter, Queenston: The Edwin Mellen Press, 1989), p. 121: 'c'est pourquoy si les femmes sont autant capables que nous de se bien conduire elles-mêmes, elles le sont aussi de conduire les autres & d'avoir part aux emplois & aux dignitez de la societé civile'. All references are to this edition, hereafter *Equality*; original spelling has been retained in all quotations; however, capitalisation has been rationalized in accordance with modern usage.

10 See, for example, Albistur and Armogathe, *Histoire*, I, pp. 225–47; S. de Beauvoir, *Le Deuxième sexe* (Paris: Gallimard, 1976. 2 vols), epigraph and I, pp. 184–85; Hoffmann, p. 291–308; C. C. Lougee, *Le Paradis des femmes: women, salons and social stratification in seventeenth-century France* (Princeton: University Press, 1976), pp. 18–21; G. Reynier, *La Femme au XVIIe siècle* (Paris: Jules Tallandier, 1929), pp. 240–71. Curiously, Poullain is not mentioned in the recent study by M. E. Wiesner, *Women and Gender in Early Modern Europe* (Cambridge: University Press, 1993). Wiesner goes so far as to argue that 'most of the other vernacular defenses of women by continental authors are not as sophisticated [as the treatises written by Marie de Gournay and Christine de Pisan]' (p. 19). See M. de Gournay, *Egalité des hommes et des femmes. Grief des dames; suivis du Promenoir de monsieur de Montaigne*, ed. C. Venesoen (Genève: Droz, 1993); C. de Pisan, *The Treasure of the City of Ladies or the Book of the Three Virtues*, tr. S. Lawson (London: Penguin Books, 1985). I trust that this essay will demonstrate that Poullain merits a place in the early modern history of feminism.

11 F. Poullain de La Barre, *The Equality of the Sexes*, tr. D. M. Clarke (Manchester and New York: University Press, 1990), p. 2 (hereafter, Clarke). See also, *Equality*, pp. xiii–xv, xxviii–xxx; H. Grappin, 'Notes sur un féministe oublié: le cartésien Poullain de la Barre', *Revue d'histoire littéraire de la France*, 20 (1913), pp. 852–67 and 21 (1914), pp. 387–89; G. Lefèvre, 'Poullain de la Barre et le féminisme au XVIIe siècle', *Revue pédagogique*, 64 (1914), 101–13; H. Piéron, 'De l'influence sociale des principes cartésiens: un précurseur inconnu du féminisme et de la Révolution: Poullain de la Barre', *Revue de synthèse historique*, 1902, pp. 153–85, 270-82; M. A. Seidal, 'Poullain de la Barre's *The Woman as Good as the Man*', *Journal of the History of Ideas*, 35 (1974), pp. 499–508.

12 See the *Journal des savants*, 16 mars 1676, p. 38, review of *Excellence*; also the *Histoire des ouvrages des savants*, septembre, octobre, novembre 1691, p. 32, review of *Egalité* (ed. of 1691) and the *Dissertation* (1692) which had originally appeared as the preface to the *Excellence* (1675). Of course, neither journalist uses the term 'feminist' which only entered the French language at a much later stage.

13 Clarke, pp. 4, 23–24, notes the connection between, on the one hand, Poullain's feminism and, on the other, his Protestantism, and the exegetical principles he enunciated in *Doctrine*; Grappin makes a similar connection and comments, in passing, on Poullain's 'esprit critique, d'un sens du relatif qui était une rareté en son temps', 'Notes', p. 860; 'A propos du féministe', p. 388. Neither critic, however, engages systematically with Poullain's exegesis. Alcover, pp. 79–92, discusses Poullain's attitude to the Bible at some length, but insists that his rationalist exegesis is subversive of the traditional understanding of the Bible as divine revelation. While I agree that Poullain's feminist exegesis is subversive of patriarchy, I get no sense from his writings that he wishes to do away with the Bible altogether.

14 Three editions of the *Egalité* have appeared in recent years, the bilingual edition mentioned in n.9; the English translation cited in n.11, and a French reprint, *De l'égalité des deux sexes* (Paris: Fayard, 1984). B. Magné is currently working on a fourth edition.

15 For example, Ruether, *Sexism*, pp. 33–37.

16 For example, B. Brown Zikmund, 'Feminist consciousness in historical perspective', in Russell (ed.), pp. 21–22; E. Schüssler Fiorenza, *Bread not Stone: the Challenge of Feminist Biblical*

Interpretation (Edinburgh: T. & T. Clark, 1990), p. xii; see also her earlier 'Toward a feminist biblical hermeneutics: biblical interpretation and liberation theology', in B. Mahan and L. D. Richesin, *The Challenge of Liberation Theology: a First Forld Response* (Maryknoll [N. Y.]: Orbis, 1981), pp. 103–05.

17 For a stimulating discussion of this issue see A. Jardine and P. Smith, *Men in Feminism* (New York and London: Methuen, 1987). See also D. Porter (ed.), *Between Men and Feminism* (London and New York: Routledge, 1992).

18 Poullain, *Equality*, p. 85: 'L'esprit n'a point de sexe. [. . .] 'il est égal & de même nature en tous les hommes, & capable de toutes sortes de pensées. On this see Clarke, pp. 9, 25; Alcover, *Poullain*, pp. 60–61.

19 Poullain, *Equality*, p. xxxii.

20 Twentieth-century theologians suggest that a hermeneutics of suspicion is the 'beginning point' of feminist interpretations of the Bible. See K. Doob Sakenfeld, 'Feminist uses of biblical material', in Russell (ed.), *Feminist Interpretation*, p. 55; Schüssler Fiorenza, *Bread*, p. xii: 'Feminist interpretation [. . .] begins with a hermeneutics of suspicion that applies to both contemporary androcentric interpretations of the Bible and the biblical texts themselves'. See also, her earlier *In Memory of Her: a Feminist Theological Reconstruction of Christian Origins* (New York: The Crossroad Publishing Company, 1983), pp. 29–30.

21 See, for example, S. Pufendorf, *On the Duty of Man and Citizen According to Natural Law*, ed. J. Tully, tr. M. Silverthorne (Cambridge: University Press, 1991), I,3.i, p. 33. It is unlikely that Poullain was influenced by this treatise since it was first published in 1673, the same year as Poullain's *Equality*. However, Pufendorf's major compendium of natural law political theory, *On the Law of Nature and Nations* appeared the previous year. It is possible, then, that Poullain was influenced by Pufendorf as he wrote the *Equality*; although it is less important to identify his actual source than to appreciate the fact, as we shall see, that he is concerned to refute the sexism of natural law political theory. The connection between Poullain and Pufendorf is made by Seidal, *Poullain*, p. 502; and Alcover, *Poullain*, pp. 38, 85–86, 93, n.4, 94–95.

22 Poullain, *Equality*, p. 23: 'Les choses estoient dans un état tres different d'aujourd'huy, il n'y avoit point encore de gouvernement, de science, d'employ, ny de religion établie [. . .] les hommes & les femmes qui estoient alors simples & innocens, s'employoient également à la culture de la terre ou à la chasse comme font encore les sauvages. L'homme alloit de son côté & la femme alloit du sien; celuy qui apportoit d'avantage étoit aussi le plus estimé'; see also *De l'éducation des dames* (Paris: Antoine Dezallier, 1679), p. 321: 'l'égalité des hommes selon la nature, & [. . .] l'obligation qu'ils ont de travailler à se conserver les uns les autres par une assistance reciproque' ('the equality of humanity in the state of nature, and the duty they have to work for mutual self-preservation by helping each other'). See Pufendorf, *On the Duty of Man and Citizen*, II.1.viii, p. 117.

23 Poullain, *Equality*, p. 23, see p. xxxii. Poullain does believe that women are weaker than men, but insistently limits this to physical weakness, see *Excellence*, pp. 59–60, and, for the patriarchal critique of his position, 158–59; see also pp. 270–71, for the argument that the women of Plato's republic, and the New World are not socially handicapped by pregnancy.

24 Poullain, *Equality*, p. 23: 'On vid la maistresse se soûmettre à son mary, le fils honorer le pere, celuy-cy commander à ses enfans'.

25 Poullain, *Equality*, p. 25: 'les femmes obligées d'y [= dans les maisons] demeurer pour élever leurs enfans, prirent le soin du dedans: [. . .] les hommes estant plus libres & plus robustes se chargerent du dehors'.

26 Pufendorf, *On the Duty of Man and Citizen*, II.1.7, p. 116 and II.2.4, pp. 121–22; Poullain, *Excellence*, p. 40: 'la domination est contre la nature; le pouvoir de se faire craindre & obeïr, qui est ce que l'on entend par domination, n'est fondé que sur le dereglement' ('domination is against nature; the power to make oneself feared and obeyed, which is what domination means, is founded on nothing less than moral disorder').

27 Poullain, *Equality*, p. 25.

28 I follow the definition given by Schüssler Fiorenza, *Bread*, p. 13; see also L. M. Russell, 'Liberating the word', and E. Schüssler Fiorenza, 'The will to choose or to reject: continuing our critical work', in Russell (ed.), pp. 15, 127.

29 Poullain, *Equality*, p. 25.

30 Poullain, *Equality*, p. 25: 'le desir de dominer'.

31 Poullain, *Equality*, pp. 25–27.

32 Poullain, *Equality*, p. xxxiii; see Seidal, *Poullain*, pp. 502–505.

33 Poullain, *Equality*, p. 27: 'Lors qu'un seigneur se vid maistre d'un peuple & d'un païs considerable, il en forma un royaume; il fit des loix pour le gouverner, prit des officiers entre les hommes, & esleva aux charges ceux qui l'avoient mieux servy dans ses entreprises. Une preference si notable d'un sexe à l'autre fit que les femmes furent encore moins considerées'.

34 Poullain, *Equality*, p. 21: 'Toutes les loix semblent n'avoir esté faites que pour maintenir les hommes dans la possession où ils sont'; see also p. 74: 'Il faut considerer que ceux qui ont fait ou compilé les loix estant des hommes, ont favorisé leur sexe' ('we must take into account that those who have made or compiled the laws, being men, have favored their sex'). Contrast this with Pufendorf, *On the Duty of Man and Citizen*, II.12.iii, p. 155. As a corrective to the gender bias of the law, Stasimaque — the male voice in *Dames* who seems to speak for Poullain — recommends the creation of 'chambres mi-parties', that is legal panels composed equally of men and women which would be empowered to legislate in all matters concerning women (p. 6).

35 ibid., p. 27: 'Pour le culte qu'on luy [= à Dieu] a rendu, il n'a esté regulier que depuis qu'on s'est assemblé pour faire des societez publiques. [. . .] les hommes qui estoient déja les maistres du gouvernement ne manquerent pas de s'emparer encore du soin de ce qui concernoit la religion'.

36 ibid., p. 29: 'ils [= les hommes] s'assemblerent en certains lieux pour en [= des sciences] parler plus à leur aise. [. . .] On fit des academies, où l'on n'appella point les femmes; & elles furent de cette sorte excluës des sciences, comme elles l'étoient du reste'. Poullain is quite confident that women intellectuals were a feature of early cultures. However, given the social codes of their time ('une bien-seance importune'), they were prevented from moving freely in public (that is, male) intellectual circles and, as a result, made no disciples (*Equality*, p. 30).

37 See Ruether, pp. 72–75 for a similar analysis.

38 See D. Spender (ed.), *Male Studies Modified: the Impact of Feminism on the Academic Disciplines* (Oxford: The Pergamon Press, 1981), pp. 1–9.

39 Spender, p. 1; see Poullain, *Equality*, p. 21: 'elles [= les femmes] n'ont esté assujetties que par la loy du plus fort' ('women have only been dominated because of the law which favors the strong').

40 ibid., p. 21: 'ce n'a pas esté faute de capacité naturelle ni de merite'; 'les femmes mêmes supportent leur condition. Elles la regardent comme leur estant naturelle'.

41 ibid., p. 163: 'ne le [= Dieu] connoissant que sur leur [= hommes] rapport'.

42 ibid., pp. 63–67.

43 ibid., pp. 171–77, see also p. 65; *Dames*, p. 334.

44 ibid., pp. 35, 67, 155–57; see also *Dames*, pp. 275–76.

45 See Poullain, *Equality*, pp. 153–55; *Excellence*, pp. 275-76; see also L. Irigaray, 'The poverty of psychoanalysis', in M. Whitford (ed.), *The Irigaray Reader* (Oxford: Blackwell, 1991), pp. 82, 92.

46 Poullain, *Dames*, pp. 14–16, 26, 133–34. See F. Poullain, *De l'éducation des dames*, ed. B. Magné (Toulouse: Université de Toulouse le Mirail, 1994), p. vi.

47 Poullain, *Equality*, p. 71: 'tout ce qu'en [= des femmes] ont dit les hommes doit estre suspect, parce qu'ils sont juges & parties'.

48 Simone de Beauvoir used this statement as one of the two epigraphs to *Le Deuxième sexe*.

49 Poullain, *Equality*, p. 101: 'les livres de l'Ecriture [..] sont authentiques [. . .] ils contiennent la veritable religion, & toutes les maximes sur lesquelles elle est fondée'; see *Dames*, pp. 309–10; *Excellence*, pp. 5–6 (Scripture as the rule of truth); p. 170 (although here the divinity of Scripture is expressed more forcefully by the male interlocuter); *Doctrine*, pp. ix, xi.

---

50 Poullain, *Doctrine*, pp. xi–xii, 23–37, 237–45. It is significant that while still a Roman Catholic, Poullain also argued that faith and behaviour should be ruled by Scripture rather than tradition, see *Dames*, pp. 309–10.

51 Poullain, *Doctrine*, p. 274: 'dans le même esprit, dans la même disposition, & suivant les mêmes règles, qu'on lit & qu'on doit lire tous les bons livres'; see Clarke, pp. 23–24.

52 See Alcover, pp. 79-92, although the conclusions she draws from Poullain's rationalism differ from my own.

53 Poullain, *Doctrine*, p. 273: 'en lisant l'Ecriture sainte, il [. . .] est [. . .] permis de rejetter comme faux tout sens qui paroit contraire aux règles de la saine raison, & de s'arrêter à ce que l'on trouve y être conforme'; see *Equality*, p. 179. See also P. Bayle, *Commentaire philosophique*, ed. J. M. Gros (Paris: Presses Pocket, 1992), I.i, pp. 85–97; and W. Rex, *Essays on Pierre Bayle and Religious Controversy* (The Hague: Martinus Nijhoff, 1965), pp. 77–193. This hermeneutical principle may be inspired by Cartesianism but it is radically different from Descartes's own insistence on the central role of the Roman Catholic magisterium in the hermeneutical process, see V. Carraud, 'Descartes et la Bible', in J.-R. Armogathe (ed.), *Le Grand siècle et la Bible* (Paris: Beauchesne, 1989), pp. 277–91.

54 Poullain, *Equality*, p. 179: 'ce qu'ont dit les autheurs sacrez par rapport aux usages de leur temps'; see Alcover, *Poullain*, p. 40.

55 Poullain, *Excellence*, pp. 4–5. This aspect of the work is noted by the *JS*, 16 mars 1676, p. 38. See also Schüssler Fiorenza, *Bread*, p. xi.

56 Poullain, *Doctrine*, pp. 278–79; see Descartes, *Discours de la méthode*, ii.

57 Poullain, *Excellence*, p. 87.

58 Poullain, *Excellence*, p. 215: 'On diroit au contraire que cette histoire qui est celle de tout le monde, n'est que l'histoire de nostre sexe. Elle ne parle quasi que des hommes, elle ne conte les generations, les familles & les empires que par eux, & ne nomme presque point les femmes dans les genealogies qu'elle décrit; & elle nous apprend que ce sont les mâles qui ont inventé les arts & les sciences, bâty les villes, formé les societez, fondé les royaumes, gouverné les estats, en un mot qu'ils ont seuls eu le soin de tout ce qui concerne la paix, la guerre, & la religion'.

59 Compare this with Schüssler Fiorenza, 'The will to choose', p. 130: 'a feminist critical hermeneutics of suspicion places a warning label on all biblical texts. Not only is scripture interpreted by a long line of men and proclaimed in patriarchal churches, it is also authored by men, written in androcentric language, reflective of religious male experience, selected and transmitted by male religious leadership. Without question, the Bible is a male book'. See also Alcover, *Poullain*, p. 87–88, whose conclusions differ radically from my own.

60 Such is the stance of 'postbiblical feminists' according to Schüssler Fiorenza, *Bread*, p. 9.

61 This is also the dilemma voiced by many twentieth-century theologians, see Trible, 'Jottings, p. 147–49; R. R. Ruether, 'Feminism and patriarchal religion: principles of ideological critique of the Bible', and L. Russell, 'Feminist critique: opportunity for cooperation', *Journal for the Study of the Old Testament*, 22 (1982), pp. 54–66, 67–71. See also the critique of this position in Schüssler Fiorenza, *Bread*, pp. 12–14.

62 Poullain, *Equality*, p. 179: 'elle [= l'Ecriture] n'est que pour servir de regle aux hommes dans leur conduite, selon les idées qu'elle donne de la justice'.

63 Poullain, *Excellence*, pp. 31–45; M. A. Farley also argues that equality and mutuality 'function as interpretive principles but also as normative ethical principles in a feminist theory of justice', 'Feminist consciousness and the interpretation of Scripture', in Russell (ed.), p. 45. Ruether, *Sexism*, pp. 22–33 argues that the prophetic critique of power relationships must be appropriated for feminist theology and hermeneutics. It is disappointing to note Poullain's rationalisation of the failure of the prophets to apply their critique of social injustice to the oppression of women (see *Excellence*, pp. 76–78). His ethical feminist hermeneutics are inspired, as a result, by rational ethical principles rather than the biblical prophetic tradition.

64 See Wiesner, *Women and Gender*, p. 11 for a brief account of biblical misogyny; see Newsom and Ringe, p. 14 for a twentieth-century feminist reading of the biblical myth of human origins. Poullain's commentary on this verse receives particular attention from Henri Basnage in his review in *HOS*, septembre, octobre, novembre 1691, p. 32; see also Alcover, *Poullain*, pp. 83–84, 86.

65 Poullain, *Excellence*, p. 45: 'Dieu [. . .] l'avertissant [= Eve] par ces paroles que le peché auquel elle avoit eu part, le [=Adam] deregleroit tellement que sans se soucier de l'égalité qui estoit entr'eux, il prendroit sujet d'exercer sur elle un empire de domination'; see Alcover, p. 43.

66 Poullain, *Excellence*, pp. 24, 274.

67 See E. Cady Stanton, *The Woman's Bible*, ed. D. Spender (Edinburgh: Polygon Books, 1985 [1st ed. 1895]) pp. 23–27: 'Then follows what has been called the curse. Is it not rather a prediction?' (p. 27).

68 Poullain's choice of names for the two female voices in *Dames* is significant. Sophie (wisdom) needs no comment, except to point to the significance of woman-wisdom in Poullain's thought (see n.86 below). Eulalia of Merida, a fourth century virgin and martyr, disobeyed the edicts of Diocletian, which decreed that all should offer sacrifices to the gods (see D. H. Farmer, *The Oxford Dictionary of Saints* (Oxford and New York: University Press, 1987), p. 153. I am grateful to my colleague, J. Simpson for drawing this to my attention). Less dramatically, though no less significantly, Eulalie is liberated by her reading of the New Testament from the various idolatries of patriarchy, as Poullain understands them.

69 Poullain, *Dames*, p. 37: 'les uns & les autres seront punis ou recompensez de la mesme façon, & pour les mesmes actions; & [. . .] les sciences n'y sont deffenduës à personne'.

70 Poullain, *Dames*, p. 28: 'les diaconesses estoient ordonnées presque avec les mesmes ceremonies que les diacres'. See Rm 16.1, 1 Tm 5.3–16; on the distinction between widows as receipient of financial support and 'widow' as the title of an early christian office, see Newsom and Ringe, 356–57.

71 Poullain, *Dames*, p. 29: 'pour faire entrer la doctrine du Seigneur dans les lieux où les hommes n'entroient point'.

72 Poullain, *Dames*, p. 31. See Rm 16.3 and Ac 18.26. Some commentators argue that Priscilla is named first because she was more prominent in the church. See *Equality*, pp. 101–03, where Poullain foresees women as theologians and Christian ministers or priests.

73 See Schüssler Fiorenza, *In Memory of Her*, p. 86.

74 There can be no doubt that Poullain is consciously creating a 'woman's Bible' on a discrete scale, since he is criticized for this feminocentric reading by the patriarchal interlocutor in *Excellence*, pp. 220–21; also p. 5.

75 Sakenfeld (p. 60) sees this positive, constructive theology as an essential part of the feminist enterprise.

76 Poullain, *Excellence*, pp. 41, 298; *Dames*, 168–71, 271.

77 Poullain, *Excellence*, p. 66: '[les] hommes [. . .] ont de la peine à rien concevoir que sous des images grossieres & sensibles'.

78 Poullain, *Excellence*, pp. 61–62: 'les masles [. . .] croyent [. . .] qu'ils approchent plus de Dieu & qu'ils en sont plus estimez parce qu'ils le font parler comme eux, en disant qu'il est roy, seigneur, pere, etc. & non pas reine, dame, mere, etc'..

79 Poullain, *Dames*, p. 20: 'une dame accomplie qui est digne des services & des soins de tout le monde'.

80 Poullain, *Dames*, pp. 20–21: 'elle [= la vérité] est brillante & lumineuse comme luy [= le soleil]. Elle éclaire nos ames, elle les fortifie & les réjoüit'; see p. 137: 'il [= Dieu] prend souvent les noms de verité, de splendeur & de soleil, pour nous faire comprendre qu'il éclaire nos esprits par la lumiere de la verité qu'il y répand' ('he [= God] often takes the name of truth, radiance, or sun to make us understand that he enlightens our minds by the light of the truth which he sheds on them').

81 Poullain, *Excellence*, pp. 298, 310: 'l'Estre qui a produit & engendré le monde'; 'la toute puissance divine qui produit [le monde] dans son immensité comme dans un vaste sein'.

82 On the use of analogy to speak about God, see E. A. Johnson, *She Who Is: the Mystery of God in Feminist Theological Discourse* (New York: Crossroad, 1993), pp. 113–17.

83 Poullain, *Dames*, p. 23: 'elle [= la vérité] est homme pour les femmes, & elle est femme pour les hommes'. On alternative metaphors for God, see S. Mc Fague, *Metaphorical Theology: Models of God in Religious Language* (London: SCM Press, 1983).

84 Poullain, *Excellence*, p. 13: 'les caracteres de la divinité se trouvent dans les femmes comme dans les hommes'; this statement is part of Poullain's feminist commentary on 1 Co 11.7.

85 Poullain, *Excellence*, pp. 298–301: 'tout l'univers en general, & chaque creature en particulier est en mesme-temps l'effet & l'image de l'amour divin. [. . .] C'est pour cela que [Dieu] a inspiré à toutes les créatures le desir de l'union qui est ce que j'entends par amour'. ('the universe as a whole, and each individual being is at the same time the result and the image of divine love. [. . .] It is for this reason that [God] has inspired all created beings with the desire for union which is what I understand by love').

86 See Prov 8.4–21; Newsom and Ringe, p. 148; Johnson, *She Who Is*, pp. 124–49.

87 Poullain, *Excellence*, pp. 293–94: 'le plus vuide de tous les phantômes que les hommes se soient forgez'.

88 Poullain, *Excellence*, p. 294: 'suivant les loix de la religion & de la raison, nous aimons une vie éloignée du trouble et des armes'.

89 See Poullain, *Excellence*, p. 304: 'comme sa [c'est-à-dire, Dieu] principale action est l'amour par lequel il produit un estre nouveau hors de soy-mesme, les choses qui luy ressemblent le plus en cela doivent avoir le premier rang' (since his [that is, God] principal action is the love whereby he brings forth a new being out of himself, the things which most resemble him in this respect should take first place').

90 Poullain, *Excellence*, pp. 317, 310: 'l'art d'aimer'; 'imitant [. . .] sa [c'est-à-dire, Dieu] bonté, sa sagesse, sa misericorde, sa providence, bien autrement que les hommes'.

91 See Cady Stanton, p. 14.

92 See Cady Stanton, pp. 5–13.

93 See Ruether, *Sexism*, pp. 75–79, for a critique of the use of dualism to oppress women.

94 Piéron (pp. 275–76), Alcover (pp. 40–41, 98–108), and Frankforter and Morman (*Equality*, p. xxvi) present Poullain's feminism as revolutionary, indeed, as an early expression of ideas which later take a more pragmatic form at the time of the French Revolution. However, Poullain repeatedly affirms that he is not calling for social change but merely treating equality as an academic question (see *Excellence*, pp. 76–78, 268, 272). Of course, it is impossible to tell if this cautious approach to the social role of women is merely a disclaimer, used by Poullain as a form of self-protection — given the far-reaching and adventurous form of his thinking. Certainly, in the conclusion to *Dames* (pp. 343–45), he dwells at length on the necessity for an outward show of conformity in order to protect the intellectual freedom of the sage.

95 If we take Henri de Basnage, the journalist reviewing the *Egalité* as a case in point, it is clear from his summary of the work that he accepts Poullain's arguments as a proof of the 'tyrannie' exercised by men over women throughout history. Although, Basnage — like Poullain — does not argue that social change is necessary, *HOS*, septembre, octobre, novembre, 1691, pp. 30–31.

96 This point is also made by Hoffmann, pp. 306–07.

97 Poullain, *Excellence*, p. 272: 'la production & l'éducation des enfans qui appartiennent aux femmes est du moins aussi importante & aussi noble que tout ce que font les hommes'. Ruether (*Sexism*, p. 44) argues that 'the doctrine of complementarity' can be used 'to restrict women to their traditional roles and spheres'.

98 I am indebted in these concluding remarks to Ruether, *Sexism*, especially pp. 109–110.

99 This essay is dedicated to the memory of my father, Patrick Joseph Whelan (18 August 1922–17 April 1995).

100 See Pr 5.3–9; 7.5; Sirach 9.3–4; 42.12–13 (hereafter Si); Poulain, *Excellence*, p. 190; see also Newsom and Ringe, pp. 147–48, 237.

101 See Si 25.24; 1Ti 2.14; Poulain, *Excellence*, pp. 201, 207; see also Newsom and Ringe, pp. 355–56.

102 See Si 42.14; Poulain, *Excellence*, p. 193.

103 See Pr 5.24–26; Si 9.5–8; 25.21; Poulain, *Excellence*, p. 192.

104 See 1 Co 7.1, 8; Poulain, *Excellence*, pp. 84–88; see also Newsom and Ringe, p. 323.

105 See 1 Co 7.34; see also Newsom and Ringe, pp. 324–25.

106 See 1 Co 7.2.

107 See Pr 18.22; see also Newsom and Ringe, p. 150.

108 See Pr 12.4; 19.14; 31.10–31; Si 26.1–4, 13–18; 36.26–30; Poulain, *Excellence*, p. 93.

109 See Pr 21.9, 19; 25.24; Si 25.13-20, 22–23; 26.6–9; Poulain, *Excellence*, pp. 84, 93.

110 See Pr 19.13.

111 See Si 22.1–6.

8. FAITH AND REASON IN THE THOUGHT OF MOISE AMYRAUT

DESMOND M. CLARKE

Disagreements about biblical interpretation in the seventeenth century derived from a variety of sources, including the following: the distinction between canonical and apocryphal texts, the literalness or otherwise with which texts should be understood, the choice of translations and, fundamentally, the role of reason and authority, especially the authority of churches, in interpreting the Scriptures. Moise Amyraut (1596–1664) addressed the last of these issues in a number of writings and provided an interesting Calvinist response to a cluster of epistemological questions which confronted both theologians and philosophers at the time.[1] In examining Amyraut's account of the role of faith and reason in religious belief, it is helpful to compare it with the views popularly presented by Cartesian contemporaries in the name of the Roman Catholic tradition and to discuss the extent to which both views can be usefully called 'rationalist'.

Bayle identifies a common feature of these two Christian traditions. He writes, in the Preface to the *Dictionnaire*:

> The *Roman Catholicks* and *Protestants* fight it out upon abundance of Articles of Religion, but they perfectly agree on this Point, That the Mysteries of the Gospel transcend Reason.[2]

Futher in the same context, he writes:

> Let us try to put this in a clearer Light. If some Doctrines are above Reason, they are out of its reach; If they are out of its reach, it can't attain to them; If it can't attain to them, it can't comprehend them; If it can't comprehend them, it can't find any Idea or principle that can afford Solutions; and consequently, its Objections will remain unanswer'd, or, which is the same thing, will be answer'd by some Distinction as obscure as the Thesis it self which is attack'd . . .
> The Conclusion from this is, That the Mysteries of the Gospel being of a supernatural Order, neither can nor ought to be submitted to the Rules of Natural Reason; They are not adapted to the Test of Philosophical Disputes; their Greatness and Sublimity hinders them from stooping to them . . . They would no longer be Mysteries if Reason could solve all the Difficulties of them...[3]

However, while Bayle concedes that both 'Catholicks and Protestants agree in this Position, that Reason is to be rejected in the judging of a

A.P. Coudert, S. Hutton, R.H. Popkin and G.M. Weiner (eds): Judaeo-Christian Intellectual Culture in the Seventeenth Century, 145–159.
© 1999 *Kluwer Academic Publishers. Printed in the Netherlands.*

Controversie about our Mysteries',[4] he also acknowledges a significant difference of opinion between the churches about the extent to which reason may determine the content of faith:

> It seems that the Papists and Lutherans ought more strongly to insist upon this Principle than the Calvinists; for the Doctrine of the Real Presence has a more particular occasion for it.[5]

Here Bayle has identified one of the central questions on which various Christian traditions disagreed. There was a fundamental question about the scope for rational criticism in biblical interpretation; and the theological context in which this question emerged most sharply, during the second half of the 17th century, was in interpreting literally or metaphorically the words of the Eucharistic liturgy, 'This is my Body' and 'This is my Blood'. Bayle's comments imply that, in defending a literal interpretation of these texts, the Roman Catholic tradition was strongly supporting the principle that the Bible is not amenable to criteria of rational analysis, while the Calvinist or Reformed Church — or, at least, some of their theologians – agreed that rational criteria provide a minimum threshold which any acceptable interpretation of a biblical text must satisfy. This was the fundamental principle to which Amyraut appealed in his interpretation of Scripture.

Moise Amyraut was appointed Professor of Theology at the Calvinist college at Saumur in 1633, and published his reflections on the role of faith and reason in the same year as Descartes' *Meditations* (1641). In *De l'elévation de la foy et de l'abaissement de la raison*,[6] he questions the suggestion that God requires the faithful merely to believe the mysteries of faith but does not require them to 'waste time in examining diligently those things which they are given to believe'.[7] He reports this view as being aptly expressed in the aphorism that, in matters of religion, 'one must elevate one's faith and depress one's reason', as if faith and reason were two sides of a simple balance.[8] Belief in transubstantiation provides a good example of this principle at work, in the opinion of Amyraut, because it requires that our reason be depressed.[9]

Amyraut, however, argues against this position and develops instead the suggestion that faith and reason are complementary, that they are two ways of coming to know God. He divides the teachings of faith into two classes; (1) those which are accessible to reason, and (2) those which cannot be comprehended [*comprises*] by reason. Among the first are those truths which are 'common to almost all nations on earth' and can be known by reason alone, for example, that there is a God, that God governs the world by his providence, and 'that there are certain immutable and inviolable moral laws which were established by nature itself'.[10]   With respect to these, faith does not 'depress' reason, as if faith and reason were on opposite sides of a balance and, when one is elevated, the other is depressed. Rather, faith illuminates and clarifies what can be discovered by reason.[11]

There are other truths which are accessible in principle to reason but are so difficult to discover that hardly any pagans have done so. However they are still such that, if announced or preached to non-christians, they can be understood and accepted by them. This group includes, for example, the claim that 'man is corrupted by sin from birth, that he has fallen from perfection from the beginning'.[12]

The second class of beliefs, (2) above, are those which cannot be understood by human reason. It includes two sub-groups, the first of which are those truths which 'are simply beyond reason but at the same time do not destroy reason' – for example, the doctrines of the Trinity and the Incarnation, which we can at least understand.[13] This suggests that we have to be able to understand a doctrine in some sense in order to believe it, 'for to believe is simply to be persuaded of the truth of something, either by reasons which prove it, or by its own evidence which shines in it'.[14] Amyraut clarifies what he means by the ability of reason at least to understand these mysteries by contrasting his approach with that of the scholastics; they tried to *explain* the Trinity, which is equivalent to taking away the authority of Scripture to support our faith. For Amyraut, the text of Scripture is the voice of God which informs us about the Trinity and therefore the authority of Scripture is compromised by scholastic efforts to make the Trinity more credible than it already is.[15]

Finally, there are 'other doctrines which are contrary to reason'.[16] These are 'doctrines which are not just above reason but directly contrary to it' and are such that:

> the subject matter falls within the scope of things that we understand adequately, and these doctrines attribute to it something against which our reason provides arguments which are so strong and so evidently correct that, in order not to follow reason, one must renounce nature itself.[17]

The paradigm of this type of doctrine, for Amyraut, is the doctrine of transubstantiation. The remainder of his book is devoted to explaining how unreasonable and incredible that doctrine is; given its allegedly irrational status, 'the Church does not have the authority to command us to believe in transubstantiation against the judgment of reason'.[18]

Thus Amyraut's position is that there are limits, established by reason, to what the Bible can be said to propose to our faith. These limits are set by the kinds of things which fall naturally within the scope of reason, so that the Bible cannot be understood as requesting us to believe what is manifestly unreasonable. However it may ask us to believe things which we cannot understand adequately.

This account of the role of reason in biblical interpretation reflects a similar position taught by one of Amyraut's senior contemporaries at Saumur, John Cameron. In his *Sept sermons sur le VI chap. de l'evangile selon S. Jean* (Geneva, 1633), Cameron develops a theory about the metaphorical or spiritual interpretation of *The Gospel according to St. John*, VI, 53 ff. in which Jesus teaches that only those who eat his body and drink his blood will be rewarded with eternal life. In his second sermon, Cameron argues that the New Testament requires us to do certain things in order to be united with Christ, including 'eating his body' in some sense.

> But how is it possible to implement this means, if we do not know it? And how could we aspire to this felicity, if we did not know in what this union consists? This is not something which we cannot in any way understand or of which we should be completely ignorant.[19]

Cameron argues that we do not understand how the world was created, but that lack of understanding about creation does not compromise our chances of salvation because we are not expected to create anything. In contrast, we need to know how to establish the union with God to which the Scriptures oblige us if we are to have any hope of salvation:

> About the following things we do not need to ask *How*? Such is the Holy Trinity, that in one single and very simple essence there are three persons, the Father, Son and Holy Spirit. He told us in his Word that this is the case. But he did not tell us how it is so; therefore we have to believe it without tormenting our minds in figuring out how it is possible.[20]

But in 'eating' the body of Christ, we do need to know what is required and how to implement it; this is a case in which some understanding is presupposed in order to observe Christ's commands. Thus Cameron argues that the kind of 'eating' involved in the Eucharist must be spiritual, since the nourishment required for a spiritual life in union with God must also be spiritual.[21]

Cameron's interpretation of these texts from St. John rely on a number of factors: the reliability of our senses with respect to their proper objects, the requirement that we understand those parts of Scripture which require our implementation, and a preference for a spiritual or metaphorical interpretation of texts which otherwise conflict with what seems rationally credible [e.g. that God is a shepherd]. All of these epistemological and hermeneutic principles are adapted to support the same conclusion by Amyraut.

The central role of the senses and of reason in discrimating what is offered to our religious faith is developed by Amyraut in a number of writings, including the *Apologie pour ceux de la Religion* (1647).[22] He argues that man is distinguished from brute animals by reason.[23] We are human beings before we are Christians and therefore the most fundamental law of all is that of nature or reason; hence our natural beliefs precede those of the faith.[24] Of course Amyraut acknowledges that God sometimes performs miracles and that it may possibly be the case that there is a miracle involved in transubstantiation. However we still have to decide whether something is miraculous and there are only three ways available for deciding this question:

> There are only three ways by which we can be persuaded of the truth of something, whether it is natural or miraculous: by the senses, by reason and by faith. The senses are for knowing sensible things, such as colour and shapes . . . Reason is for knowing those intellectual things of which we are naturally capable, in order to compare them one with another . . . Faith is to acquiesce to the divine authority in those things which transcend our understanding or, at least, what can be discovered with certainty by human intelligence, and which God has decided to reveal to us.[25]

Our senses suggest that the bread and wine remain unchanged during the liturgy. Reason may sometimes overrule the senses, according to Amyraut, but only in those cases in which the object of knowledge is proportionate to our reason. However no Roman Catholic theologian claimed that transubstantiation is something which is accessible to reason. Therefore one is left with the clear testimony of the senses, unless we are required by faith to believe in transubstantiation. Since the relevant words of Scripture should be read metaphorically rather than literally, it follows that there is no basis, either in faith or reason, for disregarding the evidence of our senses.[26] Nor can the Eucharist be understood as a miracle, because even miracles are performed in a manner which is consistent with reason, through the use of extraordinary causes.[27] In contrast, the product of this alleged miracle rather than the manner of its production 'conflicts with all the rules of reason and of understanding'.[28]

This claim — that transubstantiation in some way involves a subversion of reason — is developed by another author in the same

tradition in *Reflexions physiques sur la Transubstantiation*.[29]   In arguing
against the Cartesian theory as expressed by Jacques Rohault, this author
suggests that whether or not one body can change into another is a question
of physics. However our knowledge of physics is imperfect and therefore
one cannot decide that such a change is impossible.[30]   But, he argues, the
Calvinist argument is not that transubstantiation is impossible because it
conflicts with physical theory, but that it implies a contradiction which
undermines the most basic axioms of reason.

> The axioms on which I rely to show that transubstantiation is a dogma which
> implies a contradiction are not the simple principles of physics; but they are
> axioms of eternal truth which one cannot doubt without quenching all the light of
> reason. For example, when I say that a round and flat host cannot be the body of a
> man, which is neither round nor flat, and when I emphasise all those other
> contradictions that were mentioned above, I rely on this axiom: that a thing cannot
> both be and not be at the same time.[31]

This anonymous text accurately summarises the position of
Amyraut. There are some objects of knowledge which fall naturally within
the scope of reason and these constitute a negative criterion of what the
Scriptures invite us to believe, in this sense: whatever mysteries are
revealed, they cannot include beliefs which are irrational. Therefore if a
particular reading of the Scriptures results in an irrational belief, it is more
likely that we are misinterpreting the texts than that God is demanding our
assent to what is irrational. There are minimal rational standards which any
proposed interpretation of the Scriptures must satisfy.

Cartesians on Faith and Reason

Amyraut's resolution of the apparent conflict between faith and reason is
close to that adopted by the Cartesians of the same period; their
contribution to this debate is interesting because they were frequently
accused of being hostile towards tradition and being so persuaded of the
power of human reason to decide all questions that their scholastic critics
classified them as supporters of Calvinism. However, even in the case of
the Cartesians, the claims made on behalf of reason and its competence
were not as unqualified as might otherwise appear.

Descartes argued that God's powers are not limited by our reason.
Thus we cannot say what kinds of things God cannot do; we can only say
what we cannot understand, even if God were to act in a way which is
incomprehensible to us. For example, Descartes wrote to Henry More in
1649:

> For my part, I know that my intellect is finite and God's power is infinite, and so I set no limits to it; I consider only what I am capable of perceiving, and what not, and that I take great pains that my judgment should accord with my perception. And so I boldly assert that God can do everything which I perceive to be possible, but I am not so bold as to assert the converse, namely that he cannot do what conflicts with my conception of things — I merely say that it involves a contradiction.[32]

Although this is denying that human reason can set limits to God's power, it is a short step from saying that, because something is unintelligible to us, we have no reason to believe that it is theologically credible either. Some critics of this tradition, such as Père Rochon, rejected the '*pieuse soumission*' of Descartes as either disingenuous or as pushing the power of God too far.[33]

What we find in Descartes and in the Cartesian tradition — in contrast with the scholasticism of the period — is a distrust of sensory knowledge and great confidence in the power of human reason or understanding to establish its own boundaries and to act as final court of appeal in all epistemic questions which fall outside the scope of faith. One of the results of this was that, in defence of their religious faith, Cartesians were anxious to substitute, in place of the theology of the schools, their own efforts at making the mysteries of faith as intelligible as possible. However, there was also an acknowledged possibility that some mysteries are simply beyond the scope of human understanding and, faced with those, a consistent Cartesian could say: that involves a contradiction for us but, possibly, may not be contradictory for God.

This careful approach to the mysteries of faith is reflected in the work of Jacques Rohault, who classifies his own approach to these issues as that of a simple physicist:

> Not only have I not discussed those questions that pertain in any way to the mysteries of religion, but I have even refrained from dealing with any of those in which philosophers take the liberty of deciding about the power of God; so that, in order not to assume the role of anything more than a simple physicist, I only dealt with things as they occur in their ordinary and natural condition.[34]

However, while refraining from trying to set limits to God's power or attempting to explain the mysteries of religion, Rohault claims that the Cartesian account of what takes place in the Eucharistic liturgy is superior to that of the Scholastic tradition because it explains how the transformation in which the Catholic tradition believes is possible.

> One can entrust things to the power of God in two ways: one, by knowing positively that they are possible, and the other, by merely not knowing positively that they are impossible even though they are inconceivable to us.[35]

He goes on to say that the school philosophers succeed in saying what takes place in the Eucharistic celebration only in the second sense, whereas the Cartesian account can at least make sense of what is believed: namely, that despite appearances — which are perceptions of secondary qualities caused in us — what is actually before our eyes is the body and blood of Christ.

This represents the classic Cartesian approach to Christian mysteries: to extend the scope of the human understanding as far as possible but to leave room, at the limits, for the possibility of mysteries of faith.[36] The same rapprochement of reason and faith is attempted by other Cartesians. Malebranche argued, for example, that 'the certainty of faith depends on the knowledge reason gives of the existence of God'.[37] For, if we did not prove the existence of a non-deceiving God, we would have no reason to accept anything on faith.[38]

On this, at least, the Cartesians and Amyraut are agreed, that knowledge of the existence of God is accessible to reason. They also agree on the accessibility to reason of a basic moral law or natural law. For example, Bernard Lamy, in his *Demonstration of the Truth and Holiness of Christian Morality* (1688), rejects the suggestion that we must believe the principles of Christian morality 'because we profess a blind faith in everything prescribed by religion'.[39] Lamy argues:

> I hold a very different view. I am convinced that a well constructed Christian ethics is the most excellent philosophy. . . I am not afraid to say . . . that the Gospel teaches only what reason tells us . . .[40]

While claiming that the fundamental principles of morality are accessible to reason, Lamy also acknowledges that the mysteries of religion transcend human understanding:

> There is a great difference between the mysteries which religion requires us to believe and the laws which it wants us to observe. As regards the mysteries, one must acknowledge that one can know only what Scripture and Tradition tell us about them; reason cannot penetrate them.[41]

In contrast, 'the laws which must be observed in order to live well can be known by everyone. God has engraved them in the human heart'.[42] Thus with respect to morality, Lamy argues that true religion and reason 'are only the same thing. Reason is an interior language of God, and religion is an observable language by which God speaks to us in the Scriptures'.[43]

The complementarity of faith and reason is a familiar theme among the Cartesians. Pierre-Sylvain Régis wrote, in *The Use of Reason and Faith, or the Agreement of Faith and Reason* (1704), that 'reason is infallible in the order of nature, as the faith is infallible in the order of grace'.[44] Therefore there is no need to submit reason to faith or vice versa:

> I hold, on the contrary, that it is not necessary to do either, because reason and faith cannot conflict and any contradiction or contrariety which appears between them is only apparent.[45]

The question still remains, however, as to how an apparent inconsistency should be resolved. Régis argues in his three-volume *Cours entier*, as Descartes had earlier, that we cannot require God to act within the scope of human understanding:

> There is nothing therefore more unreasonable than the claim of those who do not think they must believe what they cannot conceive [*concevoir*] and who wish to explain the mysteries of the faith by the principles of natural reason. For knowing that there is an infinitely powerful God, one should not so much say that he could not do what is impossible according to the natural order, but that what he does could not be impossible because it was demonstrated that his will is the only rule of what is possible or impossible.[46]

This is easily recognisable as Descartes' principle that we cannot use the limitations of our understanding of the natural world as a criterion of what is possible for God. But the question still remains about what content can be given to a proposition which is offered for our belief if it seems to us to be 'against reason', for example, if it is self-contradictory. Régis avoids this issue by claiming that what might be impossible in the order of nature could be possible in the supernatural order,[47] and therefore what might initially seem impossible to us could be possible for God.

> That is what caused theologians to say that the truths of the faith are above reason but they are not contrary to reason, placing above reason the truths which our mind cannot conceive [*concevoir*], and which it has to believe simply because God reveals them to it; and holding as contrary to reason the truths which the mind cannot understand [*comprendre*] and which God has not revealed to it.[48]

From this brief review, it appears that Amyraut and the Cartesians of the same period agreed about some of the truths that can be discovered by reason and which were classified in the first group by Amyraut, namely that God exists, that he is not a deceiver, and that the basic rules of morality are accessible to human understanding. They also agreed that there are some mysteries of religion which cannot be discovered by reason alone and, in order to acquire knowledge of these, we must rely on revelation. However, while we cannot discover these without the aid of the Scriptures, once they are revealed we are able to make some sense of them or, at least, there is nothing unintelligible in what we are asked to believe. I do not know of any case where Cartesians classified a belief as unintelligible to us but still within the scope of faith. It was this apparent rationalism about belief which attracted the opposition of scholastic critics — saying that they differed little from Calvinists — and which made is easy for a Cartesian like Poulain de la Barre to move from being a Cartesian Catholic to being a Cartesian Calvinist.

Critics of the Cartesian approach to the mysteries of religion included the standard objection, made for example by La Grange, that many beliefs of the Christian tradition were expressed in the language of the schools and that any change in that language puts at risk the theological beliefs which relied on it for their expression.[49] La Grange also takes issue with another claim which he attributes to the Cartesians, namely that they use reason as a criterion of what is acceptable to the faith. In contrast, he claims that religious faith should be the criterion of what is acceptable in philosophy: 'we maintain that because his [Descartes'] philosophy is contrary to theology and the faith, it cannot be true'.[50] Louis de la Ville likewise rejects the Cartesians' disclaimer that they are mere physicists, and that the content of the faith is beyond the natural order and therefore beyond the scope of their inquiries. Instead, he argues,

> we should reason from the principles of our philosophy in such a way that we always submit them to the faith, and we should never support any principles which are contrary to what the faith teaches about our mysteries.[51]

The reason given is that

> we know that our reason is liable to deceive us and frequently to represent what is false with as much appearance of truth as the truth itself; since we are assured that the faith is infallible and that what it teaches cannot be false, what should a Christian phil-osopher do when his reason seems to be contrary to the faith? . . . Should he not cling more to his faith and assume that his reason has only a false appearance of the truth?[52]

The same kind of critique was mounted by Rochon, when he rejected what he took to be the Cartesians' suggestion that reason might discover one group of truths according to the order of nature, and a different group of truths in the order of grace or faith.[53] In fact, all the critics of this manoeuvre agreed on two issues; the unacceptability of the Cartesians' account of the Eucharist, and the instability of their distinction between what reason can know or understand, and what the faith can teach. It seemed as if the Cartesians had gone too far in protecting the role of reason — a position expressed by Clerselier as follows: 'Since we are all human, that is to say, reasonable, before we are Christians, whatever persuades reason enters more easily into the mind than whatever is taught to us by faith'.[54] — and that they were much closer than they cared to admit to the unorthodoxy of Calvin in their theology of the Eucharist.[55]

The accuracy of critics' comments on the close link between Cartesians and Calvinists is shown by the ease with which Poulain de la Barre, best known for his treatise on the *Equality of the Sexes*,[56] made the transition from being a Catholic Cartesian to being a stout defender of a Calvinist version of the same philosophy. Poulain expressed his theological views in *The Protestant Doctrine of Freedom to Read Holy Scripture* (Geneva, 1720).[57] He argues that the words 'this is my body' can be understood only 'metaphorically, and in no way in a literal or standard way'.[58] The doctrine of transubstantiation derives from a mistaken scholastic view which, 'supporting occult qualities, proposes mysteries and inconceivable powers instead of simple and natural causes, and attributes to external objects qualities which resemble the impressions which the objects make on us or the sensations which they trigger in us'.[59] When he comes to provide what he calls a 'philosophical commentary' on the words which instituted the Eucharist, he says there are three ways of interpreting Scripture: by tradition, by the authority of the church, or by reason, and he recommends the third way.

> The way of reasoning or of criticism consists in this: that each person who is zealous for salutary truths and who combines, without prejudice or scruple, the light of others with their own, examines Holy Scripture with the care and attention it deserves and takes as the true meaning — for example of these words, 'This is my Body' — whatever seems to be the correct one, after having examined them as it were before God and without any fear of men.[60]

In a word, Poulain recommends that we read Scripture as we would read any other book, that we try to discover the meaning which the author intended and that we not impose on the text any prejudicial reading which we might have learned from some other source [e.g. tradition].[61] The fundamental guide in critical reading is what he calls right reason, '*la droite raison*'. So if Scripture seems to say something which conflicts with reason — for example that God has certain bodily members — we should reject it because the idea of God as a spirit, on the one hand, and on the other, as someone with bodily members 'cannot be compatible in the mind of anyone who is sincere, attentive and who reasons'.[62]

In conclusion, one might briefly acknowledge a central issue which was not adequately addressed by the various participants in this debate. There was no problem in principle with truths which we fail to discover by our own resources but, once announced by others, we can make a decision to believe or not if we can at least make sense of them or give some content to what we are invited to believe. But a problem remains about beliefs proposed to our faith which we cannot even understand or which seem to be logically incoherent. The Cartesians proposed, in this case, that we acknowledge the possibility that some truths may appear to be impossible to us or to be logically incoherent, but that God cannot be limited by the scope of our intellects. That implies an appropriate modesty about the scope of our knowledge and intellectual powers, or about the application to God of human logic. The reality of God transcends our language and our logic. However that still does not answer the question about how we might give content to a belief which seems irrational to us. That left it open to others, including Amyraut, to take the next logical step and say that we are never requested by the Scriptures to believe something which is either unintelligible or contrary to reason. That is also the position which was later proposed and defended with such success by John Toland, whose efforts in this regard were rewarded by having his book burned not far from Marsh's Library at the hand of the common hangman.[63]

1 For a survey of Amyraut's life and writings, see Brian G. Armstrong, *Calvinism and the Amyraut Heresy* (Madison: University of Wisconsin Press, 1969).

2 *An Historical and Critical Dictionary by Monsieur Bayle. Trans. into English, with many editions and corrections, made by the author himself, that are not in the French editions.* 4 vols. (London: Harper, 1710), I, lvi.

3 ibid., I, lvi–lvii.

4 ibid., I, lviii.

5 ibid.

6 *De l'elévation de la foy et de l'abaissement de la raison en la créance des mystères de la Religion* (Saumur: Jean Lesnier, 1641).

7 ibid. p. 10.

8 ibid. p. 11.

9 ibid., p. 13.

10 ibid. pp. 33, 34, 35, 36.

11 ibid. p. 41. For an example of Amyraut's understanding of natural law, see his reflections on marriage in *Considérations sur les droits par lesquels la nature a reiglé les marriages* (Saumur: Isaac Desbordes, 1648). Amyraut argues that there are three sources of law: God, human reason, and the nature of things (p. 2). Human beings must regulate their lives by the use of reason and spread the authority of reason as far as possible (p. 77). When applied to marriage, reason shows the inequality of the sexes and the natural superiority of men! 'Et quant à l'inégalité du sexe, la superiorité se trouvera tousiours au mary, comme elle estoit en frere, & l'inferiorité en la femme, comme elle estoit en la soeur auparavant. . .', (p. 240). This natural superiority of men is so manifest that it is beyond dispute: 'pour ce qui est de l'inegalité du sexe, la seule conformation du corps, la force des membres, la majesté de la presence, & les autres avantages le monstrent si evidemment qu'il n'est sujet à aucune contestation' (p. 245).

12 *De l'elévation*, p. 43.

13 ibid. p. 51.

14 ibid., p. 59.

15 ibid. pp. 62–3.

16 ibid. p. 76.

17 ibid., pp. 76–7.

18 ibid., p. 237.

19 *Sept Sermons*, p. 63.

20 ibid., pp. 91–92. See also Sermon Six, p. 362, in which he refers to 'la Trinité, l'Incarnation, & tels autres Poincts, qui surpassent la portée de nos entendemens'.

21 ibid., p. 74.

22 *Apologie pour ceux de la Religion, sur les suiets d'aversion que plusieurs pensent avoit contre leurs personnes & leur creance* (Saumur: Isaac Desbordes, 1647).

23 *Apologie*, p. 15. See also *Considérations sur les droits par lesquels la nature a reiglé les mariages*, p. 25: 'Ainsi si l'excellence d'un homme consiste en l'usage de des facultés raisonnables, ..'. and the *Sermon sur ces paroles, Prenés, mangés; cecy est mon corps, qui est rompu pour vous* (Saumur: Daniel Delerpiniere, 1663), pp. 13–14: 'La raison est la faculté qui nous esleve au dessus de la condition des bestes, & par laquelle nous sommes hommes, en cela rendus egaux aux Anges, que nous sommes par elle capable de comprendre les choses intelligibles & de discourir dessus'.

24 ibid, pp. 46, 47.

25 *Apologie*, pp. 261–2. See also *Sermon sur les paroles, Prenés, mangés*, p. 13: 'Les sens que Dieu & la nature nous ont donnés, sont les premiers principes de nos connoissances, & qui destruit la certitude de leurs operations, quand ils sont bien constitués, & qu'ils agissent sur leurs propres objets, est aussi estimé destruire la lumiere du raisonnement, & mettre toutes choses dans une confusion extreme'.

26 ibid. pp. 265–76. The distinction between what Amyraut calls the '*signification propre*' and the '*signification figurée*' is made in a number of places, e.g. the *Sermon sur les paroles* (1663), p. 12.

27 '. . . if you prescind from considering the cause which produces miracles, and if you think of them in their own right once they have been performed, there has never been one which did not, in its constitution, conform perfectly with reason'. *Apologie*, p. 276.

28 *Apologie*, p. 280.

29 The full title is: *Reflexions physiques sur la Transubstantiation, & sur ce que Mr. Rohault en a ecrit dans ses Entretiens* (La Rochelle [?], 1675), and the author is possibly Elie Richard.

30 *Reflexions*, p. 6.

31 *Reflexions*, pp. 33–34.

32 Descartes to More, 5 Feb. 1649 (AT, V, 272; CSM, III, 363). This coincides with Descartes's standard teaching that the eternal truths were created by the will of God and that God could have created them other than they are. Thus God is not subject to the laws of logic *as we understand them*.

33 Père A. Rochon, *Lettre d'un philosophe à un cartésien de ses amis* (Paris: Jolly, 1672), p. 18.

34 Jacques Rohault, *Entretiens sur la philosophie*, ed. P. Clair (Paris: CNRS, 1978), pp. 110–11.

35 ibid, p. 118.

36 This was the interpretation of the Eucharist which was generally adopted by Cartesians. For a summary of the controversy, see Jean-Robert Armogathe, *Theologia Cartesiana* (Hague: Nijhoff, 1977).

37 N. Malebranche, *Search after Truth* (Columbus, Ohio: Ohio State Univ. Press, 1980), pp. 291. Cf. 'It is obvious that the certitude of faith also depends on this premise: that there is a God who is not capable of deceiving us'. Cf. ibid., p. 482.

38 *Conversations chrétiennes*, in *Oeuvres complètes*, IV, 14. Cf. *Conversations Chrétiennes*, in *Oeuvres*, vol. 4, 14: 'ne voyez-vous pas que la certitude de la foi vient de l'autorité d'un Dieu qui parle, & qui ne peut jamais tromper. Si donc vous n'êtes pas convaincu par la raison, qu'il y a un Dieu, comment serez-vous convaincu qu'il a parlé? Pouvez-vous sçavoir qu'il a parlé, sans sçavoir qu'il est?'

39 Lamy, *Demonstration de la vérité et de la Sainteté de la Morale Chrêtienne* (Paris: André Pralard, 1688), p. 1.

40 ibid., p. 2.

41 ibid., p. 1.

42 ibid., p. 3.

43 ibid., p. 5.

44 *l'Usage de la raison et de la foy, ou l'accord de la foy et de la raison* (Paris: Jean Cusson, 1704), p. 1 of Preface.

45 ibid., p.2.

46 *Cours entier de Philosophie, ou Systeme General selon les principes de M. Descartes*, 3 vols (Amsterdam: Huguetan, 1690), I, 143–4.

47 *Cours entier*, I, 520–521.

48 ibid., p. 521.

49 Jean-Baptiste de la Grange, *Les principes de la philosophie, contre les nouveaux philosophes Descartes, Rohault, Regius, Gassendi, le P. Maignon, &c.* (Paris: G. Josse, 1675). See the Letter of dedication to the Dauphin.

50 ibid., p. 6.

51 Louis de La Ville [le Valois], *Sentiments de M. Des Cartes touchant l'essence & les proprietez du corps, opposez a la doctrine de l'Eglise, et conformes aux erreurs de Calvin, sur le sujet de l'Eucharistie. Avec une dissertation sur la pretendue possibilité des choses impossibles.* (Paris: E. Michallet, 1680), pp. 120–21.

52 ibid., p. 148.

53 He argues in his *Lettre*, pp. 12–13, that the attempt by Cartesians to distinguish between faith and reason is untenable, because it suggests that reason could discover one set of truths while the faith requires belief in something quite different.

54 Preface to *Oeuvres posthumes de Mr. Rohault* (Paris: G. Deprez, 1682).

55 H. Fabri, *Tractatus Physicus* (Lyons: J. Champion, 1666), Introd. para. xxxv; Peter Daniel Huet, *Censura Philosophiae Cartesianae* (Helmstedt: Hammius, 1690), p. 82; Gabriel Daniel, *A Voyage to the World of Cartesius*, Eng. trans. by T. Taylor (London: Bennet, 1692), pp. 126–31; P. S. Régis, *Reponse au Livre qui a pour titre P. Danielis Huetii, Episcopis Suessionensis designati, Censura Philosophiae Cartesianae* (Paris: Jean Cusson, 1691), pp. 258–66.

56 F. Poulain de la Barre, *The Equality of the Sexes*, ed. and trans. by D. M. Clarke (Manchester: Manchester University Press, 1990): original French edition, *Discours Physique et Moral de l'Egalité des deux Sexes, où l'on voit l'Importance de se défaire des Préjugez* (Paris, 1673).

57 *La doctrine des protestans sur la liberté de lire l'Ecriture Sainte, le Service Divin en langue entendue, l'invocation des Saints, le Sacrement de l'Eucharistie.* (Geneva: Fabri & Barrillot, 1720).

58 ibid., Preface, p. xli.

59 ibid., p. 143.

60 ibid., p. 234.

61 ibid., pp. 274–5.

62 Ibid., p. 274.

63 John Toland, *Christianity not Mysterious* (London, 1696).

9. DESCARTES AND IMMORTALITY

DAVID BERMAN

-I-

In his *Philosophy and the Mirror of Nature*, Richard Rorty attacks the Cartesian mind-body problem in two ways: first, by a philosophical dissolution; then by a genetic or historical analysis. Without this second line of attack, Rorty says, we are not going to resolve anything. For to think that the first approach is sufficient for getting rid of the mind-body problem is as naive as believing that a psychiatrist can cure a patient by merely explaining to him how his condition arose. As Rorty nicely puts it: 'Just as the patient needs to relive his past to answer his questions, so philosophy needs to relive its past in order to answer its questions'. Hence 'nothing will serve [philosophy here] save the history of ideas'.[1]

Drawing skillfully on other scholars, Rorty shows how original and fateful Descartes' dualism was. How, then, did Descartes achieve this? The principal step, Rorty suggests, was Descartes' redescription of the term 'idea' to include not only thoughts and concepts but also pains, imaginings, feelings and bodily sensations. Everything else was then taken to be material or extended. The mind was a substance whose modes are ideas (in the enlarged sense); whereas matter was a substance whose mode is extension. So Descartes saw human beings as consisting of two substances: (1) a mind or 'single inner space' in which ideas 'passed in review before a single Inner Eye' and (2) an outer, extended body.[2] Before Descartes there had been other distinctions between mind and body — for example, the Aristotelian — but they were not 'between consciousness and what is not consciousness'.[3]

Hence the crucial question is, to quote Rorty again, 'how did Descartes manage to convince himself that something which included both pains and mathematical knowledge was 'a complete thing' rather than two things'.[4] To say that Descartes recognized this by intuition or clearly and distinctly is no answer, Rorty urges, for we would still need to explain 'how Descartes was able to convince himself that his repackaging was 'intuitive'.[5] Rorty then goes on to explain this by means of Descartes' notion of indubitability — 'the common factor . . . shared [by pains and thoughts, but] with nothing physical'. Indubitibility then became

A.P. Coudert, S. Hutton, R.H. Popkin and G.M. Weiner (eds): Judaeo-Christian Intellectual Culture in the Seventeenth Century, 161–171.
© 1999 *Kluwer Academic Publishers. Printed in the Netherlands.*

Descartes' 'criterion for the mental', since for him I can be as certain that I
am in pain as that $2 + 3 = 5$.

Although there are additional complexites in Rorty's explanation,
it is not my aim to elaborate or to comment on them. Instead, I want to
suggest that even if he is right, he has not satisfied the philosophical
patient, who needs to 'relive his past'.[6] For one thing, to explain how
Descartes managed to accept his repackaging is not to explain how he
managed to convince most of Europe's philosophers to do so for some 200
years. Rorty's explanation, although ingenious, is too disembodied, too
lacking in affect, to serve as a complete explanation. There must have been
a more gripping inducement as well as the verbal shuffling and
'unconscious sleight-of-hand', described by Rorty.[7] If his psycho-
therapeutic analogy is to hold, the explanation should also involve
resistance. My aim in this short paper is to argue that the makings of such a
psychological explanation can be found in Descartes' account of death.

-II-

Of course, in an important sense, there is no death, according to Descartes,
since he is a firm believer in immortality. Indeed, in the 'Dedicatory
Letter' to the *Meditations* he says that one of his two chief motives in
writing the book was to prove by philosophy that death was not THE END,
that 'the human soul does not die with the body'.[8] Some commentators
have questioned Descartes' sincerity here, even though he makes virtually
the same point in the *Discourse on Method*.[9] In my view, Descartes was
more deeply sincere than he knew. Why? Because in the 'Dedicatory
Letter' he also says that his confidence in immortality was based not only
or even primarily on reason, but on faith in Scripture and the Church's
authoritative teachings. Now the initial point I wish to make is the one
made by Locke in his controversy with Bishop Stillingfleet. In short, if
Stillingfleet or Descartes were really convinced of human immortality by
faith, either through the Gospel promise or the Church's authority, then
why should he be so anxious to prove it by philosophical reasoning as
well? Does this not show, Locke asks, that 'God is not to be believed on his
own word, unless what he reveals . . . might be believed without him'.[10]
Why, in other words, should anyone need a second suit of (philosophical)
armour against death, if he already has an invincible one?

Of course, Descartes does have an answer. The philosophical
proof, he says in the 'Dedicatory Letter', is needed for the unbelievers —
those who will only believe in immortality if it is 'proved to them by

natural reason', rather than by an appeal to faith. That helps somewhat to lessen the psychological conflict, but it does not go very far. Why? Because there is no evidence, as far as I am aware, that anyone in the sixteenth or seventeeth century — at least up to Descartes' death in 1650 — openly denied personal immortality, or refused to accept it if it could not be proven by reason. This may seem incredible. It is hard for us to appreciate the power and uniformity of fundamental religious beliefs before the nineteenth century. Thus most people — even historians — are surprised to learn that there was no avowed atheism before the late eighteenth century, and that the first published assertion of atheism, or denial of the existence of God, was in Baron D'Holbach's *La Système de la Nature*, printed in 1770.[11]

Who, then, is Descartes writing against: whom is he trying convince? Descartes goes some way towards identifying his targets on the question of immortality when he speaks of those audacious people who were condemned by the Lateran Council held under Pope Leo X. For these people, Descartes says, held that 'as far as human reasoning goes, there are persuasive reasons for holding that the soul dies along with the body'.[12] Hence they are a fitting target for Descartes' philosophical argument for immortality, based on his dualism: that the mind is entirely independent of the body. Yet this still does not help to resolve the puzzle raised by Locke, since these audacious individuals did believe in immortality, Descartes notes, although 'on faith alone'. They were, to use the technical term, conditional immortalists, who believed that, although we were not naturally immortal, we would be raised from the dead and given eternal life at the Second Coming, since it was Jesus Christ alone who 'brought life and immortality to light through the Gospel' (2 Tim. 1.10). So, again, Descartes seems to have had no real enemies: no unconditional mortalists to persuade. But if he had no enemies why is he girding his loins for battle? Why is it so important for him to persuade certain unnamed (and apparently unknown) mortalists that the soul is immortal?

Before trying to answer this question, I want to reintensify the psychological conflict by considering another of Descartes' main motives. 'The preservation of health has always been [he writes] the principal end of my studies'.[13] Descartes' passionate interest in health and longevity was known to his contemporaries. In a letter of 4 December 1637 to Huygens, he says he is working on a compendium of medicine, partly based on his own reasoning, which he hopes will lead to the prolongation of his life to 'a hundred years or more'.[14] The key seemed to him to be bodily hygiene and, especially, diet. Indeed, some of his contemporaries believed that he had discovered the secret of living for three or four hundred years.[15] Descartes speaks about the importance and great potentiality of medicine in Part Six of the *Discourse on Method*, where he says that it might free us from 'innumerable diseases' and 'perhaps even from the infirmity of old age'.[16]

Yet why should Descartes be so anxious for this-worldly health and longevity when he was doubly confident of blissful immortality in the next world? One is reminded here of a story which Bertrand Russell tells about a man who was asked at a 'dinner [party] what he thought would happen to him when he died. The man at first tried to ignore the question, but, on being pressed, replied: 'Oh well, I suppose I shall inherit eternal bliss, but I wish you wouldn't talk about such unpleasant subjects'.[17] We see the absurdity here. But is it not also odd that two of Descartes' main goals were the conservation of health *and* proving the soul's immortality? Consider, by way of analogy, a woman who not only took the oral contraceptive, but used as well a diaphragm, and was also trying to find some third (less certain) method of contraception. I think we would be forced to say that she was unnaturally fearful of conception. Similarly, I think Descartes was, at an unconscious level and by our standards, more than usually terrified by death — by THE END.

If we cannot explain something at a conscious level, then we need to move to a deeper level. The way to resolve the conflict, I believe, is to suppose that unconsciously Descartes was more than usually fearful of death and doubtful about immortality. I think I can support this hypothesis by examining Descartes' fullest account of death, which is in the *Passions of the Soul*, Part one, where he opposes the usual view that the soul is implicated in the demise of the body: 'it has been believed, without justification', he says, 'that our natural heat and all the movements of our bodies depend on the soul; whereas we ought to hold, on the contrary, that the soul takes its leave when we die only because this heat ceases'.[18] For Descartes, the mind is not a sort of thermostat that regulates the body's temperature. So death concerns the body only, according to him, not the soul. When the body loses a certain amount of heat, it dies; and then the soul leaves it, presumably because it can do nothing more with such a cold body. The soul is not wrenched painfully from the body. Descartes opposes the common view that it is the departure or separation of the soul that causes death. He also denies that the soul can directly do anything, or omit doing something, that causes the body's death. The death of the body, as Descartes graphically explains in section 6, is merely like the winding down of 'a watch or other automaton (that is, a self-moving machine)'.

Here we can see how Descartes could describe bodily death as a 'trivial cause'.[19] He is talking about the death of human body as though neither he, or anyone, had anything to do with it or fear from it. Is this psychologically feasible? *Prima facie*, it is. For if Descartes did believe that his body, like a non-human animal, is just an extended machine that has nothing to do with his real, thinking self, then he can be sure that he will not be affected by his body's death. So dualism took the sting out of death. This is one way of explaining how Descartes could be so detached and unmoved in his account of death. What is not easily explained, however, is how Descartes could be so imperturbable about death, while being so interested in bodily health and longevity. Yet on my hypothesis, these two things can be explained. For as I see it, Descartes' dualistic account was a way of denying or warding off his unconscious dread of death, a dread which was also being assuaged by the consoling belief that he was likely to live for a hundred years or more.

In his detached account of death it is as though Descartes himself is already dead. And in an important sense, he was already dead, that is, if we combine his dualism with the received view of death (the separation of mind from body). Then it will follow that Descartes was born dead and has always been dead, since his mind has always been separated from his body. Perhaps Nietzsche had Descartes or someone like him in mind, when, in his *Gay Science*, he speaks of the great privilege of the dead. 'What privilege? To die no more'.[20] In other words, Descartes' dualism constitutes a pre-emptive strike against death. To take an analogy: one way to vanquish the fear of being burgled is to give away all your possessions. That, in effect, is what Descartes did. Or, to vary the metaphor, by inocculating himself with death, Descartes lost his conscious fear of it. The result was the unnatural imperturbability, a state of attenuated death, as it were, when thinking about death. But the tremendous fear still remained at an unconscious level, producing his incongruous passion for immortality and longevity.

The incongruous elements make sense, I suggest, once we postulate Descartes' unconscious fear of death. No doubt, alternative stories might be told which do not postulate this. But I doubt whether such stories are as plausible or natural as mine, or that they can resolve the crucial problem which I mentioned above. That is, why was Descartes so concerned to attack the mortalists, those who did not believe in personal immortality, since there is no evidence that there was anyone in the sixteenth or seventeenth century — at least up till Descartes' time — who denied an afterlife. This is strange, but not if my hypothesis is accepted.

For as I see it, Descartes was splitting off and projecting his fearful, unconscious doubts about immortality onto these unnamed putative enemies. Descartes was, in effect, creating mortalistic enemies as a way of dealing with his own disturbing unconscious doubts. Projecting the doubts was one way of getting rid of them, at least to some degree; it was also a way that Descartes could make sense of his (otherwise otiose) reassuring arguments for immortality based on dualism.[21]

This sort of projection is not as uncommon as it may initially appear. Consider, for example, unjustified jealousy. This by no means rare phenomenon can be explained, Freud argues, by supposing that the jealous person feels impulses towards unfaithfulness which have come under repression. He or she can then alleviate the pressure by projecting (unconsciously, of course) the unfaithful impulses into the partner to whom faithfulness is owed.[22]

-III-

Would Descartes, the lover of truth, have accepted my interpretation? Not easily, since it would (if true) raise his disturbing fears about death. Nor could he be expected to accept my conclusion that there were paranoid features in his thinking. There is bound to be resistance to my interpretation; but this, as I stated in Section I, is what we should expect. Dualism was a death and life matter. Reliving its genesis is bound to be painful. It would not be easy for Descartes to accept either that his dualistic account of death arose from a dread of having, or being, a living mortal body; or that he dealt with this dread by withdrawing to the safety of his mind, which meant giving up his body as an irrelevant machine that had nothing to do with the real, essential Descartes.

Ideally, however, there would be no need for this strategy of dividing mind from body in order to conquer death. In an ideal world, the living human body would not be subject to death. Descartes never states directly that this is what he most wants; however, I suggest that he expresses it indirectly, fancifully, in the form of a wishful image in the *Discourse of Method*, Part three, where he speaks about the importance of bringing our desires into line with reality. Thus, he says, we should not 'desire to be healthy when ill or free when imprisoned, any more than we now desire to have bodies of a material as indestructable as diamond or wings to fly like the birds'.[23] Having a body as indestructable as a diamond was not, I take it, a stock image in Descartes' time — like having wings to fly like a bird. It was, I think, a wishful image that flowed unguardedly (in those pre-Freudian times) from Descartes' unconscious.

It is in Descartes' images that we can perhaps most directly observe his deeper, less censored wishes and fears. He wished to be an indestructable, incorruptible diamond, a bodily substance that could not be broken, but he feared that he was horribly fragile and destructible. That fear also emerges in an image he uses both in the *Meditations* and in the earlier *Search after Truth*, where he uses the image to describe the delusions of mad people. Some of them believe, he says in the First *Meditation*, that 'their heads are made of earthenware, or that they are pumkins, or made of glass'. In the *Search after Truth* he changes the image somewhat when he describes 'those melancholic individuals who think themselves to be vases'.[24] In both cases, the human body is imagined to be even more fragile and destructible than it really is. That, in my view, shows Descartes' unconscious fear. Of course, the force of my point will depend on how common this picture of madness was in the seventeenth century. If mad people were often spoken about as believing that they were made of glass or pottery, then my point will have less force. If the image (and especially that of the diamond) was idiosyncratic to Descartes, then my point and thesis will be enhanced.[25] Similarly, my main hypothesis depends on the historical fact (if it is such) that there were no avowed unconditional mortalists in the sixteenth or seventeenth century. To the extent that there were external enemies, who published accessible attacks on immortality, there will be little or no reason to accept my thesis, that Descartes was projecting internal ones.

-IV-

Having argued that the, or a, cause of Descartes' dualism and dualistic account of death was an unconscious fear of death, I shall now briefly fill in the main line of my psychological hypothesis, showing its connection with Descartes' dualism and his redescription of the concept of idea.

A person who is exposed to a fearsome threat may react in a number of ways. One way is to attack; another basic way is to withdraw or escape. But a person who is trapped in, for example, a concentration camp or an intolerable family situation cannot physically withdraw. He can, however, withdraw psychically, by a process of splitting. He can detach himself from involvement with the threatening or agonizing external objects. The interest he loses in bodily objects, he can concentrate in his mind, in his thinking and fantasies. In Freudian terms this is described as decathecting the body and cathecting or hypercathecting mental objects.[26] The body may then be experienced as dull and deadish, whereas the mind is activated by the energy or interest that had been withdrawn from the body. When interest leaves the body it can go to the head. Thinking becomes libidinized. But sexual thinking is not the same as thinking about sex. Rather, ordinary thinking is endowed with an intensity and vivacity akin to sexual love. Thoughts are also, as in the case of normal loved objects, overestimated.

The application of this model (which would be accepted, I think, by a wide range of psychoanalysts) should be clear.[27] How did Descartes' dread of death, that bodily death meant THE END, bring about his theoretical split of mind and body? It did so, according to my thesis, by causing Descartes to experience his body and bodily feelings in a detached, dullish way, and his mind and thoughts as intimate and lively. That Descartes did experience his mind and body in these ways seems supported especially by *Meditation* Six, where he describes his body as if he had only a distant connection with it; whereas he portrays his mind and its objects as glowing with vivacity.[28] The linguistic repackaging of thoughts and concepts with pains and bodily sensations was a consequence of these experiences. Because his thoughts and bodily sensations were felt to be roughly alike in vivacity or vapidity, they could be subsumed under the new, inclusive category: idea.

If we suppose that Descartes' contemporaries had a similar dread of mortality, then they, too, would have had these (largely inchoate) experiences- of a dullish body but a lively mind. It was Descartes, however, who harnessed these experiences, articulating them in his classic dualistic theory. It is at this point that Rorty's intellectual reconstruction comes in; although, unlike Rorty, I take Descartes' experiences, rather than his language, to be primary. The linguistic innovation gave expression to the raw dualistic experiences. It was because thoughts and bodily sensations did not feel so very different that they could be put into one concept. So the experiences, which were caused by the dread of death and were the mind's unconscious way of dealing with it, also helped to cope with that fear at a conscious level. They did so by prompting the repackaging of the term 'idea', thereby providing the crucial step to dualism, which in turn offered a convincing philosophical proof (according to Descartes) for the immortality of soul.

-V-

But what, we need to ask, originally activated the unconscious fear of death in Descartes and his contemporaries? What happened in the early seventeenth century that made the (unconscious) fear of death so acute? The main cause, I take it, was that the scriptural and ecclesiastical justifications for immortality were losing their hold, particularly on the educated classes, although no one was clearly avowing this. I think this is supported by what we know of the dramatic rise of scepticism in Europe, the *crise pyrrhonienne*.[29] The Reformation had damaged ecclesiastical authority; the growing interest in non-theistic religions, prompted by the study of classical texts and travel literature, was raising problems for the accepted Biblical framework; and the emerging scholarly work on the Bible was also undermining its authority and hence in the Gospel promise of resurrection and immortal life. Serious scepticism and infidelity were beginning to surface, bringing with it the terrible doubt that death might really mean THE END. Although not yet awake, Europe was stirring uncomfortably from a dream of immortality that had lasted for more than a thousand years. This overview is supported by Descartes' own remark in the 'Dedicatory Letter', in which he alludes to the growth of infidelity concerning God and immortality.

Presumably, there must have been something in Descartes' distinctive past that prefigured and disposed him to experience acutely the unconscious dread of death and the consequent dualistic sensations. I imagine this has a great deal to do with the fact that Descartes' mother died shortly after he was born, that he was a sickly child who was not expected to live long, and that his father seems to have rejected him.[30] However, given how little we know of Descartes' early years, I do not think that it can be very fruitful to pursue this line of thought. As a brilliant theoretician, Descartes was in a unique position to articulate and systematize the widespread but still latent dualistic feelings. He was bold enough to express what many were only feeling. By systematizing these feelings within a dualistic position Descartes provided Europe with a way of dealing with the great fear, a *modus vivendi* which was to last for nearly three centuries.[31]

1 Richard Rorty, *Philosophy and the Mirror of Nature* (Oxford: Blackwell, 1980), p. 33.
2 ibid., p. 50.
3 ibid., p. 51.
4 ibid., p. 56.
5 ibid.
6 ibid., p. 33.
7 ibid., p. 58.
8 *The Philosophical Writings of Descartes* (Cambridge, Cambridge University Press, 1985), translated by J. Cottingham, R. Stoothoff, D. Murdoch; vol. 2, p. 3.
9 See, for example, J. Cottingham, *Descartes* (Oxford: Blackwell, 1986), p. 111. See especially the conclusion of Part Five of the *Discourse*, where Descartes describes the 'subject of the soul' as 'of the greatest importance'; *Philosophical Writings of Descartes*, vol. 1, p. 141.
10 *Mr Locke's Reply to . . . the Lord Bishop of Worcester's Answer to his Second Letter* (1699), in *The Works of John Locke* (London, 2nd ed., 1722), vol. I, p. 565.
11 See my *History of Atheism in Britain: from Hobbes to Russell* (London: Routledge, 1990), chaps. 1 and 6, and 'Deism, Immortality and the Art of Theological Lying', in J. A. L. Lemay (ed.), *Deism, Masonry, and the Enlightenment* (Delaware: University of Delaware Press, 1987), pp. 61–78. While I do not think that there were any avowed atheists before 1770, I am not claiming that there were no avowed mortalists before Descartes' time — for example, among the ancients.
12 *Philosophical Writings of Descartes*, vol. 2, p. 4.
13 ibid., vol. 3, *The Correspondence* (Cambridge: Cambridge University Press, 1991), trans. and edited by J. Cottingham, R. Stoothoff, D. Murdoch, and A. Kenny; p.273, letter to the Marquess of Newcastle, October 1645.
14 *Philosphical Writings of Descartes*, vol. 3, p. 76.
15 Ben-Ami Scharfstein, *The Philosophers: Their Lives and the Nature of Their Thought* (Oxford: Blackwell, 1980), pp. 135–6.
16 *Philosophical Writings of Descartes*, vol. 1, p. 143.
17 Russell, 'Stoicism and Mental Health', in *Let the People Think* (London, 1941), p. 54.
18 *Philosophical Writings of Descartes*, vol. 1, 329.
19 ibid., Second Set of Replies, vol. 2, p. 109.
20 Nietzsche, *Gay Science* (New York: Vintage, 1974), trans. by W. Kaufmann, p. 218.
21 For Freud's account of projection which comes closest to my reconstruction of Descartes, see his 1922 essay 'Some Neurotic Mechanisms in Jealousy, Paranoia and Homosexuality', in *The Standard Edition of the Complete Psychological Works* (London: Hogarth Press, reprinted 1986) ed. J. Strachey et al., vol. XVIII, pp. 223–32; also see vol. I, pp. 209–12; vol. XII, pp. 66–71; XIII, pp. 61–4.
22 See Freud, *Standard Edition*, vol. XVIII, pp. 225–7.
23 *Philosophical Writings of Descartes*, vol. 1, p. 124.
24 ibid., vol. 2, pp. 13 and 407.
25 In his *Enquiry into the Human Mind* (Edinburgh, 1764), Thomas Reid mentions a (presumably) mad person who thought he was 'made of glass' (chap. 5, sect. 7).
26 See, for example, lecture xxii of Freud's *Introductory Lectures on Psycho-Analysis* (1917), in *Standard Edition*, vol. XVI, pp. 373–6.
27 See, for example, R Fairbairn, 'Schizoid Factors in the Personality', in *Psychoanalytic Studies of the Personality* (London: Tavistock Publications, 1952); Harry Guntripp, *Schizoid Phenomena, Object Relations and the Self* (London: Hogarth Press, 1968), chaps 1 and 2; R. D. Laing, *The Divided Self* (London, reprinted 1969), especially chaps 4 and 5.

28 Thus Descartes writes: 'As for the body which by some special right I called 'mine', my belief that this body, more than any other, belonged to me had some justification. For I could never be separated from it, as I could from other bodies; and I felt all my appetites and emotions in, and on account of, this body; and finally, I was aware of pain and pleasurable ticklings in parts of this body, but not in bodies external to it', *Philosophical Writings*, vol. 2, p. 52; also see pp. 51, 53–4, 58–9.

29 See J.M. Robertson, *History of Freethought* (London: Watts, 1936), Richard Popkin, *History of Scepticism from Erasmus to Spinoza* (Berkeley: University of California Press, 1979) and my 'Die Debatte uber die Seele', in *Grundriss der Geschichte der Philosophie: Die Philosophie des 17. Jahrhunderts.* 3 England (Basil: Schwabe, 1988), pp. 759–81.

30 Scharfstein, *The Philosophers*, pp. 127-8; G. Rodis-Lewis, 'Descartes' Life and the development of his philosophy', *Cambridge Companion to Descartes.*

31 Earlier versions of this paper were read at the Loyola College, Baltimore, and the University of New Mexico. I am grateful to those present and also to Dr James Hopkins for helpful comments.

10. SPINOZA AND CARTESIANISM

THEO VERBEEK

The idea that theology and philosophy are separate disciplines; that they have their own methods and their own problems and that they play their own role in society, never was very original. However, the idea that philosophy is irrelevant to theology and that whatever philosophy does is of no consequence to theology was new in the seventeenth century and seems to have been characteristic of Cartesianism.[1] In this paper, I shall discuss some aspects of the problem as it was further developed by Dutch Cartesians and, more particularly show, that Spinoza cannot be understood without this background.

The classical text on separatism in Descartes is the first rule of the so-called 'provisional moral code', which sets apart the laws of one's country and in particular the religion in which one has been brought up, before instituting a universal doubt.[2] For Descartes this was not an arbitrary decision but one that was based on a very specific theory of judgement.[3] According to Descartes, all judgement is the product of a co-operation between the understanding and the will, in which the contents — a set of ideas — are provided by the understanding and the dynamics — the act by which the truth of a given set of ideas is affirmed or denied — by the will.[4] However, the will can overrule the understanding either because the necessities of life force require it or because Divine grace compels us to accept as true ideas which by definition are not clear and distinct.[5]

Dutch Cartesians generally interpreted Descartes' first rule of the moral code as stating that, given the fact that religion was never called into doubt, it cannot be an object for philosophy either.[6] But, although they also accepted the theory of judgement that goes with it, their separation of reason and faith, philosophy and theology, could easily be interpreted as being based on a convention — a convention, moreover, Descartes had been the first to break by proposing a novel interpretation of the theological dogma of transubstantiation.[7] More to the point, Descartes' adversaries had claimed that it is impossible to exclude any particular idea from doubt.[8] Their objection shows that two conditions must be met: first, the act of judgement must be based on a free will, so that, whenever we wish to do so, we can freely doubt or exclude from doubt whatever is

A.P. Coudert, S. Hutton, R.H. Popkin and G.M. Weiner (eds): Judaeo-Christian Intellectual Culture in the Seventeenth Century, 173–184.
© 1999 *Kluwer Academic Publishers. Printed in the Netherlands.*

presented to us by the understanding; and, second, ideas must be recognized as being immune from doubt. If these conditions fail the result must be either total scepticism or a philosophical reconstruction of religion.

Cartesians reacted to this problem by defining philosophy in such a way that only clear and distinct ideas can be its object. Consequently, clearness and distinctness are not just criteria for truth but of demarcation, in the sense that clearness and distinctness qualify an idea as a possible object for philosophical investigation. Naturally, this means that philosophy is severely limited in scope. It also means that philosophy is no longer the hand-maid of, for example, theology but a discipline which, after having identified its object by means of systematic doubt, proceeds in complete independence, without having regard either to religion or to daily life both of which are covered by ideas that are not clear and distinct.

This is more or less the position of Johannes de Raey (1622–1702), from 1651 a professor of philosophy in Leiden and, from 1668, in Amsterdam, who for many years was one of the most prominent representatives of the Dutch Cartesian school.[9] De Raey always believed that philosophical knowledge is knowledge of a very specific kind.[10] From the early 1660s he underpinned this notion with an original theory of meaning.[11] According to him, the meanings of words are ideas. However, since there are two types of ideas — the clear and distinct ideas of science, which, being innate, belong to the mind alone, and the obscure and confused ideas of the senses, which the mind acquires in co-operation with the body — there are also two languages: Philosophical language and ordinary language. Consequently, the idea that philosophy can be practical or can be used in theology is according to this view incoherent because neither practical nor religious problems can be formulated in the language of philosophy. Nor can we translate into the language of philosophy a text written in ordinary language — like the Bible. Although there is considerable confusion in De Raey's mind about the implications of his view it seems to me that he has hit upon some important insights on the nature of modern science. What emerges indeed is the idea that the aim of science is to construct a (mathematical) model and provide a representation of something that by definition can never be seen. Accordingly, the only way to understand what philosophy is, is to learn the rules of its language, that is, identify the ideas to which it refers.

De Raey's philosophy is an interesting attempt to deal with a problem that was to occupy philosophers until Kant. It is the problem of the relation between the mechanical philosophy and the world of action and daily life; between the scientific world-view and common sense; between science and metaphysics. In fact, De Raey's solution of this problem is basically similar to that of Berkeley and Kant, except that his Cartesianism prevents him from turning science into a purely subjective picture of the world. Indeed, the fact that he has learned from Descartes how to interpret the clear and distinct ideas of science as a true picture of the world leads to many inconsistencies and obscurities. In any case, he isolates scientific knowledge from other kinds of cognition, in order to prevent the categories of science from being applied to the problems of religion and action. It implies of course that, strictly speaking, metaphysics is not natural theology and that it speaks about God only because that is necessary for laying the foundations of science.

Although De Raey is never mentioned in Spinoza's work (nor in his correspondence), Spinoza certainly knew about him. His first published work, *Principia philosophiæ Renati Des Cartes* (1663), was originally written for a certain Johannes Casearius (c. 1641–1677), who matriculated as a student in theology in Leiden in 1661, at a time when De Raey was the only regular professor of philosophy.[12] As a result, it seems likely not only that Spinoza was familiar with De Raey's ideas but also that his own work on Descartes' *Principia* and even the *Tractatus de intellectus emendatione* can be seen as commentaries on the ideas developed by De Raey during his lectures.[13] In the following I shall briefly discuss Spinoza's relation to the particular interpretation of Descartes that was developed by the Dutch Cartesians, concentrating more particularly on three points: His conception of metaphysics, his notion of certainty and his idea of the freedom of philosophy.[14]

According to Lodewijk Meijer's preface, Spinoza's *Principiorum Renati Des-Cartes Partes I & II more geometrico demonstratæ* grew out of a 'geometrical' treatment of Book II and part of Book III of Descartes' *Principles* and of an attempt to solve 'the principal and the most difficult questions that are generally discussed in metaphysics, which Descartes has not yet solved' — an attempt in which one easily recognizes the 'Cogitata metaphysica'. At a later stage, Spinoza was allegedly been asked by friends to complete this with a geometrical treatment of Book I, an effort which took two weeks.[15] Actually, this book is anything but a faithful rendering of Cartesian philosophy. In fact, this description is fitting only for Book II, but it is certainly not true of Book I, which is based on the appendix to Descartes' *Second Set of Replies*.[16] In this text Descartes already had made an attempt to provide a 'geometrical' presentation of the main truths of his metaphysics, in particular the existence of God and the real distinction between mind and body. This text was the source of propositions I–VIII of Spinoza's own discussion in Part I of his work. Even so, the proofs and the order of the proofs are different and sometimes there is also a shift in emphasis, which, in combination with what is said in the *Cogitata*, also implies a significant shift in meaning. It is clear, for example, that for Spinoza the importance of what has come to be called the 'ontological proof' of God's existence is not so much that it forms additional evidence about God's existence or that it shows the difference between the existence of God and that of created beings, but that being the cause of His own essence and existence is the basic fact about God's nature in general, from which all His other attributes can be deduced. In any case, there is not a one-to-one relation between Book I of Descartes' *Principia* and Spinoza's version of it.

Implicitly, Spinoza also rejects the Cartesian conception of metaphysics, if only because in the original plan there was no geometrical treatment of Book I. Accordingly, metaphysics is no longer the discipline in which the foundations are laid for the other sciences, but only the science of God and the mind. Whereas Dutch Cartesians believed that metaphysics should be dealt with only in sofar as it is necessary to justify the criterion of clearness and distinctness, Spinoza freely develops a theory of the Divine attributes. Indeed, the explicit aim of the 'Cogitata metaphysica' was to go beyond Descartes and provide the solution of those questions he had left unsolved. However, by dialectically developing the notion that God is His own cause and therefore gives Himself all the perfections of which there can be an idea Spinoza arrives at the conclusion that creation is impossible and that there is no separation between God and nature.

Spinoza's main justification for rejecting the Cartesian conception of metaphysics is that true science does not require a foundation. If we have a true idea, we automatically know that it is a true idea.[17] Truth is a sign of itself and of falsehood: 'Est enim verum index sui et falsi'.[18] Accordingly, there is no reason why one should prove the existence of God and the real distinction between body and mind before setting about to know the material world. There is no reason for systematic doubt either, because ideas become doubtful only in connection with other ideas.[19] If we imagine a flying horse we believe in the real existence of that flying horse, unless we have other ideas in virtue of which we know that a flying horse does not exist.[20] Someone who dreams believes in the reality of his dream, but someone who is awake will never mistake reality for a dream.[21] Spinoza does not, for that matter, say that all ideas are certain. A single idea is neither doubtful nor certain but simply 'that sensation'.[22] It can become doubtful only if it is contrary to another idea and certain if, eventually, it is confirmed by a true rational idea.[23] This means that, even if particular beliefs based on the imagination turn out in fact to be true, their truth is never self-evident nor certain. Any such belief may turn out to be false but the only way to know that it is, is from the view-point of reason.

Still, someone who has a sensation or an imagination (and no rational knowledge to correct or confirm it) must *feel* certain of what he experiences. Spinoza agrees with that. The dreamer feels certain about the reality of his dream. Someone who is in error — 'a waking dream'[24] — feels certain of his beliefs as long as he has no reason to assume that they may be false. Nonetheless, Spinoza refuses to refer to the psychological condition of the dreamer as 'certainty', because, as he says, certainty is not absence of doubt but 'something positive'.[25] It is not easy to see what Spinoza means, unless one realizes that, according to him, there are no innate ideas. The only idea that is always there is the idea of our body, which constitutes our soul.[26] The first and for many people the only ideas they ever have are those which are caused by an affection of their own body.[27] The ideas of the affections of the body do not conceal from our view the true ideas that we already had, but are the material from which the true ideas are developed. The idea of a *causa sui*, on the other hand, which idea is undoubtedly certain, is not innate, although it is developed from ideas everybody has and although it is clear to anybody who manages to have it. As a result, the adequate ideas we associate with the second and third kind of knowledge always appear against a background of ideas that are not adequate. Their certainty manifests itself through themselves, because they are always accompanied by an idea of themselves, and through their contrast with the ideas of the imagination, which in turn *become* uncertain in virtue of the same contrast. Finally, since the only idea that would allow us to doubt the ideas of reason, namely, the idea of a deceitful God, is contradictory, it is impossible to undermine the inherent certainty of the ideas of reason: Whenever we have a true rational idea we are certain that it is true.

Therefore, it is not necessary either to justify the clear and distinct ideas that we have or to start with a systematic doubt. If we have any true ideas we know that we have them and we know that they are true. The only preliminary task the philosopher can think of would be to try and obtain true ideas, not only for their own sake but also because they expose the falsity of the ideas we already had. Accordingly, the didactics of philosophy is not to expose the uncertainty of our ideas but to ask for definitions, which, by laying bare the causal structure of the things defined, make us understand the universal determinism of nature.[28]

It seems then that there are two ways to arrive at the same result. The first is to analyze the Cartesian idea of God, which is the way chosen in the *Cogitata metaphysica* and in the first part of the *Ethics*. This way is, of course, eminently suitable for philosophers, especially Cartesian philosophers, because it makes use of the technical notions of those familiar with the second kind of knowledge. The second way is to start with experience and to search for definitions and causes. According to Spinoza, this way is even better than the first, because, although the demonstration that everything 'depends from God for its essence and existence, is legitimate and cannot be called into doubt, it does not affect our minds as much as when the same thing is concluded from the essence of a particular thing'.[29] In both cases, however, the result is the insight that the whole of nature, including ourselves, is necessarily determined and that neither on the level of human beings nor on that of God there is any freedom.[30] Accordingly, the development of a scientific attitude is now seen to be essential for developing a *Weltanschauung*. On the way to true salvation, that is, the beatitude caused by the intellectual love of God, the second kind of knowledge is an indispensable stage.[31]

Finally, Spinoza's conception of the freedom of philosophy seems to have been developed in reaction to Dutch Cartesians. According to these Cartesians, the only freedom philosophy has is the freedom of judgement, which, if properly understood, prevents the philosopher from discussing those problems of which he cannot have a clear and distinct idea. As we already saw, this means that philosophy becomes an independent and autonomous discipline. Institutionally, the separation of philosophy and theology implied the creation of two different competencies, which in turn allowed university administrations to protect new philosophy. And, finally, the political fruit of this was, ideally at least, that the Church would have no reason to remonstrate with the authorities for the fact that irreligious doctrines were taught in their university. Accordingly, Cartesian separatism fits into a complicated pattern of political and institutional motives, which are very characteristic of seventeenth-century Dutch society in general.

The subject-matter of Spinoza's *Tractatus theologico-politicus* is, according to its title, to show that 'the freedom to philosophise can not only be granted without injury to Piety and the Peace of the Commonwealth, but that the Peace of the Commonwealth and even Piety are endangered by the suppression of this freedom'.[32] Most commentators interpret *philosophari* as 'think' or even 'speak'. The object of the *Tractatus* therefore would be the freedom to think and to speak, a freedom which is not only harmless but also necessary, both for the peace of the commonwealth and for 'piety'. This, however, is misleading or rather downright false. In the seventeenth century, *philosophari* means only one thing, namely, to do philosophy, a discipline which still involved a highly technical method and a number of highly technical concepts. As a result, the true subject of the Tractatus is the freedom of philosophy, which can be equated with the freedom to think only because the argument is not on academic philosophy, which is taught by public officials, but about philosophy as it is done by and for free citizens. In other words, Spinoza is dealing with a particular philosophy, his own if only because that is the only one that is true and known to be true. Of this particular philosophy it is shown that it is harmless because the morality it advocates is conducive to social harmony. Since, on the other hand, the morality of reason is the same as that prescribed by religion, a philosophy whose only concern is truth does not harm the interests of religion. In brief, a philosophy that fully develops the idea that there is no distinction between God and nature is politically and religiously harmless, in spite of the fact that from a more conventional point of view it would be legitimate to characterise such a philosophy as atheist.[33]

This accounts for the first half of the title. It remains to be shown why philosophy (that is, true philosophy) is necessary both for the peace of the commonwealth and even for piety (*ipsaque pietate*). According to Spinoza religion is any form of free and virtuous behaviour that is inspired by ideas of the imagination.[34] Accordingly, he defines faith as any idea (or ideas) of the imagination that makes such behaviour possible.[35] Its criterion, therefore, is thoroughly pragmatic: 'Faith requires not so much true dogmas as pious dogmas, that is, such as move the heart to obedience'.[36] For example, if to act 'religiously' it is necessary to believe that one is free, this belief counts as true faith.[37] Also, if it is necessary to believe that we will be saved, belief in salvation is true faith, although the idea that we are immortal is patently false.[38]

This raises the question why revelation is necessary, especially because, as Spinoza explicitly says, God is known better by reason than by revelation.[39] This, however, is the very reason why revelation is necessary, namely for those who are unable to use their reason. Accordingly, the main use of religion is social and political.[40] It is a substitute for rational knowledge, not in the sense that it makes us know or understand whatever we know or understand by reason, but in the sense that it leads to the same kind of behaviour. However, if there is no sense in which $2 + 2 = 5$ is more false than $2 + 2 = 7$ it is difficult to see why one should make a distinction between religion and superstition. Yet, this distinction seems to be of overriding importance in the *Tractatus theologico-politicus*.[41] According to the preface, people would never be superstitious if 'if they were able to exercise complete control over all their circumstances, or if continuous good fortune were always their lot'.[42] Since this is rarely the case, they are the 'wretched victims of alternating hopes and fears', and 'their credulity knows no bounds'.[43] Like religion, therefore, superstition is rooted in the imagination and, like it, is made superfluous by reason, because there is neither hope nor fear — but, presumably, knowing anticipation only — if there is true knowledge of nature.[44] Accordingly, the best anti-dote against superstition is philosophy because, simply by presenting a true picture of reality, philosophy dispels any false picture of the world. So much is certain, philosophy makes both religion and superstition superfluous for those who understand it.

A key to the distinction between religion and superstition is provided in a few passages of the *Tractatus theologico-politicus*, for example, where Spinoza says that those narratives must be selected from the sacred histories 'that are most effective in instilling obedience and devotion'[45]; that Scripture 'merely employs such order and such language as is most effective in moving men to devotion'[46]; that historical narratives 'teach and enlighten men as far as suffices to impress on their minds obedience and devotion'[47]; that words (and books) become sacred if they are 'so arranged that readers are moved to devotion'[48]; that Moses introduced 'religion into his commonwealth so that his people would do their duty not by fear but from devotion'.[49] The key-word in all these texts is 'devotion' (*devotio*). Devotion, however, is essentially different from hope and fear because it is a form of love.[50] Therefore, although both religion and superstition have their roots in the imagination, their general difference is that between a doctrine based on fear and one based on love.

From the point of view of the *Ethics* the distinction between love and fear certainly is significant, because love strengthens the soul, while fear makes it weak and dependent. But the distinction is perhaps even more important to the ruler, because fear makes people unreliable and unpredictable. Accordingly, it is both necessary and possible to make the distinction between religion and superstition because it makes all the difference between a peaceful commonwealth and a commonwealth that is continually divided by internal strife. Accordingly, a free philosophy, that is, a philosophy that allows itself to freely address the problem of religion, is indispensable for a well-ordered commonwealth, because philosophy alone provides the criteria for making the distinction between religion and superstition. After all, even a truly religious person is unable to make it because, living in the sphere of the imagination, he has no certain criteria. Accordingly, if we are to decide which particular religion is superstitious (that is, which we are not going to tolerate), philosophy is indispensable.

By describing as superstitious any religion that is based on fear Spinoza turned the tables on the orthodox Calvinists. It is the official creed of the Seven Provinces that is denounced as superstitious and as a liability for any well-ordered commonwealth. The actual political situation comes into view both where Spinoza emphasizes the link between a monarchical form of government and superstition, and where he blames the intrusion of the law into the realm of speculative thought.[51] For not only had there been active measures against his friends Lodewijk Meijer and Adriaan Koerbach — quite often instigated by Cartesians — but there was also an increasingly powerful coalition between Calvinist ministers and the Prince of Orange. Separatism turned against those who, in the interest of the public order, had insisted most on the separation of the Church and the State; of theology and philosophy; of faith and reason. Indeed, according to Spinoza, the only politically viable solution was to subordinate the Church to the State; to allow philosophy to become religiously and politically meaningful; and to introduce a pragmatic criterion for faith. This is also the meaning of the expression *theologico-political*, the sense of which derives from *politico-theological*. This was used as a term of abuse by orthodox theologians to designate all those who, in the interest of political or ecclesiastical unity, declined a too strict formulation of the creed. In this way, the Orthodox said, they subordinated truth to unity and theology to politics. According to Spinoza, however, true political unity can be achieved only if the theology's task is redefined in the light of truth.

As a result, the title of Spinoza's *Tractatus* contains a programme, the main point of which is that philosophy should be free to discuss and criticize religion, because only an enlightened religion can fulfil its aim, which is to make people obey. In that programme Cartesian philosophy cannot be missed, except that it must lift its own limitations. Enlightenment, on the other hand, is achieved, not simply by applying to religion the method of Cartesian science, but by a *reductio ad absurdum* of Cartesian metaphysics on the one hand, and a complete reversal of the classical order of Cartesian philosophy on the other. Once that is achieved, the true aim of religion can become visible and the distinction between religion and superstition be made.

1 Cf. Paul Dibon, 'Connaissance révélée et connaissance rationnelle: aperçu sur les points forts d'un débat épineux', in: *Regards sur la Hollande du siècle d'or* (Naples, 1990), pp. 693–719; for Descartes himself, see Henri Gouhier, *La Pensée religieuse de Descartes* (Paris, 1924), pp. 217–235.

2 '...to obey to the laws and customs of my country, holding constantly to the religion in which by God's grace I had been instructed from my childhood'. *Discourse on method*, III, *AT*, VI, 23; *CSM*, I, 122. All other relevant texts are collected and discussed in Gouhier, *op. cit.* Descartes will be quoted after the Adam-Tannery edition (hereafter *AT*, followed by volume and page number) and after the English translation by Cottingham, Stoothoff and Murdoch (hereafter *CSM*, followed by volume and page number).

3 Cf. Descartes, *Discours de la méthode*, ed. É. Gilson, pp. 237–238.

4 *Meditations*, IV, *AT*, VII, 56–60; *CSM*, II, 39–41; *Principles*, I, art. 32–39, *AT*, VIII-A, 17–20; *CSM*, I, 204–206); cf. G. Nuchelmans, *Judgment and proposition* (Amsterdam, 1983), pp. 36–54.

5 *Principles*, I, art. 35, *AT*, VIII-A, 18; *CSM*, I, 204; cf. *Meditations*, IV, *AT*, VII, 58; *CSM*, II, 40–41. For religion, see Gouhier, *La pensée religieuse*, pp. 206–208.

6 Cf. Joh. Clauberg, *Initiatio philosophi* (1656), I, 25, in: *Opera omnia philosophica* (Amsterdam, 1691; repr. Hildesheim, 1968), p. 1137.

7 Martin Schoock, *Admiranda methodus* (Utrecht, 1643), sect. III, ch. 1; see Descartes/ Schoock, *La querelle d'Utrecht*, ed. Theo Verbeek (Paris, 1988), p. 267–269.

8 J. Revius, *Methodi cartesianæ consideratio theologica* (Leiden, 1648).

9 On De Raey, see A.J. van der Aa, *Biographisch woordenboek*, vol. XVI, pp. 43–44; C. Louise Thijssen-Schoute, *Nederlands Cartesianisme*, (Amsterdam 1954; reprinted Utrecht, 1989); Theo Verbeek, *Descartes and the Dutch* (Carbondale, 1992); idem, 'Tradition and novelty', in: Tom Sorell (ed), *The Rise of Modern Philosophy* (Oxford, 1993); idem, *De vrijheid van de filosofie* (Utrecht, 1994). Misled by Poortman's *Repertorium der Nederlandsche wijsbegeerte* (Amsterdam, 1948) I have in other publications given the year of his death as 1707. It is 1702.

10 Cf. Johannes de Raey, *Oratio de gradibus et vitiis notitiæ vulgaris* (Leiden, 1651), re-published in *Clavis philosophiæ naturalis* (Leiden, 1654), pp. 1–34; 2nd ed (Amsterdam, 1677), pp. 1–32, and in *Cogitata de Interpretatione* (Amsterdam, 1692), pp. 343–375.

11 This theory is developed in various disputations and essays, all collected in *Cogitata*.

12 On Casearius, see W. Meijer, 'Johannes Casearius', *Nederlandsch Archief voor Kerkgeschiedenis*, 1 (1902) 398–417 (in Dutch); idem, 'De Joanne Caseario', *Chronicon Spinozanum*, 3 (1923) (in Latin). He matriculated atLeiden University as a student of theology on 21 May 1661. In 1665 he continued his studies in Utrecht and was admitted to the ministry in Amsterdam, on 5 October 1665. In 1668 he took service with the East Indian Company at Malabar and provided the drawings for a botanical work, *Hortus Malabaricus* (1678), by the local governor Hendrik Adriaan van Reede tot Drakenstein. He gave his name to a family of plants (the 'Casearia').

13 There are two manuscript copies of De Raey's course on Descartes' *Principia*, one of which certainly dates from the Leiden period: Leiden University Library, Department of Western Manuscripts, BPL 907; Amsterdam University Library, Manuscript Department, X B 7. Both courses also contain lectures on the first three parts of the *Discourse on Method*.

14 My discussion will be brief and, I am afraid, unsatisfactory for many people. Some of it was covered in my Utrecht inaugural lecture as Thijssen-Schoute professor in the history of ideas, *De vrijheid van de filosofie* (Utrecht, 1994). The problem will be treated more fully in a book.

15 *Correspondence*, Ep. 13.

16 Descartes, *Second set of Replies*, *AT*, VII, 160–170; *CSM*, II, 113–120.

17 *Ethics*, II, prop. 43.

18 *Correspondence*, Ep. 76; *Ethics*, II, prop. 43 (with scholium).

19 *Tractatus de intellecta emendatione* (hereafter *TIE*), §§ 77–80, Gebhardt, II. 29–30.

20 *Ethics* II, prop. 49, schol; cf. *Ethics* II, prop. 17, schol.

21 'Soo dan iemand die de Waarheid heeft en kan niet twyffelen dat hy ze heeft; dog iemand die in Valsheid of doling steekt, die kan wel waanen dat hy in waarheid staat: gelyk als iemand die droomt wel denken kan dat hy waakt, maar nooyt kan iemand, die nu waakt, denken dat hy droomt'. *Short Treatise*, II, xv, Mignini, 73. The *Korte Verhandeling* is quoted after the edition by Filippo Mignini (L'Aquila, 1986).

22 'Dubitatio itaque in anima nulla datur datur per rem ipsam, de qua dubitatur, hoc est, si tantum unica sit idea in anima, sive ea sit vera, sive falsa, nulla dabitur dubitatio neque etiam certitudo: sed tantum talis sensatio'. *TIE*, § 78, Gebhardt, II, 29.

23 *Ethics*, II, prop. 42.

24 'Error autem est vigilando somniare'. *TIE*, Gebhardt, II, 24.

25 *Ethics*, II, prop. 49, schol.

26 ibid., II, prop. 13.

27 ibid., II, prop. 14–16.

28 *TIE*, §§ 95–98, Gebhardt, II, 34–36.

29 *Ethics*, V, prop. 36, schol; cf. *Ethics*, V, prop. 24.

30 ibid., I, app.

31 ibid., V, prop. 28.

32 '*Tractatus theologico-politicus continens dissertationes aliquot, quobus ostenditur libertatem philosophandi non tantum salva pietate et reipublicæ pace posse concedi; sed eandem nisi cum pace reipublicæ ipsaque pietate tolli non posse*'. The translation is Shirley's, with some alterations (hereafter, *TTP*).

33 According to contemporary definitions, an atheist would be anyone who holds the wrong ideas about God with the ultimate aim to ignore God's will; cf. H.-M. Barth, A*theismus und Orthodoxie: Analysen und Modelle christlicher Apologetik im 17. Jhdt* (Göttingen, 1971); idem, A*theismus: Geschichte und Begriff*, (München, 1973).

34 For a survey of the use of 'religio' and 'godsdienst' see Emilia Giancotti-Boscherini, *Lexicon Spinozanum* (The Hague, 1970), vol. II, pp. 920–928; 1204.

35 'Faith must be defined as the holding of certain beliefs about God such that, without these beliefs, there cannot be obedience to God, and if this obedience is posited, these beliefs are necessarily posited'. *TTP*, ch. 14, Gebhardt, III, 175 [Shirley, 222].

36 *TTP*, ch. 14 , Gebhardt, III, 176 [Shirley, 223].

37 'The revelation of Cain teaches us only that God admonished him to live the true life [...] Therefore, although the wording and reasoning of admonition seem clearly to imply freedom of the will, we are entitled to hold a contrary opinion'. *TTP*, ch. 2 , Gebhardt, III, 42–43 [Shirley, 86]; cf. Gen. 4. 7–15.

38 I am aware of the fact that Matheron holds the opposite interpretation. It rests however on the assumption that the relation between obedience and salvation is not an object of moral certainty but of mathematical certainty. This however is wrong not only because the certainty of those to whom virtue is obedience is never more than a moral certainty, but also because it is only in particular cases that obedience leads to salvation. Indeed, although there is an intelligible link between virtue and salvation (in the sense of having a better chance for survival) there is no intelligible link between obedience and virtue. Accordingly my argument stands: The belief that, if we obey, we will be saved, is a necessary condition for obeying the will of God as it is 'revealed', but it is rationally true only in sofar as it makes people act virtuously. See Alexandre Matheron, *Le Christ et le salut des ignorants selon Spinoza* (Paris, 1971).

39 *TTP*, ch. 1, Gebhardt, III, 15–16 [Shirley, 59–60].

40 'How salutary this doctrine is, and how necessary in the state if men are to live in peace and harmony and how many causes of disturbance and crime are therefore aborted at source, I leave for everyone to judge for himself'. *TTP*, ch. 14, Gebhardt, III, 179 [Shirley, 226].

41 There is hardly any mention of it in other works; cf. *Lexicon Spinozanum*, II, pp. 1047–1048; 1269 ('overgelovicheit').

42 *TTP*, præf., Gebhardt, III, 5 [Shirley, 49]; cf. *Ethics,* III, prop. 50, schol.

43 *TTP*, præf., Gebhardt, III, 5 [Shirley, 49].

44 'Wat dan de Hoope, Vreeze, Verzekertheid, Wanhoop en Belgzugt aangaat, het is zeeker dat zy uyt een kwaade opinie ontstaan. Want gelyk wy al vooren bewezen hebben, alle dingen hebben haar noodzaakelyke oorzaaken, en moeten zodanig als zy geschieden, noodzakelyk geschieden'. *Short Treatise*, II, ix, Mignini, 64.

45 *TTP*, ch. 5, Gebhardt, III, 79 [Shirley, 122].

46 *TTP*, ch. 6, Gebhardt, III, 91 [Shirley, 134].

47 *TTP*, ch. 5, Gebhardt, III, 77–78 [Shirley, 121].

48 *TTP*, ch. 12, Gebhardt, III, 160 [Shirley, 207].

49 *TTP*, ch. 5, Gebhardt, III, 75 [Shirley, 118].

50 *Ethics*, III, aff. def. 10; cf. *Ethics,* III, prop. 52, schol.

51 *TTP*, præf., Gebhardt, III, 7 [Shirley, 51].

11. LA RELIGION NATURELLE ET RÉVÉLÉE PHILOSOPHIE ET THÉOLOGIE: LOUIS MEYER, SPINOZA, REGNER DE MANSVELT

JACQUELINE LAGRÉE

L'objet de cette étude est de comparer sur quelques points essentiels et de façon systématique la façon dont trois livres qui se répondent[1] l'un à l'autre en très peu de temps la *Philosophia S.Scripturae interpres* de Louis Meyer, médecin et ami de Spinoza de 1666, le *Tractatus theologico-politicus* de Spinoza de 1670 et l'*Adversus anonymum Theologo-politicum liber singularis*[2] de 1671 essaient de résoudre une question suscitée par Descartes sans être vraiment tranchée par lui: celle de la possibilité et de la pertinence d'une apologétique cartésienne. Si le *Tractatus theologico-politicus* occupe dans notre propos une place centrale, c'est non seulement qu'il reprend pour la trancher de façon complètement différente, la question soulevée par L. Meyer de l'articulation de la philosophie et de la théologie, et qu'il est à son tour réfuté par Mansvelt, mais c'est surtout parce qu'il constitue un tournant décisif, un événement critique, une ligne de démarcation entre ceux qui croient pouvoir fonder une apologétique nouvelle et plus forte sur la méthode et les premiers principes de la métaphysique cartésienne et ceux qui voient dans le péril spinoziste la preuve du caractère aporétique ou pire, carrément dangereux de ce projet. Mansvelt meurt trop jeune pour être accusé de spinozisme. D'autres critiques, tels que Wittich ou Velthuysen,[3] seront attaqués et très durement alors même qu'ils s'efforçaient de nier une filiation naturelle entre Descartes et Spinoza.

Meyer, Spinoza et Mansvelt réfléchissent sur le statut de la révélation à partir d'un horizon intellectuel commun marqué par la philosophie de Descartes qui impose de penser la différence entre concevoir et comprendre, entre indéfini et infini ou l'affirmation d'une distance infinie entre le fini et l'infini. L'affirmation de l'infinité divine donne lieu chez le calviniste Mansvelt à la justification du caractère incompréhensible de l'économie de la grâce — que l'on songe à l'adage des métaphysiciens calvinistes: *finitum non est capax infiniti* — tandis qu'elle s'accompagne, chez Meyer et Spinoza, d'une homogénéité de nature des entendements finis et infini et du refus de toute surnature.

A.P. Coudert, S. Hutton, R.H. Popkin and G.M. Weiner (eds): *Judaeo-Christian Intellectual Culture in the Seventeenth Century*, 185–206.
© 1999 *Kluwer Academic Publishers. Printed in the Netherlands.*

Autour de la question de la révélation, c'est non seulement l'accès au divin, le statut de l'Ecriture Sainte, la promesse de salut et de béatitude pour l'homme qui se joue, c'est-à-dire des questions éthiques et religieuses, mais encore toute une théorie épistémologique, celle des modalités et de la puissance de la connaissance humaine, celle du rapport entre imagination et raison ainsi qu'une détermination métaphysique de l'unité du réel et de ses lois dont le révélateur est le concept de loi divine ou la théorie du miracle, impensable et impie s'il est vrai que la nature naturante ou Dieu agit toujours selon les mêmes lois, ce qui fait que la nature que nous connaissons, la nature naturée, est une et toujours la même.

Pour en donner un avant-goût, prenons l'exemple du concept de révélation:

L. Meyer rabat toute la révélation sur la connaissance acquise par la lumière naturelle donc la réduit à un discours faible, (connaissance par ouï-dire ou d'imagination) et à une propédeutique à la science.

R. de Mansvelt, dans le droit fil d'une théologie calviniste, défend les droits de la révélation mais pour sauver Descartes de l'accusation d'être *architectus spinozismi* il lui donne une extension maximale en y intégrant la connaissance naturelle.

Spinoza conserve à la révélation (identifiée à l'Ecriture Sainte) un statut et un domaine de validité propres mais, en proposant un concept radicalement nouveau de religion à la fois naturelle et révélée, il ruine la distinction de la nature et de la surnature impliquée par le concept traditionnel de révélation. Il n'accorde pourtant pas à cette notion plus que L. Meyer et moins que Mansvelt; il la subvertit en déplaçant complètement la problématique des modes et des finalités de la révélation, ce qui implique une distinction stricte entre philosophie (ou science) et révélation (ou foi) et débouche sur l'exigence irrécusable de la liberté de philosopher.

Rappel Biographique

LOUIS MEYER: fait partie du petit groupe d'amis à qui fut dicté le *Court Traité*; éditeur des *Principes de la philosophie* et des *Opera posthuma*, marqué par Descartes et par Spinoza, il évoque Descartes et le Spinoza du *Court Traité* à la fin de l'*Interpres*:

> Nous pensons qu'il vaut mieux connaître peu de choses mais avec certitude plutôt que de prendre et de faire prendre à autrui beaucoup de choses fausses ou douteuses pour vraies et certaines. En outre nous sourit une grande espérance: en ces temps où son principal fondateur et propagateur, René Descartes, a illuminé le monde des lettres et lui a légué son exemple, la philosophie verra son territoire

agrandi en tous sens par ceux qui souhaitent marcher sur les traces de cet auteur; et l'on verra paraître sur Dieu, l'âme rationnelle, la suprême félicité de l'homme et les moyens de parvenir à la vie éternelle, des pages qui feront autorité sur l'interprétation de l'Écriture Sainte et qui prépareront et aplaniront la voie pour réunir et rassembler dans la douceur de l'amitié, l'Eglise du Christ jusqu'ici divisée et déchirée par des schismes continuels.[4]

RÉGNER DE MANSVELT, issu d'une bonne famille d'Utrecht, fit ses études à Leyden et Utrecht (où il étudia le grec, l'hébreu, la philosophie et la théologie); devenu ministre, il succéda à Utrecht à Daniel Voetius sur la chaire de philosophie; il y 'enseigna la philosophie ancienne et nouvelle et se fit beaucoup d'honneur dans sa profession. Il remplit avec beaucoup de sagesse et de zèle l'emploi de recteur pour lequel il fut choisi. C'était un homme très laborieux mais à qui les occupations de cabinet et les méditations les plus profondes ne faisaient rien perdre de sa politesse et de ses manières affables. Il mourut épuisé par l'étude au mois de mai 1671, à la fleur de son âge. Près de mourir, il dit à ses amis que la vraie philosophie n'était que la méditation de la mort. Il a publié un traité *De legitima ratiocinandi ratione* & diverses dissertations. Après sa mort, on imprima son ouvrage contre le traité théologique et politique de l'impie Spinoza. Il avait aussi composé un commentaire sur L'*Enchiridion* d'Epictète'.[5]

L'*Adversus anonymum* réunit dans une même désapprobation L. Meyer & Spinoza et rapporte la discussion sur leurs livres à un débat théologique aussi ancien que l'Eglise chrétienne, celui *de usu rationis in theologia*. La préface de l'éditeur reconnaît à Mansvelt le mérite d'avoir été le premier et le seul (*primus et unicus*) à avoir entrepris de réfuter le *Tractatus theologico-politicus* de cet anonyme du début jusqu'à la fin,[6] récusant ainsi par avance l'accusation lancée par Stouppe:[7]

> Entre les théologiens qui sont dans ce pays, il ne s'en est trouvé aucun qui ait osé écrire contre les opinions que cet auteur avance dans ce Traité. S'ils continuent dans le silence on ne pourra s'empêcher de dire ou qu'ils n'ont point de charité en laissant sans réponse un livre si pernicieux ou qu'ils approuvent les sentiments de cet auteur ou qu'ils n'ont pas le courage et la force de les combattre.[8]

Mansvelt associe L. Meyer et Spinoza[9] et, comme Velthuysen,[10] considère que le second a mis ses pas dans ceux du premier en faisant paraître clairement l'entreprise de destruction de la foi qui se cache sous le projet explicite de défense de la paix religieuse. Discutant la formule scolastique qui fait de la philosophie la servante de la théologie, il entend défendre contre les deux anonymes l'accord et le secours mutuel des deux vérités, philosophique et théologique et il écrit:

Surtout, une occasion en a été offerte très récemment par l'Anonyme qui, sur l'interprétation de l'Écriture Sainte, a écrit de façon non seulement paradoxale mais hétérodoxe, comme ce fut démontré par des gens très savants. [.] Un autre Anonyme a suivi ses traces; récemment, sous le même prétexte, des très denses ténèbres de son cerveau, il a porté au jour un traité qu'il faudrait plutôt condamner aux ténèbres éternelles, *Tractatus theologico-politicus* pour démontrer avec des philosophes récents, combien il faut éviter tout mélange de théologie et de philosophie.[11]

On pourrait certes, objecter à la pertinence de l'examen de ce gros traité,[12] le mépris dans lequel le tint Spinoza. Dans une lettre à J. Jelles du 2 juin 1674[13] il écrit ceci:

J'ai vu exposé à la devanture d'un libraire le livre qu'un professeur d'Utrecht a écrit contre le mien et qui a été publié après la mort de l'auteur: le peu que j'en ai lu m'a fait juger que ce livre ne valait pas la peine d'être lu, encore moins d'être réfuté. J'ai donc laissé là le livre et son auteur. Les plus ignorants, me disais-je, non sans sourire, sont souvent les plus audacieux et les plus disposés à écrire. Ces gens là me paraissent exposer leur marchandise à la vente comme des fripiers qui montrent d'abord ce qu'ils ont de plus mauvais. Nul, dit-on, n'est plus rusé que le diable, pour moi je trouve que la complexion de ces gens là l'emporte encore beaucoup en ruse.[14]

On a peut-être trop vite suivi le conseil ironique de Spinoza et abandonné la lecture de Mansvelt qui est sans doute moins instructive pour la compréhension de Spinoza ou même pour la réception du *Tractatus theologico-politicus* comme tel, qu'elle ne permet d'éclairer d'un jour particulier les difficultés rencontrées par l'apologétique cartésienne après la publication de l'*Interpres* et du *Tractatus theologico-politicus*. Dès lors, le travail de Mansvelt apparaîtra moins comme une simple réfutation d'un texte honni que comme une défense des positions du groupe de théologiens hostiles à la scolastique[15] et désireux de fonder une apologétique rationaliste sur les principes de Descartes; notamment sur les deux première vérités découvertes par la philosophie première, à savoir la certitude de l'ego comme *res cogitans* et l'existence d'un Dieu *ens perfectissimum et sufficientissimum*,[16] d'où découle la démonstration de l'immortalité de l'âme et de la dépendance de la créature par rapport au créateur. Mansvelt a besoin, pour son projet apologétique, de sauver la raison de montrer comment elle intervient préalablement à et pendant la révélation et de lui faire avouer ses limites pour qu'elle prépare à la révélation et accepte de s'y soumettre. Réduire la révélation à une préparation à la philosophie comme Meyer ou séparer rigoureusement les domaines de validité pour restreindre la portée de la révélation à un enseignement moral comme Spinoza, et cela en prolongeant la démarche cartésienne comme le montre l'exposé spinoziste des *Principia* et plus encore la préface de L.Meyer à ce même texte constituait bien pour les théologiens cartésiens un péril mortel.

Philosophie et Theologie: Ejiciatur Ancilla?

> Les philosophes chrétiens récents, philosophant bien plus sainement, ont distingué avec exactitude la théologie de la philosophie et, reconnaissant à chacune des principes très différents, des moyens tout à fait autres et des fins parfaitement distinctes mais découlant toutefois du même Dieu n'ont pas admis, pour cette raison, d'accommodation de la seconde à la première ou de la première à la seconde, de peur qu'elles ne se corrompent l'une par l'autre, bien qu'ils aient admis qu'il ne fallait pas condamner l'usage de la seconde dans la première. Cette question a recommencé à être agitée à nouveaux frais; l'occasion en fut offerte principalement par l'Anonyme qui a écrit sur l'interprétation de l'Ecriture Sainte de façon non seulement paradoxale mais hétérodoxe comme des gens très savants l'ont démontré, s'affirmant du nombre de ces philosophes récents dont, en cette affaire, il n'était pas moins éloigné que le ciel de la terre.[17]

Un tel propos manifeste clairement le souci de rejeter Meyer avec Spinoza du groupe des *philosophi recentiores,* à savoir des cartésiens, et d'éliminer tout risque de contagion entre les deux. De façon plus mesurée et plus objective, Leibniz, dans le Discours préliminaire à la *Théodicée*, fait un rapide état de la controverse entre 'théologiens rationaux et non rationaux', sur la place respective de la philosophie et de la théologie:

> La question de l'usage de la philosophie dans la théologie a été fort agitée parmi les chrétiens et l'on a eu de la peine à convenir des bornes de cet usage quand on est entré dans le détail.[18]

Il rappelle le débat suscité par la publication du livre de L. Meyer,[19] les diverses réfutations qui s'ensuivirent[20] et la reprise de cette dispute contre les Sociniens. Reprenant l'ancienne métaphore des Pères de l'Eglise, celle de la servante Agar (qui symbolise la philosophie) que Sarah, sa maîtresse (la théologie), veut chasser de sa maison après avoir utilisé ses services, parce qu'elle risque d'usurper sa place, Leibniz refuse l'éjection de la philosophie mais recommande la distinction entre ce qui est absolument nécessaire (d'une nécessité métaphysique à laquelle même les mystères ne sauraient contredire) et ce qui est hypothétiquement nécessaire, d'une nécessité physique, celle de lois de la nature, que Dieu peut lever.

> Il y a quelque chose de bon dans ces réponses mais comme on en pourrait abuser et commettre mal à propos les vérités naturelles et les vérités révélées, les savants

se sont attachés à distinguer ce qu'il y a de nécessaire et d'indispensable dans les vérités naturelles ou philosophiques d'avec ce qui ne l'est point.[21]

Pour nos auteurs, qu'en est-il?[22] L.Meyer fait assurément de la philosophie la maîtresse de la théologie contre la tradition qui la tient pour servante conservée et non pas rejetée tandis que Spinoza récuse complètement toute relation de collaboration comme de maîtrise/ servitude, en séparant rigoureusement les deux domaines de la foi[23] et de la philosophie. Cela ne peut se comprendre qu'en reprenant les définitions respectives des deux concepts en jeu et en rappelant l'horizon polémique du débat. Que cette question soit absolument décisive, on en prendra seulement pour preuve le fait que Mansvelt qui, par ailleurs, commente chapitre par chapitre et page par page, le *Tractatus theologico-politicus*, consacre les 5 premiers chapitres de l'*Adversus anonymum* à définir ce qu'est la philosophie ou révélation divine par la nature, ce qu'elle est à l'origine (sapience) et ce qu'elle est devenue après le péché originel (amour et désir de la sagesse), ce qu'est la théologie ou révélation divine par l'Écriture et enfin la distinction, l'accord et le secours mutuel des deux révélations.

En dépit des divergences que nous nous employons à souligner, il y a bien un fond commun aux trois: ils s'accordent sans peine sur les méfaits de la scolastique,[24] le désir de retour à la pureté doctrinale de l'Eglise primitive et l'approbation des progrès que Descartes a rendus possibles en philosophie.[25] Mais là où Meyer et Spinoza dénoncent les méfaits de la haine théologique, Mansvelt voit plutôt la perversion de l'enseignement primitif et pérenne de l'Eglise par le mélange avec des spéculations philosophiques.[26]

Pour comprendre la subversion que Spinoza fait subir au concept théologique de révélation et l'extension outrancière de ce concept chez Mansvelt, nous partirons donc de leurs définitions respectives de la philosophie et de la théologie.

Définitions

1. La philosophie:

Louis Meyer la définit ainsi:

Sous ce nom de philosophie [nous entendons] la connaissance vraie et très certaine que la raison, libre de tout voile de préjugés soutenue par la lumière naturelle et la pénétration de l'entendement, cultivée et secondée par l'étude, l'application, la pratique, l'expérience et l'usage des choses, découvre et place

> dans la lumière très certaine de la vérité, en partant de principes immuables et connus par soi et en passant par des conséquences légitimes et des démonstrations apodictiques, perçues clairement et distinctement.[27]

Cette définition est assez proche de celle de Mansvelt: la philosophie est l'espèce naturelle du genre de la révélation ou dévoilement de la vérité,[28] dont l'autre espèce est la connaissance par révélation divine. La philosophie, comme désir et amour de la sagesse, désigne tout usage correct de la droite raison, quel que soit son domaine d'application: droit, science, théologie.[29] C'est ce que devient la sapience naturelle, ou connaissance révélée par la nature, après la chute et l'affaiblissement de la raison humaine: une connaissance certaine, tirée méthodiquement des notions communes inscrites par Dieu dans l'âme humaine.[30] Sans connaissance de Dieu, il ne peut y avoir science certaine de rien. Or cette connaissance, possible à la raison, a été obscurcie par le péché et doit être complétée et corrigée par la révélation divine. Par exemple, la raison enseigne à tous qu'il faut se connaître soi-même mais la révélation complète ce que la droite raison eût pu enseigner même aux païens: *nosce Deum et te ipsum*, connais Dieu en toi et toi-même en Dieu.[31] Au sens propre:

> la philosophie signifie, pour nous, l'étude que l'homme corrompu fait avec une diligence sans faille, à partir de la raison droite qui lui reste et la connaissance acquise par cette étude à partir des notions innées, grâce à l'usage correct des reliquats en lui de la raison incorrompue, tant de ce qu'il faut connaître que de ce qu'il faut faire.[32]

La philosophie, ainsi définie et limitée, est sans doute moins aisée et moins rapide que la révélation naturelle initiale mais elle est certaine dans son ordre et la grâce divine la soutient et la complète dans les domaines qui la dépassent: la béatitude céleste et la connaissance exacte de Dieu et de l'économie du salut.

Pour Spinoza, les choses sont moins simples. Non seulement il ne définit jamais la philosophie dans le *Tractatus theologico-politicus* mais il n'emploie le terme que de façon démarcative pour la distinguer de la théologie.[33] La philosophie est caractérisée par son but: la vérité, par son fondement: les notions communes, mais pas par sa méthode; rien n'est dit ici, notamment, de la différence entre connaissance du deuxième et du troisième genre.[34] La philosophie y est plutôt évoquée à propos des controverses d'écoles, donc comme source de divisions et, au fil de l'ouvrage, le terme de philosophie en vient, notamment dans le ch. XV, à être remplacé par un équivalent qui met l'accent sur le mode de connaissance, à savoir la raison.[35]

Il y a donc bien, chez les trois, un fond commun de la critique de la philosophie: la philosophie a été et demeure pour une bonne part une école de disputes;[36] Descartes a ouvert la voie pour la sortir du scepticisme et la conduire, par la méthode, sur la voie sûre d'une science.[37]

2. La théologie

Si L. Meyer qualifie la théologie de 'discipline la plus excellente', ce n'est pas par son objet, ni par son mode de savoir, mais par son but: 'elle excelle de bien des lieues sur tout le reste puisqu'elle montre aux mortels le chemin du bonheur et de la vertu et qu'elle peut les conduire au salut éternel qui est ce qu'il y a de plus éminent et de plus désirable'.[38] Tout l'enseignement de la théologie se tire de l'Ecriture Sainte puisque la première vérité théologique (analogue, en son statut de principe, à la découverte du *cogito* en philosophie première) est que 'les livres de l'Ancien et du Nouveau Testament sont le Verbe infaillible de Dieu très bon et très puissant'.[39] La question portera donc sur la norme infaillible de l'interprétation de l'Ecriture (la philosophie) et sur le statut de la théologie, une fois la vérité qu'elle enseigne découverte philosophiquement.

Chez Mansvelt en revanche, [40] la théologie est définie par son objet et sa fin comme 'tout discours sur Dieu, qui provient de Dieu, face à Dieu et pour sa gloire'.[41] Il y a donc de fausses théologies, celles de Varron, et une vraie, celle des Apôtres. La théologie étant totalement identifiée à la révélation scripturaire, la question essentielle concernera son contenu, à savoir la nature de Dieu en tant que sa connaissance excède les capacités de la raison humaine, l'économie de la création et du salut et la rédemption gratieuse par le Christ.

Chez Spinoza la théologie est identifiée avec la Parole de Dieu[42] quand on la confond avec son fondement et le coeur de son enseignement (la loi morale) ou encore à la foi.[43] Elle fait l'objet d'une certitude seulement morale;[44] elle est trop souvent le lieu des préjugés et d'un discours indigne de Dieu dont elle parle, confondant les natures et les espèces, comme d'un homme parfait.[45]

Si l'on compare systématiquement ces trois positions sur la théologie, on obtient le tableau suivant:

Théologie	Meyer	Mansvelt	Spinoza
objet	Vérités encore inaccessibles à la raison	mystères divins supérieurs à la raison	enseignement moral et piété
but	connaissance	gloire de Dieu	vraie vie
dogme fondamental		salut par la grâce du Christ. Primat de la foi	salut par l'obéissance. Primat des œuvres.
norme d'interprétation	philosophie	inspiration de l'Esprit Saint	Ecriture seule
méthode	réduction à la science	demander l'aide de la grâce divine[46]	enquête historique
certitude	faible & outeuse	morale & indubitable[47]	morale forte

En dépit des divergences qui sont fortes, ce qui est remarquable ici c'est l'horizon commun qui situe l'analyse et la résolution des difficultés de la théologie à partir d'un modèle de la communication linguistique et symbolique. C'est très net chez L. Meyer qui consacre une part importante de l'*Interpres* à l'examen du sens du mot *interpres* (ch.2), puis aux raisons d'ambiguïté ou d'obscurité d'une phrase, d'un passage (ch. 3), à la différence entre sens vrai et vérité (ch.4), au caractère conventionnel du langage (ch.11). C'est vrai aussi de Spinoza si l'on songe non seulement au chapitre VII du *Tractatus theologico-politicus* mais aux longues et précises analyses, dispersées dans le traité, sur le sens de certains mots hébreux, sur les différentes tournures ou modes de parler propres à telle langue ou telle culture.[48] C'est encore vrai de Mansvelt qui consacre une bonne partie du chapitre IV sur la révélation divine, à présenter des traits décisifs du fonctionnement de la commmunication: (a) le caractère conventionnel des signes; (b) le passage de la perception d'un signe à la pensée que ce signe entend signifier; (c) l'affectation originaire à un mot courant d'un sens obscur véhiculant des pensées fausses, en raison de l'institution du langage par le vulgaire.[49] Par ex. on parle du chien comme s'il éprouvait des pensées semblables à celles des hommes, alors qu'on sait bien que le chien ne perçoit, ne veut et ne comprend rien avec conscience comme le fait l'homme.[50] D'où, conformément à une tradition héritée de l'humanisme érudit, l'attention portée au contexte, au but visé par la communication, aux jeux rhétoriques, à l'évolution de la langue, toutes choses qui rapprochent Mansvelt de Spinoza ou des exégètes de l'Ecole de Saumur.

D'où vient alors le désaccord qui est, au sens propre, radical? Sans entrer dans le détail, il faut souligner que, sur cette question de l'articulation de la philosophie et de la théologie, Spinoza répond à Meyer en déplaçant ses propositions et en refusant, quoiqu'en dise Velthuysen, de mettre ses pas dans ceux de son ami. Mansvelt, lui, dans sa surdité au propos spinoziste, témoigne de la radicale nouveauté de ce discours et de l'affrontement sans médiation ni conciliation possible de deux univers de pensée. Reprenons donc la question de l'articulation des deux disciplines, philosophie et théologie.

3. Articulation philosophie / théologie

Chez Meyer, la philosophie commande la théologie puisqu'elle est à la fois sa norme d'interprétation et son terme. [51] La théologie n'apparaît plus, dans l'Epilogue, que comme un discours imaginatif utile aux ignorants pour les inciter à réfléchir sur Dieu, la suprême béatitude des hommes et le moyen d'y parvenir.[52]

Chez Mansvelt, la raison joue un rôle préliminaire et auxilaire:[53] (a) elle prouve l'existence d'un Dieu vérace, condition de possibilité du fait même de la révélation;[54] (b) elle discrimine entre vraies et fausses révélations;[55] (c) elle sert à convaincre les infidèles.[56] En retour, la théologie renforce et étend plus loin la lumière naturelle, en lui faisant connaître des attributs divins et l'économie du salut qu'elle n'aurait pu atteindre seule. Mansvelt se présente d'ailleurs lui même comme un rationaliste mesuré, qui fait résolument l'éloge de la raison mais garde la juste mesure entre l'excès de confiance des sociniens et le défaut de confiance des sceptiques.[57]

Spinoza, en défendant la séparation stricte des fondements, des méthodes et du but des deux disciplines, répond à la fois à Meyer et à Mansvelt qui, en des sens et des fins opposés, confondent tous deux sens vrai et vérité. [58]

Spinoza	philosophie	théologie
fondement	notions communes	révélation
but	vérité	salut par l'obéissance
méthode	déduction rationnelle	enquête historique

Contre Meyer, Spinoza refuse de réduire l'enseignement de l'Ecriture à un enseignement spéculatif présenté de façon confuse et métaphorique; contre Mansvelt, il récuse la thèse d'un complément doctrinal sur les attributs de Dieu ou l'ordre du monde et de l'histoire de l'humanité. La confusion des deux domaines, corrélative à l'assimilation du sens vrai et de la vérité, aboutit chez Meyer à confondre vérités spéculatives et enseignement moral et chez Mansvelt, obéissance et vérité. Spinoza lui s'emploie à *distinguer*: les modes de connaissance (rationnel versus imaginatif), les domaines de validité, les destinataires, les types d'autorité. C'est cette distinction seule qui empêche l'inféodation, comme chez Meyer, de la lecture de la Bible à une caste de lettrés, à un nouveau clergé intellectuel, ou, comme chez Mansvelt, à un clergé de type traditionnel qui s'arroge le monopole de l'inspiration. Derrière la stricte séparation entre philosophie et théologie, ce qui est en jeu c'est la liberté de l'interprétation et l'accès potentiel de tous les hommes à une voie de salut conduisant à la vie vraie ainsi que la liberté politique de philosopher. On le voit bien dans les dernières pages de l'*Adversus anonymum* de Mansvelt qui approuvent les lois civiles qui restreignent et encadrent la liberté de penser.[59]

La Liberté de L'Interprétation

Sans reprendre tout le débat sur l'interprétation de l'Ecriture, sa norme, ses finalités et ses enjeux, il faut souligner l'originalité de la thèse spinozienne de l'*accomodatio* et ses enjeux pratiques ainsi que les résistances que cette thèse suscite chez Mansvelt.[60]

Spinoza, généralement considéré comme l'un des fondateurs de l'exégèse moderne c'est-à-dire philologique et historique, s'inscrit en fait dans une tradition inaugurée par les grands hébraïsants de la fin du XVIe et du début du XVIIe siècles. Sur ces points, sur la nécessité d'une connaissance précise des langues de l'Ecriture,[61] sur l'évolution de la langue et les difficultés propres à l'hébreu, Mansvelt exprime très souvent son accord avec Spinoza et voit dans cette difficulté une incitation divine à l'étude; il souligne les progrès récents de l'exégèse, en insistant sur l'apport des dictionnaires et grammaires, notamment de Bochart et Cocceius.[62] Mais il refuse les conclusions de Spinoza sur le droit pour chacun à la libre interprétation des dogmes fondamentaux. Le credo minimum du chapitre VII, doit être complété par l'affirmation de la création et de la conservation continue. Pour autant, l'accommodation ou l'adaptation de Dieu à la finitude des esprits humains ne porte, selon Mansvelt, que sur les modes de la révélation et non sur l'interprétation de son contenu.

L'accommodatio

Une des thèses les plus fortes et les plus scandaleuses en son temps
de la lecture spinozienne est, en effet, l'affirmation d'un droit pour tout
individu, à la libre réinterprétation des textes sacrés, en fonction de sa
complexion et de son histoire propre:

> Chacun, nous l'avons déjà dit, est tenu d'adapter ces dogmes de foi à sa
> compréhension et de se les interpréter de la façon qui lui semble les faire adopter le
> plus facilement, sans aucune hésitation et de grand coeur, afin d'obéir à Dieu sans
> réserve et de tout son coeur.[63]

Cette adaptation seconde répond en écho à une première adaptation,
celle de Dieu même qui s'est plié à la complexion, aux préjugés et au type
d'imagination des prophètes auxquels il a révélé son enseignement.[64] Cette
adaptation, considérée comme pédagogique et provisoire par Meyer, est
insoutenable pour Mansvelt dès lors qu'elle porte sur le contenu de la
vérité révélée. Pour lui, il n'y a pas d'adaptation possible entre deux vérités
puisque toute vérité est naturellement conforme à toute autre. Si le vrai
s'adapte au faux (notamment aux préjugés) il devient faux; quant au faux
qui tente de s'adapter au vrai en prenant la forme du vraisemblable, il n'en
reste pas moins faux. Cela parce que tant Meyer que Mansvelt supposent
que la révélation consiste en une communication directe *a mente ad
mentem* que Spinoza réserve exclusivement au Christ.[65] La récusation de la
double adaptation, celle de Dieu à l'*ingenium* des prophètes, celle du
lecteur moderne face aux dogmes de foi, a pour conséquence de ne pas
pouvoir rendre compte du langage métaphorique, anthropomorphique,
inadéquat dont la Bible parle de Dieu. On en prendra pour exemple le cas
de la 'jalousie de Dieu'. Pour Spinoza, Moïse a bien cru que Dieu était
jaloux (cette jalousie s'exprimant également sous la métaphore qui dit que
Dieu est un feu dévorant) quoique cette thèse soit contraire à la raison; la
recherche du sens vrai conduit à déclarer que telle fut la croyance de Moïse
mais que toute autre est la vérité puisque Dieu n'est pas sujet aux
passions.[66] En revanche Mansvelt tente seulement de distinguer la jalousie
divine de la jalousie humaine: la jalousie divine est 'la volonté ardente et
déterminée de punir les profanateurs de sa gloire qui offrent à d'autres
l'honneur qui n'est dû qu'à lui seul'; elle est donc une réaction légitime de
Dieu contre le péché par excellence qu'est l'idolâtrie;[67] la jalousie humaine
est 'le chagrin qu'éprouve l'âme impuissante qui craint qu'un autre ne
jouisse d'un bien qu'elle estime à tort n'être dû qu'à elle seule'.[68] Le

langage anthropomorphique n'est nullement contesté et le Dieu de la Bible est bien un dieu jaloux qui défend sa gloire.[69]

De quoi nous assure la Bible?

Finalement accepter ou refuser la thèse de la liberté de l'interprétation *ad captum sui* dépend de la détermination de ce dont la Bible est censée nous assurer, donc des enjeux pratiques de sa lecture. Meyer et Mansvelt restreignent la liberté d'interprétation à deux castes de clercs, doctes ou religieux, toute autre forme d'interprétation n'étant le fait que d'ignorants ou de méchants, mais il est vrai que chez eux la Bible ne nous assure pas de grand chose: pour Meyer, de rien puisqu'elle est un instrument pédagogique provisoire, voué à s'effacer dès que la vérité est connue par la voie de la science; pour Mansvelt, elle annonce le salut de quelques uns par la grâce incompréhensible de Dieu transmise par le Christ.

En revanche chez Spinoza, la Bible, et elle seule, assure le philosophe que tous les hommes, savants et ignorants, sont susceptibles d'être sauvés: les uns, les ignorants, par la voie de l'obéissance, les autres par celle de l'intelligence des lois de la nature, par la vertu sous la conduite de la raison, mais par l'obéissance aussi dans la mesure où ils ne sont jamais uniquement conduits par la raison.

> Je veux signaler expressément l'utilité et la nécessité de l'Ecriture Sainte ou de la révélation que je tiens pour très grandes. Car puisque nous ne pouvons saisir par la lumière naturelle que la simple obéissance est un chemin de salut mais que seule la révélation enseigne que cela a lieu par une grâce singulière de Dieu que notre raison ne peut comprendre, il en résulte que l'Ecriture a apporté aux mortels une grande consolation. Puisque tous absolument peuvent obéir, et que peu seulement, comparativement à l'étendue du genre humain, parviennent à la pratique habituelle de la vertu sous la conduite de la raison, si nous n'avions pas le témoignage de l'Ecriture, nous douterions du salut de presque tous les hommes.[70]

La question est de savoir si le salut et la vraie béatitude peuvent être conçus comme naturels. Mansvelt le nie et reprochant à Spinoza de concevoir un salut *ex natura* et non pas *ex gratia Christi*, il l'accuse d'une confusion subreptice entre philosophie et théologie, contraire à son but explicite, qui est de les distinguer. Si nous ne connaissons clairement la pensée des prophètes que pour les choses qui sont connues clairement par la lumière naturelle, si 'le salut véritable et la béatitude consistent dans le repos de l'âme et que nous ne pouvons trouver ce vrai repos que dans les choses que nous connaissons très clairement',[71] alors la règle d'interprétation pour chacun de l'Ecriture est bien la lumière naturelle commune à tous et Mansvelt n'a pas tort de dénoncer un retour masqué de la philosophie dans la théologie.

Enjeux Théoriques & Pratiques

Les enjeux de cette dispute sont à la fois métaphysiques et pratiques. Mansvelt s'appuie sur des thèses fondamentales de la métaphysique cartésienne pour défendre le projet d'une apologétique rationnelle. On a besoin de la raison pour prouver les deux premières vérités sans lesquelles il n'est pas d'acceptation raisonnable de la révélation: ce sont, rappelons-le, l'existence de Dieu comme *ens perfectissimum et sufficientissimum* et la déterminatio de l'*ego* comme *res cogitans*. Mais Mansvelt va plus loin dans la fidélité à Descartes. Commentant le passage du chapitre IV sur la nécessité des propriétés géométriques du triangle il rejette la thèse spinoziste selon laquelle 'la nécessité de l'essence et des propriétés du triangle en tant que conçues comme vérités éternelles, dépend de la seule nécessité de la nature divine et de l'entendement divin, non de la nature du triangle, ce qui fait que ce que nous appelons volonté ou décret de Dieu n'est qu'une idée de son entendement. Il la récuse en rabattant, à l'inverse de Spinoza, l'entendement divin sur la volonté divine. La vérité du triangle dépend de la seule complaisance éternelle de Dieu. La nécessité d'une vérité éternelle ne dépend pas de la nécessité de l'entendement divin mais de la perfection du bon vouloir divin:

> Comme cette vérité [la nature du triangle et l'égalité de ses angles à 2 droits] n'est telle que par la seule complaisance éternelle de Dieu et n'est contenue depuis l'éternité dans la nature divine par aucune autre nécessité que par cette complaisance très parfaite de Dieu, en tant que vérité éternelle découlant, selon son arbitre, de la vérité première et essentielle de Dieu; ce n'est que par sa complaisance que Dieu a en soi les idées de toutes les choses extérieures à lui, qu'il comprend en soi. [72]

Ce qui veut dire qu'en dehors de l'idée de soi-même, toutes les idées que Dieu pense et comprend en soi dépendent de sa libre volonté (*pro ejus arbitrio*). Essences, existences et événements ont le même statut d'êtres dépendants de la toute puissance et de la liberté de Dieu:

> La complaisance des décrets divins est éternelle mais elle n'en est pas moins libre. Car la liberté est une perfection et une propriété inséparable de l'essence éternelle et très parfaite. Ce que Dieu a voulu par sa complaisance éternelle se produit infailliblement. Mais cependant, on ne peut pas dire que ce qui arrive de la seule nécessité de la nature divine possède sa nécessité d'essence: le vrai provient de la complaisance éternelle et très parfaite de l'essence divine nécessaire par laquelle

seule, sont et peuvent être toutes les choses qui, en dehors de Dieu, sont ou peuvent être. Car, sans la complaisance de Dieu, rien ne peut obtenir de Dieu sa vérité ou son essence.[73]

Dire qu'aucune essence ne peut exister ou avoir de vérité sans Dieu et sans sa complaisance, c'est reprendre en des termes légèrement différents, la thèse cartésienne de la libre création des vérités éternelles. Alors que Spinoza nie la pertinence du concept de volonté divine en le rabattant sur l'entendement, Mansvelt à l'inverse, affirme la primauté du vouloir ou de la liberté en Dieu. Ce faisant, il entend sauver la transcendance et la toute puissance de Dieu. Ce qui est en jeu ici, c'est la façon de concevoir le rapport et la distance entre fini et infini. Spinoza pense cette distance infinie en intègrant le fini dans l'infini comme mode et il affirme donc l'immanence de l'infini au fini; Mansvelt la pense comme la distance infinie du créé au créateur. D'où la dépendance des essences éternelles elles-mêmes à l'égard du bon vouloir divin. C'est parce qu'il s'accorde en bien des points avec Spinoza sur la méthode érudite d'interprétation de l'Ecriture mais qu'il refuse la thèse de l'adaptation qui réduit le mystère divin et sa transcendance que Mansvelt, défenseur de la gloire de Dieu, ne peut accepter la thèse de la libre interprétation par chacun des dogmes fondamentaux. Pour éviter cette conséquence, à ses yeux scandaleuse, du système, il présente, avec une mauvaise foi manifeste et sans références textuelles cette fois, l'identification du dieu spinozien à l'univers ou à la masse corporelle.

Les autres oppositions, le rejet de la religion universelle, naturelle et revélée, le refus du salut par les oeuvres ou par l'obéissance au profit du salut par la foi, don gratieux de Dieu, ne se comprennent bien que sur le fond de cette ligne de partage radicale entre d'une part l'affirmation de la transcendance incompréhensible de Dieu et d'autre part le refus de la surnature.

La religion universelle

Spinoza défend à plusieurs reprises ce qu'il appelle la *religio catholica*,[74] *lumine naturali et prophetice revelata*, formule qui fait écho à celle de Mansvelt sur la double révélation par la lumière de la nature et par la lumière de l'Ecriture.[75] La conception est toutefois radicalement différente puisqu'ici l'Écriture enseigne la même chose, mais autrement, que la lumière naturelle: que la vraie vie consiste dans l'amour de Dieu lequel se résume dans l'amour du prochain.[76] La détermination de la religion universelle ne passe plus, comme chez les rationalistes religieux du XVIIe siècle, par le comparatisme religieux ou par une théologie naturelle.[77] Elle résulte entièrement de l'interprétation rigoureuse de la Bible qui en dégage le fondement universel et l'enseignement moral constant.[78]

Il est clair que cette détermination de la religion est irrecevable pour un croyant: de ce point de vue, Mansvelt a raison d'objecter qu'une obéissance sans égard à la vérité, donc une obéissance aveugle, débouche inévitablement sur la soumission entière à l'Etat, thèse plus explicite dans le *Traité politique* que dans le *Tractatus theologico-politicus*. En outre, la totale liberté d'interprétation ruine la notion même d'Eglise, c'est-à-dire de communauté de croyants liés par une même foi. Au mieux, elle conduit à la constitution d'Eglises nationales; au pire, comme le craint Mansvelt, à une multiplication de chapelles.[79]

Alors que pour Meyer, la religion universelle est un concept vide puisque la religion est marquée par l'imagination, les préjugés, l'erreur, donc constituée selon un principe de dispersion, pour Mansvelt, la religion universelle n'est plus là ou pas encore: elle est située dans un passé très archaïque, celui de l'Église des premiers temps avant l'alliance qui particularise la révélation, ou dans un futur eschatologique; pour Spinoza, en revanche, elle est indiscutablement toujours au présent, cultivée par tous les hommes et il y en eut de tout temps qui ont pratiqué la loi de justice et de charité. C'est le mélange de philosophie et de foi qui engendre les divisions ecclésiales.[80] La séparation des deux règnes garantit la paix civile et le développement parallèle du savoir et de la vertu.

Si l'on prend la peine de lire l'ennuyeux traité de Mansvelt, on comprend bien pourquoi il était si capital et si urgent, pour un théologien cartésien enseignant à Utrecht de se démarquer de Spinoza et de réfuter page à page le *Tractatus theologico-politicus*. Ce n'était pas seulement oeuvre pie à l'égard des étudiants ou du public cultivé, amateur de nouveautés. C'était véritablement prendre les armes pour défendre la possibilité même d'une apologétique cartésienne. La tentative de Mansvelt est d'autant plus remarquable qu'écrivant en 1671, il ignore les *Opera Posthuma* et donc l'*Ethique*. Ce n'est donc pas sur la définition de Dieu comme *causa sui*, sur la distinction des attributs, sur le statut des modes finis et sur la causalité immanente qu'il peut attaquer Spinoza, comme le feront après lui Wittich, Aubert de Versé ou le Père Lamy. S'il a témoigné d'une évidente mauvaise foi en interprétant le *Deus sive natura* comme identité de Dieu et de l'univers corporel, c'était là une façon desespérée de refuser la thèse immanentiste et de chercher à sauver la transcendance divine et la coupure entre le monde sacré divin, et le monde profane, humain, mise à mal par l'affirmation spinozienne de l'unité de la nature.

On le voit clairement dans le commentaire du chapitre sur la loi divine: si la puissance de l'homme est une partie de la puissance de la nature, et par là-même une partie de la puissance de Dieu, *adeo homo sibi deus suus,* l'homme devient alors son propre dieu. C'est donc bien en définitive à cette thèse métaphysique de la transcendance de l'infini et du statut du fini par rapport à l'infini (dépendance stricte ou dépendance et intégration) que se nouent les thèses herméneutiques sur la méthode de lecture, savante et profane de l'Ecriture et les thèses politiques sur la liberté de philosopher et le *jus circa sacra*.[81] C'est bien aussi pourquoi seule une autre détermination métaphysique de l'infini et une autre conception du rapport entre sagesse et toute puissance divines, celle de Leibniz, permettra de dépasser le débat stérile entre théologiens rationaux et non rationaux.

BIBLIOGRAPHIE:

Meyer, L., *Philosophia S.Scripturae interpres, Exercitatio paradoxa in qua veram philosophiam infaillibilem S. Literas interpretandi normam esse apodictice demonstratur et discrepantes ab hac sententia expenduntur ac refelluntur.* Eleutheropolis (Amsterdam 1666); trad. néerl., *De Philosophie d'uytleghster der H. Schrifture* (Vrystadt 1667) ; 2de éd. publiée à la suite du *Traité théologico-politique de Spinoza,* en 1673 et 1674; 3ème éd. (Magdeburg 1776). Trad. fr. J. Lagrée & P.-F. Moreau *La philosophie interprète de l'Ecriture Sainte* (Paris, Intertextes, 1988).

Spinoza, B., *Oeuvres complètes en quatre volumes publiées par Carl Gebhardt,* (Heidelberg réédition de 1972) et plus particulièrement *Tractatus theologico-politicus* (Amsterdam 1670) ; G. t. III (édition citée pour la pagination); trad. Appuhn, *Traité théologico-politique* Paris, GF,II, 1965.

Mansvelt, Regneri A., *Adversus Anonymum Theologo-Politicum,* liber singularis in quo omnes & singulae *Tractatus theologico-politicium Dissertationes examinantur & refelluntur, cum praemissa disquisitione de Divina per Naturam, & Scripturam Revelatione. Opus posthumum,* (A. Wolfgand, Amsterdam, 1674) (cité *Adversus anonymum*).

Descartes, René et Martin Schoock, *La querelle d'Utrecht,* Textes établis, traduits et annotés par Theo Verbeek (Paris 1988).

Lagrée, Jacqueline, *La raison ardente, religion naturelle et raison au XVIIe siècle,* (Vrin, Paris 1991).

Verbeek Theo, *De vrijheid van de filosofie, reflecties over een Cartesiaans thema, Quaestiones infinitae, Publications of the department of philosophy* (Utrecht University 1994).

1 Le *Tractatus theologico-politicus TTP* est une reprise déplacée de certains thèmes de l'*Interpres*, notamment une récusation de la manière dont Meyer conçoit les rapports entre philosophie et théologie; l'*Adversus anonymum theologico-politicum* (*Adversus anonymum*) est clairement une réfutation du *Tractatus theologico-politicus*. Le *Tractatus theologico-politicus* occupera donc naturellement une place centrale dans notre examen.

2 Publié en 1674 à Amsterdam; parfois relié avec la *Brevis enervatio* de Bredenburg de 1675 ou à la suite du *Tractatus theologico-politicus* de Spinoza.

3 Cf. Wilhelm Schmidt-Biggemann, 'Spinoza dans le cartésianisme', *L'Ecriture Sainte au temps de Spinoza et dans le système spinoziste*, T & D 4 du Groupe de Recherches Spinozistes (Paris, 1992), pp. 71–89.

4 *Philosophia S. Scripturae interpres*, Epilogue, trad. Lagrée-Moreau, *La philosophie interprète de l'Ecriture Sainte*, p. 249.

5 *Moreri Dictionnaire* (Paris 1759), T.VIII, p. 180b. L'éloge mortuaire est dû à J.G. Graevius (*Oratio in obitum Regneri Mansveldi*).

6 *A capite ad calcem*: de la tête au talon.

7 La réfutation de Mansvelt, écrite en 1671, peu après la sortie du *Tractatus theologico-politicus*, ne fut publiée qu'après sa mort en 1674.

8 Stouppe, *La religion des Hollandais représentée en plusieurs lettres écrites par un officier de l'Armée du Roy à un pasteur et professeur en théologie de Berne* (Cologne, chez Pierre Marteau, 1673), p. 67.

9 LA *PSSI* et le *Tractatus theologico-politicus* furent réédités ensemble et condamnés ensemble en même temps que le *Léviathan* de Hobbes et un recueil de textes sociniens en juillet 1674.

10 Cf. Lettre XLII de J.Osten à Spinoza.

11 'Praecipue nuperrimam occasionem praebente Anonymo qui de Sacrae Scripturae interpretatione non modo paradoxe sed etiam heterodoxe ut a viris Doctissimis demontratum fuit, scripsit . . . Hujus item vestigia secutus est alterus Anonymus qui nuper, sub eode praetextu, ex densissimis cerebri sui tenebris in lucem edidit Tractatum ad aeternas potius tenebras condemnandum, Theologico-politicum, quasi cum recentioribus philosophis demonstraturus quam necessario evitanda sit omnis Theologiae & philosophiae mistura'. *Adversus anonymum*, ca.I, p. 3.

12 364 pages in 8°. Plus d'une fois et demi le *Tractatus theologico-politicus* qui, dans la même dimension et avec des caractères plus gros, ne fait que 233 pages.

13 Donc juste après la parution de la réfutation de Mansvelt.

14 Lettre L, Trad. Appuhn, modifiée, IV, p. 284; G.IV, 240–41.

15 Les attaques contre la scolastique sont omniprésentes chez Mansvelt qui la qualifie de *monstrum monstruosissimum*.

16 *Adversus anonymum*, II, p. 21.

17 *Adversus anonymum*, XX, p. 2: 'Verum recentioribus Philosophis Christianis longe sanius philosophantibus & Theologiam a Philosophia accurate discernentibus, & utriusque diversissima agnoscentibus principia, media plane aliena & fines omnino distinctos, sed tamen ab eodem Deo profluenta & idcirco nullam admittentibus accomodationem hujus ad illam aut illius ad hanc, ne aut haec per illam, aut illa per hanc corrumperetur, quamvis hujus usum in illa non contemnendum admitterent, de novo haec quaestio agitari coepit, praecipue occasionem praebente Anonymo qui de Sacrae Scripturae interpretatione non modo paradoxe sed etiam heterodoxe, ut a viris doctissimis demontratum fuit, scripsit, inter recentiores illos Philosophos a quibus tamen non minus quam coelum a terra in hac causa distabat, suum nomen professus'.

18 Leibniz, *Théodicée*; discours préliminaire, § 16.

19 Nommément cité et distingué de Spinoza à qui l'*Interpres* a parfois été attribuée; cf. § 14.

20 Wolzogen, Vogelsang, Van der Weye, cités au § 14.

21 Discours préliminaire, *Théodicée*, § 17.

22 Sur ce thème de l'ancillarité: Spinoza, *Tractatus theologico-politicus* XV, 'neutra neutri ancilletur sed quod unaquaeque suum regnum sine ulla altrius repugnatia obtineat' (G. III 188:11–19), et *Ep.* 63. *Adversus anonymum*, I, p. 2.

23 Terme qui supplante celui de théologie: *Tractatus theologico-politicus* XIV, (G.III 179:26).

24 Sp: *Tractatus theologico-politicus* XIII, Ap. p. 168 'La doctrine de l'Ecriture n'est pas une philosophie, ne contient pas de hautes spéculations mais seulement des vérités très simples qui sont aisément perceptibles à l'esprit le plus paresseux . . . Qu'on cherche quels sont ces mystères cachés dans l'Ecriture visibles pour eux, on ne trouvera rien que des inventions d'Aristote ou de Platon'. *Adversus anonymum*, I, p. 7: 'multi quidem Christianorum varios suos errores in quos per Aristotelicorum & Platonicorum speculationes inciderant'.

25 *Philosophia S. Scripturae interpres*, prologue, p. 25 et V, 4, p. 109; *Adversus anonymum*, ch. I, p. 4; ch. III, 19, p. 32, avec la reprise de l'image traditionnelle: Descartes a dissipé les très épaisses ténèbres de l'esprit humain. Spinoza, *Principia*.

26 *Philosophia S. Scripturae interpres*, prologue; Spinoza: préface du *Tractatus theologico-politicus*.

27 *Philosophia S. Scripturae interpres*, V, 2, p. 106.

28 *Adversus anonymum*, II, 1, p. 9: 'Revelatio, si nomen spectetur, proprie est veli detractio, qua id quod eo velatum & occultum erat, oculis patet'.

29 ibid., III, 12, p. 26: 'Theologi, Jurisconsulti & omnes qui huc collimant, suum studium, quemadmodum faciunt, quodammodo Philosophiam dicere possunt'.

30 ibid., II, 20, p.17; les deux premières notions sont, dans le droit fil des *Méditations* de Descartes, celle de l'ego comme *res cogitans* et de Dieu comme *ens perfectissimum & sufficientissimum*.

31 ibid., II, 21, p. 17.

32 ibid., III, 12, p. 26: 'Nobis vero Philosophia significat & studium quod homo corruptus ex recta ratione in se reliqua continua diligentia impendit & eam quam illo studio ex innatis sibi notionibus per rectum usum in se reliquarum incorruptae Rationis reliquiarum sibi comparat notitiam tam de iis quae cognoscenda quam quae agenda sunt'.

33 Sur ce sujet cf. Pierre-François Moreau, 'Qu'est-ce que la philosophie? Spinoza et la pratique de la démarcation', *Hobbes et Spinoza, Scienza e politica* (Bibliopolis Naples 1992), pp. 53–69 et plus particuliérement p. 62, n. 16.

34 Sauf pour le Christ qui a connu Dieu immédiatement d'esprit à esprit, donc par une connaissance du troisième genre. *Tractatus theologico-politicus* I, p. 7 & V, p. 64.

35 *Tractatus theologico-politicus* XV, p. 184. Tandis que le doublet philosophie / théologie fonctionne pour souligner leur pseudo opposition ou subordination, le couple Raison / Théologie prend sa place pour évoquer leur légitime distinction.

36 *Philosophia S. Scripturae interpres*, prologue, *Adversus anonymum*, III, 16; Spinoza *Tractatus theologico-politicus* préface.

37 Descartes 's'est efforcé de construire la connaissance par degrés à partir des notions premières, absolument certaines et indubitables, innées, de Dieu et de l'Ego (Dei et Sui). Il a si bien réussi que ses thèses ainsi démontrées, sont considérées par beaucoup d'esprits très compétents comme des démonstrations très vraies et non comme des oracles et des propos dignes de foi. Dans toute l'Europe, des gens très savants découvrent de plus en plus de choses à partir de ces principes selon cet ordre; ils suppriment un nombre infini de questions et de doutes de sorte que leurs travaux pour connaître la vérité par la nature ont fait faire de nombreux et d'immenses progrès et découvert d'infinies erreurs; la lumière innée de connaître a été libérée d'innombrables ténèbres et la droite raison, mise en nous par Dieu et qui nous est restée partiellement depuis la chute, a été largement reconduite à son usage légitime', *Adversus anonymum*, III, 19, p. 33.

38 *Philosophia S. Scripturae interpres*, Prologue, p. 23.

39 ibid., Prologue, p. 27.

40 *Adversus anonymum*, ch. IV, intitulé *De la révélation divine par l'Ecriture ou théologie*.

41 'Omnis quidem sermo de Deo, qui sit ex Deo, coram Deo & ad gloriam ejus, Theologia denominatur'. *Adversus anonymum* IV, 3, p. 34.

42 *Tractatus theologico-politicus*, XV, p. 185, 12–3: *theologia sive verbum Dei.*

43 ibid., XIV, 179.

44 ibid., XV, 185–9.

45 *Ep.* 23.

46 *Adversus anonymum*, XII, 16, p. 178.

47 ibid., IV, 11.

48 Par exemple ceux qui hébraïsent en grec, comme Jean.

49 Par exemple pour l'âme humaine qui signifie ce par quoi l'homme pense, veut, comprend: détermination plus marquée par la philosophie cartésienne que par la philologie latine, quoi qu'en dise Mansvelt.

50 *Adversus anonymum*, IV, 5, pp. 36–7. Là encore, il est impossible de ne pas penser à la distinction cartésienne de la pensée et de l'étendue et à la thèse des animaux-machines.

51 *Philosophia S. Scripturae interpres*, V, 1, p. 115sq.

52 Epilogue, p. 247–8.

53 *Adversus anonymum* V, 5.

54 ibid., V, 3.

55 ibid., V, 11 mais Mansvelt ne donne ni critère ni méthode pour discerner entre vraies et fausses révélations.

56 ibid., XX, 21.

57 ibid., XX, 3 où il rejette la thèse de la double vérité.

58 La formule de la lettre XLIII (à J. Osten) où Spinoza affirme avoir réfuté la thèse de 'ceux qui nient que la raison et la philosophie soient les interprètes de l'Ecriture' tout comme celle, inverse, de Maïmonide (et de Meyer), s'applique aussi à Mansvelt.

59 *Adversus anonymum*, ch. XXV, 36, p. 363.

60 Cf. J. Lagrée, *La raison ardente* (Paris, Vrin, 1991), ch.V.

61 L'hébreu mais aussi l'arabe, le chaldéen, le syriaque et le grec. *Adversus anonymum*, XII, 2, p. 168.

62 *Adversus anonymum*, XII, 7 & 8, pp. 172–3.

63 *Tractatus theologico-politicus*, XIV, G III, 178, 30–32.

64 ibid., II, G.III, 42.

65 'Les décrets de Dieu qui conduisent les hommes au salut ont été révélés [au Christ] immédiatement sans paroles ni visions'. *Tractatus theologico-politicus* I, G.III, 21, 5–6.

66 *Tractatus theologico-politicus*, VII, G.III, 101, 15–22.

67 Pour Mansvelt l'opposé de la théologie ou connaissance droite de Dieu est l'idolâtrie; pour Spinoza c'est la superstition.

68 *Adversus anonymum*, XX, 16.

69 ibid., XII, 3, p. 168.

70 *Tractatus theologico-politicus*, XV, G.III, 188.

71 *TTP* VII, G.III, 111.

72 'Cum ea veritas non nisi sola aeterna complacentia talis sit & nulla alia necessitate quam perfectissimae illius complacentiae divinae ab aeterno in natura divina contineatur, tamquam aeterna veritas a prima & essentiali Dei veritate pro ejus arbitrio profluens; non nisi sua complacentia in se habet ideas omnium quae praeter se intelligit in se'. *Adversus anonymum*, IX, 5, p. 137.

73 *Adversus anonymum*, IX, 5, p. 138: 'Aeterna quidem est decretorum divinorum complacentia: sed tamen ideo non minus libera. Nam libertas aeternae & perfectissimae essentiae inseparabilis proprietas & perfectio est. Infallibiliter etiam fit quicquid Deus aeterna sua complacentia voluit. Sedtamen ideo dici nequit quicquid fit ex sola necessitate naturae divinae suam habere necessitatem essentiae: verum ex aeterna & perfectissima necessariae essentiae divinae complacentia; qua sola sunt

& possunt esse omnia quae praeter Deum sunt aut esse possunt. Nam absque Dei complacentia nihil a Deo suam veritatem aut essentiam obtinere potest'.

74 Il s'agit là, comme toujours en milieu protestant de la religion universelle et non pas de celle de l'Eglise romaine. Les références sont les suivantes: Religio catholica sive *lex divina* per Prophetas et Apostolos universo generi revelata (*Tractatus theologico-politicus*, préface G. III, 10, 5–7); Ne quis putet religionem catholicam etiam indigere Pontifice (*Tractatus theologico-politicus*, VII, G. III, 116, 23–24); Nempe quod verbum Dei … proprie significat legem illam Divinam, hoc est, religionem *toti humano generi universalem*, sive catholicam, ubi verum vivendi modum docet, qui scilicet non in caeremoniis, sed in charitate, et vero animo consistit, eumque legem, et verbum Dei promiscue vocat. (*Tractatus theologico-politicus*, XII, G III, 162, 18–22); Religio catholica quae *maxime naturalis* est. (*Tractatus theologico-politicus*, XII, G III, 163, 15); Quare hoc ipsum mandatum unica est totius fidei catholicae norma, et per id solum omnia fidei dogmata, quae scilicet unusquisque amplecti tenetur, determinanda sunt (*Tractatus theologico-politicus*, XIV, G. III, 174, 33–35).

75 Lettre XLIII. G. IV, 225, 11–12.

76 Sur l'identité vie vraie religion et sur son établissement par la raison, cf. *Ethique*, IV, P. LXXIII, sc.

77 Cf. Herbert de Cherbury ou Wissowaty. Voir J. Lagrée, *La raison ardente* (Paris, Vrin, 1991).

78 *Tractatus theologico-politicus*, XI, G.III, 156, 8–10: 'Le fondement essentiel de la religion consiste principalement en enseignements moraux'.

79 *Adversus anonymum*, XIX, 11, p. 252: 'adeo discerperentur omnia Ecclesiae membra in partes minutissimas ut tota non nisi dissensio foret & plane inordinata turba'.

80 *Tractatus theologico-politicus*, XI, G.III, p. 157–8.

81 *Adversus anonymum*, IX, 1, p. 129.

12. STILLINGFLEET, LOCKE AND THE TRINITY

G.A.J. ROGERS

Introduction

Until recently Edward Stillingfleet has featured in histories of philosophy only as the opponent of John Locke in their famous controversy on the implications of Locke's philosophy for the doctrine of the Trinity. In recent years, however, he has been looked at as a thinker in his right by, amongst others, Richard Popkin, Robert Carroll and Sarah Hutton.[1] As a result of their work Stillingfleet is beginning to emerge from the shadow of Locke and attention has somewhat shifted away from that famous exchange and towards other of his writings. In particular Sarah Hutton has emphasised that in his uncompleted second version of *Origines Sacra*, published after his death in 1702, Stillingfleet reveals a knowledge of contemporary philosophy and science and an engagement with it that is very much aimed at defeating contemporary Moderns as their positions support or tend towards atheism. He focuses especially on Hobbes, Descartes and Spinoza. Stillingfleet, as Hutton puts it, sees 'these three figures as *philosophers* who undermine the generally received proofs of the existence of God and providence and 'attribute too much to the mechanical powers of matter and motion'.' She goes on to argue, contrary to Popkin's reading, that Stillingfleet was concerned not merely with sceptical argument. He 'perceived the hydra of atheism and unbelief to be philosophical in origin, and that its roots were not the corrosive effects of sceptical arguments but mistaken doctrines produced by supposedly rational minds'.[2] Popkin had earlier given an apparently different reading of Stillingfleet's place in the seventeenth century. He emphasised his commonsense approach against the arguments of the sceptics: 'In the new scientific, philosophical and theological context he sought to show how an intelligent, reasonable man could maintain his religious views as more probable than their denials'.[3]

What I have to say in this paper does not substantially dissent from either of these judgements, which are themselves not as far apart as they might at first appear. Rather, I wish in general to endorse them. But I also wish to take the issues further and to explore the nature of Stillingfleet's philosophical position in some more detail. In the light of this it will be

A.P. Coudert, S. Hutton, R.H. Popkin and G.M. Weiner (eds): Judaeo-Christian Intellectual Culture in the Seventeenth Century, 207–224.
© 1999 *Kluwer Academic Publishers. Printed in the Netherlands.*

possible to turn to his famous confrontation with Locke and to place it
within Stillingfleet's wider objectives, and thereby, I hope, to appreciate
what his particular worries about Locke were, what his place in the
philosophical debate was and to make some gesture towards placing him in
the history of philosophy. In examining these aspects of Stillingfleet's
position I shall want to emphasise that in his earlier work especially
Stillingfleet adopts positions which were entirely in keeping with the
Moderns, as we have learnt to call them, and, more specifically, with the
new Way of Ideas which have come to be associated especially with the
philosophy of Descartes and Locke.[4] It was only in his later years that
Stillingfleet seems to have detected trends in that movement that he came
to see as dangerous, and which emerged as positive hostility in his
confrontation with Locke. So although Carroll could characterise this
conflict as one between Stillingfleet the Scholastic and Locke the Modern,[5]
this cannot be seen as an accurate picture of Stillingfleet's earlier position,
and almost certainly overstates his scholastic commitments at the end of
his life. At an earlier stage at least Stillingfleet was one of the modern
young men at Cambridge, very close in many of his beliefs to the
Cambridge Platonists, especially Henry More, who was perhaps the
leading philosopher in the university whilst Stillingfleet was at Cambridge
(even though Stillingfleet never adopted their full range of metaphysical
commitments) and standing close as well to Descartes on many central
philosophical issues. Evidence for these claims, and their implications, will
be offered in what follows.

Stillingfleet and the Existence of God

Much of *Origines Sacræ* (Version 1)[6] is historical, but in the Preface
Stillingfleet tells us that in the third book, inter alia, he has 'manifested the
certainty of the foundation of all religion, which lie in the being of God
and the immortality of the soul'. In other words, Stillingfleet is going to
argue a philosophical justification for these central claims and not rely
solely on the historical argument that is contained in the first two books.
He sets out to establish three propositions:

> 1. That the true notion of a Deity is most agreeable to the faculties
> of men's souls, and most consonant to reason and the light of
> nature.

2. That those who will not believe there is a God, do believe other things on far less reason, and must by their own principles deny some things that are apparently true.

3. That we have as certain evidence that there is a God, as it is possible to have, considering his nature.[7]

We may note the limited nature of the claims that Stillingfleet is making. He is not suggesting some kind of metaphysical certainty for these propositions. But he does think that they can convincingly be shown to be true.

When he turns to the first of these he sees that to make his case he must clarify the notion of God. We of course cannot have an image of God, he says. But that is not to the point, as if human beings had no 'higher faculty in their souls than mere imagination'.[8] But the idea of God must be understood in a more general sense than this. And to explain this Stillingfleet falls back on the language of Scholastic philosophy:

> it is commonly said in the schools that the Divine intellect doth understand things by their ideas, which are nothing else but the things themselves as they are objectively represented to the understanding. So that an idea, in its general sense, in which we take it, is nothing else but the objective being of a thing as it terminates the understanding, and is the form of the act of intellection.[9]

He then goes on to explain this further in language which is likely to sound very familiar to any student of Locke: 'that which is then immediately represented to the mind in its perception of things, is the idea or notion of it'.[10] We will recall that Locke in the *Essay Concerning Human Understanding* explained the word *Idea* as: 'that Term, which. . . serves best to stand for whatsoever is the Object of the Understanding when a Man thinks, I have used it to express whatever is meant by *Phantasm, Notion, Species*, or whatever it is which the Mind can be emply'd about in thinking'.[11] In the *Epistle to the Reader*, in explaining what he means by 'determined Idea' Locke again uses language very reminiscent of Stillingfleet. Amongst other features, they have, he says, this character: 'Some immediate object of the Mind, which it perceives and has before it distinct from the sound it uses as a sign of it'.[12]

So the first point that I wish to make here about Stillingfleet's philosophical position is that his language is by 1662 already the language of the new Way of Ideas. Indeed, he is one of the first philosophers writing in English to make great use of this terminology much more, for example, than any of the Cambridge Platonists or even the intellectually closer Joseph Glanvill. The point is important for an overall assessment of

Stillingfleet's philosophical position, because it will emerge that the conflict between Locke and Stillingfleet, when we finally reach it, is not between a representative of the New Way of Ideas and somebody who has always represented an older tradition, for at this stage at least, they are both within that new tradition. The young Stillingfleet, then, was no defender of the Ancients against the Moderns.

When we attempt an identification of the sources for Stillingfleet's position the catalogue of his library gives us plenty of suggestions. The most obvious are the French philosophers of the previous generation of whom the most important were Descartes, Gassendi, and Arnauld. Stillingfleet's library held their works and their impact on his thinking, especially that of Descartes, is substantial. To those, however, must be added the English philosophers of the period whose imprint is also clearly visible, of whom perhaps the most important is Boyle, but others too may be detected, including More and, perhaps surprisingly, Hobbes, both of whose works, once again, are prominent in the library.

I shall begin with some remarks about the relationship between Stillingfleet and Descartes. In the end there are vast differences between them, and Stillingfleet is going to make much of his assault on the Cartesian rejection of final causes. But in his account of ideas Stillingfleet is very much in the French philosopher's debt. It is not that Stillingfleet here draws on particular passages from Descartes, though some remarks come close to being that, but that the mode of presentation and the claims made are entirely within the Cartesian conception of philosophy. Thus, in considering the nature of ideas and how they may be true or false Stillingfleet says: 'an idea in the soul may be considered two ways. 1. As it is a mode of cogitation, or the act of the soul apprehending an object'.[13] So understood it cannot be considered false 'for as it is an act of the mind, every idea hath its truth. For whether I imagine a golden mountain, or another, it matters not here; for the one idea is as true as the other, considering it merely as an act of the mind'.[14] We may compare this with Descartes in the *Meditations*: 'as far as ideas are concerned, provided they are considered solely in themselves and I do not refer them to anything else, they cannot strictly speaking be false; for whether it is a goat or a chimera that I am imagining it is just as true that I imagine the former as the latter'.[15]

Second, says Stillingfleet, 'the idea may be considered with regard to its objective reality, or as it represents some outward object. Now the truth or falsehood of the idea lies in the understanding passing judgment concerning the outward object'. And Descartes had written immediately after the passage quoted above: 'Thus the only remaining thoughts where I must be on my guard against making a mistake are judgements. And the chief and most common mistake which is to be found here consists in my judgeing that the idea which are in me resemble, or conform to things located outside me'. It would be tedious to multiply examples of the way in which Stillingfleet's text has such correspondences with that of Descartes and I shall not do so more than is necessary. But whether or not Stillingfleet is consciously drawing on Descartes here (and I suspect he was probably not), there are a number of important similarities between their two positions. There are also important differences to which we shall come. But first something more about the similarities.

The first point that I wish to emphasise is a philosophical one, indeed, an epistemological one. It is that Stillingfleet cannot be accurately represented as a direct realist in his account of perception and judgement. In these passages he reveals himself to be every bit as committed as Descartes was to some kind of distinction between ideas as apprehended by the mind and objects which exist independently of the mind. Stillingfleet's language a few lines later brings the matter home conclusively. At the same time he comes very close to offering an account of experience which anticipates Locke's distinction between simple and complex ideas. Both matters arise in the context of a consideration of the status of fictional objects, *'entia rationis'*, 'chimeras, centaurs, &c'. He explains these as the product of the understanding. The latter would not be able to 'compound such things, were they not severally represented to the mind', he tells us, 'as unless we had known what a horse and a man had been, our minds could not have conjoined them together in its apprehension'.[16]

It looks at first sight as though Stillingfleet may be making the point central to Locke's epistemology that there are some ideas that it is impossible for the human mind to make. Although Stillingfleet seems to be at least half way towards that conclusion his actual position is rather different. Locke's argument, which is a great deal more sophisticated than anything ever considered by Stillingfleet, is, in outline, that experience is atomic in structure. The atoms of experience, Locke's simple ideas, cannot be created by the mind, we are just passive recipients of them. But, once the mind has the atoms, it can arrange them as it will, indeed by acts of will, to produce new complex ideas of, for example, fictional entities such as that of the chimera. Our inability to create new simple ideas is a brute metaphysical necessity about our condition comparable to nature's inability to create a new atom of matter.[17]

As Stillingfleet has nothing corresponding to Locke's simple ideas in his account he cannot offer that explanation of the origin of ideas. But he does offer another. Like Locke he has to be able to explain the origin of our ideas of non-real entities, or, as he calls them, ideas that 'have no congruity at all in the order of the universe'.[18] He tells us that: 'although the idea itself be a mere creature of the understanding, yet the mind could not form such an idea but upon preexistent matter; and some objective reality must be supposed, in order to the intellectual conception of these anomalous entities'.[19] He goes on to invoke matter and motion as the source of these ideas: 'So that had there never been any such things in the world as matter and motion, it is very hard to conceive how the understanding could have formed within itself the variety of the species of such things, which are the results of these two grand principles of the universe'.[20]

Stillingfleet's language here is interesting. The invocation of the words 'two grand principles of the universe' and their identification with matter and motion anticipates Robert Boyle's phrasing in his *Origin of Forms and Qualities*: 'These two grand and most catholick principles of bodies, matter and motion, being thus established'.[21] Boyle's work was not published until four years after that of Stillingfleet, but such a striking similarity might cause us to wonder if it was no anticipation at all. Perhaps Boyle had shown his manuscript text to the young cleric, with whom he was acquainted well enough to send him a copy of the second edition of *Spring and Weight of the Air* in 1662 and which Stillingfleet acknowledged by letter.[22] At all events, as we shall see, the very same passages from Boyle are indeed cited in the much later Version 2 of *Origines Sacræ*. Stillingfleet's phrasing also underlines the fact that he was well versed in contemporary physical theory, a fact which his library catalogue endorses,[23] once again supporting the judgement that he must be seen as very much one of the Moderns.

Stillingfleet, then, explains the possibility of our ideas of fictional objects in terms of the existence of an independent physical world. As he puts it:

> I grant those we call *entia rationis* have no external reality, as they are such; but yet I say, the existence of matter in the world, and the corporeal phantasms of outward beings are the foundations of the soul's conception of those entities, which have no existence beyond the human intellect.[24]

In other words the only reasonable explanation of the possibility of having ideas of fictional objects lies in the fact that there is a physical world independent of the mind.

This argument is very important for Stillingfleet as it plays a crucial part in his demonstration of the existence of God. The first move in his argument is to show that we do indeed have an idea of God, contrary to those, such as Hobbes, who say that we can have no such thing. (We might in parentheses note that Hobbes's denial of our ability is not part of any attempt on his part to deny that God exists. It is, rather, part of his argument that it is absurd to argue about God's nature as it is wholly incomprehensible to us, but that is another story.) Stillingfleet's claim that we can and do have an idea or notion of God can obviously only be sustained if we agree that ideas or notions are not images, because all agree that images of any kind of infinity are impossible for us to have. But to distinguish ideas from images is a perfectly standard use of the word *idea* and one in which he had been preceded by Descartes and was to be followed by Locke.

Stillingfleet's discussion of the notion of the infinite is deeply influenced by Descartes' treatment of the same matter. I will comment on two ways in which this occurs, the first of considerable importance for the later parts of my argument. It is that Stillingfleet adopts the Cartesian terminology of clear and distinct ideas, 'though infinite as infinite cannot be comprehended, yet we may clearly and distinctly apprehend a Being to be of that nature'. Thus he is committed to utilizing the criterion of clear and distinct ideas as a means of determining the existence of God.

A second way in which his account in indebted to Descartes is that he also accepts the Cartesian view that infinity as applied to God, and in contrast with its application to such things as space and time, is a *positive* idea: 'the Being which is infinite we apprehend in a positive manner, although not adequately, because we cannot comprehend all which is in it'.[25] And Stillingfleet gives us an analogy with seeing the sea, which we can do clearly and distinctly even though we cannot see it all.

Stillingfleet, however, is no dogmatist. He does not claim that, as a matter of necessity, our idea of God guarantees God's existence. It only seems 'highly probable, and far more consonant to reason than the contrary'. But he does go on to give his reasons for supposing so in some considerable detail. Without following every stage in his argument the essence of it is that the idea of God could not have come from any experience that we might have of the physical world. Further, the unity of that idea cannot plausibly be explained except on the assumption of its cause being an object which itself had that unity, which could only be God himself.

Having conceded that the argument is less than logically compelling Stillingfleet has now to offer reasons which make it plausible. This he proceeds to do. The first central line of thought is essentially *ad hominem*. It is that we accept many other things as true on less evidence. The Epicureans, for example, accept that the origin of the universe is the product of the fortuitous concourse of atoms, a much less plausible claim than that it is the product of a deity. If that is granted then there is nothing unreasonable about the theist's hypothesis.

We cannot follow Stillingfleet through all his theological considerations, but there is one element in his account which is directly relevant to the claims of this paper. He makes much of the fact that the idea of God is, more or less, a universal one. God, he says,

> hath imprinted an universal character of himself on the minds of men; and that may be known by two things. 1. If it be such as bears the same importance among all persons. 2. If it be such as cannot be mistaken for the character of any thing else.[26]

The argument to support the first of these claims is not defeated, Stillingfleet urges us, by individual contrary examples. We can find special circumstances to explain away the apparent counter-instances. Once again, it would, he says, be totally implausible to suppose that so many people in so many different ages could have accepted a deity if it were not true. And he goes on to claim that the idea of God, like the 'common notions' of logic must have been innate in our minds at our entry into the world. It was, in other words, a rejection of the empiricist principle, and it was a rejection clearly made:

> If then our knowledge of truth comes in by our senses, and sensation doth wholly depend upon the impressions of outward objects, what becomes of all common notions, and of the prolepsis of a Deity?[27]

Leaving aside the merit or otherwise of Stillingfleet's argument, we will all know that it was precisely this doctrine of innate ideas that Locke was so forcefully to challenge in the opening book of the *Essay Concerning Human Understanding*. It would be somewhat surprising if Stillingfleet was not alarmed when, much later in his life, he was to open Locke's work and find its early chapters devoted to a refutation of one of his central beliefs. It was hardly the kind of start to endear its author to the, by then, up and coming bishop, so up and coming, indeed, that the Queen herself was soon to champion him for Canterbury.[28]

We have seen that Stillingfleet eschews pretensions to dogmatic certainties for his argument. But in the end he could not resist the temptation to make his case the stronger by claiming a form of necessity for his proof of a Deity. Here, once again, it appears that Descartes is the source, though he is not given the credit. Stillingfleet outlines his proof thus:

> *1. That clear and distinct perception of the mind is the greatest evidence we can have of the truth of any thing. 2. That we have this clear perception that necessary existence doth belong to the nature of God. 3. That if necessary existence doth belong to God's nature, it unavoidably follows that he doth exist.*[29]

This, which we know as the Ontological Argument, and that most famously had its modern expression in the fifth of Descartes' Meditations, rests heavily on the Cartesian conception of clear and distinct ideas, and in his account of the first premise of his argument Stillingfleet, though now with due acknowledgement to both Descartes and Henry More, draws heavily on the French philosopher. There could be, he says, no higher principle than that of clear and distinct ideas and to deny that its application resulted in certainty would be 'as much as to say our faculties are to no purpose'.[30] Stillingfleet is not, however, content to let his argument rest there. And his next move, quite contrary to that of Descartes, is to offer us proof for a deity drawn from the design that nature so evidently exhibits in so many ways.

Once again we must resist the temptation to follow his argument in detail. But it should be apparent from what I have said, that his claims whilst drawing on Descartes to a remarkable degree also go beyond him with regard to the Argument from Design. In this he closely follows More's *An Antidote against Atheism* of 1652. And he combines these positive claims with an assault on the empiricists, as represented by the classical atomists, and very much in the style of the Cambridge Platonists. He argues, for example, that the distinction made by some (he does not himself support or reject it) between what were to be called the primary and secondary qualities of objects could never be made without rejecting that sensation caused by particles of matter was the ultimate source of knowledge.[31] And later when he is arguing for the existence and immortality of the soul he claims — again following Henry More — that it is impossible for the mind to arrive at knowledge that, say, the sun is a large object, simply on the basis of ideas conveyed by sense in the way the materialists like Epicurus supposed.[32]

Thus far we have focused on Stillingfleet's first version of *Origines Sacræ* and my objective has been to show how that work reveals much of Stillingfleet's early philosophical position. I have in particular laid emphasis on the way in which he is much indebted to Descartes, especially in his allegiance to the criterion of clear and distinct ideas and in the commitment to the Ontological Argument. But I have also wanted to reveal Stillingfleet's hostility to classical empiricism, his commitment to innate ideas, and his claims, not always followed, that he was sticking to probabilities, not certainties. I have, however, also stressed his commitment to the new Way of Ideas and to some similarities between his own position and that of his later opponent, John Locke. Now I wish to turn to his later position, both as it emerges in the second version of *Origines Sacræ* and in his controversy with Locke, and finally try to explain why it was that he saw himself at such great distance from Locke when, in truth, their two positions had been so much closer than he would allow.

Origines Sacræ (Version 2)

Book I, Chapter I of Stillingfleet's manuscript of his second version of *Origines Sacræ* is devoted to 'The general Prejudices against Religion in our Age examined; and the old atheistical Hypotheses considered'. It draws substantially on ancient authors but Stillingfleet also cites many contemporaries including Hobbes (both *De Homine* and *Leviathan*), Ray, Hooke, Scaliger, father and son, and a host of recent travel writers, not dissimilar to Locke's use of such texts for rather different purposes in Book I of the *Essay*.[33]

When we turn to the second chapter, prefixed with the words, 'The modern atheistical Hypotheses examined, and the Unreasonableness of them shewed', it is Descartes who features most prominently as the source for Stillingfleet's attack and it is Descartes' search for absolute certainty and his rejection of final causes that are his most prominent targets. The objections that Stillingfleet raises to Descartes are not particularly original. As he acknowledges, many of them had already been made by Gassendi and Mersenne and in all of these criticisms it is probably true that his position was at one with Locke. Indeed, it is the trio of Hobbes, Descartes and Spinoza who are the butt of Stillingfleet's assault: all three of them too materialist, and in the case of Hobbes even atheistical, and all searching for a kind of certainty that as human beings is bound to elude us.

Although Hobbes and Spinoza receive substantial criticism it is Descartes with whom Stillingfleet has the most sustained disagreement.

Not only is Descartes guilty of rejecting final causes, but in requiring unreasonable standards of proof he also claims too much for his method. Stillingfleet cites Descartes' letter to Mersenne in which he wrote that 'he should think he knew nothing in physics, if he could only tell how things might be; if he could not demonstrate that they could be no otherwise'.[34] Furthermore, '[i]n setting up a notion of matter, or corporeal substance independent of the power of God' and '[i]n undertaking to give an account of the *phænomina* of the *universe from the mechanical laws of motion, without a particular Providence*',[35] Descartes' philosophy tended to atheism. Similar worries led Henry More to move away from his early admiration for Descartes. It is not that Stillingfleet rejects the corpuscular philosophy. On the contrary, he quotes Boyle favourably and at length in its support, but, like the Cambridge Platonists, he always claims that it can never explain all the phenomena that we know to exist.

The citation from Boyle is of more general interest and worth further exploration. We have already noted that a passage in the first version of *Origines Sacræ* appears to anticipate remarks by Boyle. Those very same passages in Boyle now feature (again?) in Stillingfleet's text. This time, however, the source is clearly identified as that of that 'truly Christian virtuoso' and author of *The Origin of Forms and Qualities*. Stillingfleet says that he has no difficulty in accepting Boyle's account of matter and its properties, and he succinctly and accurately outlines its main features, including Boyle's distinction between primary and secondary qualities. But Stillingfleet underlines his hostility to too strong a commitment to empiricism: 'I can no means agree' he writes, that 'there are no other qualities in bodies but what relate to our senses'.[36] And then, apropos a further reservation, he interestingly goes on to quote Thomas Sydenham who had emphasised in his medical work the difficulty and often impossibility of knowing the natures of complex things like animals and the human body and the inadequacy of accounting for them in purely mechanical terms:

> That we may know enough for our general direction what to do, but that the secret causes are so hidden from us, as we have reason to admire the supreme Artificer in what we know, and to adore him in what we do not.[37]

When we read these words we might be forgiven if we thought them to express not the sentiments of Sydenham but those of Locke who, in the *Essay*, many times emphasised the limited nature of our understanding of the internal causes of physical things. Thus he writes: 'But whilst we are destitute of Senses acute enough, to discover the minute Particles of

Bodies, and to give us *Ideas* of their mechanical Affections, we must be content to be ignorant of their properties and ways of Operation'.[38]

That Stillingfleet should choose to quote both Boyle and Sydenham is itself of interest. For it was first with Boyle in Oxford and then with Sydenham in London that Locke had conducted his most important scientific research. Neither is it the only Boyle work cited by him. Another is identified as *Experiments of Air*, which, if correctly identified as Boyle's *General History of the Air* of 1692 has a particular Locke connection as it was Locke, acting as Boyle's literary executor who prepared it for the press after Boyle's death and included in it a table of weather reports which Locke had made over the years. That Stillingfleet should also draw on them, and with considerable sympathy, is a pointer towards one of my conclusions.

In similar vein, we might note that the final paragraph of the manuscript of *Origines Sacræ* (Version 2), also links with the modern philosophers of nature. For here Stillingfleet turns to Newton as a support for his anti-mechanical philosophy. Newton, he tells us, had admitted that gravitation as expounded in the *Philosophia Naturalis Principia Mathematica* could not be explained on mechanical principles alone but also required a force directed by divine power and wisdom. So again like the Cambridge Platonists, Stillingfleet finds in the phenomena and in their explanation further reason to reject the materialist philosophy. That he should find support for his views in the *Principia* is again worth noting for its author was yet another friend and collaborator of Locke, this time primarily, though not exclusively, in theology.

Finally of Version 2 we may ask the question why did Stillingfleet see it as necessary or at least desirable to write it? One explanation might be this. The earlier version had indeed borrowed much from the new Way of Ideas, indeed, more than the older Stillingfleet, in the light of what he saw as its misuse by its proponents, could now accept. In the philosophy of the Unitarians and the Deists and in the persons of Toland and Locke it was the unacceptable face of empiricism. It was to defeat this powerful trend that Stillingfleet began his rewriting of *Origines Sacræ* and challenged Locke's philosophy. In doing so he was in no small part rejecting his own earlier beliefs. So we should see the later Stillingfleet as revisionist.

Stillingfleet and the Trinity

It is quite possible that Stillingfleet and Locke had become acquainted in London in the late 1660s or early 1670s. It was at Lord Shaftesbury's request in 1674 that the Bishop of Lincoln had granted Stillingfleet the living of North Kelsey. And as Locke had been acting as Shaftesbury's Secretary for Presentations immediately before this it is very likely that he actually dealt with the original request.[39] But there is no evidence of any further contact or connection before Stillingfleet's assault on the *Essay* in *A Discourse in Vindication of the Doctrine of the Trinity* (1697).[40]

The *Vindication* was a product of the Socinian controversies that flared in the 1690s.[41] As one might expect in a defence of the doctrine of the Trinity Stillingfleet's discourse has three objectives. It is to make it appear:

> 1. That the Churches Doctrine, as to the Trinity, as it is expressed in the Athanasian Creed, is not liable to their charges of Contradiction, Impossibilities and pure Nonsense.
> 2. That we own no other Doctrine than what hath been received by the Christian Church in the several Ages from the Apostles Times:
> 3. And that there are no Objections in point of reason, which ought to hinder our Assent to this great point of the Christian Faith.[42]

Much of the early part of the work is historical, although there are excursions into matters of philosophy, as in the discussion of persons, which is obviously a central concept for the dispute. But it is only in the last chapter of the book, Chapter X, 'The Objections against the Trinity in Point of Reason answer'd', that Stillingfleet engages with the issues that are to lead to his exchange with Locke. Stillingfleet's entry into Locke's *Essay* in the *Vindication* is via Toland's famous Deist work *Christianity Not Mysterious* which had appeared the year before.

If this was indeed Stillingfleet's first encounter with the argument of the *Essay* then it is surprising. For not only did Stillingfleet own the first, 1690, edition of Locke's *Essay*,[43] which almost certainly he would have to have bought well before 1696, but also on general grounds one would expect him to have anyway bought it immediately on its publication. But, for whatever reason, there can be little doubt that Stillingfleet's reading of Locke is through the interpretation attributed to it by Toland.

To explore that reading in detail is beyond the scope of this paper. All that I shall attempt to do here is to show how Stillingfleet distorts not only Locke's but his own philosophical position (as judged by the *Origines*

Sacræ) in his determination to refute both Locke and the Deists and to draw some wider conclusions.

The argument of Chapter X of the *Vindication* is complex. Not only does it invoke two other philosophical works it also presupposes familiarity with much other literature. But there are several strands which may be identified and assessed without sliding too deeply into impossibly prolix exegesis. The one from which I shall begin is that Stillingfleet is determined to saddle Locke with the position that nothing is certain unless it is the product of clear and distinct ideas. Thus, conceding for the sake of argument Locke's empiricist principle that all ideas are the product of sensation or reflection, he writes:

> Let us suppose this [the empiricist] Principle to be true. . . I ask then, how we come to be certain that there are *Spiritual Substances* in the World, since we can have no *clear and distinct Ideas* concerning them?

Locke, it will be recalled, is indeed committed to denying the possibility of an idea of substance beyond it being 'something we know not what' which is the substratum in which properties, either mental or physical, inhere. But in his reply to Stillingfleet's charges he makes the sound point that he never claimed that we can only have knowledge where we have clear and distinct ideas:

> I do not remember that I have any where said, that we could not be convinced by reason of any truth, but where all the ideas concerned in that conviction were clear and distinct; for knowledge and certainty, in my opinion, lies in the perception of the agreement or disagreement of ideas, such as they are, and not always in having perfectly clear and distinct ideas.

Sometimes, Locke goes on, we can be certain of something even though it depends on obscure ideas. 'I exist' is one such, which combines the clear idea of existence with the obscure relative idea of 'support', which he calls substance.[44] So we can know things about which we have obscure ideas. But this is exactly what Stillingfleet in *Origines Sacræ* (Version 1) had also said about our ideas of God and, to remind you of his example, the sea. So it would appear that Locke and Stillingfleet are not really as far apart as Stillingfleet claims, a thought which seems often to have come to Locke too as he ploughed through the Bishop's responses.

Further evidence that their position is closer than Stillingfleet is prepared to allow is to be found in their shared recognition of the limited nature of the things about which we can be absolutely certain. Here both of them distance themselves from Descartes. the problem is that the language which each uses to characterise his own position tends to obscure their shared outlook. On the one side Stillingfleet makes much of the fact that he holds various things to be certain, but with a common sense certainty that does not claim any kind of metaphysical absolutes. On the other, Locke claims that we cannot reach certainty on many matters but can only have justified belief. But the line between these two positions is often hard to draw. Further, both believe that it is possible to demonstrate the existence of God — Locke, if anything, with more certainty than Stillingfleet. And both favour arguments drawn from the order of nature for evidence of a divine providence.

On the great sceptical question supposedly raised by the Way of Ideas, namely how can we know that there is anything external to the ideas which we have, Stillingfleet appears to hold that Locke and his like have no satisfactory answer. But if what we have seen already to have been Stillingfleet's earlier position, then he too was in the same camp, for he too, as we have seen, was, or had been, of the new Way of Ideas. It is not, however, so clear that Stillingfleet was as heavily committed to the doctrine of ideas by the time that he came to write *Origines Sacræ*, Version 2, as he had been earlier. There is a real dearth of any such language in the later work. It looks as though Stillingfleet may deliberately have moved away from the language of ideas in his later years, though this is by no means obvious from the *Vindication* itself, even though when it is used it is usually in the context of identifying the positions of his opponents. So at this stage I would not place this as a firm conclusion, but rather more as a possibility that would bare further investigation.

There is one large difference between Locke and Stillingfleet, however, which cannot be so easily explained away. And that is the explanation of general ideas. Stillingfleet can see no satisfactory way of accounting for these on the basis of simple ideas and holds to some kind of innate ideas doctrine. To that extent it would not be unfair to see him as a Platonist. Although he does not develop a full assault on this aspect of Locke's work it is clear that he would have to reject Book I of the *Essay* almost totally.

Conclusions

Stillingfleet occupies something of a mid position both temporarily and intellectually between the Cambridge Platonists and Locke. But he is markedly more close to Locke than he himself allows because he reads Locke through his Deist interpreter whom he rightly sees as a real threat to standard doctrines of which that of the Trinity was, for the Anglican church, the most important. But there is another dimension to the exchange with Locke that also plays a role in the dispute that is only now coming to the fore. It is that Locke was troubled by Stillingfleet's assault because it came too close to the truth about his own beliefs. That is to say Locke was himself probably convinced that the doctrine of the Trinity was not to be found in the Scriptures. Although he probably did not believe it was contrary to reason (though it was, if true, above reason) it was nonetheless a doctrine for which he could find no compelling evidence. It was this dimension of Stillingfleet's attack that came close to his own secret position. He believed that nothing of that was revealed in the argument of the *Essay*, and on that he was probably correct. But Stillingfleet, by coming at Locke via Toland, was able to see that Locke's position did not exclude the possibility of Unitarianism being true. Locke was probably genuinely concerned that the Bishop's attack might soon become too warm for comfort on an issue about which Locke was very relectant to engage in public controversy.[45]

And finally, a suggestion about the development of Stillingfleet's thought. The young Stillingfleet, I have suggested, was very close to his philosophical mentors in Cambridge, of whom Henry More was almost certainly the most prominent. As such he saw himself in the vanguard of the new philosophy, strongly influenced by Descartes, and moving rapidly away from the tradition of the Schools. In his later years, however, no doubt very conscious of the impact of that new philosophy on the rising generation, and aware too of what he perceived as a rising tide of materialism and other threats to Christian orthodoxy, he came to abandon many of his earlier positions and attempted to consolidate a philosophical outlook that would resist these newer trends. This he was never able to do. For his own philosophy was neither certain enough or deep enough to provide a lasting opposition to either Locke or the deists. As a result Stillingfleet was never anything other than an interesting minor figure in the history of late seventeenth century philosophy. As such he is an important weathervane of the contemporary philosophical climate.

1 Richard Popkin, 'The Philosophy of Bishop Stillingfleet', *Journal of the History of Philosophy*, 9 (1971), pp. 303–319; Robert Todd Carroll, *The Common Sense Philosophy of Religion of Bishop Edward Stillingfleet* (The Hague: Martinus Nijhoff, 1975); Sarah Hutton: 'Edward Stillingfleet, Henry More, and the Decline of *Moses Atticus*: a Note on Seventeenth-Century Anglican Apologetics', *Philosophy, Science and Religion in England, 1640–1700*, Richard Kroll, Richard Ashcraft, and Perez Zagorin (eds), (Cambridge: Cambridge University Press: 1992), pp. 68–84; Sarah Hutton: 'Science, Philosophy, and Atheism, Edward Stillingfleet's Defence of Religion', *Scepticism and Irreligion*, R.H. Popkin and Arjo Vanderjagt (eds), (Brill: Leiden, 1993), pp. 102–120. For a recent assessment of Stillingfleet's place in Anglican theology, which gives due credit to him as a philosopher, see Martin I.J. Griffin, *Latitudinarianism in the Seventeenth-Century Church of England* (Leiden: Brill, 1992) a work dating from 1962. The published work contains annotations by Richard Popkin.

2 Hutton, 'Science, Philosophy, and Atheism', 1993, pp. 110–111, n.1.

3 Popkin, 'Philosophy of Stillingfleet', p. 303, n.1.

4 The *locus classicus* for this is John W. Yolton: *John Locke and the Way of Ideas* (London: Oxford University Press, 1956; reprinted Bristol: Thoemmes Press, 1994). But see also Yolton's many later writings which develop these and related issues.

5 Carroll, *Common Sense Philosophy*, p.86, writes that his argument against Locke 'was essentially one based on scholastic rationalistic metaphysics'.

6 I shall follow Sarah Hutton in calling the 1662 edition Version 1 and that of 1710 Version 2.

7 *Origines Sacræ: or a Rational Account of the Grounds of Natural and Revealed Religion*, 2 Vols. (Oxford: Clarendon Press, 1817), vol. I, p. 331.

8 ibid.

9 ibid.

10 ibid., pp. 331–32.

11 *An Essay Concerning Human Understanding* (1690). Quotations are taken from Peter Nidditch's edition (Oxford: Clarendon Press, 1975) and references are by Book, Chapter, and Section number, and the page number of this edition. This quotation is from I, I, 8, p. 47.

12 *Essay*, pp. 13–14.

13 *Origines Sacræ*, version 1, vol. 1, p. 332.

14 ibid.

15 'Third Meditation', *Meditations on First Philosophy* in *The Philosophical Writings of Descartes*, edited by John Cottingham, Robert Stoothoff and Dugald Murdoch (Cambridge: Cambridge University Press, 1984–1991) 3 vols, vol. 2, p. 26.

16 ibid., p. 332.

17 Cf. *An Essay Concerning Human Understanding* (1690), edited by Peter H. Nidditch (Oxford: Clarendon Press, 1975), Book II, Chapter II, Section 2, pp. 118–119. Further references will be to this edition.

18 *Origines Sacræ*, p. 333.

19 ibid., p. 332.

20 ibid., p. 333.

21 *Origin of Forms and Qualities*, Part I, The Theoretical Part, *The Works of the Hon. Robert Boyle*, 6 vols. (London, 1772), vol. 3, p.16.

22 There is a letter of thanks for the book from Stillingfleet to Boyle of 6 October 1662 in *Works*, vol. 6, p. 462. *Spring and Weight of the Air* is the short title given by John F. Fulton to *New Experiments Physico-Mechanicall, Touching the Spring of the Air* (London, 1660, 2nd edition, 1662). Cf. Fulton, *A Bibliography of the Works of Robert Boyle* (2nd Edition, Oxford: Clarendon Press, 1961), pp. 9–14.

23 Besides the expected wealth of theological works the library contains a very high proportion of the most important scientific works from Copernicus onwards, including a large number of medical works.

24 *Origines Sacræ*, version 1, p. 333.

25 ibid., p. 335.

26 ibid., p. 346.

27 ibid., p. 348.

28 This was on the death of Tillotson in 1694.

29 ibid., p. 357.

30 ibid., p.358.

31 Compare ibid., pp. 358–9.

32 ibid., pp. 372–73. Henry More had used a similar argument.

33 Thus, whilst Locke uses the travel sources to argue that there is no innate idea of God Stillingfleet claims that deeper investigation reveals this not to be the case.

34 *Origines Sacræ*, version 1, vol. II, p. 327.

35 ibid., p. 327.

36 ibid., p. 324.

37 ibid., p. 325. the quotation is taken from Sydenham's *Tractatus de podagra et Hydrope* (London, 1683), p. 160, which is in the Marsh Library, Catalogue M2, Fol. 449.

38 *Essay*, IV, III, 25, p. 556. See also the whole of this particular chapter 'Of the Extent of Human Knowledge' for other similar remarks on the limits of human understanding.

39 For Lincoln's letter telling Shaftesbury of Stillingfleet's appointment see Peter King, *The Life of John Locke*, 2 vols., (London, 1830, reprinted, Bristol, 1991), vol. 1, p. 360. Locke was appointed Secretary of Presentations in 1672 a post which he relinquished when Shaftesbury ceased to be Lord Chancellor in November 1673.

40 *A Discourse in Vindication of the Doctrine of the Trinity: with An Answer to the Late Socinian Objections against it from Scripture, Antiquity and Reason. And a Preface concerning the different Explications of the Trinity and the Tendency of the present Socinian Controversie. By the Right Reverend Father in God, Edward, Lord Bishop of Worcester. The Second Edition. London, Printed by J.H. for Henry Mortlock at the Phoenix in S Paul's Churchyard, 1697*. The first edition was also 1697. There is no first edition in the British Library. The only copy listed in the *Union Catalogue* is supposedly a first edition (also 1697) but this copy and Locke's own copy (cf. John Harrison and Peter Laslett: *The Library of John Locke* (Oxford: Oxford Bibliographical Society, 1965), p. 240, book No. 2787) have the same pagination as the so-called second edition.

41 For a recent discussion of these see, J.A.I. Champion: *The Pillars of Priestcraft Shaken. The Church of England and its enemies 1660–1730* (Cambridge: Cambridge University Press, 1992), esp. pp. 116–120. For the context see also John Spurr: *The Restoration Church of England* (New Haven: Yale, 1991).

42 *Discourse*, Preface, p. vi.

43 It is in the Marsh Library catalogued under P.1, fol. 465.

44 *Mr Locke's Letter to the Bishop of Worcester* in *The Works of John Locke* 10th edition (London, 1823), vol. 4, p. 42.

45 A reason why Locke would not wish to engage in any kind of public discussion of the doctrine of the Trinity, besides the obvious one of danger, is that Locke thought it none of anybody else's business what he thought on the matter, it was between him and God (and possibly Mr Newton). On this see G.A.J. Rogers: 'John Locke, Conservative Radical' in Roger Lund (ed): *The Margins of Orthodoxy* (Cambridge: Cambridge University Press, 1995), pp. 97–116.

13. 'THE FIGHTING OF TWO COCKS ON A DUNG-HILL': STILLINGFLEET VERSUS SERGEANT

BEVERLEY SOUTHGATE

Introduction

The quotation in my title comes from *Origines Sacrae* (1662). Edward Stillingfleet is not in fact describing himself and his adversary John Sergeant, but rather making a general observation about the nature of philosophy after its alleged degeneration: historically, he claims, philosophers grew more concerned with innovating than with seeking truth; so they engaged in 'disputes and altercations, which helped as much to the finding of Truth, as the fighting of two Cocks on a dunghill doth the finding out the Jewel that lyes there'.[1]

That, then, may serve conveniently to introduce my subject and to make some connection with the Marsh Library. My subject is a series of 'disputes and altercations' between Stillingfleet and Sergeant, and both these men are well represented in the catalogue of this institution. In their squabbling, they seem to me at times closely to resemble two cocks fighting on a dung-hill, but somewhere at their feet they believe there lies a jewel that can belong to only one of them. That jewel is the jewel of religious truth; but it gleams through layers of history, is refracted through history, and has to be evaluated in relation to history. So the theological search raises questions of historiography, specific questions relating to the subject of Biblical authenticity, but also more general questions about the validity of any historical accounts of the past.

First, though, it has to be admitted that John Sergeant's connection with Marsh's Library, as coming through Stillingfleet, is not entirely happy; for little love or even respect came to be lost between the two men. Few holds were barred in the theological controversies of the time, and Sergeant himself was a cock-sure fighter who ruffled many feathers. Protestants accused him of being 'an ill natur'd, absurd fellow, in perpetuall squibbles with everyone', as well as 'a great Drunkard, seldom out of a Tavern, or Alehouse';[2] and some even held him responsible for the death of his adversary Henry Hammond through so battering 'the man's inflated ego that shame made him catch a fatal disease'.[3] Hammond's

A.P. Coudert, S. Hutton, R.H. Popkin and G.M. Weiner (eds): *Judaeo-Christian Intellectual Culture in the Seventeenth Century*, 225–235.

seventeenth-century biographer records how he was as a student 'never engag'd (upon any occasion) into fights or quarrels', and he was later to pay heavily for that 'pacifick temper'.[4] Sergeant in turn seems to have been lucky to die in his bed, or at his desk, still with vitriolic pen in hand. Having been accused of hurling fire-balls during the Great Fire of London, he only escaped by pleading his physical inability to have done any such thing: the ambition may have been there, but unhappily he had been left by the plague as 'a mere Skeleton, nothing but Skin and bones'. Later, following an anti-Catholic proclamation by Charles II, he again escaped arrest — this time, having mercifully regained his strength, by fleeing to France at an hour's notice.[5] And that returns us to Stillingfleet, for it was allegedly he who (with Tillotson) planned to have Sergeant apprehended. It is hardly surprising that the refugee came to have little respect for a man 'who as I see plainly by constant Experience, has none at all for Truth, but practices and pursues all over Study'd Insincerity';[6] but his flight from Stillingfleet does provide another link with this conference, for in Paris he encountered none other than the Bishop of Dublin. Peter Talbot initially proved friendly; but he later denounced Sergeant as a heretic, published an anti-Blackloist tirade,[7] and became determined in Bishop Richard Russell's words to 'rake out' of Sergeant's writings 'all the dirt' he could.[8]

Contributions to the dung-hill thus came from a variety of sources, and our two protagonist cocks, Sergeant and Stillingfleet, were not simply engaged in a personal skirmish. Their confrontations had to do, most obviously, with Catholicism and Anglicanism, but they fought too as representatives of opposing camps that had not only theological but also wider intellectual concerns. In particular, Sergeant was associated with the notorious Thomas White and his 'cabal'[9] of 'Blackloists' (a minority 'faction' of English Catholics who derived their name from their leader's singularly unconcealing alias). Sergeant had in fact come into contact with White's ideas as a young man in Lisbon in the 1640s, and he remained associated with Blackloist ideas until his death.[10] It was through White that he was appointed to the influential position of Secretary to the English Catholic Chapter in 1655,[11] and during the high point of Blackloist influence Sergeant was invariably perceived as White's disciple, or as having, in John Warner's words at that time, 'put himself entirely into the hands of White (alias Blacklow) to be trained and taught by him'.[12]

'Blackloism' included a whole package of theological and political policies, but it implied, perhaps above all, a commitment to defying the perceived menace of sceptical philosophy. White's own position on this is clear: his repudiation of what he calls the Pyrrhonist 'contagion' is most evident in his rebuttal of Joseph Glanvill with his trendy talk of dogmatism's 'vanity';[13] but it is a consistent theme throughout his many works, and that anti-sceptical plank of Blackloist philosophy is kept afloat by Sergeant in his latter-day attempts to formulate and expound a convincingly 'solid philosophy'.[14]

This interweaves, again, with Catholic attempts to establish an absolutely certain 'rule of faith' at the expense of their Anglican opponents; and it brings us to the heart of Sergeant's long-running dispute with Edward Stillingfleet. Thus, Sergeant revealingly describes how his rival had mocked him, or 'had cast a jeer upon me. . . calling me 'the man of principles and demonstration''.[15] For the pragmatic Anglican Bishop, Sergeant's uncompromising refusal in theological matters to accept any level of doubt, or the sufficiency of 'moral certainty', seemed ridiculous: mere humans had to accept the reality of their condition, and accommodate their principles to that. But for Sergeant himself conversely, Stillingfleet appeared as a 'Man of No Principles', and amazingly complacent in the face of the demonstrable inadequacy of his so-called 'Rule of Faith', which amounted in fact to nothing better than a 'Rule of Hope'.[16] The two men's opposing views on this theological matter may now seem to be of rather parochial concern, but their approach to scepticism impinges on historiographical issues of far wider importance; and some facets of the jewel in the dung-hill may not entirely have lost their allure.

The Rule of Faith and Historiography

The 'Rule of Faith' debates between the two men open, as is well known, in the 1650s, develop in the 1660s, and continue intermittently through the next decade.[17] Then they resurface with a vengeance in the 1680s, when Sergeant's friend Peter Gooden issued a public (and by this time rather unoriginal) challenge to the Protestants, to demonstrate the absolute certainty of their grounds for faith; and Sergeant himself stepped in once again to represent the Catholic cause.[18] These continuing debates are of course concerned fundamentally with the status of the Bible, but they impinge importantly on more general philosophical and historiographical concerns. For the central issue is, in Tillotson's words, 'by what way and means the knowledge of Christ's Doctrine is conveyed certainly down to us, who live at the distance of so many Ages from the time of its first delivery'.[19] The *theological* matter of Christ's Doctrine is intimately bound up with its *historical* conveyance and its *certain* delivery; and it is in relation to this, the certainty of history, that something of a paradox is revealed in the positions of both our contestant cocks.

Stillingfleet

For Stillingfleet, a historiographical problem already emerges in *Origines Sacrae*. There he confronts the ever-growing body of contemporary 'atheists', and he notes how those undesirables purport to derive their position from three premises: first, the irreconcilability of scriptural and pagan histories; second, the irrationality of believing the scriptures; and third, the possibility of providing a scientific account of the origin of things, without any need to resort to the scriptural version. These three allegations of the atheists share one common factor: a questioning of, or repudiation of, the authority of the Bible.[20] And it is of course just that authority that Stillingfleet is determined to maintain, as underpinning Protestant claims to have a certain basis for their faith.

He is concerned, then, to confirm the validity of historical accounts recorded in the Bible, and so he attempts, for example, to give mathematical demonstrations of the practical possibility of the Flood-story and of its aftermath.[21] But it is in his approach to the first of the three atheistical issues, the irreconcilability of scriptural and pagan histories, that Stillingfleet's problematic position in relation to historiography is most obviously revealed. For his immediate response is to seek to undermine the whole of ancient history: if the scriptural record of past times fails to cohere with alternative accounts, it is the latter that have to be shown to be at fault; and he therefore sets about exposing their 'apparent defect, weakness, and insufficiency'. Lack of contemporary records, weak memories, deficient language, preoccupation with basic necessities, a nomadic life, barbarism, ignorance, and wars — all these left 'no leisure, nor opportunity for any Arts and Sciences to flourish', and militated against the possibility of any reliable history in remote antiquity. And even when one reaches supposedly historical times, things are not much better. The deficiencies are obvious: what the earliest Greek historians wrote was notoriously mere poetry, 'invented for nothing but to please silly people'; the credibility of the early chronicler Aristeus[22] is seriously compromised by his claim to have been able to let his own soul out of his body and then retrieve it; the accepted 'Father' of history (Herodotus) was suspected of falsehood even by his own contemporaries; and Thucydides himself confessed ignorance of anything that happened before the Peloponnesian War. All in all, profane history stands condemned for 'uncertainty, confusion and ambiguity'; and its inconsistency with the Word of God is therefore hardly surprising.[23]

For the Word of God itself, defying all the difficulties of transmission just noted, stands infallibly revealed in the Scriptures: in contradistinction to other historical accounts, the Biblical tradition is claimed to be both credible and certain. For, to avoid intolerable uncertainties and anxieties about our own salvation, we need to be assured that the whole of past history has been under the control of Divine Providence; and to confirm that, we need a reliable record of those former times. Had there been no such permanent record of God's providential ordering, we would need claims constantly renewed in every generation and that would expose us to 'an innumerable company of croaking Enthusiasts . . . continually pretending commission from heaven';[24] to preserve us from which, a benevolent God authorised in Moses a uniquely reliable historian, whose work now justifiably stands as the basis of Protestant certainty.

Moses' own reliability and the authenticity of his writings, are for Stillingfleet beyond reasonable doubt: the Jews of all people would early have detected any attempted deceptions; Moses himself had the benefit both of an excellent Egyptian education, and of direct contact with the historical tradition that led straight back, via Noah, to Adam; as chief actor in the recorded events, he was their most reliable historian, needing no rhetoric 'to court acceptance', but *demanding* belief through his patent 'Majesty and authority'. Moses in short 'was no pretender to divine revelation, but was really imployed as a peculiar instrument of State under the God and ruler of the whole world'. To distrust the authenticity of Mosaic history is tantamount to distrusting the veracity of God himself; for it is surely 'most gross and unreasonable incredulity, to distrust the certainty of anything which comes to us with sufficient evidence of divine revelation'.[25]

And there we reach the crux of the historiographical issue, and of the wider debate with John Sergeant: for what is essentially in dispute is precisely when 'incredulity' is 'unreasonable' and when 'evidence' is 'sufficient'; or when in other words 'Moral Certainty' is to be adjudged acceptable. In this respect, Stillingfleet is finally forced by Sergeant to retreat to a position from which he must concede the sufficiency of moral certainty, not only in secular historical writings but also in the Scriptures themselves. So by 1677, his aspirations are modest: 'All that I desire is that you will give an assent of the same Nature to the History of the *Gospel*, that you *do* to *Caesar*, or *Livy*, or *Tacitus*, or any other ancient

Historian'.[26] For Stillingfleet it has always been *unreasonable* to doubt the veracity of the Mosaic account in the Scriptures, but he comes to concede that it must be equally unreasonable to doubt those other historical accounts of which he has previously been so critical; for we can hardly repudiate reports of everything that we have not personally experienced. 'Either we must destroy all *Historical faith* out of the world, and believe nothing (though never so much attested) but what we see ourselves, or else we must acknowledge, that a *moral certainty* is a *sufficient foundation* for an *undoubted assent*'.[27] Admittedly, there must always remain a remote possibility of some error, but that risk seems minimal; and Stillingfleet seems unconcerned that the basis of Protestant faith thus becomes no more reliable than those ancient historians whom he himself has been previously concerned to discredit.

Sergeant

This is far from good enough for John Sergeant: for him 'moral certainty' is by no means 'a sufficient foundation for an undoubted assent'; and we are returned to our cock-fight. For Sergeant likens his adversary's confidence in mere probability to 'those comfortable lights which both parties have when they lay even wagers at Cock-fighting and such games; giving good *hopes* to *both* sides, but good *Security* to *neither*'.[28] The requisite 'good security' can, Sergeant believes, still in fact be found: refusal to accept the *probable* odds of 'moral certainty' does not imply for him, as it does for Stillingfleet, the inevitable destruction of '*all* Historical faith'.

But there remains for Sergeant no less than for Stillingfleet an historiographical problem. As a Blackloist, he is bound on the one hand to maintain some basis for ascribing certainty in those vital areas (such as science, religion, and morality) where the effects of scepticism seem particularly pernicious; while on the other hand, he has to undermine his opponent's grounds of faith, grounds that on the face of it seem to be enclosed within that very territory that he seeks to defend. In short, the fervently anti-sceptical Sergeant, needing to question the basis of Protestant dogma, has himself to assume a highly sceptical position in relation to the historical validity of the Holy Scriptures; and that has implications for his attitude to other aspects of historical study. For in attacking the authority of the Bible, Sergeant would endanger also some strategically important collateral territory: if the validity of the Biblical record comes into question, what historical accounts of the past, including that required to substantiate Catholic claims to continuing links with the early Christian tradition, could possibly remain immune to similarly sceptical threats? Where in short can the basis of some historical faith be found?

In his refusal to accept the 'new realities' of 'moral certainty', Sergeant sounds like an unreconstructed 'Ancient', but he proceeds very much in the 'Modern' manner to insist on an empirical rather than purely verbal approach to historical evidence. In fact, this late-seventeenth century Aristotelian sounds remarkably like an early-seventeenth century Baconian, as he accuses his opponents of maintaining a merely *verbal* approach to knowledge. Like Bacon's earlier scholastics, they 'are convinc't not to study Things, but Words', with Stillingfleet himself contriving 'to leade his Reader into a Wilderness of Words (whole Libraries of Authors) where, by his way of managing Citations, which is by Criticising, upon ambiguous words and phrases, they may dance in the Maze till they be weary'. Protestants, in short, through their reliance on the written scriptures, are condemned 'to study vapour in *wordish learning*'.[29]

An escape from the vaporous maze of wordish learning is provided by a proper application of empiricism. As Bacon again had claimed, this in the first place has the advantage of being more democratic, since even babies and children and 'the rudest vulgar' can understand the evidence of 'our Eyes and Ears'; but secondly and most importantly, it guarantees real certainty. And such empirically-based certainty is precisely what is provided, in matters of faith, by Catholic tradition: instead of taking refuge in such Protestant havens as 'inward Light or knowledge infus'd extraordinarily', Catholics can rely on a tradition which is 'the way of coming to Faith by the open use of our Senses'. Those senses are utilised in an *oral* or *practical* tradition; and it is by means of that, that reliable historical records are transmitted — including of course the record of Christ's message. Sergeant's claim is, then, that certain matters have been transmitted from generation to generation by means of a living tradition — not by a 'dead' written account, but by 'a Delivery down from hand to hand (by wordes, and a constant course of frequent and visible Actions conformable to those Words) of the Sence and Faith of Forefathers'.[30] One vitally important parcel of material thus transmitted contains the Christian message, relayed like a baton from generation to generation in an essentially *empirical* way to contemporary Catholics; but other outstanding historical events have been similarly kept alive.

Not all historical events of course are actually outstanding: some are comparatively insignificant, and witnessed by only a few at the time; so that even Alexander the Great's private acts and conversations were 'of small Concern or Note, and seen or heard but by a few'. These, then, cannot lay claim to any reliable reporting. But the record of his conquest of Asia is another matter: that was a public event which made an immediate impression on a great number of people; and its memory, passed on not through literary records but through a continuing practical tradition, has been retained as 'fresh and lively'.[31] The workings of that infallible historical tradition can be clarified by reference to a fashionably mechanical analogy: it persists through 'working on their Senses, as that in a long chain of Iron, one link drawn should draw all the rest; or, that the turning the First wheel, should move a thousand distant ones depending on its motion'.[32] No-one, then, can reasonably doubt the historical truth of such episodes, unless 'besotted and un-mann'd' by 'Speculative Scepticism'; and in historical study generally, one can actually lay claim to 'most Certain Truths'.[33]

In the particular case of the Christian message transmitted through Catholic tradition, there is even more reason for wholehearted assent; and Sergeant is again scathing of his Protestant adversaries who take refuge in something less. As far as he is concerned, there can in respect to scepticism be no half-measures: one is either certain or uncertain; and one cannot afford uncertainty about something as important as the grounds of faith. Even in the cases of highest probability, one can after all prove mistaken and lose one's wager: houses in London have fallen down contrary to all expectations; and the sun has defied every inductivist's example by actually failing to rise. In the matter of salvation, one cannot afford to get it wrong: even at odds of a thousand-to-one, there is a one-in-a-thousand chance of damnation, and that is too great a risk; 'the Basis of Mankind's Salvation must be incomparably more secure than that which we usually have for the attainment of a Bag of Money, a Place at Court, Merchandise from the Indies, and such-like trivial Concerns'.[34]

Sergeant believes, then, that his Catholic faith provides a bastion against the militant inroads of scepticism. The Scriptures, as a written record of the past, may be subject to varied interpretations, and it is that which results in the proliferation of individualistic Protestant sects.[35] But the uninterrupted oral, practical, empirically-based 'tradition' of Catholicism, ensures absolute certainty in the conveyance of historical truths, and acts as a benchmark by which to establish a definitive interpretation. Historians, therefore, as well as theologians can be assured of at least some certainties. Written records may be intrinsically unreliable and potentially subject to personal misinterpretation, but they can be checked against a continuing and authoritative source; and true certainty can thus be guaranteed.

Conclusion

It is true certainty that is the jewel over which our two 'Marsh-infesting' cocks have been fighting, and it is in the light of that that their differences become clear, as well as their own internal inconsistencies. Edward Stillingfleet, having initially argued against the validity of secular history, in order to boost his own claims for the certainty of scriptural history, is later forced to concede their practical equivalence. Neither can furnish more than moral certainty: probability has to suffice, not only in historiography but also by implication in theology. So he resigns himself to a modernist (or even post-modern) position, from which the jewel of certainty appears as only artificial anyway. For John Sergeant, on the other hand, there could be no such concessions. So having initially, for theological reasons, repudiated the adequacy of any historical account, including that in the scriptures, he later seeks to confirm the validity of certainty as an historical goal. For some sort of *historiographical* certainty is needed, and must be shown to be attainable, in order to confirm the possible retrieval of that ancient jewel of *theological* certainty, in comparison with which Christians would 'practically repute all other things as *Dung*'.[36]

---

1 Edward Stillingfleet, *Origines Sacrae, or A Rational Account of the Grounds of Christian Faith* (London, 1662), p. 429.

2 John Sergeant, *The Literary Life* (dated Paris, 3 September 1700), p. 55. My page references are to the MS, but the work has been published in *Catholicon*, vols. II and III (London, 1816).

3 Bishop Richard Russell, in *Lisbon College Register*, p. 175. For Sergeant's low opinion of Hammond, see *Literary Life*, pp. 13, 31–2. It is small wonder that John Tillotson largely refrained from controversial writing as being 'irksome and unpleasant', believing further that a 'Man that hath once drawn Blood in Controversie... is seldom known ever perfectly to recover his own good Temper afterwards'. *Works* (6th edn., London, 1710), p. 583, quoted by R.T. Carroll, *The Common-Sense Philosophy of Religion of Bishop Edward Stillingfleet, 1635–1699* (The Hague, 1975), pp. 44, 56.

4 John Fell, *Life of Henry Hammond* (1661), pp. 7, 8; quoted by J.W. Packer, *The Transformation of Anglicanism, 1643–1660* (Manchester, 1969), p. 17.

5 *Literary Life*, pp. 64, 69, 106–7.

6 *Fifth Catholick Letter* (London, 1688), Preface.

7 Lominus [i.e., Peter Talbot], *Blakloanae Haeresis* (Ghent, 1675).

8 Russell also described Talbot as a 'Creator of Mischief' and the most 'troublesome person alive'. See his letters to Watkinson, 26 February and 9 September 1676, in Russell Papers, Lisbon Archives, Ushaw College. Even after his death, Sergeant's notoriety lived on: as late as 1714, it was unanimously resolved by the Catholic general assembly that his books 'containing sharp and severe reflections upon his brethren of the chapter be suppressed and destroyed'. G. Anstruther, *The Seminary Priests*, vol. 2 (Ushaw, 1975), p. 288.

9 So Robert Pugh, who describes Sergeant as being a member and 'of evil reputation', in his collection of allegedly incriminating letters entitled *Blacklo's Cabal* (1680), Epistle to the Catholick Reader.

10 Cf. Sylvester Jenks: 'J.S. is dead. But I had rather write his faction had been dead'. BL Add. MS 29612, f. 60.

11 George Leyburn, *Encyclical Answer* (Douai, 1661), p. 86. Leyburn notes that White found his young protegé 'very nimble, wanton and active as to maintaining and spreading his new doctrines'.

12 John Warner, *The History of the English Persecution of Catholics*, ed. T.A. Birrell (London, 1953), p. 230.

13 Glanvill's *Vanity of Dogmatizing* (London, 1661) provoked White's *An Exclusion of Scepticks* (English translation, London 1665); and the debate continued in Glanvill's *Scepsis Scientifica* (London, 1665) and 'Of Scepticism and Certainty', in *Essays on Important Subjects in Philosophy and Religion* (London, 1676). See B.C. Southgate, "Cauterising the Tumour of Pyrrhonism': Blackloism versus Skepticism', *Journal of the History of Ideas*, 53, 1992, pp. 631–645.

14 Here I take issue with R.T. Carroll, who describes Sergeant's position as 'sceptical and fideistic' (*Stillingfleet*, pp. 44, 62). For Sergeant's late anti-scepticism, see *The Method to Science* (London, 1696) and *Solid Philosophy Asserted against the Fancies of the Ideists* (London, 1697).

15 *Literary Life*, p. 103.

16 *Errour non-plust* (n.p., 1673), subtitle, *Literary Life*, pp. 95–6.

17 Sergeant dates the origin of the debate to Henry Hammond's *Of Schisme. A defense of the Church of England against the. . . Romanists* (London, 1654), to which he responded in *Schism Disarm'd* (Paris, 1655). See also esp. *Sure Footing in Christianity* (London, 1665); *Faith Vindicated* (Louvain, 1667); *Reason against Raillery* (n.p., 1672); *Errour non-plust* (1673); John Tillotson, *The Rule of Faith* (London, 1666); Edward Stillingfleet, *A Reply to Mr. J. Serjeant* (London, 1666).

18 Sergeant was willing enough to intervene since he had not liked the way his old sparring-partner had recently been 'glancing at him uncivilly [and] provoking him causelessly'. *Six Catholick Letters* (London, 1688), Preface (handwritten).

19 John Tillotson, *The Rule of Faith*, pp. 6–7. A similar definition is given by Sergeant in his Preface to *Reason against Raillery*; again, he stresses the conveyance of Christ's teachings 'without the least danger of Errour'; and cf. his *Fifth Catholick Letter* (London, 1688), Preface.

20 This theme, of the 'mean Esteem of the Scriptures', is later identified by Stillingfleet as having become 'common. . . among the Scepticks of this Age'. *Letter to a Deist* (London, 1677), Preface.

21 Stillingfleet here uses calculations made by Sir Walter Raleigh, and cites confirming evidence from (otherwise discredited) ancient historians. *Origines Sacrae*, pp. 543f. Cf. Thomas White's not dissimilar attempts to establish the practical possibility of the Biblical Deluge in his *Peripateticall Institutions* (London, 1656), Theologicall Appendix.

22 Or Aristeas, cited by Herodotus (Bk. IV, ch. 13) as a source of information on the one-eyed Arimaspi and gold-guarding Griffins.

23 *Origines Sacrae*, Preface, pp. 15f., 61f., 73. Despite his professed scepticism about the reliability of Herodotus and Thucydides, Stillingfleet goes on to use them as evidence for his own views: see, e.g., pp. 124, 561.

24 Cf. Thomas Sprat on 'the late extravagant excesses of Enthusiasm [and] the infinite pretences to Inspiration and immediate Communion with God'. *History of the Royal Society* (London, 1667), pp. 375–6.

25 *Origines Sacrae*, pp. 132–138.

26 *Letter to a Deist*, p. 27.

27 *Origines Sacrae*, p. 112.

28 *Errour non-plust*, p. 162

29 *The Method to arrive at Satisfaction in Religion*, appended to *Errour non-plust*, p. 267; *Sure-Footing*, pp. 165, 68.

30 *Sure-Footing*, pp. 41, 47, 109.

31 The number, as well as the quality, of the original witnesses is important for Sergeant: see, e.g., *Second Catholick Letter* (London, 1687), p. 43.

32 This indicates Sergeant's interest in the new science, another interest that he shared with his Blackloist friends, Kenelm Digby and Thomas White.

33 *Sure-Footing*, pp. 41, 221, 228, 237; *Method to Science* (London, 1696), p. 341. Sergeant suggests bitterly that one can easily envisage the indefinite perpetuation of the memory of events which cause popular excitement, by considering the Gunpowder Plot, with its annual ceremonies of bonfires and fireworks, and 'spitefull Preaching against All Catholicks indifferently'. It is clear that the memory of such events can be kept alive and fresh by perpetuating practical traditions. *Fifth Catholick Letter*, p. 7.

34 *Faith Vindicated*, pp. 146–147; *Reason against Raillery*, pp. 146–147, Preface.

35 The Protestant John Biddle was notorious for having interpreted the Scriptures as being even 'plainly against a Trinity and Christ's Divinity' (*First Catholick Letter*, p. 29); and Thomas White, who expressed some admiration for Biddle as a co-heretic, had calculated the likelihood of textual corruption in the Bible at 15 or 16 to one. Rushworth, *Dialogues* (2nd edn., Paris, 1654), p. 95. It is precisely because the Scriptures alone are unreliable, 'their sense. . . oftentimes obscure and very difficult to be discovered and penetrated into, that an authoritative tradition is necessary: *Controversy-Logicke* (Paris, 1659), p. 50; cf. p. 87.

36 *Faith Vindicated*, p. 86.

14. LIMBORCH'S *HISTORIA INQUISITIONIS* AND THE PURSUIT OF TOLERATION*

LUISA SIMONUTTI

The work and its publication

In 1692, Philippus van Limborch dedicated the volume of the *Historia Inquisitionis* to the Archbishop of Canterbury, John Tillotson:[1]

> The book which I now publish, and my History of the Inquisition prefixed to it, appeared to me worthy of Your Grace's Patronage, rather than any other Person's living, when I considered the Subject treated of in both of them, and that high Station, which in these most difficult Times You support with the greatest Honour and universal Applause of all good Men, for the common Advantage of the Reformed Churches.[2]

The special bond between the Dutch Arminians and those sectors of the Anglican clergy sympathetic to anti-predestination and an emphasis on the ethical rather than the dogmatic message of true Christian doctrine goes far beyond the personal friendship between Limborch and Tillotson. Such a relationship dates to the time of Arminius and his critical assessment of English Puritanism. In the first decade of the seventh century, Hugo Grotius called the attention of King James to the Remonstrant sect.[3] This led to the participation of the English delegate John Hales in the Synod of Dordrecht and the subsequent repercussions his reports and memoirs had on the English court and Anglican clergy.[4]

The foundation of the theological school by Episcopius in 1634 and the endorsement it received from the Frenchman Etienne de Courcelles marked a strong revival of the Remonstrant community after the years of exile following their condemnation at the Synod of Dort. In the second half of the century, spurred on by Petrus Grotius (the son of the well-known jurist and ambassador to the Swedish court), two professors at the Remonstrant Seminary, Arnold Poelenburg and Philipp van Limborch, presented the works of the fathers of Arminianism (Arminius, Episcopius, and Courcelles) to the principal exponents of Latitudinarianism and Neoplatonism at Oxford and Cambridge. The two theologians, who were committed defenders of religious liberty and toleration, resolved to solicit the further attention of those sectors of the English clergy most sympathetuc towards Remonstrant doctrine and ethics. For their part, the liberal English Protestants, by virtue of their distance from Puritanism and Protestantism with strong predestinationist and dogmatic tendencies,

A.P. Coudert, S. Hutton, R.H. Popkin and G.M. Weiner (eds): Judaeo-Christian Intellectual Culture in the Seventeenth Century, 237-255.
© 1999 *Kluwer Academic Publishers. Printed in the Netherlands.*

proved receptive to the Remonstrants' criticism of Calvinist theology of a
Gomarist stamp.

The meetings, exchanges of letters and published works, and the
common themes in their respective writings testify to the affinity between
the Dutch Remonstrants and liberal English theologians. In the last quarter
of the century, Limborch, the principal representative of the Remonstrant
wing, had close relationships with the Cambridge Neoplatonists Henry
Moore and Ralph Cudworth[5] and their allies at Oxford and Cambridge.[6] He
also corresponded with the principal representatives of the English
Latitudinarians such as John More, William Lloyd, John Tillotson and,
through them, with Edward Stillingfleet, John Pearson, and Gilbert Burnet,
with whom he formed a strong friendship during Burnet's sojourn in
Holland.

Turning to these theologians, Limborch sought to gather the views
of moderate Protestants who were open to the ideal of religious concord
and the toleration of dissident groups.[7] He admired the open and candid
('aperte et candide') freedom with which religious debate was conducted by
the Latitudinarians, whose moderate position would have been endorsed by
both the Remonstrants and contra-Remonstrants.[8] Not only the works but
also the personal histories of the Latitudinarian clergy revealed an openess
toward a plurality of positions and interpretations of the Scriptures.
Archbishop Tillotson was a case in point. The influence that moderate
Protestants such as Chillingworth and Whichcote had on his intellectual
formation, together with his ties with Wilkins, contributed to making
Tillotson 'an eclectic man, and not one to bind himself to opinions', to
quote the words of his first pupil, John Beardmore.[9]

The Glorious Revolution found many Latitudinarians among its
supporters. The Latitudinarian clergy could depend on a growing consensus
during the early 1690s that recognized the importance of the Latitudinarian
interpretation of Anglicanism within the ecclesiastical hierarchy. Thus
Tillotson was promoted to the Archbishop's seat at Canterbury in 1691. He
would be succeed by another Latitudinarian, Thomas Tenison, while
Stillingfleet would become the Bishop of Worcester, Moore the Bishop of
Norwich, Fowler the Bishop of Gloucester, and Burnet the Bishop of
Salisbury.[10]

A Manuscript to be Published

Given this situation it is understandable why Limborch placed the *Historia
Inquisitionis* under the protection of the Latitudinarians and especially of
Tillotson. His intention was to present this work to a broader audience, not

simply to the Dutch public, because he was convinced of its usefulness not only for the doctrinal debate that animated Dutch Protestants but also for the English clergy and for the entire Christian world. Furthermore it was thanks to his English friends John Locke and Benjamin Furly that Limborch became passionately involved with this editorial project, and it was with their protection and encouragement that he edited the text.

The *Historia Inquisitionis* is made up of two parts. The first consists of an ample and documented historical introduction written by Limborch and describing inquisitorial persecution from the Middle Ages through the modern era. The second part contains the transcription made by Limborch of the precious late Medieval manuscript entitled *Liber sententiarum inquisitionis Tholosanae*. This codex was a compilation of the sentences handed down by the Toulouse inquisitors during the period from 1307 to 1323. According to Limborch, the harshness of the language and the cruelness of the descriptions in the inquisitors' reports demonstrated more clearly than any polemical work possibly could the illegitimacy of an Office that described itself as 'Holy' while defending the Catholic faith with a violence that completely contradicted the teachings of the Bible.[11] Having taken such a clearly critical position, Limborch entered into the lively contemporary debate on liberty of conscience and the persecution of heretics. He did not condemn or list the errors of the Inquisition as strongly as others had before him; he simply and deliberately presented the medieval codex in a complete and philologically correct edition, allowing the text itself, without any further comment, to reveal the cruelty and irrationality of Catholic persecution, indeed, of any religious persecution.

From the very beginning of the work Limborch emphasizes the central point of his argument against persecution by pointing out how dubious the term 'heretic' actually is:

> By an Heretick, therefore, I understand one condemned for Heresy by the Church of Rome. I could not rehearse their Decrees but in their own Words, and was therefore forced always to use them, unless I would have interrupted the Course of the History, by repeated and innumerable Alterations, and thereby rendered it less pleasing and acceptable. Let it therefore suffice, once for all, to say, that, by the Word Heretick, when I ever speak of the Inquisition against Hereticks, I do not mean one who is truly an Heretick, but accounted an Heretick by the Church of Rome, taking the Word in the Popish Sense of it. In the mean while, those who are Hereticks in their Account, are not so in mine; and I sincerely believe, that those which the Church of Rome hath condemned for Heresy, have died, and gloriously endured the Punishment of Fire for the Testimony of Jesus Christ, and the maintaining a good Conscience.[12]

He stresses the necessary of contextualizing the interrogators' reports, the sentences, and the executions of those political figures and common people who had fallen into the hands of the Holy Office, accused of being Albigensians, Waldensians or Beguins (one of the denominations of the Spiritual Franciscans).

He thus began the *Liber sententiarum inquisitionis Tholosanae* with a brief history of the medieval French, Spanish, Italian, and Central European Inquisition, complete with an accurate description of the role of the vicars, notaries, etc. and of the workings of the tribunals. He reserved a great deal of space for the analysis of the canon law on which the Holy Office was based and which established the kind and gravity of the crimes the heretics were accused of. This broad and detailed introduction, which takes up half of the large volume, concludes with a description of the methods and the procedures used to judge and condemn the heretics. Limborch leaves to the codex itself the task of directly and incisively revealing the sentences passed by the Tribunal and the nature of those condemned to execution.

In the pages that precede the text of the *Sentences* Limborch vaguely mentions the provenance on the manuscript, thus raising the question that has aroused the curiosity of church historians and of scholars of the Inquisition for nearly three centuries: how did he obtain the manuscript and from whom?[13] The little he says on the subject is far from satisfactory:

> Dear reader, here is a book published for you, of a sort hitherto unknow to the Christian world. It is agreed on indubitable evidence that the manuscript itself, which I have had in my possession for four whole years thanks to the generous consent of its owner, was written by notaries of the Inquisition, and is an authentic exemplar taken from the archives of the Inquisition of Toulouse.[14]

The document, compiled by four Inquisition notaries (Limborch lists their names and seals[15]), contains the *Sentences* passed by the important and infamous inquisitorial judge, Bernard Gui.[16] The Liber is, in fact, made up of sixteen 'sermons' containing rules of inquisitorial procedure and the relative penalties for the heretics, most of which were pronounced by Gui in the Cathedral of Tolouse in collaboration with such prelates as Geoffroy d'Ablis, Jean de Beaune, Gaillard and Preyssac, Bishop of Tolouse, as well as others.[17] The manuscript also contains an alphabetical index of locations, dates, and names of those tried by the Inquisiton in the period from 1307 to 1323. The *Sentences* is the fruit of Gui's inquisitorial experiences. It provided the documentary basis for his better known *Pratica Inquisitionis heretice pravitatis*,[18] used for more than three centuries as a fundamental document in the history of the medieval Inquisition, for which even today there are very few documentary sources. Historians, who considered the manuscript lost, believed that Limborch had compiled his edition from a copy, most likely an imperfect one, of the *Sentences*; they were not, however, able to explain either how Limborch had come to possess the codex or who the generous donor had been.

From the early 1970s, however, a scrupulous reconstruction of the history of the manuscript's passage from France to Holland and then to England, where it was eventually acquired by the British Museum in 1756,[19] revealed the authenticity of the codex as well as the role John Locke and his friend and correspondent, the merchant Benjamin Furly, played in its acquisition and the overseeing of its publication. Locke in particular followed the preparation of the text and all the phases of its publication for four years.

Writing to Furly early in 1688, Locke expresses a certain envy for Furly, who had recently been lent the manuscript by its last owner, the knight Sir William Waller. Locke had himself seen the document, or a copy of it, during his sojourn in Montpellier in 1677, and he had even taken some notes from it. At that point the codex had probably belonged to Waller, with whom Locke had been in contact at the end of 1676. The document had obviously kept Locke's attention, for some ten years later he added a note to his Journal mentioning the presence of the manuscript in Nimes.[20]

In the course of their correspondence in the early months of 1688, Locke and Furly discuss the importance of publishing the *Liber sententiarum* in order to put such an important document before the public. It therefore became essential to explain the origins of the heretical movement condemned in it from a historical point of view.[21] A few days after his return to Rotterdam from Amsterdam, where he had been for several months, and while a guest of Furly's, Locke wrote to Limborch, stressing the importance of publishing the document:

> On my suggestion and incitement our Friend Furly has sent you through van Helmont a book in manuscript, with a view to its remaining in your keeping whilst arrangements are made for printing it. When you see the contents I think you will agree with us that it deserves to see the light; for it contains authentic records of events in that rude age, of which historians have given us either negligent or faulty accounts. I would prefer, and, unless I am mistaken, all lovers of truth would be with me preferring, such artless narratives, drawn from the very fountain-head, to the flowers of rhetoric offered by historians, which are ornaments in the writer, indeed, but deceive the reader and lead him into errors.[22]

Locke's decision to entrust the edition to Limborch indicated the common cultural interests he and Limborch shared, which had taken root during the years Locke spent in Amsterdam.[23] While there, Locke participated on an almost weekly basis in the meetings attended by Limborch and many like-minded friends and colleagues such as Pieter Guenellon, Egbertus Veen,

Mattheus Sladus, as well as other Remonstrants. In the letters which
bridged the distance between them over the subsequent years, particularly
those written after Locke's move to Rotterdam at the beginning of February
1687, the two men kept each other informed about their thoughts and
activities and the appearance of their respective works. Locke himself
recognized and noted the help he received from Limborch and his circle of
friends in the drafting and revision of his works and in their presentation to
a broad public through their publication in erudite Dutch journals.
Limborch also benefited from his friendship with Locke to the point that he
was concerned to mantain the friendship right up to Locke's death. Locke's
influence on Limborch is revealed by the attention Limborch pays to
Locke's ideas in his own writings beginning in the 1680s. The affinity of
the views of the two friends, above all on religious matters but also in
regard to the ties between reason and religion and the search for truth, form
the background for their collaboration and criticism of the Inquisition for its
persecution of heretics.

In one of his first letters to Limborch written in the beginning of
1685, Locke expressed his interest in a work that Limborch was in the
process of finishing, his *De veritate Religionis Christianae Amica Collatio
cum Erudito Judaeo*.[24] When this work was published two years later,
Limborch wrote to thank his friend for his critical contribution during the
revision of his work.[25] He also thanked Locke for keeping him informed
about the views of the Amsterdam Jews concerning the legitimacy of
engaging in religious debates with Christians.[26]

During these months Locke was extremely interested in the
doctrinal and ethical questions discussed in Limborch's work, which he had
already had occasion to analyse closely. He was also concerned with the
experiences that Balthasar Orobio de Castro, the erudite Jew who had
agreed to conduct this amicable debate with Limborch, had with the
Inquisition Tribunal.[27] Locke asked Limborch to send him a detailed
account of Orobio's experiences so that he could compare the methods
used by the Spanish Inquisition with those described in the recent work on
the Portuguese Inquisition in the colonies in India at Goa.[28] Limborch had in
fact received an account of the torture suffered by Orobio straight 'from his
own mouth.'[29] Subsequently he did not hesitate to include the account in the
chapter dedicated to torture in his *Historia Inquisitionis* in memory of his
now deceased friend. Given this significant convergence of interest, it was
natural that once he had the *Liber sententiarum* at his disposal, Locke
would think of Limborch (perhaps with the help of a mutual friend Jean Le
Clerc) as the scholar best suited to prepare the edition and to resolve the
editorial and economic difficulties in which he and Furly had found

themselves as a result of their attempt to prepare the *Liber sententiarum* for publication.[30]

It was only natural that Limborch's interest in the question of toleration and the persecution of heretics — evidenced in all of his work — would be aroused with his reading of the *Liber sententiarum*. Graciously agreeing to edit the manuscript, he confessed to Locke in March of 1688 how engrossed he had become in the project: 'I am now so imbued with its expressions that they have become second nature to me.' In the same letter he commented on the importance of publishing the manuscript: 'I am glad to have seen that book; in my opinion it is entirely in the interests of Christianity that it should be published, and the more I read of it the more eagerly I desire its publication.'[31] Within a few days he again wrote to inform Locke that he already begun to make arrangements with the publisher Hendrik Wetstein, who was, in his view, better suited to undertake this kind of publication than Abraham Wolfgang (whom Le Clerc would have preferred[32]), about procuring the right to publish from the owner of the manuscript and meeting the expenses involved.[33]

In the months and years before the the work was finally published in September 1692, there are constant references in the correspondence between the two friends to the transcription of the manuscript,[34] the gathering of historical materials, the drafting of the introduction,[35] and the many difficulties Wetstein had with printing[36] and publishing it,[37] as well as the reaction to it.[38] For example, in March 1691, Limborch sent Locke a detailed report on the contents of the four books which made up the historical introduction, with a precise summary of the contents of the chapters.[39] When the work was almost completely printed, Limborch sent the letter he had written dedicating the book to the Archbishop of Canterbury to Locke for his opinion. He also sent Locke the list of historical references which he had been used in the compilation of *Historia Inquisitionis* and which he planned to insert in the volume to show the historical and philological accuracy of the work.[40] Limborch's great care and determination in overseeing the publication of the manuscript met with the support and complete approval of Locke, who even after his return to England continued to concern himself with the publication of *Historia*, which he, standing in for Limborch, eventually presented to the Earl of Pembroke, the Bishop of Salisbury and the Bishops of Bath and Wells.[41]

Between Philology and History

Limborch begins his historical introduction by citing important passages from Tertullian, Ciprianus, Lactantius, and other Church Fathers to stress the fact that 'the primitive Christians opposed with the greatest vigour, all cruelty and persecution for the sake of Religion.'[42] He condems the use of force in religion on the grounds that the constraint of will does not lead to devotion or faith and is contrary to the spirit of Christian doctrine. Citing Lactantius, Limborch shows that early Christians believed Christian doctrine should be defended by the sword of reason and could only be preserved by the sole evidence and strength of truth.[43]

Limborch attributes the rise of persecution in the Christian Church to the fact that civil power was placed placed in the hands of the Christians as a result of the Council of Nicene and to the conversion of the Emperor Constantine. With the consequent mixing of religion and politics, civil law became a means of punishing those sects, such as the Arians, defined as heretics by the Council with ever more rigor and severity, even to the point of total extirpation. According to Limborch, these developments in the relationship between the Church and the State gave birth to a 'degenerate Posterity.'[44] The writings of the Church Fathers, especially those of Athanasius, who condemned religious persecution as an invention of the Devil and certainly not in accord with the teachings of the saints, were ignored. Nor was the rejection of persecution found in the writings of Hilarius, Gregory Narianzen, Chrysostom, and other Church Fathers heeded. Not even the position of St. Jerome who, although advocating a certain degree of persecution never desired the death of heretics, could stop the increasing resort to persecution or the increase in the Pope's tyrannical power.[45]

Another turning point came with Saint Augustine. Although he had always been against forcing people's consciences in their choice of faith, the Donatist heresy convinced him that persecution was necessary. Heretics merited punishment and even death. Their elimination was 'the chief duty towards God.' Limborch concludes:

> But the Minds of Christians have been perverted . . . through the Prevalence of Self Love; so that when they could prevail with the Civil Power to assist them, they have pronounced all that differed from them Hereticks, and then exercised all Kinds of Cruelty against them.[46]

In the following chapters, Limborch analyses the doctrine of the Albigensians and the Valdensians and the rise to power of the Tribunal of the Holy Office in various European countries in the years before the Reformation. He highlights the at times conflicting but generally mutually supportive relationship between civil and ecclesiastical power that accompanied the rise of the Inquisition. The relationship between the Emperor Frederick II and Pope Gregory IX and the introduction of the Inquisition in Spain are examples of such an affiliation. But, in Limborch's view, historical factors were not enough to understand the *Liber sententiarum* in all its complexity. Consequently he devoted most of the introduction to an accurate description of canon law and the rules which governed the procedures of the tribunals. He also analysed the roles and tasks of the different inquisitors, notaries, ordinary judges etc., and their relationships with political rulers, the national churches, and Rome.

Following this, Limborch examines the various categories of heresy, in the form of schismaticism, Judaizing, witchcraft, polygamy, blasphemy, and the production and distribution of prohibited books, and he gives a description of the rules of procedure and the methods used by the inquisitors. He analyses the various stages of the inquisitorial hearings: the accusation, denunciation, interrogation of the witnesses and prisoners, the role of the lawyers, the appeal, the sentencing procedure, and the different results obtained, from acquittal to abjuration, to torture, to auto da fé, to death. He concludes with a brief chapter on the abuses and injustices of the Inquisition.

In order to avoid being charged with anti-Catholic bias, Limborch used almost exclusively Catholic sources (ecclesiastical annuals, the writings of Catholic priests and theologians, famous inquisitors manuals), providing a bibliography of these at the beginning of the work. The authors cited include Bernard of Como, Simancas, Zanchini, Juan de Rojas, Emerycus, Pegna, Ludovicus of Paramo, Sousa, Fulcodi, Carena, Sarpi, and the contemporary work of Dellon.[47] The only Protestant work he mentions is that of Montanus, which was published pseudonymously.[48] Dellon's book, which met with great success at the end of the seventeenth and the beginning of the eighteenth centuries, told the story of Dellon's misadventures with the Portuguese Inquisition in the colonies of India.[49] Limborch knew this work well and drew inspiration from the historical notes and the engravings depicting an auto da fé and the procession of the condemned.[50]

Limborch included similar engravings in his own work, but he accentuated the public aspect of the ceremonies by adding numerous figures from the nobility and lower classes who intently watch the procession of the condemned from behind windows and doors, on balconies and roof tops, and from the ramparts, forming an aisle for the procession of the condemned all the way to where the pyre is set.[51] These engravings emphasized the political, social and religious significance of the executions. The ceremony during which the heretics were formally condemned to death actually took place on a wooden stage with an altar in the background, flanked by two pulpits, one bearing the ensign of the crown and reserved for a representative of the king, the other surmounted by a cross and thus reserved for a papal envoy.[52]

Limborch's *Historia Inquisitionis* is not only important for its historical value because it draws on both ancient and recent sacred history but also for the philological rigor with which Limborch edited and annotated the text. Furthermore, in the few pages that proceed the *Liber sententiarum*, where he discusses the transcription and publication of the codex, he describes the collation between the apographo and the autographo texts and the grammatical and linguistic rules used to modernize the medieval text. We must not forget that until the twentieth century, many scholars considered Limborch's work the first historical-critical work on the Tribunals in a truly modern sense. In his desire to provide an accurate and philologically correct text and to make this text comprehensible from a historiographical point of view and in terms of its political and religious significance, Limborch distanced himself from contemporary anecdotal and romanticised tales of the Inquisition trials like those of Dellon, Leti, or the later work of Marsollier.

Religion and Politics in Limborch's Thought

In his research on the history of Remonstrant beliefs, on one hand, and his own systematization of Remonstrant doctrine, on the other, Limborch was faced with the problem of the relationship between political and ecclesiastical power. This, in turn, led him to a critical analysis of the concept of heresy and, eventually, to a defense of religious toleration and liberty of conscience.

From the time of his first polemical writing against the rigid Calvinism of Jacobus Sceperus in 1661, Limborch defended moderate Protestants who rejected the doctrine of predestination and advocated a more tolerant interpretation of Protestantism.[53] In ensuing works, particularly in the editions of the works of Arminius, Episcopius, and Courcelles, as well as in the two editions of *Praestantium ac Eruditorum virorum Epistolae*,[54] he proposed to his learned contemporaries throughout Europe a Christian way which expressed itself not so much through a dogmatic or theocratic system but rather through a rational ethic that clarified the relationship between ecclesiastical and political institutions. He discussed the issues of liberty of conscience and heresy in all his writings, from his polemical pamphlets against Breedenburg through his work on systematic theology, in which he outlines the basis of Remonstrant belief, reducing it to what he felt was a widely comprehensible and fundamental creed acceptable to all Christians.[55] Significantly, he concludes his *Theologia christiana*[56] with four chapters in which he addresses the definition of heresy and of a heretic and raises the question of the legitimacy of the punishment of those who err. While endorsing the condemnation — but only in a moral and spiritual sensed — of idolatry and of beliefs opposed to the foundations of Christianity (and hence, in his opinion, inimical to, peace and concord), he defends the ideals of liberty of conscience and mutual toleration among Christians. In these chapters he refers to the much milder condemnation of ancient heretical doctrines by the Church Fathers and to their conviction that because of the irrepressibility of conscience, the need to regulate public religious practice, and out of respect for civil law a wide margin should be left for the liberty of individual conscience.

Even in the subsequent works such as *De veritate*,[57] the historical works on the synod of Dordrecht of 1618,[58] and various unpublished texts the issue of heresy and persecution remained focal points of Limborch's thought. In the unpublished manuscript with a preface dated October 1710[59] and entitled 'Reformatorum de poena haereticorum sententia ex variis autoribus et ecclesiarum responsis collecta et exemplis aliquot demonstrata', heresy and toleration are obviously central issues. Gathering together the ideas presented in the final chapters of *Theologia christiana* and in *Historia inquisitions*, he completes the trilogy with this unpublished work, providing an inventory of the ecclesiastical opinions and commentaries of theologians and of authors on the subject of heresy and how the church should deal with it.

The *Historia inquisitionis* does not simply have a special place in Limborch's intellectual biography; it was conceived as a decisive contribution to the politico-religious debate that occurred during these very years and involved Locke, numerous English exiles and French refugees, as well as those Huguenots, Liberal Protestants, Latitudinarians, and dissidents who had remained in there own countries. Some of the first Dutch readers of the treatise, in particular those amoung the Contra-Remonstrants, such as Triglandius, immediately grasped that Limborch's intention in this work was to criticize the condemnation of the Remonstrants and the death and exile to which they had been subjected by the synodal decrees of Dordrecht. The very orthodox Triglandius understood that Remostrants like Limborch drew a parallel between these decrees and the summary procedures and persecutions of the Catholic Inquisition.[60] Like the Remonstrants, liberal Protestants also emphasized the affinities between the contemporary debate on heresy and some of the medieval heretical sects condemned in the *Liber sententiarum* and described by Limborch at the beginning of his historical analysis. For example, in his *Histoire de l'Eglise*[61] Henry Basnage followed in Limborch's footsteps. Critically analysing the doctrines of the Cathar-Albigensian and the Valdensians, he recognizes that in important ways they anticipated ideas characteristic of the Protestant Reformation:

> . . . on trouve une idée si juste et si precise de la Religion, qui'il est impossible de ne l'y pas reconoître. On y rejette les mêmes erreurs que les Reformez rejettent; on y combat l'Eglise Romaine par les mêmes raisons que nous employons contr'elle, et on y établit la même doctrine que nos Eglises professent aujourd'hui. . .[62]

Limborch was fully aware that the publication of the *Liber sententiarum* in a philologically and historically unassailable edition was highly relevant to the persecution and intolerance of his time. He mentions this on more than one occasion in his letters to Locke. As he wrote to his friend:

> While this subject *(the Historia)* is my own daily occupation, lo and behold in this country of ours those whom it least behoved, people who themselves have barely escaped the hands of persecutors, have decided to show us an exemplar of the Holy Office. Jurieu, such is his theological clemency, has set himself by fair means or foul to work the ruin of a certain Hamburg minister...[63]

Describing the trial of the Hamburg minister, he continues:

> Jurieu, indignant at being removed from the judges' bench and borrowing a distinction from Holy Office procedure, desires to be counted not as a prosecutor but as a denunciator, and accordingly demands to be given a place among the judges. . .

At the end of the same letter, Limborch asks: 'Do you not seem to be listening to the Holy Office pronouncing sentence on a heretic 'convicted on denial''?[64] In his reply Locke agreed: 'Theological zeal, as I see it, is always and everywhere the same and proceeds in the same way.'[65] The care with which Limborch analyses the relationship between ecclesiastical and political power in his historical introduction and his discussion of the significance of their alignment for the history of Christianity from its debut up to his own time is further confirmation of his modern sensitivity in grasping these relationships.

The Reception of Limborch's Work

Limborch's historical discussion of the procedures, methods, and activities of the Inquisition, together with his own ideas about religion and toleration, were diffused to a vast public in contemporary learned journals, which provide gold-mines of information about the religious controversies and intellectual climate of the period. When it appeared, the *Historia* was immediately reviewed in a long and detailed article by Limborch's friend and co-religionist, Jean Le Clerc, in his 'Bibiliothèque Universelle et Historique.'[66] Le Clerc emphasized the historical and rigorous philological background provided by Limborch, which, in his view, both protected the work from any easy refutation and highlighted the cruelty and injustice of inquisitorial persecution.

> L'injustice et la cruauté sont si visibles, qu'il suffit de dire simplement et naturellement les choses telles qu'elles sont, pour faire conclurre à tout homme raisonnable, que ce Tribunal ne sauroit avoir été établi, que par les inspirations de celui qui s'est déclaré l'Ennemi du Genre humain, dés le commencement du Monde.[67]

Within a few months an equally incisive, but less analytical, review appeared in the Huguenot Basnage de Beauval's 'Histoire des Ouvrages des Savans.'[68] Although the review did not overlook the historical and philological aspects of the edition, it put more emphasis on the contemporary religious debate. Banage's review is striking in terms of the prominance it gives to the role of politics in the Inquisition's assertion of authority.

The review which Limborch most eagerly awaited was without doubt the one published in 'Acta Eruditorium Lipsiensis'[69] both because of the prestige this journal enjoyed among contemporary scholars but also and above all because although the Journal represented Protestant opinion, it was removed from Limborch's circle of Remonstrant and refugee friends. In the brief space of a few pages 'Acta' listed the contents of the chapters of *Historia* and underlined its historical and scholarly importance. This journal, along with the ones mentioned above, constituted a very important vehicle for the diffusion of the work. To give an example, the Neapolitan scholar Giuseppe Valletta first came across Limborch's work in the pages of 'Acta' and only later did he read the text itself. Even though he did not quote Limborch directly, which would have risked censorship by the Neapolitan clerics, he was very much influenced by him, and in his own writings, particularly the unpublished ones, he critically analysed the Inquisition's development from a political and religious point of view rather than a legal one.[70]

At the beginning of the eighteenth century renewed interest in Limborch's work, particularly in his historical introduction, emerged among the English public. A brief extract from the introduction appeared in London in 1734, published with the intention of revealing to 'the common people' the cruel aspects of the Inquisitions's persecution of Protestants.[71] The anonymous editor recalled that when Limborch's work first appeared, it met 'with great approbation by all understanding men,'[72] and lamented the fact that it was no longer accessible to the 'ordinary reader.' The brief economical abridgement, stripped of its documentary apparatus and references, would, however, remedy this and be within the reach of every enemy of superstition and of Catholicism in England.[73]

But the most assiduous promoter of Limborch's work was the non-conformist Samuel Chandler.[74] While Limborch had tried to present the work in as non partisan way as possible, Chandler, on the contrary, wanted to emphasize the polemical aspect of the work and its relevance to the current debate, which not only involved dissidents in open dispute with the Catholic Church but also the issue of the establishment of the Anglican Church. This last issue, which had been bitterly debated in England in the second half of the seventeenth century was still of vital interest in the first ten years of the eighteenth century.

Chandler's translation and edition of Limborch's *Historia Inquisitionis*,[75] which appeared in 1731, was not identical with the original. For example, it lacked the documentary support Limborch had provided. Chandler also printed a preface to Limborch's historical introduction in which some additions were included that came from Limborch's own annotated copy of the work. This had been given to Chandler by Limborch's son, Francis. Chandler also added a long introduction, in which he retraces the history of religious thought from its classical Greek and Latin origins through the first ten years or so of the seventeenth century. Here he defends the legitimacy of liberty of conscience and demonstrates the political and religious benefits of a policy of toleration.

These pronouncements, made by an author who certainly did not shy away from dispute, produced an immediate reaction on the part of orthodox Anglicans and led to an acrimonious exchange of pamphlets between Chandler and William Berriman, an Anglican minister.[76] With Berriman, however, this confrontation would soon shift to a personal level. Chandler's edition of Limborch's work was clearly a significant event. It is sufficient to scan the long list of the subscribers to Chandler's edition to realize that with its publication we are in the midst of the political and religious battles on deism and on the path to European Enlightenment.

* An earlier version of this paper was given at a seminar series organised by Anonio Rotondò, at the Department of History of the University of Florence. I want to thank Anonio Rotondò for his support and encouragement while I was doing research for the paper, and for the detailed and stimulating discussion on the occasion of the seminar.

1 Tillotson professed his approval of *Historia Inquisitionis* ('Ingens quidem Opus, magno labore et industriâ, nec minori fide et judicio perfectum, expletumque omnibus suis partibus et numeris') and his gratitude to Limborch for his dedication. Cf. unpublished letter, Amsterdam, Universiteit Bibliotheek (abbreviated in UBA), UBA, M. 38, 10 February 1692–93, VS. The Archbishop's library includes among its volumes the splendidly bound copy donated by Limborch. *Bibliotheca Tillotsoniana; or a Catalogue of the curious Library of Dr. John Tillotson late Lord Archbishop of Canterbury* (Cambridge and Oxford, 1965), p. 25.

2 Philippus van Limborch, *Historia Inquisitionis cui subjungitur Liber Sententiarum Inquisitionis Tholosanae ab anno Christi 1307 ab annum 1323* (Amsterdam: Henry Wetstein, 1692). This and other quotations are taken from the English edition of *The History of the Inquisition, by Philip a Limborch, translated by English by Samuel Chandler, In Two volumes, To which is prefixed a large Introduction concerning the Rise and Progress of Persecution, and the real and pretended Causes of it* (London: J. Gray 1731), *The Dedication.* In Chandler's edition Limborch's Dedication to John Tillotson opens the second volume.

3 The Arminians of Holland assumed the name Remonstrants after the presentation of the Remonstrance containing the most salient points of their interpretation of Calvinism to the minister of the States of Holland in 1610.

4 cf. A.W. Harrison, *The Beginnings of Arminanism to the Synod of Dort* (London, 1926); idem, *Arminianism* (London: Duckworth, 1937); C. Bangs, *Arminius. A Study in the Dutch Reformation* (New York: Abingdon Press, 1971); L. Simonutti, *Arminianesimo e tolleranza nel Seicento olandese. Il carteggio Ph. van Limborch-J.Le Clerc* (Florence: L.S. Olschki, 1984); see also N. Tyacke, *Anti-Calvinists. The Rise of English Arminianism* (Oxford: Clarendon Press, 1987).

5 cf. R.L. Colie, *Light and Enlightenment. A Study of the Cambridge Platonists and the Dutch Arminians* (Cambridge: Cambridge University Press, 1957); L. Simonutti, 'Reason and Toleration: Henry More and Philip van Limborch,' *Henry More (1614–1687) Tercentenary Studies*, ed. S. Hutton (Dordrecht: Kluwer, 1990).

6 cf. L. Simonutti, 'Liberté et vérité. Politique et morale dans la correspondance hollandaise de More et de Cudworth', G.A.J. Rogers, J.-M. Vienne and Y.-C. Zarka (eds), *The Cambridge Platonists in Philosophical Context* (Dordrecht: Kluwer Academic Publishers, 1997), pp. 17–37.

7 cf. Limborch's letter to William Lloyd dated 21 February 1678 (UBA: III D 16, c. 123): 'Agnovi statim Ecclesiae Anglicanae moderationem, qua omnem in dogmate arduo de praedestinatione divina decisionem, ut temerariam, damnant, utriusque sententiae tolerationem sancivit, et tum Remonstrantes quam Contraremonstrantes genio suo complectitur.' Similarly he wrote some years earlier to another Latitudinarian Bishop, John Pearson (UBA: III D 16, cc. 120v–121; letter of 22 February 1675).

8 idem, Limborch to William Lloyd, 21 February 1678.

9 Cited in Martin I.J. Griffin, Jr, *Latitudinarianism in the Seventeenth-Century Church of England* (Leiden: E.J. Brill, 1992), p. 17.

10 cf. W.M. Spellmann, *The Latitudinarianism and the Church of England, 1660–1770* (Athens, Georgia: University of Georgia Press, 1993), ch. 7.

11 'My History of the Inquisition gives Light to the *Book of Sentences.* My Design in it was to give a Representation of that Tribunal, not in a false Disguise, nor deform'd by unnatural and hideous Colours, but in living and genuine ones; I mean, to draw the Picture of that horrible Court, which makes its principal Boast of the Title of Sanctity, to the Life, not from the Writings of those who separate from the Church of Rome, but that there may be no Room for Calumny, from those of the Popish Doctors, and even Inquisitors themselves; that hereby the vast Power granted to the Inquisitors, the most cruel

Laws of it, and the injust Method of Procedure, quite different from the usage of all other Courts, might appear to the whole World, and that hereby the Papacy it self might be known to all Mankind to be what it really is.' Philippus van Limborch, *The History of the Inquisition, The Dedication to John Tillotson.*

12 ibid., *Preface to the Reader.*

13 cf. Charles Molinier, *L'Inquisition dans le midi de la France au XVII et au XIV siècle* (Paris: Sandoz et Fischbacher, 1880), Introduction, pp. ii–iii; Pia Cremonini, *Storia della storia dell' Inquisizione, Storia dell' Inquisizione*, in H.C. Lea (ed), *Fondazione e procedura* (Milano: Bocca, 1910), pp. xvi–xvii.

14 'Benevole Lector, ecce tibi librum, qualem typis editum hactenus non vidit Christianus Orbis. Ipsum autographum, quod possessoris benevola voluntate integro quadriennio in manibus meis fruit, scriptum est et ubique subscriptum manu Notariorum Inquisitionis, indiciisque indubitatis constat, esse authenticum exemplar ex Archivis Inquisitionis Tholosanae depromptum.' He also continues: 'Authenticas indicia adeo sunt manifesta, ut sola voluminis inspectio mox omne dubium inspicienti adimat. Volumen constat ex pergameno, et intras duas laminas ligneas compactum est. Laminarum alteri hic inscriptus est titulus, *L. Sentenciarum*' (Philippus van Limborch, *Historia Inquisitionis cui subjungitur Liber Sententiarum Inquisitionis Tholosanae, Liber Sententiarum, Praefatio ad lectorem.* Neither the Preface nor the *Liber Sententiarum* was published in Chandler's edition of *Historia Inquisitionis.*

15 Bernardus Sutor, Gulielmus Julian, Petrus de Claveriis, Jacobus Marquesius.

16 cf. Celestin Douais, *Les sources de l'histoire de l'Inquisition dans le midi de la France aux XII et XIV siècles* (Paris: Palme, 1881); idem, *Documents pour servir à l'histoire de l'Inquisition dans le Languedoc* (Paris: Renouard, 1900); H.C. Lea, *A History of the Inquisition of the Middle Ages* (Cambridge, Massachusetts: Heffer, 1956); H. Kamen, *The Spanish Inquisition* (London: Weidenfeld & Nicolson, 1965) and the most recent bibliography cited in Jean-Baptiste Guiraud, *Elogio della Inquisizione* (Milano: Leonardo, 1994).

17 cf. the description of the code Add. MS. 4697, ff. 2–8 mentioned in the catalogue of the British Library of London.

18 The work was published for the first time by the canonical C. Douais (Paris: A. Picard, 1886).

19 cf. the accurate reconstruction provided by M.A.E.Nickson, 'Locke and the Inquisition of Toulouse,' *The British Museum Quarterly* 36 (1972): 83–92.

20 cf. *The Correspondence of John Locke*, ed. E.S. De Beer, 8 vols. (Oxford: Clarendon Press, 1976–1989), letter n. 991. Cf. in particular the manuscripts conserved at the Oxford, Bodleian Library: *Journal*, Ms Locke, f.2., cc. 18–34; e Ms. Locke, c. 27, c. 48. Locke mentions this codex and another one relating to the inquisitorial reports in the South of France (*Correspondence*, n. 1473).

21 cf. *Correspondence*, nn. 993, 1004 and in particular n. 1023.

22 cf. *Correspondence*, n. 1023.

23 On Locke and the religious and cultural environment in Amsterdam during the first years of his exile see L. Simonutti, 'Religion, Philosophy and Science: Locke and the Limborch Circle" in J.E. Force and D.S. Katz (eds) *Everything Connects. In Conference with Richard H. Popkin* (Leiden: Brill, 1998).

24 Locke writes: 'I beg that you will give me the opportunity of perusing once again those writings of your own and of Don Balthasar which you lent me some time ago. If they may be handed to the bearer, my servant, they will be duly delivered to me, and I will return them shortly with my best thanks' (*Correspondence*, n. 810). Limborch's work was published at Gouda by J. Ab Hoeve in 1687.

25 When Limborch received the first unbound copy of his work in the beginning of September, 1687, he wrote to Locke: 'Here at last is a copy of my discussion with the learned Jew which is now after long delays to see the light. I regret that I have none to hand as yet in bound form, but I am to have some in a few days, of which I shall send you one. I did not wish to be guilty of detaining this copy by me for a single day; for it is to you, if to anyone on earth, that it becomes me to offer it first, seeing that it is through your care that this whole discussion is appearing in a more polished form. You have removed numerous blemishes, you have supplied arguments that had escaped me, and you have

embellished the whole work of my pen; a service which I shall ever acknowledge with gratitude and proclaim to the world' (*Correspondence*, n. 958).

26 cf. *Correspondence*, nn. 963, 964.

27 On Orobio de Castro and his relationship with Limborch see Richard H. Popkin, 'The Marranos of Amsterdam,' *The Third Force in Seventeenth-Century Thought* (Leiden: Brill, 1992), pp.149–171; and Yosef Kaplan, *From Christianity to Judaism. The Story of Isaac Orobio de Castro* (New York: Oxford University Press, 1989), especially ch. 10.

28 cf. *Correspondence*, n. 979.

29 cf. Limborch, *Historia Inquisitionis,* pp. 323–324; and the English edition *The History of the Inquisition,* lib. II, ch. xxix, pp. 221–222.

30 cf. *Correspondence*, n. 1023.

31 *Correspondence*, n.1033.

32 idem. The letter from Limborch to Furly, in which he presumably explained the details of the publication to the owner of the document, is missing (none of the letters between Limborch and Furly seem to have been conserved).

33 cf. *Correspondence*, n. 1034.

34 ibid. nn. 1034, 1134, 1148, 1158, 1172.

35 ibid. nn. 1058, 1178, 1215.

36 Limborch writes to Locke: 'I have now read right through the book of the Inquisition at Toulouse; I have carefully collated the copy with the original and have offered it to Wetstein; he is delaying the business for some other reasons; I do not know whether it is the dearness of paper or the discouragement he has received from his brother that is making him slower to proceed with publication; it may be indeed that he desires to put off for a time the payment of the money still due, and that this is why he has asked that the copy may remain in my hands' (*Correspondence*, n. 1215. Cf. Also n. 1229). Limborch also writes to Locke: 'The publication of the book of the Holy Office is held up by the very high cost of paper; for this reason, glad as I should be to see it appear, I cannot hurry it on very much; nor can one hope for any fall in the price while this war continues, as all trade with france is strictly forbidden by law; this is what is keeping the work of the press at a standstill here and allowing so very few books to be printed' (*Correspondence*, n. 1233. Cf. also *Correspondence*, nn.1262, 1283, 1393, 1447.

37 ibid., nn. 1518, 1539, 1553.

38 ibid., nn. 1572, 1581, 1671, 1692.

39 ibid., n. 1368.

40 ibid. nn. 1516 e 1539.

41 cf. *Correspondence*, n. 1539.

42 Limborch, *The History of the Inquisition,* lib. I, ch. ii, p. 4.

43 ibid., lib. I, ch. ii, p.6.

44 ibid., lib. I, ch. iii.

45 ibid., lib. I, ch. v and vii.

46 ibid., lib. I, ch. vi, p. 40.

47 For the bibliographic description of the texts see E. van der Vekene' *Bibliographie der Inquisition* (Hildesheim: Olms, 1963).

48 cf. B.A. Vermaseren, 'Who was Reginaldus Gonsalvius Montanus?' *Bibliothèque d'Humanisme et Renaissance* 47 (1985): 47–77.

49 Gabriel Dellon, *Relation de l'Inquisition de Goa* (Leida: Gaasbeek, 1687). Reprinted in Paris in 1688 as well as numerous times in the course of the eighteenth century. In 1688 it appeared for the first time in English in London, in two editions; and in the same year the first German edition also appeared, while the Dutch edition appeared in 1697.

50 cf. *Correspondence*, n. 979.

51 cf. Engraving n. 1 and n. 2. Francisco Bethencourt discusses Limborch's debt to Dellon's engravings but emphasizes the way in which the engravings were enriched. See his article, 'The *auto da*

fé: ritual and imagery,' *Journal of the Warburg and Courtauld Institutes* 55, (1992): 155–168. Another influence may have been the religious processions and the King's procession. Cf. Frances A. Yates, 'Dramatic religious procession in Paris in the late Sixteenth Century,' *Annales musicologiques* 2 (1954): 215–270. Both Dellon's images and the images in Limborch's *Historia Inquisitionis* were continously reproduced uip to the present; see, for example, the cover of E. van der Vekene's bibliography.

52 cf. engraving n. 3.

53 Limborch, *Korte Wederlegginge van 't boexken onlangs uytgegeven by Iacobus Sceperus genaemt Chrysopolerotus* (Amsterdam: J. Rieuwertsz, 1661).

54 The first edition appeared in Amsterdam in 1660, edited by Limborch and Chr. Hartsoeker. The work was subsequently enlarged (Amsterdam, 1684 and 1704).

55 On Limborch see, P.J. Barnouw, *Philippus van Limborch* (The Hague: Mouton, 1963); on some aspects of his thought see also J. M. Hicks, *The Theology of Grace in the Thought of Jacobus Arminius and Philip van Limborch: a Study in the Development of Seventeenth-century Dutch Arminianism* (Ann Arbor, MI: UMI Dissertation Services, 1985).

56 *Theologia Christiana ad praxin pietatis ac promotionem pacis Christianae unice directa* (Amsterdam: H. Wetstein, 1686).

57 *De veritate Religionis Christianae, amica collatio cum erudito judaeo* (Gouda: J. van der Hoeve, 1687).

58 *Relatio historica de origine et progressu controversiarum in Foederato Belgio de Praedestinazione. Tractatus posthumus*, p. 4., in *Theologia christiana ad praxin pietatis ac promotionem pacis Christianae unice directa*, (Amsterdam, 1686). This work, which appeared posthumously, was added to the volume of *Theologia christiana* from the fourth edition, which appeared 1715.

59 UBA, Ms, III G 28, 199 ff. Although Limborch declared that this work is destined for private use, the internal organization of the text and the presence of the preface leads one to think Limborch had plans for its publication. Cf. also A. des Amorie van der Hoeven, *De Joanne Clerico et Philippo a Limborch dissertationes duae* (Amsterdam: F.Muller, 1843), see in particular Appendix E.

60 Limborch writes to Locke: 'Not long after the publication of my *Historia* Professor Trigland among others was in company with Mr. de Volder. He saw my *Historia* and after he had looked at it a little de Volder asks him whether he has seen and read it. He says no, and adds, 'These men believe that they were wronged in the year '18 of this century, and therefore are wont to insist on it and repeat it in season and out of season.' De Volder replies that nothing of that, not so much as a single word, is to be found in this whole *Historia,* unless perhaps he supposes that readers who see here the proceedings of the Inquisition painted to the life will believe that the acts of the year '18 are similar to them in all respects, and for that reason these acts are condemned in this book. Many of the Contraremonstrants are buying and reading it; so far however I have not heard any unfavourable opinions' (*Correspondence*, n. 1640).

61 Henry Basnage de Beauval, *Histoire de l'Eglise depuis Jesus-Christ jusqu' à present* (Rotterdam: R. Leers, 1699), especially pp. 1410–1437.

62 ibid. p. 1412.

63 *Correspondence*, n. 1317.

64 *Correspondence*, n. 1317. Cf. also n. 1447.

65 *Correspondence*, n. 1473. Some months later, welcoming the upcoming publication of the work, Locke added: 'I am glad that the publication of a work I have so long wanted, and which I judge to be most useful to the reformed world at this time, is now imminent' (*Correspondence*, n. 1518. Cf. also n. 1509).

66 *Bibliothèque Universelle et Historique*, 3 (1692): 360–409.

67 idem, p. 362.

68 *Histoire des Ouvrages des Savans*, 1693: 496–511.

69 *Acta Eruditorum* 1693: 323–333. Cf. *Corrispondence*, nn. 1640 and 1668.

70 cf. Vittor Ivo Comparato, *Giuseppe Valletta, un intellettuale napoletano della fine del Seicento* (Napoli: Morano, 1970).

71 *A brief representation of the cruel and barbarous proceedings against protestants in the Inquisition. Extracted from* The History of Inquisition . . . *To which is prefixed a preface, relating to the present great complaint of the increase of Popery in this Nation* (London: J. Roberts, 1734).

72 idem, Preface.

73 The UBA has a copy of the *Historia inquisitionis* with numerous corrections and annotations in the hand of Limborch. In particular, Limborch gives an account of the trial of Galileo Galilei and reproduces the text of his abjuration, with the intention of adding these pages to the end of chapter 30 of the *Historia* as the last example of illegal and unjust persecution.

74 Samuel Chandler completed his studies in Leiden in 1716. A non-conformist, he was one of the writers most active in the controversies in favor of toleration and of 'reasonable' Christianity.

75 *The History of the Inquisition by Philip a Limborch . . .Translated into English by Samuel Chandler, in two volumes. To which is prefixed, a large Introduction concerning the Rise and progress of Persecution, and the real and pretended causes of it* (London: J. Gray, 1731).

76 William Berriman, *Some brief remarks* (London, 1733); *A review of the remarks* (London, 1733). Chandler's replies in *An answer to the brief remarks* (London, 1733) and *A vindication* (London, 1734). See also the anonymous *A letter to a Friend occasioned by Mr. Chandler's History of Persecution. With a Postscript concerning his Answer to Dr. Berriman* (London: J Brotherton, 1733) and Zachary Grey, *An examination of Mr. Samuel Chandler's History of Persecution* (London, 1736).

INDEX

ARCHIVES INTERNATIONALES D'HISTOIRE DES IDÉES
*
INTERNATIONAL ARCHIVES OF THE HISTORY OF IDEAS

137. Otto von Guericke: *The New (so-called Magdeburg) Experiments* [Experimenta Nova, Amsterdam 1672]. Translated and edited by M.G. Foley Ames. 1994   ISBN 0-7923-2399-8
138. R.H. Popkin and G.M. Weiner (eds.): *Jewish Christians and Cristian Jews*. From the Renaissance to the Enlightenment. 1994   ISBN 0-7923-2452-8
139. J.E. Force and R.H. Popkin (eds.): *The Books of Nature and Scripture*. Recent Essays on Natural Philosophy, Theology, and Biblical Criticism in the Netherlands of Spinoza's Time and the British Isles of Newton's Time. 1994   ISBN 0-7923-2467-6
140. P. Rattansi and A. Clericuzio (eds.): *Alchemy and Chemistry in the 16th and 17th Centuries*. 1994   ISBN 0-7923-2573-7
141. S. Jayne: *Plato in Renaissance England*. 1995   ISBN 0-7923-3060-9
142. A.P. Coudert: *Leibniz and the Kabbalah*. 1995   ISBN 0-7923-3114-1
143. M.H. Hoffheimer: *Eduard Gans and the Hegelian Philosophy of Law*. 1995
ISBN 0-7923-3114-1
144. J.R.M. Neto: *The Christianization of Pyrrhonism*. Scepticism and Faith in Pascal, Kierkegaard, and Shestov. 1995   ISBN 0-7923-3381-0
145. R.H. Popkin (ed.): *Scepticism in the History of Philosophy*. A Pan-American Dialogue. 1996   ISBN 0-7923-3769-7
146. M. de Baar, M. Löwensteyn, M. Monteiro and A.A. Sneller (eds.): *Choosing the Better Part*. Anna Maria van Schurman (1607–1678). 1995   ISBN 0-7923-3799-9
147. M. Degenaar: *Molyneux's Problem*. Three Centuries of Discussion on the Perception of Forms. 1996   ISBN 0-7923-3934-7
148. S. Berti, F. Charles-Daubert and R.H. Popkin (eds.): *Heterodoxy, Spinozism, and Free Thought in Early-Eighteenth-Century Europe*. Studies on the *Traité des trois imposteurs*. 1996
ISBN 0-7923-4192-9
149. G.K. Browning (ed.): *Hegel's* Phenomenology of Spirit: *A Reappraisal*. 1997
ISBN 0-7923-4480-4
150. G.A.J. Rogers, J.M. Vienne and Y.C. Zarka (eds.): *The Cambridge Platonists in Philosophical Context*. Politics, Metaphysics and Religion. 1997   ISBN 0-7923-4530-4
151. R.L. Williams: *The Letters of Dominique Chaix, Botanist-Curé*. 1997   ISBN 0-7923-4615-7
152. R.H. Popkin, E. de Olaso and G. Tonelli (eds.): *Scepticism in the Enlightenment*. 1997
ISBN 0-7923-4643-2
153. L. de la Forge. Translated and edited by D.M. Clarke: *Treatise on the Human Mind (1664)*. 1997   ISBN 0-7923-4778-1
154. S.P. Foster: *Melancholy Duty*. The Hume-Gibbon Attack on Christianity. 1997
ISBN 0-7923-4785-4
155. J. van der Zande and R.H. Popkin (eds.): *The Skeptical Tradition Around 1800*. Skepticism in Philosophy, Science, and Society. 1997   ISBN 0-7923-4846-X
156. P. Ferretti: *A Russian Advocate of Peace: Vasilii Malinovskii (1765–1814)*. 1997
ISBN 0-7923-4846-6
157. M. Goldish: *Judaism in the Theology of Sir Isaac Newton*. 1998   ISBN 0-7923-4996-2
158. A.P. Coudert, R.H. Popkin and G.M. Weiner (eds.): *Leibniz, Mysticism and Religion*. 1998
ISBN 0-7923-5223-8
159. B. Fridén: *Rousseau's Economic Philosophy*. Beyond the Market of Innocents. 1998
ISBN 0-7923-5270-X
160. C.F. Fowler O.P.: *Descartes on the Human Soul*. Philosophy and the Demands of Christian Doctrine. 1999   ISBN 0-7923-5473-7

ARCHIVES INTERNATIONALES D'HISTOIRE DES IDÉES

*

INTERNATIONAL ARCHIVES OF THE HISTORY OF IDEAS

161.   A.P. Coudert, S. Hutton, R.H. Popkin and G.M. Weiner (eds.): *Judaeo-Christian Intellectual Culture in the Seventeenth Century.* 1999   ISBN 0-7923-5789-2

KLUWER ACADEMIC PUBLISHERS – DORDRECHT / BOSTON / LONDON